On the Art of Writing Copy

Writing

Copy

2nd Edition

On the Art of Writing Copy

2nd Edition

Herschell Gordon Lewis

AMACOM

American Management Association

New York • Atlanta • Boston • Chicago • Kansas City • San Francisco • Washington, D.C.

Brussels • Mexico City • Tokyo • Toronto

This publication is designed to provide accurate and authoritative information in regard to the subject matter covered. It is sold with the understanding that the publisher is not engaged in rendering legal, accounting, or other professional service. If legal advice or other expert assistance is required, the services of a competent professional person should be sought.

Library of Congress Cataloging-in-Publication Data

Lewis, Herschell Gordon, 1926–
    On the art of writing copy / Herschell Gordon Lewis.—2nd ed.
        p. cm.
    Includes index.
    ISBN 0-8144-7031-9
        1. Advertising copy.   2. Business writing.   I. Title.
    HF5825.L44 1999
    659.13′2—dc21   99-043415

Printing number

10 9 8 7 6 5 4 3 2 1

CONTENTS

Chapter Twenty-Seven

Addendum

PREFACE

About a decade has passed since publication of the first edition of this book.

Has anything changed? Do we have a reason to update this text instead of just putting it back on the press?

You're darned right things have changed. You're darned right we have a reason to update the text.

One major development is the World Wide Web, which didn't exist when the first edition of this compendium of easy-to-apply rules for force-communication first hit the bookstalls.

The Web has influenced all other media; still, it maintains and constantly expands its own set of rules, some of which parallel those of conventional media and some of which don't. Trying to force rules for on-line communications into a mold not built for those rules parallels writing a television commercial as catalog copy. It's kind of similar—a third cousin—but it isn't what professional force-communicators do.

Other media evolve. The 21st century (goaded by television and e-mail) moves toward conversational, informal copy . . . which suggests reasons to depart from the trend. Some copy, as samples in this book will show, border on bad taste. Or do they? Bad taste, like obscenity, is in the mind of the beholder, based on that individual's personal experiential background. Anyone who was around in the 1960s and 1970s would have been shocked to see an ad that said, "This product kicks others' butt." Today, the phrase is a cliché (see Figures X-1, X-2, X-3, and X-4). Chapter 2 includes a discussion of in-your-face advertising.

Are we moving into a no-holds-barred era? Kenneth Starr's report, which listed President Clinton's peccadilloes in excruciatingly explicit detail, opened wide a Pandora's box of directness that had been pried ajar by rap music and increasingly explicit television and motion picture scenarios. In-your-face advertising (see Chapter 2) may leave a permanent imprint on communications. But, as is true of all evolution and devolution, the Shock Diminution Rule applies: Shock diminishes in exact ratio to repetition. What once was forbidden, and then was mildly naughty, eventually becomes ho-hum.

So yes, this new edition incorporates changes.

The degree of change, relative to your own professional approach to copywriting, depends on your creative flexibility as well as your willingness (plus your ability) to generate a selling climate. What does your reader, viewer, or listener want to see or hear? What words can transform apathy into enthusiasm?

You're in Command of Your Army of Words

Is writing a chore for you? A delight? A tedious way to spend an afternoon? A challenge you meet with lance at the ready or with sweaty palms?

Depending on how you approach writing, you will or won't be thrilled to see some hard rules in print. The notion of superimposing principles on an art form may gall you because it's unseemly to replace—or even modify—talent with mechanical principles. But isn't it time, in a computerized, word-processed era, to figure out why some word sequences sell and some don't?

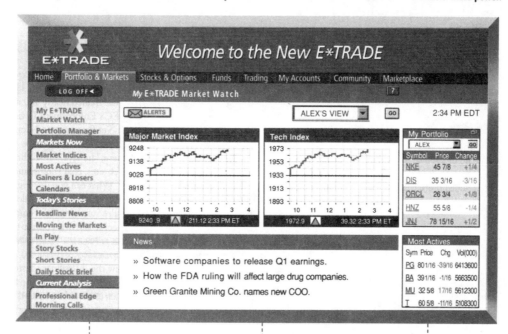

Figure X-1: A headline such as this would have been both daring and distasteful only a few years ago. Today, "kicks butt" has become so common it's a cliche.

Democrats!

If you want to kick some Republican butt, we're your phone firm.

In today's **hard charging, fast turn around, no excuses** political world, **NTS stands alone** as the telephone calling form of choice for democratic committees, labor unions, and progressive groups that are dead serious about their phoning activities.

NTS provides voter **ID, persuasion, issue advocacy, GOTV, grassroots outbound, grassroots inbound, and patch through phoning** to clients who mean business.

7000 predictive dial phone stations in **79 phone centers coast-to-coast** give NTS the leading edge. **Fifty million phone calls** in 18 years are a testimonial to NTS experience.

If you absolutely, positively want it done the right way right from the start call **Mac Hansbrough** today at **1-800-234-7770** or email chansbrough@aol.com

NTS is the number one political and public policy telephone communications company in the world.

National Telecommunications Services, Inc.

1-800-234-7770

Figure X-2: Ads succeed or fail based on their ability to connect with the targets at whom they're aimed. This one uses the butt-kicking vernacular in a hard-hitting, direct message that will offend some . . . and attract others.

Figure X-3: Does this ad communicate, or does it, as too many ads do, substitute getting attention for generating a response?

Have you ever sold shoes in a department store on a commission basis? Then you know a peculiar truth: One salesperson, week after week, outsells all others. That person may be male or female; he or she isn't the best looking, doesn't have the best vocabulary, isn't the best dresser, doesn't have the best knowledge of stock on hand, and (most frustrating to the other salespeople) doesn't fight to confront a new customer wandering into the department. Yet, when sales are toted up, that same nondescript salesperson invariably has the highest total.

Book after book tries to explain why. Most books on salesmanship deal with (and laud) perseverance or personality or deliberate psychological matchup with the customer. Great. I agree. The winning salesperson has all these, plus an implicit knowledge of how to communicate on the prospect's level of understanding.

What has puzzled me, right up to the publication date of this new edition, is that nobody has added to the rules of salesmanship in media advertising outlined in the first edition of this book.

Every year we have another ton of books on mass communications. But how about some more rules the writer can use? How about some more codified, organized techniques to transform the guesswork of everyone-can-write-it copy to I'm-beating-the-odds copy? How about a few tips on how to add that magical ingredient, *rapport*, to the marketing mix?

I'm a copywriter-chauvinist, and I'm quick to defend my profession when critics claim (even though they're often justified) that we don't know what we're doing. "You guys put words on paper, and somebody reads, sees, or hears them," our critics chide. "You don't know why your words sell, if they do. You're still in the Stone Age."

Not so. I, for one, am firmly convinced that we're starting to forge some iron spears. At last we're bringing into organized focus a handful of the rules for force-communication that have been hovering elusively in the "copywriter's heaven" above us.

A professional copywriter may know the rules implicitly, but now we begin to recognize them explicitly. The difference isn't one of content; it's one of organization.

A bright-eyed student, copywriter-to-be, enrolls in a college course. The student typically wants to write clever copy; the instructor encourages or discourages, based on an individual prejudice that in turn is based on an experiential background that may or may not be valid.

The instructor transmits and superimposes a set of copywriting fiats without regard for (or, often, knowledge of) universal truths. Hard rules for selling a "what" to a "whom" are offered in the guise of tradition: "This is how I learned to do it, so it's how I'll teach you to do it."

Kick derrière.

It is the most powerful luxury SUV on the continent. It pampers seven passengers in three rows of leather-trimmed seats. While it tows up to 8,100 pounds. Over a mountain. With an attitude. Call 1 800 446-8888, visit www.lincolnvehicles.com or see an authorized Lincoln Navigator dealer.

Lincoln Navigator. What a luxury [ ] should be.

Figure X-4: Lincoln neatly balances its sedate image against contemporary "with it" language, by gentrifying the phrase and making it somehow seem charming: "Kick derrière."

A mathematics instructor who taught, "Two plus two are seven because I like it that way," would be laughed out of class within the first two minutes. The geography teacher who taught, "The Monongahela River is the longest river in the world; it's the only river I've navigated, and it's long," would last only until a student became forever cynical by learning that the teacher was substituting his own limited sphere of knowledge for incontrovertible, tested, proven fact.

Why can't the budding copywriter have the benefit of rules? Why can't an experienced copywriter, shifting from consumer to business copy, know which gears to engage? Why can't a nonwriter doggedly apply rules and write as well as someone who labels himself or herself a professional? Well, one reason is that the people we're trying to influence don't run on tracks. Or do they? You'll have to decide, after plowing through whichever sections of this book interest you.

If you say to me, "In three words, tell me how to write effective copy," I'll answer: "Sure. The three words are *clarity, benefit*, and *verisimilitude*. Combine those three qualities and your copy can't miss." (Not to worry if that third word isn't familiar: Verisimilitude, a truly magical ingredient, is explained in this text. It may be the most worthwhile element any communicator might ever want to control.)

You may wonder, If it's that easy, why have I turned my brains into mashed potatoes by isolating, culling, and refining solid rules? Why do we need hundreds of rules when we can get by with the three-word formula?

You know the answer, of course. Knowing the three magic words is like spotting intelligent life in another galaxy through a powerful telescope. You know they're out there, but to get to them you first have to invent faster-than-light drive. The rules in this book are just the beginning. They'll tell you how to hold the screwdriver to open the crate of parts.

To my successor, a hundred years down the road, who picks up the torch, who adapts the rules of force-communication as a changing society changes buyer attitudes, who might be kind enough to cancel my mistakes, and who is born into a copywriting climate made a shade more hospitable by this uncertain beginning, I say—as Columbus might have said to Rand McNally—Greetings! I may have had only the vaguest notion of where I was going, and I may not have known where I was when I got there, and I may have thought west was east . . . but I got there first!

Herschell Gordon Lewis

ACKNOWLEDGMENTS

Two lovely young ladies, both named Nelson, helped immeasurably in the preparation of both editions of this book. Peggy Nelson organized and typed many of my original notes and, thank goodness, questioned some dubious conclusions, forcing me to realize they were prejudices rather than conclusions. Carol Nelson, my coauthor in several books, was the source for much updating as well as information and examples relating to electronic media copywriting.

My perspicacious son (and coauthor of *Selling on the Net*), Robert Lewis, who can spot an oxymoron, a cliché, or an overused superlative at sixty paces, pointed out many examples of these curios. And because he is a world-respected authority on the techniques of on-line marketing, his input on that subject undoubtedly has been more valuable than my output.

My editor, Ellen Kadin, is my heroine because she not only clarified my own vision of what this new edition should be and ruthlessly blue-penciled my stupidities but also relentlessly badgered me to deliver the manuscript on time.

But anyone who knows how I work and live also knows who should get credit for these words appearing at all—my wife and business partner, Margo. Not only is she the world's best sounding board for ideas and its foremost clipping service for samples, but she's the world's number one originator of ideas. How lucky I am!

My thanks to all—and to you, for reading the result.

INTRODUCTION

What This Book Will Do for You

Should you write "3" or "three"? "30 minutes" or "half an hour"? Should you lie a little in an e-mail headline to prevent the recipient from clicking the mouse and getting rid of you forever? Should you show a toll-free number in a television spot throughout its length, or will that ploy dull the viewer's reaction?

These questions are typical of the miniproblems besetting the 21st-century copywriter, who faces targets whose skepticism and even antagonism would have been regarded as impolite a generation ago. Impolite? The very meaning of that word has changed, as courtesy becomes a less frequent commodity in society. And we, after all, don't create social mannerisms; we just reflect them and cater to them.

Every word counts . . . so which one should you use?

The answers are in this book. Deciding logically and deliberately whether to use "3" or "three" can be the beginning of a transformation from copywriting-as-art to copywriting-as-science.

We sit at our keyboards. We sift through the layers of experience and intellectual scar tissue. We make decisions, some of them automatic and some of them tortured. Are we right or are we wrong when we change "Can you . . ." to "Will you . . ."?

If you picked up this book and are reading the Preface, you're serious about copywriting. You want your words to be dipped in the magic bucket of power.

Should you write "This is the information you requested" or "This is the information you asked for"?

When should you avoid using asterisks?*

How many ways are there to write a guarantee? What should you promise and what should you avoid?

What's a better word for the word *should*, which appears so often in these first paragraphs?

Do you write "A historic" or "An historic"?

Should (do) you write "One mile"? "5,280 feet"? Do you leave out the comma and write "5280 feet"? (And what's the difference?)

What's a simple test you can give a writer who wants to work for you?

What's wrong with this seemingly harmless line of copy: "The manufacturer has told us the quantity we are to receive will be small"?

What changes in spelling and word construction do you make when you want your copy to appear British?

What's wrong with using the word *disbelieves* in a radio spot?

If you're inventing a brand name, what's the difference between an "ush" syllable and an "usk" syllable?

Do you know the three can't miss tips for writing news releases?

---

* All the time.

What's wrong with paragraphs starting with the word "as"?

The answers to these questions are only a handful of the tips, rules, laws, and commandments—covering just about every commercial-writing circumstance and medium I can think of—in this book. As far as I know, this is the first time anyone (or should it be "anybody"?) has stuck his head in the lion's mouth by attempting to codify rules of copywriting. Even if the book doesn't help you, it has a certain historic value.

Depending on how you approach writing, you will or won't be thrilled to see some hard rules in print. If you welcome the notion that at last it's possible to check your copy against a statutory base, anticipate the marketplace in the year 2025: By then, I'm convinced, you'll have a wide choice of computer programs incorporating these rules. Make a mistake and a red flag will go up. (No, this isn't parallel to those CD-ROMs offering a menu of boilerplate letters, where all you do is fill in the names. We're after genuine creative help—rules, not templates.)

If you think that reducing the creative process to a series of rules is a serious offense—breaking and entering the writer's hallowed seat-of-the-pants domain, a sacred land violated only by nonthreatening (because they're uncreative) researchers—then you'll find the whole concept repulsive, and I guess we aren't going to convince each other of anything.

I think I'm safe. Why? Because if you pooh-pooh the concept behind this book—that writing deliberately and confidently is better than writing haphazardly and fearfully—you wouldn't buy a book whose whole premise, cover to cover, fights your own philosophy.

Okay, if you're ready, let's plow ahead. Welcome to the shining new world of thoughtful, dynamic copy.

H.G.L.

On the Art of Writing Copy

2nd Edition

Chapter One

FORM OR SUBSTANCE: WHICH MAKES FOR MORE EFFECTIVE COPY?

Why Rules Mean Better Copy

This book is jam-packed with rules, laws, commandments, concepts, precepts, principles, and savage opinions.

Why, after all these years, does the copywriter need some rules, laws, and all the rest of it? I'll tell you why: Organized society is becoming more and more dependent on communicators.

We've moved from the safe, shallow waters of an industrial society to the roiling seas of a communications society. It's unthinkable that an event, an individual, or an invention could achieve significance without media attention. So isn't it high time that we began codifying the rules of the road?

Form or substance: Which makes for more effective copy?

Psychology and communications push upward through the crust of human activity, like twin giant volcanoes changing the landscape. During the maturation process over the last 200 years or so, psychologists and communicators alike have ignored the bond they need to dominate 21st-century thought: Psychologists aren't good communicators and communicators are at best seat-of-the-pants psychologists.

Microchips and microthinking

This first chapter begins what I hope will be an ongoing welding of psychology to communications . . . plus the formalization of rules that good copywriters sense but haven't had available to them in organized form.

We're late with this. One reason is that the puppet strings of mass communications have been pulled and tugged by individuals who recognize and are comfortable with the techniques of communication, but who don't give equal status to semantics or phonetics. They're uneasy with linguistics and philology, the study of the words.

Glorification, especially in art-directed communications, has been of *medium*, not *message*. That's how a writer or an artist builds a portfolio, leading to a better-paying job; that's where the cycle of creating good-looking ads continues.

Did the ads pull? Who cares? They look good, don't they?

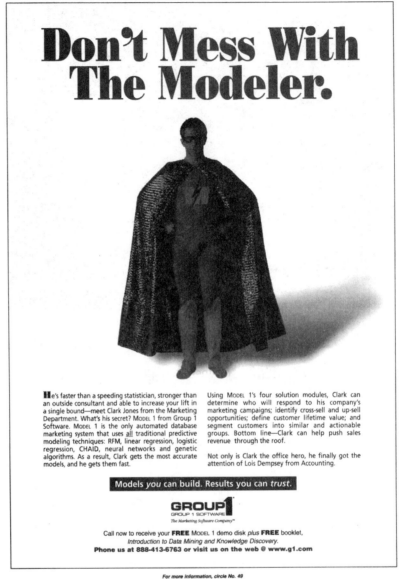

Figure 1-1: An ad generating a "Huh?" reaction is dangerous. Here the Illustration Agreement Rule (see Chapter 13) is discarded in an attempt to substitute cleverness for communication. What possible advantage could there be of trying to force the message to conform to the graphic instead of having the graphic illustrate the message? The text reveals benefits; many readers will never see them.

Three key rules for wordsmiths

For the foreseeable future, I plead that those who go into battle carrying the title wordsmith observe three key rules:

1. the Form Worship Maxim (coming right up)
2. Roget's Complaint (With all the specific descriptive words available, the writer who regards neutral, nonimpact words such as *needs*, *quality*, *features*, and *value* as creative should agree to work for no pay).
3. the Clarity Commandment (the overriding determinant of word choice) When choosing

words and phrases, clarity is paramount. Let no other component of the message mix interfere with it. The reader invariably will apply a negative interpretation to statements that violate the Clarity Commandment.

Want proof that copywriting is approaching the wonderful intersection beyond which logical rules can prevent mistakes? There it is! Observing those three rules (and any beginner can put them to use during the first five minutes at the keyboard) will result in usable copy.

But I don't mean . . .

We can't overlook the one big difference between copywriting as a science and some of the more natural sciences: If you screw up a chemical formula, your compound won't work. Not at all. Zero. But if you screw up a copy formula, your ad still may bring in some business. It won't pull as well as it would have if you'd written it according to the rules, but it probably won't draw a total blank.

The enormous distribution of most advertising messages tilts the odds against zero pull in the writer's favor. Your miscreated formula reaches thousands, even millions of people. On the Internet, it has the potential to touch tens of millions. Even if you make every copywriting mistake in the book, some will get the message.

The point? "The ad didn't draw a blank" is no reason to discard the rules.

For the last time: form or substance?

Is copywriting an art or a science? I say it's about one-third of the way across the bridge from art to science. What makes the current position uncomfortable is the absence of professional standards. Until we have professional standards, anyone can hang out a shingle and claim to be a copywriter. What, for example, is the message transmitted in Figure 1-1? Poseurs have no difficulty aping the form of an ad or a mailing piece someone else has created; their difficulty lies in paralleling substance. For those who believe mechanical tricks can cover or replace imaginative sterility, I propose the Form Worship Maxim: The writer who puts form ahead of substance implicitly admits a creative deficiency. Communications infected with this deficiency call attention to format rather than to what they say. Invariably the writer has a way to transmit the message more effectively than the one he used.

Figure 1-2: What was your quick first reaction to this ad? Mine too.

This may not be the most prudent investment strategy on
Wall Street. But with Williams, you get BOTH
energy AND communications.

NYSE: WMB

Respect for Dave's stock savvy was waning. Time to
regain confidence with Williams' energy AND
communications businesses.

NYSE: WMB

Williams wants you to know that you can easily be
overlooked by the behemothic phone company.

Thanks to the exceptional service offered by
Williams communications; Ed could share
quality time with the family.

Figures 1-3A, 1-3B, 1-3C, 1-3D: This is a campaign by a company called Williams,
proposing . . . what? The assumption, "Everyone knows who we are," is both poor
logic and poor marketing strategy.

The Five Great Motivators

In the Age of Skepticism, we recognize the Five Great Motivators. Remember when primitive classes in advertising taught that food, clothing, and shelter were motivators? Remember when instructors talked about primary needs and secondary needs? No more. We're in the Age of Skepticism, and anyone who might be moved by food, clothing, or shelter isn't worth your promotional dollars. Gourmet food? Yes. Designer clothing? Yes. Status-laden shelter? Yes. But it's the qualifier words that give us the motivators, not the basic requirements of life.

If you want your message to work, you can't consider primary needs and secondary needs. First, the word *needs* is a generalization that won't connect solidly when it comes up against a specific appeal. (Please: For the rest of your life plus six months, don't use *needs* as a noun in any copy you write. Thank you.)

Second, you're way, way off the center of the target if you even consider secondary sales arguments. It's a competitive marketplace, and you have to whang them right between the eyes.

Figure 1-4: This is the cover of a freestanding insert. While "New merchandise" is too general to have much impact, and "no more clipboards" may confuse the uninitiated, that huge coupon is a grabber—a classic use of the *great* motivator greed. The purpose of this cover is to spur the casual reader to open the insert, where actual merchandise is shown.

Figure 1-5: An advantage of greed as a motivator: The ad doesn't have to be pretty, just clear.

So you lean on one of the Five Great Motivators:

1. fear
2. exclusivity
3. guilt
4. greed
5. need for approval

If you're particularly astute and have the opportunity, you frost the cake with either or both "soft" motivators:

▶ convenience
▶ pleasure

If you write clearly and within the reader's experiential background, and present benefits based on an appeal to one of these motivators, you can't miss!

As the mass communications juggernaut rumbles well into the super-sophisticated 21st century, a sixth motivator is showing promise. Actually, it's almost a combination of the second Great Motivator, exclusivity; the Soft Motivator, pleasure; and a smidgeon of the others. Almost, but not quite. We'll keep an eye on it. If you're reading this after the year 2005, you might decide to add it to the hallowed list:

6. ego gratification (maybe)

It's increasingly safe to build a sales appeal around ego gratification, conglomeration of motivators that play to a combination of fear, exclusivity, guilt, greed, and need for approval. That conglomeration, like cosmic dust hardening into a planet, may become the sixth motivator on its own.

Figure 1-6: Does this ad make its point? The theme is, "We're a lot more concerned with your deal than our image." Two questions arise: 1) How might this financial services company have better projected that concept? 2) Is the concept powerful enough to warrant prime position in the company's advertising tactic?

Ego gratification isn't new, but as a valid motivator it's the natural child of the "I deserve everything" attitude that seems to infect all strata of society.

Ego gratification gathers to itself these ingredients:

- ▶ praise from others
- ▶ being in style
- ▶ emulating and being recognized by those we admire
- ▶ attracting an admirer or lover of our own
- ▶ having our lifestyle become congruent with lifestyles we regard as superior

You can see the evolution: Each of these could be sandwiched into one of the Five Great Motivators. Together, they're forming a new one—ego gratification. It's still too naked an appeal to stand alone, but it's getting close. Close.

And how about envy?

How about envy? Unquestionably, copy with a "Don't you wish you could be like . . . " theme has substance, although I'm not enamored of headlines beginning with "Don't."

Remember the motion picture *Close Encounters of the Third Kind*? François Truffaut (playing a distinguished scientist) says to Richard Dreyfuss (playing a clodlike antihero), "I envy you." The effect on the viewer is electric; it's the denouement of the movie. In *Titanic*, the plot swings on a rich girl's envy of the free and easy lifestyle of a boy traveling in steerage. Envy has power.

Years ago, when television was an expensive luxury, a radio commercial had a young child pleading plaintively, "I want a television Christmas . . . a world of magic all my own!" So dynamic was this message that various parent groups lobbied to have it banned.

But how often can we as writers mount an envy appeal without betraying our own position of greed? We're handling live grenades, hot radium. Envy, like the prime mover fear, isn't for the beginner. It's for the maestro who knows the reader, listener, or viewer. It's for a trained or instinctive master psychologist. Safety lies in the Five Great Motivators. With them, you can't miss; stray from them and your message—and you—can wind up in the wastebasket.

How Much Do You Tell Them?

In transmitting their messages, copywriters walk the tightwire between puffery and dullness. How much should you say about what you're selling? A safe rule is the Rule of Partial Disclosure: Tell the target individual as much as you can about what your product or service can do for him or her. If you have space or time left over, don't move down to the next information level (facts unrelated to benefit); instead, restate or illustrate some of the benefits.

The First Canon of Salesmanship wasn't created exclusively for writers, but its aptness applies to every force-communication message: When the prospect says yes, quit selling.

Overtransmission of integrity

Totality of facts—an encyclopedic recitation of every scrap of information about what you're selling—not only may bore people out of buying but also can unsell by including facts they see as negative, even if you don't. The frantic obsession with emptying the information bag mixes desperation with exhibitionism: Total disclosure is undressing in public.

More possibilities than you ever imagined in a single box.

Consider the variety of service alternatives and application demands you face today. Wouldn't it be nice to have a single box that lets you choose the best service for each application and, at the same time, saves you money? Now you can, with ATLAS.

ATLAS is a new integrated access system from ADTRAN. Capable of both dedicated and switched access, this versatile host-site platform consolidates voice, data, and video onto a single digital circuit—lowering monthly payouts, optimizing your pipeline and reducing network management to its simplest form. And it's available for a fraction of what most alternatives cost.

ATLAS. It's the only network access solution that covers the spectrum.

ATLAS 800
The new integrated access system from ADTRAN

CALL 800 9ADTRAN (800 923-8726) FOR A FREE BROCHURE.
www.adtran.com/atlas

T3 ▪ SNMP ▪ T1 ▪ FRAME RELAY ▪ ISDN ▪ REMOTE ACCESS

ADTRAN, Inc.
P.O. Box 140000
Huntsville, AL 35814-4000

ADTRAN

Figure 1-7: Eye-catching . . . but is it image-enhancing? This ad appeared in an Internet trade magazine. How far does the reader have to penetrate the text to discover what's being sold?

Here is an example of copywriting without the sense or discipline of discrimination. Copy for a talking telephone has these four bullets:

▶ Can be taught to respond to one voice only.
▶ Made to conform to U.S. government regulations.
▶ Pulse/Touch-Tone switchable.
▶ 16-number memory.

I hope your question is the same as mine: What is that second bullet doing there? The word "Made" is considerably weaker than the word *manufactured*, but the biggest objection to this bullet is its reference to a point that 1) has no apparent benefit to the reader and 2) has negative overtones. The word "regulations" is deadly in selling copy, especially when any form of the word *approved* might be a substitute. For heaven's sake, use positive words instead of neutral or negative words when you're trying to sell!

When a writer becomes Pandora, opening wide the box of evils locked in a corner of every business enterprise, often the opening has as its justification the integrity of the writer. If you write copy like this and begin to feel that your dispassionate and enlightened viewpoint is superior to your employer's desire to sell something, quit before you're fired. You're in the wrong job.

What bothers me far more than an occasional misguided eruption of conscience is seeing or hearing the result of such an eruption in print or broadcast ads. Somebody had a noble idea and somebody else okayed it. Even more puzzling, a born-again advertiser thinks the public will applaud utter honesty that makes him look bad.

Yes, I know the fifteenth Way to Thwart the Age of Skepticism—admit an Achilles' heel. (See "Skepticism" in Chapter 26 of this book for the other fourteen ways.) But the admission is supposed to temper what otherwise is an incredible claim, not to become the linchpin selling argument.

We hear this radio commercial:

Sheehan Leasing isn't the lowest-priced leasing company. But does cheap really fit your lifestyle? Isn't it worth a little more—not a lot more, a little more—to get Sheehan service? . . .

and we quit listening. Sheehan has admitted an Achilles' heel, all right, but that's the only one of its aspects the company has described. We're not tempering incredulity and thereby adding verisimilitude; we're blurting out a negative that overpowers the mildest of positives—"Sheehan service," an unexplained molecule of puffery.

The commercial typifies the negative information ads we see too often. Why write ads that raise more questions than they answer?

A catalog description of the robot zoids has this copy:

Each uses two C batteries and Terox also requires two AA batteries for lights (no batteries included).

Analyze those words: "no batteries included." Can you think of a more negative way to transmit this information? Why not the standard *batteries not included*, which at least doesn't violate the Rule of Negative Transmission: Unless you want the reader or viewer to think you're the originator or generator of the reason for negative information, don't put this information aggressively.

IT'S THE NECKLACE INSPIRED BY THE MOVIE TITANIC

And Here's The Hottest News – It's only $19⁹⁵

By Liz Peterson
(Special Advertising Supplement)

Have you seen the necklace that's taking the nation by storm? Well, it's called the *Blue Heart Jewel* and we'll even tell you how to get it.

Lindenwold Fine Jewelers has been swamped with people wanting to buy the *Blue Heart Jewel* necklace.

But when word got out that this stunning necklace costs only $19.95, Lindenwold Jewelers had to work miracles to insure they could keep up with the demand.

The *Blue Heart Jewel* is designed just the right size for everyday wear. It looks great with simple denim jeans or is equally perfect with an evening gown.

Even though everyone is trying to get one, Lindenwold Fine Jewelers is still taking orders for the *Blue Heart Jewel* necklace. They have even promised that, at least for now, they will still sell the necklace at this amazing low price.

HERE'S HOW TO GET YOUR OWN BLUE HEART JEWEL NECKLACE

We'll give you the direct telephone number and address so you can immediately get your own *Blue Heart Jewel* necklace. If you have a credit card (VISA, MasterCard, Discover/Novus or American Express), call toll free, **1-800-757-0660**, and ask for Dept. 1539.

To order by mail, send $19.95 check, cash or money order to: Blue Heart Jewel, Dept. 1539, Lindenwold Fine Jewelers, 20 Lindenwold Ave., Canton, Ohio 44767. You must add $5.95 for shipping and handling.

The *Blue Heart Jewel* necklace comes with a full, lifetime money-back guarantee. And, even though so many people are requesting more than one, all orders are normally shipped within 72 hours.

Hopefully, you'll be one of the lucky ones who can get the *Blue Heart Jewel necklace*, because, right now, it's definitely the hottest status necklace anywhere. Enjoy! ■

©1998 (HS® S-4107 OF3272R-1

HOT: Hollywood heartthrob Jensen Ackles (star of Days of our Lives) sizzles with Titanic fever as he shows off the Blue Heart Jewel for all his gal pals.

THE SUN JOURNAL • NEWSPAPER REPRINT WITH PERMISSION

Necklace Makes Huge Splash With Movie Fans

Hollywood Report — The blockbuster movie *Titanic* has inspired a necklace that movie fans can't get enough of. If you liked the movie, you'll have to have one...

Now it has inspired the *Blue Heart Jewel*, designed [and] specially sized... for comfortable everyday wear by Lindenwold Fine Jewelers.

The jeweler says, "People will not believe their eyes when they actually see someone with the *Blue Heart Jewel* necklace. It draws unforgettable attention to anyone seen wearing it."

With all the attention the movie is getting, fashion experts are predicting that blue heart necklaces may become the hottest jewelry trend of all time, especially at the low price of only $19.95.

Lindenwold Fine Jewelers is providing a special order request line. Call toll free, 1-800-757-0660, and ask for Dept. 1539. The necklace is being released on a first-come, first-served basis.

■ **BLUE HEARTS SPARKLE AT BOX-OFFICE.** Super model Colleen Capell (Right) and Kara Murphy, look like a million wearing the *Blue Heart Jewel* necklace inspired by the blockbuster movie *Titanic*.

Figure 1-8: Yes, it's a lot of copy, but a lot of copy is the way to sell with a single shot. A mail-order ad has to generate response now or it fails; image is inconsequential if response isn't there. Notice the technique of an apparent newspaper story insert: The intention is to give what appears to be a third-party validation to the claims made in the rest of the ad.

Mona Lisa   *Leonardo Da Vinci (1452-1519)*

To Know The Secret To
Building Business You Need Talent.

Painter, inventor, scientist. The depth and variety of Da Vinci's body of work is a tribute to human talent. And talent makes the difference between being good and being great. With Metromail, you know you are working with the most talented people in the industry. The combination of the best people, state-of-the-art technology and extensive experience, is the secret to great direct marketing.

Metromail emphasizes *partnership* between our people and yours as the best tool to provide you with more and better information. Information that will improve your perspective and add value that will enhance your business. What we bring to the partnership is talent and attention to detail. Our expertise assures you of the very best in marketing products and services.

So let the marketing artists at Metromail help you design your message for your best audience. They'll work with you to put together a portrait of who you want to reach so that your next direct marketing effort will be a masterpiece.

The Art of Building Business

Metromail
AN R.R. DONNELLEY & SONS COMPANY

Lombard (800) 321-8013   Lincoln (800) 228-4571   Oak Brook (708) 574-3800
Sherman Oaks (818) 382-4600   Atlanta (800) 541-0524   New York (212) 599-2616

Booth #1812 Fall 1995 DMA Show

Metromail is a member of the Direct Marketing Association (DMA), and as such believes in and adheres to DMA's guidelines for Ethical Business Practices, Personal Information Protection, Mailing List Practices, Marketing by Telephone Guidelines, and Fair Information Practices. By using our lists, our customers agree they will market to individuals on these lists in accordance with these guidelines and practices.

For more information, circle No. 49

Figure 1-9: The *Mona Lisa* has been used in many hundreds of ads. Does it work here? If your answer is (as mine was), "What's the tie between the *Mona Lisa* and Metromail?" the conclusion is that it's a stretch.

Specifics Sell—Nonspecifics Don't

The writer who substitutes generalities for specifics has a real problem: That writer is automatically selling less than he or she could. If the generalities stem from lack of information, the problem lies in the transmission of salesworthy facts; writer and source should attack the problem jointly. But if the generalities stem from the copywriter's own philosophy, the problem is far more severe because the procedure suggests a deficiency in the writer's professional qualifications.

IDG CONFERENCE MANAGEMENT COMPANY PRESENTS

Spotlight 98
is a winning combination of people discussing and dissecting creativity, innovation, and profit.

[**Register today!**
w w w . s p o t l i g h t . c o m]
or call **1-800-633-4312**

spotlight

Figure 1-10: When art direction becomes so paramount the message is obscured, effectiveness is damaged. This not only is hard to read; the illustrations seem to make no point.

Example: What's wrong with this copy, the total description of an item in a page of travel items?

A sleeping bag or a bed? Travasleep gives you the convenience of both.

Right! No specifics. What are the individual conveniences? We're left to interpret . . . and to sell ourselves. The writer has said to the reader, "You know more about this than I do, so you

Figure 1-11: Read the entire top paragraph. Does this weak collection of generalizations generate as strong a desire to follow up as even a single specific might?

fill in the gaps." The reader logically says, "Forget it." Certainly the writer has enough information to replace the nonspecific puffery with what appears to be specific information:

> A sleeping bag or a bed? Travasleep gives you the "sleep anywhere" convenience of a sleeping bag with the restful comfort of a soft, downy bed.

Since nonspecifics are a key no-no, let's add another example. Here's part of a letter selling a privately printed magazine:

> We don't claim your magazine would be as good as *Modern Executive*, but we do point out that . . .

You caught it, of course: "As good as" isn't as good as a specific might be. Replace it with specifics and the argument springs to life. Even knowing nothing about *Modern Executive*, we can replace "as good as" with a better "as" phrase. Pick one or invent your own:

▶ as professionally edited as . . .
▶ as beautifully printed as . . .
▶ as perfectly targeted to today's executive as . . .
▶ as big a bargain as . . .

Specificity equals felicity

Specific words generate a far greater emotional reaction than generalized words; the more specific the words, the more the writer controls emotions. (On the World Wide Web, multiply that point by four.)

Example: A writer referred to a rock musician as "dirty." Yes, dirty is an emotion-loaded word, but overtones differ from intent. An editor, after discussion with the writer, changed *dirty* to *unwashed*—the description the writer actually intended. The editor asked and answered the question the writer should have asked and answered: What conclusion do I want the reader to draw?

Aw, they know what I mean

Writing is conscious, not unconscious. You can ruminate to yourself almost unconsciously because you have no trouble decoding what you mean. But copywriting is aimed at a target.

Suppose I write "the oldest group of members." What does it mean? Are these the members who are the oldest in age? Or are they the ones who have been members for the longest period of time? I've committed the same hit-and-run mistake as many other writers, damaging the message the way static damages radio reception. The message recipient hesitates because of possible misinterpretation, and hesitation weakens impact.

If we, casual readers, can replace nonspecifics with specifics, how much better a piece of copy the original writer might compose with even a little thought. After all, the writer has ammunition we lack—all the facts.

Figure 1-12: What image does this ad project? Isn't it one of antiquity, being out-of-date with obsolete equipment? A double "then/now" photograph might have provided the effect the advertiser intended.

Figure 1-13: What makes the hat at lower right the "Management" hat? Is emphasizing hat-wearing the strongest way to make this advertiser's point—that management should be able to focus on growth and not be distracted by time-consuming peripheral details? "Reducing employment costs" is a crucial sales weapon, buried as an apparent afterthought.

And We're Off!

Even from this mild beginning, you can see how copywriting has the seeds of logical analysis in its structure. Depending on logic kills creativity? Heck, no. Don't fear it any more than you'd fear a newly discovered antitoxin for a noxious disease. It's parallel to a spelling-checker, not to a creativity suppressor.

Is seat-of-the-pants copywriting on the way out? I certainly hope so. It would be good for advertising writers' claim of professionalism if practitioners could replace "This copy worked" with "This copy worked because . . ."

Chapter Two

YOU, ME, AND WHAT MAKES US RESPOND

How to Put *You* Into the Mix

Unless the reader regards himself as the target of your message, benefit can't exist. Benefit demands a we/you relationship.

What, then, is wrong with this opening?

The person whose name appears on the label is entitled to . . .

Right! The writer is Pygmalion. He creates and his reader reacts accordingly. His dispassionate copy generates a dispassionate reader. Uninvolved, the reader remains an observer, not a participant. Emotion is sapped out of the decision-making process (see "How to Make Emotion Your Powerful Advertising Weapon" in this chapter and "Emotion vs. Intellect" in Chapter 26). When the vendor is uninvolved, the buyer is uninvolved. And when the buyer is uninvolved, the vendor loses.

So we change the approach just a hair:

If you're the individual whose name appears on the label, you're entitled to . . .

"I am the greatest" copy generates a ho-hum reaction at best. On down days, when our brains are out of gear but deadlines loom, any of us may have written an advertising headline such as the following:

There is a difference in quality and service, and the difference is *Alpha Omega.*

Suppose we're bright enough to replace those deadly words "quality" and "service." Have we helped the ad enough to make it professional? In my opinion, no. There's still a zero *you* factor in this headline.

Putting *you* into the mix doesn't just mean inserting the word *you* into self-aggrandizing copy. Don't make your copy a megalomaniacal mirror. Go through the looking glass. That's the tactical difference between Figure 2-1, which projects specific benefits, Figure 2-2, which assumes recognition, and Figure 2-3, which has a clichéd concept with boilerplate copy.

An assumptive, strutting, preening attitude results in advertising copy such as:

We're Moving!
Our new building and expanded facilities
will enable us to serve you better!

Figure 2-1: The typical meeting planner might regard Guatemala as a low-possibility choice. This ad, in a publication circulated to meeting planners, might well move that destination up the ladder because it names specific benefits.

Figure 2-2: This ad is assumptive. In a competitive ambience, assumption may not be heavy enough competitive artillery.

DOUBLETREE GIVES YOUR MEETING THE STRATEGIC PLANNING IT DESERVES.

Across the board.

Attentive service. Professional staff. Outstanding facilities.

Comfortable accommodations. They all add up to a successful agenda for you.

Just a phone call away. Plus chocolate chip cookies at over **175** locations.

DOUBLETREE HOTELS 🍒 **GUEST SUITES & RESORTS**™

FOR GROUPS 800-233-6161

Sweet Dreams

©1998 Promus Hotel Corporation. www.doubletreehotels.com

Circle #573 on Free Information Card

Figure 2-3: Can this ad—a total cliché, including the illustration—compete with meeting-site ads that specify benefits? Suppose a meeting planner asked, "Why should we choose you?" Would any sane sales executive expect the copy in this ad to carry the day?

They will, huh? How? Will you speed up my order, and if so, by how much? Will you carry a bigger inventory of the items I order? I'm the skeptical ad receiver of the 21st century. I don't care about you; I care about me. Unless you show me benefits, I regard your "new building" ad as another piece of puffery. If you want me to react to your move, give me some specifics, aimed at me. Don't give me empty self-flattery.

The "You First" Rule—Tell the reader, listener, or viewer what's in it for him, not for you—can be a moneymaker for you.

Everybody knows this, you say? Not the writer of this communication, mailed to "Resident":

1. I AM YOUR COLDWELL BANKER KLOCK COMPANY REPRESENTATIVE I AM A FULL-TIME PROFESSIONAL, enjoy my work, and am determined that you will receive the finest real estate service possible!
2. I have available the FINEST REAL ESTATE SALES TRAINING PROGRAM IN THE NATION!

They can climb stairs,
take care of upholstery,
pick up spills in the kitchen,
clean carpets and bare floors,
work indoors, work outdoors and
keep your car looking like new.

(Let's see a pen and pencil set do all that.)

Eureka's Boss Lite® Cordless and Boss® Hand Vacs are handy incentives to have around. Powerful. Lightweight. Easy-to-use. Fully-loaded with great brand recognition—thanks in part to their broad TV exposure — high perceived value and broad consumer appeal. Boss Lite® and Boss® Hand Vac.

Just two in a proven line of sought-after incentives that include Eureka uprights, cannisters, wet/dry vacs, steam cleaners and the environmentally-friendly Enviro Vac™ with true HEPA-sealed filtration systems.

They do everything you can ask an incentive to do. Except write the orders.

Boss®
Hand Vac
Model #74

Boss Lite®
Cordless
Model #93B

For your nearest Eureka representative call 888-800-2706.
Or visit our web site: www.eureka.com

© 1996 The Eureka Company, Bloomington, IL 61701   In Canada: Cambridge, Ontario N3H 2N7   In Mexico City: Andromaco 16 C.P. 11520

Figure 2-4: Suppose you had an assignment: Write an ad selling vacuum cleaners as a sales incentive. Would you have thought of an eye-catching, motivating concept such as this one?

3. I am supported by a DYNAMIC, FULL-TIME MANAGEMENT TEAM who have the time to help me help you! . . .

This exercise in consummate modesty has ten statements in all. Nine begin with the word "I" and the tenth, for variety, begins with "Our." Its egocentricity parallels the bore who, after talking about himself for half an hour, says, "Enough about me. Let's talk about you. What do you think of me?"

How to Make Emotion Your Powerful Advertising Weapon

An article in *Advertising Age* was headed, "Emotion, a powerful tool for advertisers."

As an example, the writer used a MasterCard campaign whose theme was "So worldly, so welcome." That's about as emotion-laden as a volume of 19th-century legal statutes. Think for a moment: What emotional satisfaction can MasterCard bring you? You might argue that it makes you feel worldly; in turn, the emotional side of you argues the relative emotionalism of worldly. Welcome? This word is too generalized to have any emotional impact.

For its 1999 models, Buick actually trademarked this slogan:

Isn't it time for a real car?™

Another example described in the article was a campaign by Minolta: "Only from the Mind of Minolta." Referring to an automatic-focusing camera called the Maxxum, the writer commented, "To anyone who has missed a shot while fiddling with a focusing ring, the fact of auto-focus is emotional enough."

Seems to me this commentator missed a shot. Product per se isn't emotional. "Only from the Mind of Minolta" is crowing self-encomium that leaves the reader out.

The Minolta Maxxum was an innovative and superior product; that's why it sold well, despite the nondescript theme lauded by the article in *Advertising Age*. True emotionalism is the reverse of intellectualism. Here's proof that "Only from the Mind of Minolta" doesn't qualify: The word "Mind" is an intellectual word; *brain* is more emotional. Whatever stimulators the creator of that theme may have intended to apply, emotion wasn't one of them.

The Rule of Emotional Mandate

Active voice, not passive, is a major component of emotional copy. A help-wanted ad in an advertising publication, recruiting a director for a university's graduate program in corporate communications/public relations, listed these qualifications, among others:

▶ Evidence of scholarly capabilities through publishing and research is required.
▶ Previous classroom teaching experience is mandatory.
▶ Practical industry experience is highly desirable.
▶ Proven administrative abilities are necessary as the candidate will be responsible for curriculum development.

Let's say you qualify for this job. Unless you were desperate for food, would you, as a professional in communications and public relations, feel comfortable answering this ad? The standoffish tone, the icy words such as "mandatory" and "required," the Kafkaesque avoidance of "we" as the source, the reference to you as a candidate—these will bring in the bureaucrats, not the creatives. Result? The gap between academia and the real world gets a little wider.

Are You Less Than Egg-cited
About Your Promotional Materials?

Are they lacking that special something your competitors seem to have? Are your materials outdated and in need of a fresh

new look? At Imagine That! Creative Services, we can design your corporate brochure, new logo and identity package,

or that perfect ad that stands out and gets noticed. Whatever your design needs, Imagine That! can help.

In fact, we're eggs-hilarated at the very thought.

Corporate Identity Packages • Brochures • Custom Publishing • Advertising Design
Product Catalogs • Cigar Bands • Box Design • Newsletters • Catalogs

1701 W. Hillsboro Blvd. • Suite 305 • Deerfield Beach, FL 33442 • (954) 252-9393 • (888) SKARCO-1
Fax (954) 252-9391 • e-mail: skarco@gate.net • A Division of SKARCO Press

Figure 2-5: This company specializes in creating promotional materials. Based on this ad, would you hire them?

Help-wanted classified ads aren't exempt from human reaction; in fact, they should be more aware of it. The Rule of Emotional Mandate is a handy one to keep in your hip pocket: Unless you want to avoid reader involvement in your message, always write in the active voice.

Let technicians write for one another's uninvolved nonreactions. To sell, you need reader involvement, and that means looking for a reaction, not giving a recitation.

Figure 2-6: The word "geek" has highly emotional overtones. In this usage, it unquestionably results in greater readership of the message. Body copy, less than complimentary, isn't as much of a rapport builder as it might be.

Emotion in fund-raising—a *must*

In fund-raising copy, it's suicidal to start reciting statistics, leaving the reader's emotions safely locked away. This copy leaves the reader uninvolved:

> These girls must live—and study—in wooden huts.

I've pointed this out elsewhere: If you can't think of any other way to involve your target, ask a question:

> What's it to you if these girls have to live—and study—in wooden huts?

While we were putting air in the tires, we fixed the transmission too: We changed "must" to "have to." We didn't mess with the word "study," which can get in the way of fund-raising by suggesting they can't be *in extremis* if they have the time and facilities for organized education.

How to Put Psychology to Work for You

Some of the easiest rules of communication are rules of psychology (psychology + communication = salesmanship). We stumble upon these rules by asking ourselves, "Why did I react that way?" and then chipping away personal prejudices and other impurities. What's left is a shining, valuable rule that benefits communicators by letting us play virtuoso cadenzas on the psychological strings of our targets.

While writing a direct-mail offer, I decided to strengthen the money-back guarantee by changing the risk-free inspection period from thirty days to one month. Then, like Archimedes in the bathtub, I yelled "Eureka!" as the reason for the change hit me—the Generic Determination Rule: The generic determines reaction more than the number.

And what, you ask, does that mean? You can feel relief when you see how what appears to be a pedantic rule is instead one of the most useful weapons in your arsenal.

One month is a longer time than *thirty days*. Oh, not really; *perceived* time is the psychological key that can unlock the door of buyer receptivity. What the rule means is that a generic (in this case, month and day) exercises greater control over human reaction than the number associated with it (in this case, *one* and *thirty*).

Does it work? You bet. *Half an hour* is a "longer" time than *thirty minutes*. The generics are *hours* and *minutes*. The numbers are *one* and *thirty*: One half-hour . . . thirty minutes. The rule says generics determine reaction more than numbers. That being true, sixty *minutes* seems to be less time than one *hour*. (If the television show were named *One Hour*, ratings would plummet.)

Similarly, sixty *seconds* seems to be a shorter span of time than one *minute*. Twenty-four *hours* appears to be a shorter span of time than one *day*. We pay attention to the generic unit—seconds, minutes, hours, or days—not to the number.

This piece of information is not trivial. You can control the reader's reaction without changing the facts.

If you want to suggest that you process claims in a shorter time, you write "forty-eight hours"; if you want the time to seem longer, you write "two days." Shorter distance: "Five thousand, two hundred and eighty feet"; longer distance: "one mile." Smaller quantity: "one pint"; larger quantity: "half a quart." Less weight: "eight ounces"; more weight: "half a pound."

Want proof that the Generic Determination Rule changes the perception without changing the facts? How's this: What if McDonald's Quarter Pounder were called McDonald's Four Ouncer?

Let's move up to the second level: Which of these seems to imply a longer period of time: "Established 1981" or "More Than 20 Years at This Location"?

Let's expand the Generic Determination Rule to cover this second-level concept, the Chronology Rule: Does the experiential background of your primary targets include a date within their adult experience? Then numbers of years, months, or days appear longer.

Using these two allied rules, we can widen our generic determinations in both directions. If an event is supposed to be recent, it didn't happen three months ago; it happened last April ("back in April" artificially pumps up the time gap). "I haven't seen you for ten years" suggests a considerably longer gap than "I haven't seen you since 1990."

Likewise, "You've only had it since 2000" is less time, in 2002, than "You've only had it for two years."

The psychology of tense selection

Present tense: "This sells elsewhere for $100."
    Past tense: "This sold elsewhere for $100."
    What's the difference? Plenty. Present tense has the power because right now somebody else is selling this for $100. Past tense loses strength because it's history, not current events.
    What do you do if you can't claim a current competitive marketplace at $100? Simple: You split the difference by moving into the present perfect tense: "This has sold elsewhere for $100."
    Present perfect links the immediacy of the present with the factual comfort of the past. Don't worry about terminology or the forgotten sentence parsing of Miss Norwalk's third-grade class. Keep repeating, as I do: Copywriters are communicators, not grammarians. What matters isn't your knowledge of which tense is which; it's your knowledge of how to transform the lead of drab fact into the gold of lustrous attraction.
    One exception: Use *sold,* not *has sold* or *have sold,* when suggesting a break with the past, especially in headline copy: Thousands Sold at $100!
    Why is "This has sold . . . " usually better copy than "These have sold . . . "? Two reasons:

1. Exclusivity is one of the Five Great Motivators. Singularity suggests exclusivity; pluralizing makes both what you're selling and those to whom you sell it anonymous.

2. The singular implicitly suggests quantity limitation. It's the same impulse-building syndrome that brings crowds to the door half an hour before a store opens: "Only 11 at This Price!"

(The reason for the word "usually" in the explanation: When quantity is small, pluralizing emphasizes fewness.)
    When writing accomplishment copy, present perfect creates an immediacy you can't achieve with past tense. Example: A piece of copy about miniaturized firearms read:

    Sr. Alberti created a perfect working replica . . .

which lost the selling hook by turning Sr. Alberti's accomplishment into a historical incident. The work becomes a current event with a single word change:

    Sr. Alberti has created a perfect working replica . . .

    Check your copy for lost timing. You can lose the reader's or listener's interest by wandering through history, and you can yank that interest back into the present by a tense change. Instead of

    The work had a profound effect . . .

which doesn't have a profound effect, since it seems to have come and gone before your target individual came onto the scene, you can write:

    The work has had a profound effect . . .

    The profundity seems to have continued right up to the moment your words hit the paper. "Has had" can be even more dynamic than "is having" because present tense can have a subtle overtone of incompleteness or a changeable circumstance.

"In Your Face" Advertising

Even a few years ago, readers would have been shocked by space ads with copy like that appearing in Figure 2-7:

"What does your Smirnoff vodka make you?"
"A kick-ass martini."

Figure 2-7: How hip can you get? Even a handful of years ago, copy such as this would have caused an uproar and probably been rejected by many publications. We might consider this a marker of societal change, whether good or bad.

They would have wondered why Glenfiddich vodka had to have the word "damn" in its ads (Figure 2-8).

Some would have written nasty letters complaining about headlines such as the one in Figure 2-9:

Should we call it E*TRADE 98?
E*TRADE 2.0? Or E*TRADE kicks butt?

Figure 2-8: Would this ad have succeeded if the word "damn" were dropped from "Made the same damn way since 1887"? Probably not, on a raw attention-getting basis . . . unless the copywriter had been able to think of another adjective, one that combined the suggestion of superiority with attention-getting. For some Scotch aficionados, this ad damages the brand's upscale image.

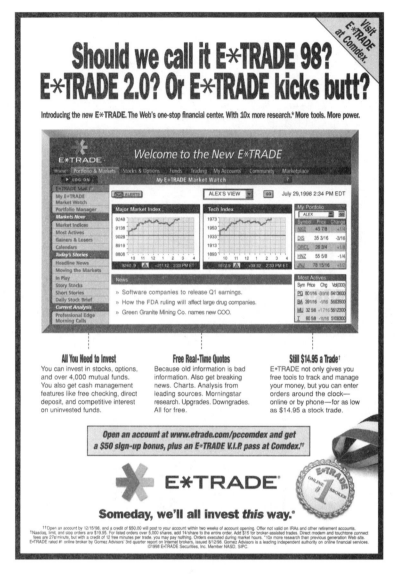

Figure 2-9: As Figures X-1 through X-4 exemplified (see Preface), the phrase "kicks butt" has become commonplace as some advertisers adopt "In your face" campaign concepts. "Kicks butt" is well on its way to becoming so commonplace that it has little impact. The significance lies in the marketing assumptions it represents: Shocking sensibilities is good salesmanship.

It is, after all, only language. And since the invention of language, what one person finds offensive another person finds provocative.

Is responsibility for the slackening of moral codes on the shoulders of radio talk-show hosts, who now regularly use words that a few years ago would have had them banned from the air? Does responsibility lie in the Internet, with no informational filters and thousands of easily available porn sites? How about movies, where the NC-17 rating means little or nothing? Why not television, which now telecasts adult-theme dramas at hours when the under-13s are viewing? Or maybe it's the schoolyard, where dirty words are now commonplace.

And why run ads showing models with pierced noses and lips, such as those in Figure 2-10? These models become role models, as do basketball players who dye their hair green.

Put the muscle of one million pre-recruited cooperative respondents into your research.

Could your research benefit from the strength of the largest Internet research capability in the business? Harris Black International has the answer. Through the Harris Poll Online we've created a cooperative respondent panel of over one million people. Very soon, that number will be close to two million and include respondents from around the world.

With HBI you'll get more research for the dollar...and you'll get it faster than

ever. You can even conduct 10,000 five-minute complex questionnaires per hour. Other advantages include:
• Pre-qualified database
• Faster, higher response rates
• Respondent friendly polling
• Low incidence sample identification

Call or email us today to find out how the power of Internet research can improve your business. Because when it comes to quality respondents, our database just can't be beat.

Harris Black International, Ltd.

135 Corporate Woods,
Rochester, NY 14623-1457
1 (888) 557-7492 • michelles@harrisblackintl.com • www.harrisblackintl.com/whatsnew_fr.html
Louis Harris & Associates • Harris Interactive • Harris Black International Consulting • Gordon S. Black Corporation • Data Collection Services • Harris Black International Network

Figure 2-10: A curiosity of today's marketing climate is the appearance of advertising messages that attract some targets and repel others.

The communicator is a mirror of society, not its creator. Two rules apply to the use of "in your face" messages.

▶ The "In-Your-Face" Message Rule: The effectiveness or annoyance of an "in-your-face" message depends entirely on its synchronization with the attitude of the message recipient.
▶ The Shock Diminution Rule: Shock diminishes in exact ratio to repetition.

Is that a hard drive in your pocket or are you just happy to see us?

Exciting, isn't it? With DirectorSearch you have 24-hour online access to an intelligent database

of directors and production companies, all organized by specialty, location, product category,

client and other criteria. View selected :30 second spots and order reels for next day delivery,

right from your computer. For a free trial, visit our website. Eeewww, that's not a hard drive!

director search

1 - 8 7 7 - 2 8 7 - 0 0 0 7

w w w . d i r e c t o r s e a r c h . c o m

Figure 2-11: You may have thought you had graduated from suggestive humor such as this when you graduated from high school. A play on words often ranks cleverness above communication. Ads aimed at creatives sometimes claim the right to cross the border of taste.

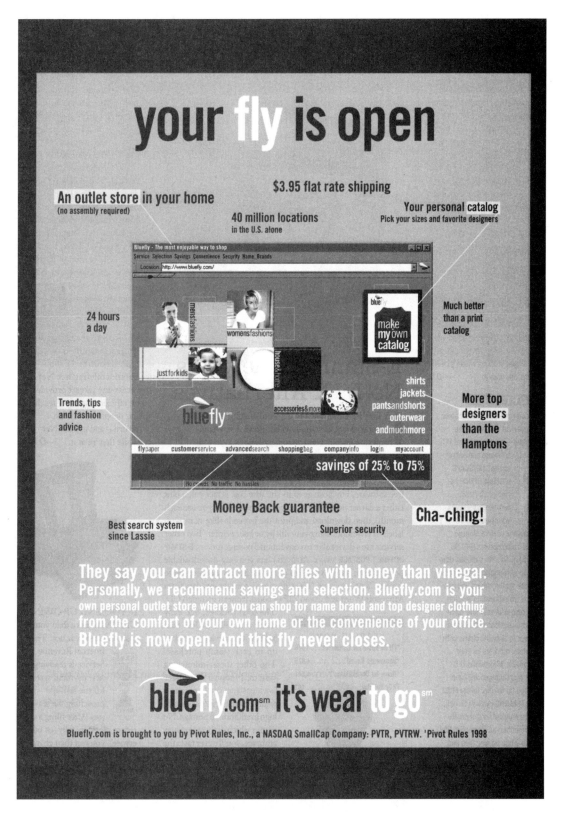

Figure 2-12: As the current prime mover in marketing message evolution/devolution, the Internet knows few rules. Ads in Internet magazines can smirk without causing a single red face.

They give you Dick.

We give you Richard.

That's the Senior V.P. Richard who lives in L.A., drives a BMW and wants to buy a DVD player and a kayak.

We know this because we're PointCast, the leading Internet news network with a 100% registered viewership of 1.2 million upscale, business consumers (22% of whom plan to buy a DVD player*). And with an average HHI of $114,000, they can afford it. So reach Richard and his 1.2 million colleagues with a PointCast 30-second, interactive, motion graphics spot that won't be wasted on some Dick. Call us at (408) 990-6413 or visit us at www.pointcast.com/richard.

Figure 2-13: To those who have never heard the obscene expression, this ad might refer to an ill-fated Miller Lite campaign centered around an obnoxious character named Dick, or it might simply be the difference between calling somebody Dick or Richard. Chances are very strong that the writer of this ad did intend to lean on the obscenity because otherwise the comparison is both weak and flat.

SURGEON GENERAL'S WARNING: Smoking
Causes Lung Cancer, Heart Disease,
Emphysema, And May Complicate Pregnancy.

WINSTON BOX

16 mg. "tar", 1.1 mg. nicotine
av. per cigarette by FTC method.

No additives are in our tobacco, for true taste

"*I've played so much guitar
it'd make your ass hurt.*"

—The late *Guitar Gabriel, Music Maker beneficiary*

Figure 2-14: Cigarette manufacturers assume they can be excused for running ads such
as this. They face limitations not only in what they can say but where they can say it.
Nevertheless, the rationale behind the language in this ad is hard to defend.

Figure 2-15: Powerful language doesn't have to be obscene, as this ad in a freestanding insert proves.

Maximizing Image

What's wrong with this copy?

> Joseph's SuperValue Warehouse is located on Cambridge Highway, on the corner of Central, Suite 902.

The mixed message destroys the size impression we want. How can a warehouse be in Suite 902? For advertising purposes, leave that suite number out. It makes the enterprise seem to be a one-room company. (Which it may be, but why advertise a negative?)

Procter & Gamble can use a post office box; most medium-size companies look better and bigger if, instead of having P.O. Box 897 as an address, they use either Box 297 or Lock Box 297. It's the same information, but the image is stronger.

Does your post office have a name? You can adopt it and gain luster: Box 297, Grand Central Post Office or (but check with the local postmaster first to get approval, which you'll probably get because post offices have their own ZIP codes) Box 297, Grand Central.

If you've won a meaningless award, either glorify it or convert it to a generic. Example: You've won the North Belle Vernon, Pennsylvania, "Best Grocer Award." To glorify it, add a descriptive word: "Winner of the coveted North Belle Vernon Best Grocer Award"; or convert it to a generic: "The award-winning store." Careful: If you claim to be "Winner of the coveted Best Grocer Award," be sure it's in context. Never let puffery expand into lying.

You Don't Have to Be a Poet

One advantage you will have from knowing a few rules is that you won't have to wait for inspiration to hit you. If you think using logic instead of waiting for inspiration isn't a healthy notion because you abandon your creative genius mantle, you've never had a deadline.

For those of us who can't stall but who pray that our feeble creative fires will start to burn brightly: Awareness of logical rules is the sign of professionalism.

Chapter Three

THE LEAN MACHINE: HOW TO USE WORDS

Good Writing Is Lean Writing

You've heard it many times before: Good writing is lean. Don't mistake leanness for anorexia. You want to get rid of fat, not muscle. Most first drafts are heavily insulated with fat, and exercising your editing muscle will break down and flush away those greasy globules without cutting into the meat.

Here's a quick test: This is one of five bullets describing a portable radio:

▶ Has a stereo/mono switch that helps you pull in weak or distant stations.

You have to leave the meat alone. So "stereo/mono switch" has to remain intact. How can you tighten and strengthen this line?

▶ Stereo/mono switch helps you to pull in weak or distant stations.

Notice anything else? What's the word "to" doing there? It's part of the fat, not the meat, so you slice it out and you have:

▶ Stereo/mono switch helps you pull in weak or distant stations.

A slash would go even further:

▶ Stereo/mono switch picks up weak/distant stations.

I don't agree. This turns leanness into anorexia. Instead of taut, the overcondensed bullet seems frantic. There's a rule for this, the Tightness Rule: Keep copy tight enough so it fits the reader's skimming without forcing a comprehension stop.

Live or Dead Words

The copywriter's job is to bring an image to life. Did a copywriter have anything to do with this line of copy?

This toothpaste is specially made to prevent cavities.

Even a beginner should be able to spot the weakness in the word "made." One doesn't need five years of postgraduate copywriting training to recognize how much more power lies in words such as *compounded* or *formulated*. Why? Because by using *compounded* or *formulated*, the writer bestows accomplishment on the toothpaste. Anyone can *make* something.

From an automobile manufacturer came this limp line:

Mazda trucks provide a new standard of quietness.

Can't you see the word "provide" draining strength out of the truck? *Provide* is an accountant's or economist's term. In the dynamic and competitive world of salesmanship, you write copy in color, not black-and-white.

The dictionary does list the word *quietness*, but the word is altogether too peaceful for truck copy, even compared with *quiet*.

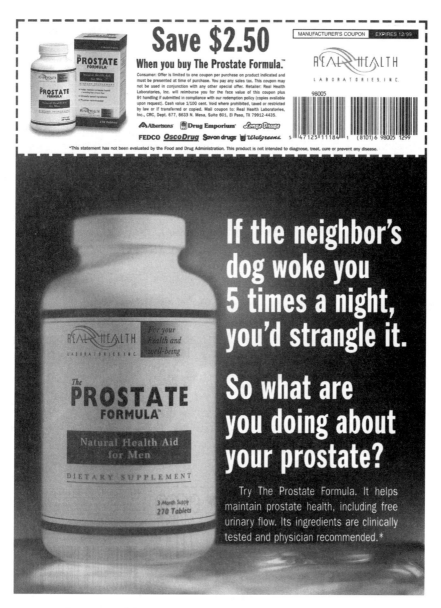

Figure 3-1: The power of this simile doesn't depend on exotic words or a huge vocabulary. Power stems from a hard direct connection with the target reader's state of mind.

"I wish to . . . " has a limp-sponge impact; "I want to . . . " indicates character and position. A billboard for a restaurant has this line of copy:

All baking done on premises.

Did a lawyer write that? A copywriter would have written:

We do all our own baking.

If the writer knew the restaurant business, the copy would have a little more specificity:

We bake our own rolls, bread, cakes, and pies.

A manufacturer's camera magalog (a catalog set up in magazine format) has this line:

The Professional MAXXUM is the fastest operating camera available today.

That word "available" is the leech in this sentence. Like *quality* and *service, available* is a neutral word, marking time. Take out the word; isn't the sentence stronger without it?

If your copy is consistently flat, don't go mad with a riot of color; add pastel tints with an occasional flare. Exotic words can be land mines. What good is a word if the reader or listener doesn't know it? *Goodbye* is colorless, but does your target individual know what *auf Wiedersehen* means? If you're sure, use it. If you're not sure, *farewell* is a word everyone knows, and it has hue.

Don't strain for it, but when you're word picking, think of a bin of corn at the supermarket: Every ear costs the same, so why not pick the biggest, juiciest ones in the bin?

How to Use Words as Ammunition and How to Avoid Firing Blanks

You and I both know writers who have favorite words and phrases. They're comfortable with those terms and take a proprietary view of them. One writer's copy has become recognizable because of overuse of the word *captured*: "In a single painting he has captured . . . "; "This book captures the spirit of . . . "; "She captured the flavor of . . . " *Captured* is a perfectly acceptable word, but it isn't worth a love affair.

Another writer just has to use *What's more* in every piece of copy. It's like a trademark, and that's what's wrong; a professional copywriter shouldn't have a trademark. Words should fit what you're selling, and when you try to fit what you're selling to your favorite words, you have inferior copy. That's the reason for the Rule of Word Matching: Use words that match the image you're trying to build. An out-of-key word changes the image.

Word matching picks up steam when some of your key words not only fit the subject but have color. Look for colorful words to tint your copy with imagery that fires the reader's imagination.

To coin a cliché . . .

A not-so-gentle warning to those who write news releases, broadcast copy, and direct mail, with an all-media alert: Comb your copy for clichés.

A cliché bleaches the color out of writing. What a paradox! Consider how many writers, fishing around for colorful phraseology, give up and pepper their copy with the blandest of seasonings—clichés. Awareness is the key to cliché elimination. If you're cliché-prone, start life-extending treatment for your copy by using these phrases less than you used to:

A breed apart.
Add years to your life and life to your years.
As far as (WHATEVER) is concerned . . .
Ask us about our . . .
. . . as we possibly can.
At this point in time . . .
The best in . . .
Bright-eyed and bushy-tailed.
Due to the fact that . . .
Each and every . . .
Enclosed please find . . .
[AND or DESPITE] the fact that . . .
The finest in [WHATEVER].
First-class quality, first-class service.
Great (especially "Feels great" or "Tastes great") . . .
Heartwarming . . .
Hustle and bustle.
I couldn't care less.
If you can find a better [WHATEVER], buy it.
. . . in any way, shape, or form.

In other words . . .
In view of the fact that . . .
Knock your socks off (see Figure 3-2).
Let's face it.
[WHATEVER] means business.
New and improved . . .
No customer too big or too small.
Prioritize.
Quite simply,
Regardless of race, color, or creed.
Revolutionary . . .
Sit up and take notice.
State of the art.
You've tried the rest. Now try the best.
. . . very . . .
Watch for it.
We hear you.
When you think of [WHATEVER], think of [WHATEVER].
When you want the best.
Why settle for [WHATEVER] when you can have [WHATEVER]?
World class . . .
Your pleasure in . . .

Colors are much abused by cliché users. A short list: red tape, rosy future, tickled pink, purple passion, blue funk, green with envy, brown study, white as snow. They put us in a black mood, or make us white with anger or red with rage, because they're permanent—usually dyed-in-the-wool.

No copywriter can have an unblemished career. Clichés creep into our writing when our thoughts wander. An occasional cliché may actually bring relief to a torrent of tortured rhetoric. But when a writer looks at his copy sheet, sees "If you can find a better automobile, buy it!" or "Our computers mean business," and doesn't do something about it, it's time to cover the keyboard. As the saying goes, "When clichés become thick as fleas, it's time to avoid them like the plague."

Schlock words

Schlock words aren't onomatopoetic (see Chapter 4). They aren't clichés. They're lowbrow. Only about 5 percent of the schlock words we see in ads have the strength of the same description

Figure 3-2: Is there any excuse for this heading, which not only is a cliché but has a zero degree of relevance? The dedicated copywriter never settles for easy but weak crutches such as "Knock your socks off," "Means business," or "When it comes to . . . "

properly presented. (You should know them, though, even though it's only 5 percent.) Here are some schlock words:

brite	nite
kleen	thru
lite	xtra

Having seen these samples, can you tell when you should use them? Right: when you're writing for bottom-end buyers.

Other words and phrases you should never use in copywriting

access (as a verb)	indeed (as first word of a sentence)
at this point in time	in terms of
define	meaningful
despite the fact that	muchly
due to (instead of "because of")	needs (as a noun)
etc.	paradigm (a pomposity)
[the] fact is	prioritize
for (instead of because)	remember (imperative followed by a comma)
frankly	
has got, have got	thusly
however	utilize (instead of use)
I could care less	what's more
I mean (followed by a comma)	-wise (as a suffix— "price-wise," "wisdom-wise")
impact (as a verb, although this has become common)	you know (as a substitute for "uuuuh")
importantly	

Don't expect to win every battle. Some nouns have been turned into part-time verbs, beginning in the 1970s with *impact* and *access*, which until that time had nestled safely in the womb of nouns. My own exasperation peaked when a speaker used *architect* as a verb.

Weak words you sometimes have to use

available	quality
[the] fact that; [in] fact	receive
feature, features (as verbs)	value
one of the most	

Redundancies

Some redundancies, such as *free gift*, help credibility, a benefit that transcends the weakness of repetition. For example, "100% aspirin free" is a redundancy Anacin used successfully for years. (If it's aspirin free, it has to be 100% aspirin free. But like *free gift*, this redundancy adds emphasis.)

Figure 3-3: If you were in the jewelry store, would any professional salesperson use as the key selling argument, "Quality is a fact"?

The Redundancy Control Rule tells you when to repeat and when to strip out the extra words: Use redundancies only when you want the reader to know you've repeated or doubled words to show emphasis.

Redundancy control suggests you question constructions that seem to be padding:

actual fact	little babies
advance planning	necessary requirement
another alternative	new breakthrough
beginning of a new era	new innovation
consensus of opinion	old adage
depreciate in value	postpone until later
8 A.M. in the morning	reasonable and fair
final expiration date	safe haven
foreign import	uniformly consistent
last year's recent achievements	young child

Compare the weakness of these redundancies with the power of the next examples. The reader recognizes your intention to emphasize, and reader recognition is your justification:

genuine leather
I myself
last and final opportunity
my personal attention
satisfaction 100% guaranteed

We stumble inadvertently into redundancies as we fight for stronger emphasis. It doesn't work that way. Adding words is adding bulk, not power. An example: *My company has never done business that way, and we aren't about to change now.*

The weakness might be hard to spot if we weren't concentrating on redundancy. The word *now* is a classic power adder, but not when it's a redundancy. "We aren't about to change" is stronger than "We aren't about to change now" because the redundancy becomes a qualifier.

For some readers, this line of copy would cause confusion: *Heinz Veuhoff is an in-house staff designer for Olympic Litho Corporation of Brooklyn, New York.* An in-house staff designer? What does *staff* add to *in-house*? The two words are the same to the reader, but because this company is named Olympic, somehow we get the impression that Mr. Veuhoff designs staffs. Why add bulk without adding information?

The definitive word about redundancies: They're copy weakeners.

Chapter Four

HOW TO WRITE MOTIVATIONAL COPY

How to Tell the Reader What to Do

The Fourth Great Law of mass communications is Tell the reader what to do. It's the easiest law to follow, which may be why it's so often ignored. (For all Four Great Laws, see Chapter 26.)

The beginner who takes my word for it and writes with slavish obedience to this law might be surprised at how effective copy becomes. If the writers of Figures 4-1, 4-2, 4-3, 4-4, and 4-5 had considered this law, their messages might have had some impact.

Three principal reasons are interlocking rules that tie the law to grammar. If you stay away from *would* or *could* constructions, you'll have more octane in your word mix. The conditional is never as compelling as the definitive.

Here are the three rules. I've given each one a high-sounding name:

1. The Conditional Declension Syndrome—The more conditional the statement, the weaker it is.
2. The Comparative Conditional Declension Syndrome—The conditional isn't as impelling as the imminent.
3. The Subjunctive Avoidance Commandment—Avoid the subjunctive. It denies actuality.

How to change weak conditional statements

Obviously, if conditional statements are feeble, they're implicitly weaker than imminent statements. Let's take a look at how changing a conditional statement to an imminent statement pumps power into what you say:

> We'll squeeze every nickel and stretch every dollar, but we're desperately close to running out of money. If we did, we'd have to cut back on programs that might have been the only act of friendship for helpless children.

The rules tell us to change a couple of words, closing the loophole the first draft gave the reader. Can you see how much stronger a suggestion of imminent problems is than a conditional statement?

> We squeeze every nickel and stretch every dollar, but we're desperately close to running out of money. If we do, we'll have to cut back on programs that might be the only act of friendship for helpless children.

Figure 4-1: Other than watching for a grand opening, what is the reader supposed to do as the result of observing this ad? A reader who has no idea who or what Whitaker is would shrug and turn the page; a reader who does know who or what Whitaker is would have no reason to react.

We have a different way of
looking at reprints!

Reprint Management Services will
give you a new perspective on
editorial reprints.
Contact us for
grown-up information.

REPRINT
MANAGEMENT
SERVICES

147 West Airport Road • PO Box 5363 • Lancaster PA 17606-5363 • 717.560.2001 • fax: 717.560.2063 • email: reprints@rmsreprints.com • www.rmsreprints.com

Figure 4-2: This company is (I think) selling a serious business service. The copywriter
seems to need rhetorical diapers.

Figure 4-3: The illustration, a destructive teenager, does nothing to help sell this advertiser's wares and much to damage the possibility of selling them. What if, instead of this sophomoric play on words, the advertiser had simply said, "If your ads or Web pages are tired, it's time to call in the pros. That's us."

Figure 4-4: News for this advertiser: The Colosseum wasn't in ruins when the game score was Lions 3, Gladiators 0. Mightn't this ad have had more zip if it had made even a single suggestion as to how the advertiser can save your company some money?

Figure 4-5: Would you look forward to having this creature as your homeroom teacher? If that's InfoBeat, then no, we don't want to meet her.

This same principle underlies the difference between *can* and *will*. Which word would you use?

You've helped us before. (Can) (Will) you, again?

Right! *Can* is conditional; it gives the donor an out. *Will* puts the act right where it belongs—within the donor's control. The effectiveness works both ways. If you're making a health claim, using *can* instead of *will* might save you from a batch of legal troubles.

In this same category are "as . . . " phrases. I don't include the invaluable *as you know*; "as . . . " limpness pertains to the likes of "as previously stated" or "as mentioned above." At best, this phraseology is a holding action; at worst, it's a strength sapper.

Even in the active voice, an "as" phrase probably is weaker than the same phrase without it. "As I told you, we'll . . . " has far less impact than "I told you we'll . . . "

Solving a Predicament Means Writing Winning Copy

If your copy leads readers into visualizing themselves in a predicament and then leads them out, you're writing a winner.

"Predicament" copy is one of the most venerable forms of professional copywriting. Two of the best-known ads of all time use a predicament as their setting—John Caples's masterpiece, "They Laughed When I Sat Down at the Piano," and the Sherwin Cody School's classic, which ran for forty-five years, "Do You Make These Mistakes in English?" (A "knockoff" of the Caples ad is reproduced as Figure 9-13.)

Most professional writers have a loose knowledge of the value of predicaments. Where so many fall flat is in failing to know or care about the difference between a credible predicament and an incredible predicament.

I still remember, with amusement and some contempt, this predicament set up by a television writer: "The most important conference of my life . . . and you switch deodorant soaps!"

How much more powerful is the predicament in which the viewer can visualize himself. One example: A group enters a conference room. One group member, obviously the boss, points at an attractive woman, sniffs, and nudges his assistant, saying, "I don't want to sit next to her."

Writing predicament copy is easy. A single rule covers it, the Predicament Method Principle: Establishing a predicament as a sales argument has these five sequential components:

1. Create a predicament the reader, viewer, or listener finds credible.
2. Put your target individual into that predicament, either by unmistakable association or by hard use of the word *you*.
3. Demonstrate whatever you're selling as the solution to the predicament.
4. Restate the circumstance with a happy conclusion.
5. Have the central character in the predicament state satisfaction.

The Predicament Method Principle is one of our most mechanical rules, which makes this procedure a can't-miss cushion on days when nothing coherent seems to flow out of your keyboard.

Hucksterism

More than half a century ago, right after World War II, a man named Frederick Wakeman wrote a book about advertising called *The Hucksters*. The book rightly ridiculed some of the creative

Figure 4-6: Hucksterism lives! "Tailored solutions" . . . so we show a needle and thread, see? And we use garment terms such as "off-the rack." Gee, how clever can you get?

techniques springing up during that period. The term *hucksterism* has stayed with us over the years. It describes the obnoxious procedure of coattail riding behind a phrase, a saying, or a slogan that has no relationship to what's being sold. An example is a loose deck card (see Chapter 22) with this headline:

> SCORE BIG!
> Direct Press Gives You the
>   Scoring Point
> That Will Keep You Ahead of
>   the Game!

The illustration is a football referee, raising his hands to indicate a touchdown. What's being offered for sale? Printing. We have a pure case of hucksterism on both levels:

- ▶ The headline can refer to any type of business.
- ▶ The graphics relate to the non-relevant headline, not to whatever the advertiser is selling.

Elsewhere in this text is a group of Unassailable Loser Statutes. Statute III declares: Illustration should agree with what we're selling, not with headline copy.

On this basis alone, hucksterism fails. But it fails on a far more serious level: It has no motivators. A distressing aspect of hucksterism is the business classification that seems to use it most—mass communications.

You've already guessed my opinion: Don't write huckster ads. All you have to do is ask, "Why should somebody buy what I have to sell?" and put the answer to that question into your copy. There's no way you'll end up with hucksterism.

Figure 4-7: Hucksterism lives! "More teeth from your Web host". . . so we show a shark with all those teeth, see? And we use teeth terms such as "More than a mouthful." Gee, how clever can you get?

Figure 4-8: Hucksterism lives! "Windows". . . so we show a bunch of window washers, see? And we use window-washer terms such as "Get your windows done." Gee, how clever can you get?

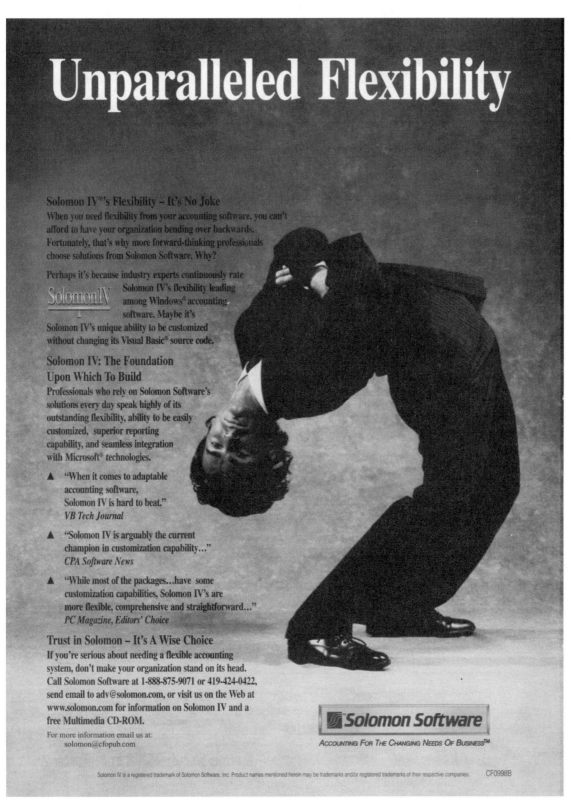

Figure 4-9: Hucksterism lives! "Unparalleled flexibility". . . so we show a guy flexing, see? And we use gymnastic terms such as "bending over backward." Gee, how clever can you get?

FOR A LIMITED TIME, GET BIG REWARDS WITH KINGSTON

 NETWORKING. Save up to $315 by purchasing select Kingston® network hubs, switches and adapters. With special offers like these, you're sure to come out a winner. So act fast. Contact your preferred Kingston source today or call Kingston at **(800) 337-7039** and you will be richly rewarded.

www.kingston.com/network

10Mbps Hubs	$20 Instant Reseller Rebate		
	KNE16TP/SE	16-port 10Mbps Stackable Workgroup Hub	$20 instant rebate
	KNE16TP/WG	16-port 10Mbps Workgroup Hub	$20 instant rebate
	KNE16TP/RS	16-port 10Mbps Rack-mountable/Stackable Hub	$20 instant rebate
100Mbps Hubs	Earn Free 6-packs of Fast EtheRx VP PCI 10/100 TX Adapters		
	KNE8TX/RS	8-port 19" Rack-mountable/Stackable Fast Ethernet Hub	Free KNE110TX/6 (6 pack)
	KNE12TX/RS	12-port 19" Rack-mountable/Stackable Fast Ethernet Hub	2 Free KNE110TX/6 (6 packs)
Switches	$100 Instant Reseller Rebate		
	KNS208/R	8-port 10Mbps Switch w/2 10/100 uplink ports	$100 instant rebate
	KNS216/R	16-port 10Mbps Switch w/2 10/100 uplink ports	$100 instant rebate
Adapters	Earn Free Multi-packs of 10Mbps ISA Ethernet Adapters		
	KNE20T/6	6-pack 10Mbps ISA Ethernet Adapter	2 Free KNE20T
	KNE20T/20	20-pack 10Mbps ISA Ethernet Adapter	Free KNE20T/6 (6 pack)
	KNE20T/100	100-pack 10Mbps ISA Ethernet Adapter	Free KNE20T/20 (20 pack)

Kingston TECHNOLOGY
NETWORKING PRODUCTS DIVISION

Figure 4-10: Hucksterism lives! "Make the big save". . . so we show a soccer goalie making a save, see? And we use sports terms such as "you're sure to come out a winner." Gee, how clever can you get?

Need a Custom Fit?

Make sure all the components fit!

Introducing CSIOpen...A program that makes all your components work!

Concentric Systems, Inc. has been selected as a Channel Partner with the AOpen Custom PC...that means you're assured all components of a PC we customize for you have been certified by AOpen to work flawlessly.

With CSIOpen, all products and parts are meant to work together...you and your customers never need worry about reliability, compatibility, and ease of upgradibility.

CSIOpen --the customizable solution for your customers! Our flexibility is tailored to your specifications and needs, as well as quick turnaround. Built and ready to go in 48 hours or less! We're here to help you meet your customer's needs FAST!

Call CSI today at **1-800- 995-4274 ext 100** to learn how the CSIOpen Program can help you build your business with that custom fit!

Watch your mailbox for your chance to win a FREE AOpen CustomPC by CSIOpen.

Figure 4-11: Hucksterism lives! "Need a custom fit?". . . so we show a tailor measuring pants, see? Oh, the pants already have cuffs, so why is he doing that? It's the idea that counts, Stupid. Gee, how clever can you get?

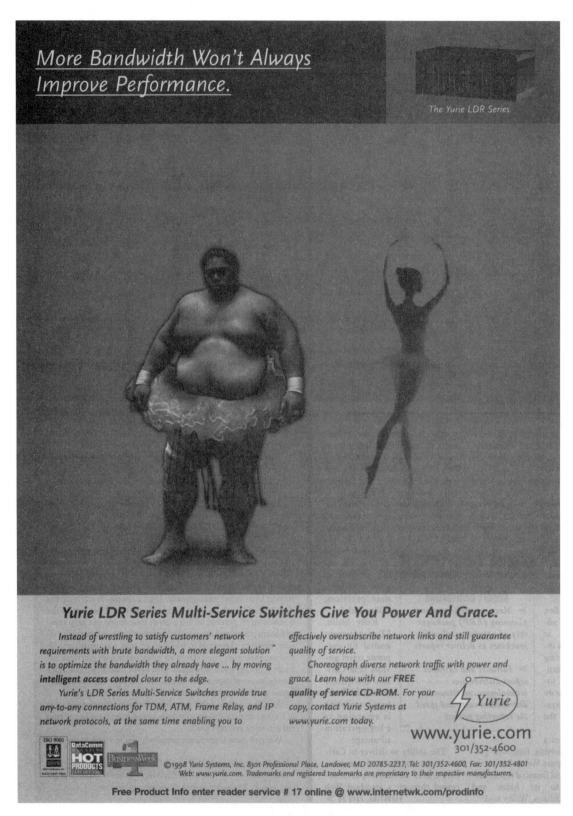

Figure 4-12: Hucksterism lives! "More bandwidth". . . so we show a fat guy who's obviously wide, see? And we compare him with a ballet dancer and use Sumo terms such as "wrestling." Gee, how clever can you get?

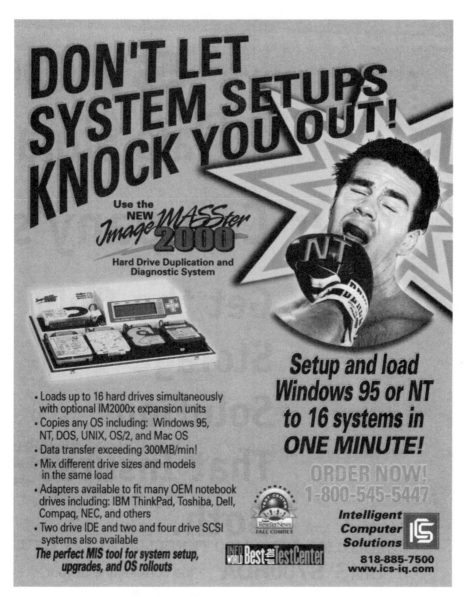

Figure 4-13: Hucksterism lives! "Don't let system setups knock you out!". . . so we show a guy getting knocked out, see? And that effectively makes it necessary to set our selling message in mice type. Gee, how clever can you get?

Figure 4-14: Hucksterism lives! "The Right Stuff". . . so we show an astronaut, holding a projector for a presentation to Mars, about 200 million miles away, see? And we use NASA terms such as "explore" and "light-years." Gee, how clever can you get?

Figure 4-15: Hucksterism lives! "Let IT Service Vision Be Your Ringmaster". . . so we show a circus ringmaster, see? And we use circus terms such as "wild beast" and "juggle" and "jump through hoops." Gee, how clever can you get?

How to Move Them Off Dead-Center

Implicit in the Fourth Great Law, Tell the reader what to do, is that the writer has to know what the reader is supposed to do. A writer is only as effective as the information source. I can't tell you what to do if I don't know what I want you to do. But copywriters can't abandon responsibility by wailing, "Nobody told me what I'm supposed to say."

Unless legal restrictions forbid absolutes, use strong, recognizable words. If you tell the reader what to do, you've done a big hunk of the job and you've moved your seat away from the amateur bullpen and into the big leaguers' dugout.

Using colorful words in copy

Within the active vocabularies of most individuals and all successful copywriters are words touched with spice. Use them as you'd use spice in a recipe—to enhance flavor without overwhelming or desensitizing the palate.

When you have a flavorful word, consider all forms of it. For example, *triumph* is a noun or verb, with *triumphant* the adjectival form. Most of the words I've included in the preliminary list are adjectives, but please don't look for adjectives only. Nouns have the power and verbs have the action. Many adjectives also have a noun variation.

Here are a few samples of colorful words you can start using today:

adventure	fiery	mellow	saucy
bagatelle	flaming	melody	savage
bazaar	frivolous	meteoric	scorching
bewitching	glow	naughty	scramble
bizarre	graceful	nimble	sensuous
buccaneer	gritty	opulent	serene
danger	haughty	preposterous	sizzling
devilish	innocent	provocative	smoky
enchanting	jaunty	pugnacious	spicy
executive	luminous	pulse-pounding	splendor
explosive	lusty	quit	startle
famish	lyrical	radiant	stunning
ferocious	majesty	regal	sultry
fierce	marvel	rogue	sumptuous

sunny	tranquil	vibrant	wicked
thrilling	transform	vicious	wild
thundering	urbane	vigor	wiry
torrid	valor, valiant	vital	

These are words inside the vocabularies of most adults. To unlock their spice, use them obliquely. For example, "a wicked person" is too straightforward to be spicy, "a wicked tennis serve" has spice, and "a delightfully wicked evening dress" is spice saturated.

Don't use colorful words to show off your vocabulary. The Concept of Reader Dominance should temper the very human desire to show the reader the size of your vocabulary. It states: The writer's knowledge of the colorful words in a piece of copy is inconsequential. What matters is whether or not the reader knows them.

Words like *fustian* and *bombast* and *diffident* can kill you instead of your target because using words your message recipient doesn't understand violates the all-important Clarity Commandment. A college sophomore, trying to bolster a knowledgeable image, might put it this way: Eschew obfuscatory adages. We say simply: For the sake of your professionalism, obey the Clarity Commandment.

Steely or spongy words

We've long known that tiger is a more powerful word than lion. It's time we began to formalize the reasons. We know that William is wearing his necktie today, that Bill is out bowling, that Will is a lawyer, that Willie likes to make harmless practical jokes, and that Billy is from the Southwest.

Of course that's nonsense. And of course, too, it's the instant image that leaps to mind until we know that William, Bill, Will, Willie, and Billy are the same guy.

This is what we call the Humphrey Bogart Syndrome. The name Humphrey suggests bookishness—a person who fondles his violin instead of a Saturday Night Special. But the late Humphrey Bogart conjures up an entirely different image. We know who he was.

But we don't know the fellow in the beer commercial. We're safer calling him Bill than we would be if he were William or Willie. That's the point. We might as well benefit from another of the human realities that help us form rules of copywriting.

We know that Mike is a tough guy and Michael is a poet and Mickey is easygoing. We know that rock is harder than stone. We know that a stag may be dangerous, but an antelope isn't. We know that, as a fast food, beef is tastier than meat. We know that farewell is more dramatic than good-bye. We know that artificial isn't good for us but man-made is. We know that half a pound is a greater quantity than ½ pound. We know that an engine seems more complicated (ergo, worth more money) than a motor. We know that slim looks good and thin looks unhealthy. We know that a trip is a shorter journey than a voyage. We know that naked is more sensual than nude and that kissing someone on the mouth is sexier than kissing that same person on the lips. For that matter, we somehow know the sexiness of the word wet, the result of a language sense outside the help any dictionary or thesaurus can give us.

Tricks With Words

Oxymorons

Oxymorons are skyrocketing in popularity. The only explanation I can offer is the equivalent sky-rocketing of the "That-which-is-different = That-which-is-better" cult.

An oxymoron combines two contradicting words into a single phrase: "Wise fool" is not only an oxymoron; it explains the word itself, *oxys* being ancient Greek for sharp and *moron* meaning just what it means today.

Tongue-in-cheekers say that word combinations such as *legal ethics* or *postal service* or *government efficiency* or *military intelligence* are oxymorons because in each instance the two words are an impossible combination. Maybe so, but we're ad people and our job is to make words work for us. What we learn from those examples is that 1) creating oxymorons can be fun, and 2) the two words don't have to be exact opposites, although most advertising use does pick opposites.

Years ago, Revlon shook up the world of cosmetics with a product line called "Fire and Ice"—an oxymoron. The arthritis rub Icy Hot is a current oxymoron. "Where Business Is a Pleasure" is a mild oxymoron, as is "The Birth of a Legend." Less convincing is "A New Family Heirloom," too tortured and contrived to be effective. "Old New Mexico" has a peculiar ring to it.

Constructing an oxymoron is one of the simplest of all mechanical grammatical tricks. Just pick a word and look up its antonym. String the two words together with "and" or use one as an adjective to modify the other. "Young senior citizen" is obvious because young is the antonym of old. "Tiny monster" or "giant midget" or "dawn at sunset" are oxymorons, and all are nonsense because they draw no word image at all.

"Poor little rich girl" and "benevolent despot" are popular oxymorons; "dumb genius" is another we understand—someone is bright but lacks common sense. "He is regarded as an unknown" appeared in print; it's nonsense because if he's regarded as anything, he can't be unknown.

A wonderful oxymoron is this overline on a full-page ad for a beauty product:

Famous Hollywood Secret Revealed . . .

If it's famous, how can it be a secret? The writer was carried away by a desire to excite the reader.

Officials from the city of Philadelphia ran an image ad with this headline:

Bring Your High-Heeled Sneakers

It's a true oxymoron. Sneakers can't have high heels. It's a brilliant play on words, and we might or might not understand this headline. Yes, we think we do, but our interpretation could differ from the writer's. That is the problem with it and with most oxymorons, relative to some readers: We're never quite sure we understand what the message is supposed to be. Think about the "High-Heeled Sneakers" headline; in a few seconds, you probably could come up with a clearer one. And don't forget salesmanship. Clarity is the gun; salesmanship is the bullet. "Bring Your High-Heeled Sneakers" has two positives: It's imperative and it's bright enough to grab attention. It also has one negative: It can be interpreted in many ways, including a contrary analysis.

For product or company names, an oxymoron might be a catchy mnemonic device: For some years now, golf club manufacturers have been selling "metal woods." Or if you're at a loss for a slogan or a headline, with a deadline at hand, an oxymoron can bail you out. But except for the rare inspired combination, an oxymoron is at best a chewing gum patch on the radiator.

Continental variations: writing for British publications

The obvious note: When writing Britishisms for U.S. readers, make only those changes the typical reader can accept comfortably. The issue you as copywriter face isn't whether your words are proper Britishisms but whether the reader will accept them as such.

Although in Great Britain you might write "I shall be there directly" instead of "I'll be there soon," most Americans don't recognize *directly* as a parallel to *soon* . . . so don't use this construction. In any type of writing, clarity should be paramount.

The obvious changes are using *s* in some words instead of the soft *c* or *z* (organisation, practise, realise) and *our* instead of *or* (colour, favour). Put the period outside quotation marks for titles of articles.

▶ Instead of *aluminum*, write *aluminium*.
▶ Instead of the committee *is* . . ., write the committee *are*.
▶ Instead of *defense*, write *defence*.
▶ Instead of *elevator*, write *lift*.
▶ Instead of *in the hospital*, write *in hospital* (even though *in future* is correct, American readers are uncomfortable with it; use *in the future* as you normally do).
▶ Instead of *jewelry*, write *jewellery*.
▶ Instead of *tire* (for a car), write *tyre*.
▶ Instead of different *from*, write different *to*.
▶ Instead of *pharmacist*, write *chemist*.
▶ Instead of *program*, write *programme*.
▶ Instead of *right away*, write *straightaway*.
▶ Instead of *skepticism*, write *scepticism*.
▶ Instead of *subway*, write *underground* (*subway* is a walkway).
▶ Instead of *traveler's check*, write *traveller's cheque*.
▶ Instead of *truck*, write *lorry*.

Be careful with these words

Some words have too much power for most advertising copy. When they appear in a headline or copy block, they taint the whole message. *Sex* used to be one of these words, although *sexy* had no negative implications. *Sex* no longer needs a more acceptable substitution, but the writer should use *sexual* cautiously.

Use the following words with care. You'll look for them and their fellows when your emphasis is negative or when you want to shake up the reader or listener.

bitch	garbage	ooze	suck
bleed	grisly	rot	vomit
damn	hell	scum	worm
decay	labor	slimy	
decompose	leprosy	snake	
filth	mess	soil	

Within your own field, compellingly negative words come to mind. Add them to this list, labeling them "For Emergency Use Only."

Theorems of Word Construction

We know many words that sound like what they are. As the first shovel in a groundbreaking that ultimately will result in a multistory structure with interlocking cubicles, we have the First Theorem of Word Construction, which should surprise nobody: When naming or describing product or company, matching word sounds to the intended effect will heighten that effect until repetition blurs it.

The Second Theorem of Word Construction states: One-syllable words are harder, tougher, and stronger than their softer, more reasonable multisyllabic equivalents. (The second theorem may be of value when writing about foods and transportation.)

The Third Theorem of Word Construction tells us: Flat vowels are crisper and are spoken faster than long vowels, so the words they represent seem crisper and faster.

A new road, not yet fully paved

The road down whose mysterious length we walk has never been trod before . . . except by gremlins laying land mines. How brave, how rash we are to take even the first step.

Our goal shouldn't be the search for words whose meanings are at variance with the suggested implicit syllable psychology. Don't look at *ama*, which in this list suggests "display," and exclaim, "Aha! What about *Alabama* and *pajama*?" Assail the notion if you like, but not because of exceptions.

Here we go! (An obvious note: We don't need a book on writing copy to tell us that the prefix *ante* means before and *post* means after, that *tri* means three and *quad* means four. These are well-known prefixes, and it would be sophomoric and presumptuous to list them here. The items on the following list are distant cousins to such components. The list looks into the "feel" of words and gives a loose idea of how the writer can use word-feel to help create a flavor.)

> ag = unsettled
> agon (as suffix) = exotic
> ama (as suffix) = display
> bl = breaking loose
> bla + soft consonant = weak, helpless
> cag = tough, in motion
> com = total, electronic
> cr = rough, harsh, dynamic
> eal = weak, unwholesome
> eep = low and slow
> esh = mushy
> ette (as suffix) = miniature, feminine
> fic = childish, harmless, primitive
> ga = open, wide, stretched
> gr + vowel + hard consonant = rough
> har = trim, sharp, strident
> iam = weakly foreign

ilee = happy
imp = weak or stupid
ish = weak, nonthreatening
j = nonthreatening
j + (vowel) + (soft consonant) = happy beginning
k (as replacement for c or ck) = unsophisticated emphasis
ka = odd
kh = exotic, Mongolian
lot = neatly sorted
ock = hard
oin = mushy, meaty
oke = agricultural, bucolic
onic = smartly contemporary
oon = funny
oor = weak, feeble
orc or ork = bizarre, meaty
org = bloated, electronic
poo = harmless
qui + soft consonant = peaceful, dependable
ram = hard, powerful
rce (as ending) = action
shl, shm, shn = messy, inferior
shr = disconnecting, loosely raucous
sk = hardness (sch does not have this overtone)
sl = skewed, wetness
sn (as prefix) = unpleasant, underhanded
spl = bursting out
squ = messy
str = incorruptible, organized, power
thr = action
tor = unhappy
tr + (vowel) + (soft consonant) = bright, happy, neat
u (short) = slightly nasty
ump = awkward
urk = evil, grotesque, abnormal
ush = wet, soft
usk = rough, exotic, animal-like
v = action
xton (as ending) = contemporary, smartly done
z + (short vowel) + (hard consonant) = controlled fast action
zz = bizarrely awry

Onomatopoeic Value for the Copywriter

Onomatopoeia is a tongue twister whose definition is simpler than its pronunciation: a word whose sound when spoken parallels what the word is describing.

One of the most famous onomatopoeic inventions is the word *chortle*, coined by Charles

Dodgson (Lewis Carroll) in the poem "Jabberwocky." Chortle sounds like what it is, and people who have never heard of "Jabberwocky" know the word. For the copywriter, using onomatopoeic words pays off in doubled emotional impact. Many are one-syllable words with implicit emotional power.

True onomatopoeia

A starter kit of onomatopoeic words:

boom	growl	pop	smack
burst	hiss	power	smash
buzz	luminous	rock	spurt
crash	melt	rumble	zipper
fizz	muck	scratch	
gristle	poof	shriek	

Manufactured words

Some words are manufactured to represent an effect. These aren't onomatopoeic in the true sense, but we're copywriters, not philologists. Some of these manufactured words:

aargh	glarp	phooey	whack
bam	glop	slop	wham
bash	goof	slurp	yuck
blooper	gunk	smog	zap
gack	oof	ugh	

And Tomorrow We'll Have . . .

This is an elastic—and iconoclastic—chapter. Language evolves; today's innovations become tomorrow's clichés, and some of these concepts will flare like novas and then shrink into obsolescence.

As other rules for copywriting become accepted principles, the value of word-use knowledge will move out of the icy innards of the computer and into the happy daylight of creative writing, as a standard space-age weapon.

This chapter is only a beginning, a minor foundation on which you'll build your own lists. Practice with words even when nobody is paying you to do it. That's the way to become a virtuoso of the keyboard.

Chapter Five

How to Use "If," "Can," "Will," and Other Pitfalls

Statement or question? Which is more persuasive copy?

Why not see for yourself?

or

See for yourself.

How about these?

Shouldn't you cut down on your smoking, starting today?

or

Cut down on your smoking—starting today.

The answer may not please you: It depends.

Use a statement when you, the message source, take an expert or authoritarian position. The statement itself emphasizes: You know more than your message recipient. To accept a controverting opinion weakens your Olympian posture.

Use a question when you want to suggest that the buyer has a choice. If you have great guts, drop all persuasion from the question.

When to Use Which Type of Question

The persuasion-dropping decision makes little difference in the message when you use conditional questions. Instead of "Why don't you . . . ," the persuasion dropper might be phrased, "Wouldn't you . . . ," ending with "Would you . . ."

In the hands of the writer playing Russian roulette, "Shouldn't you . . . ," "Won't you . . . ," or "Can't you . . ." becomes "Should you . . . ," "Will you . . . ," or "Can you . . ."

In my opinion, drop the negative inclusion *n't* only when you're issuing a challenge or a dare. The danger lies in the reader asking a question of his own: "Who are you to confront me?"

Harvard Business Review

60 Harvard Way
Boston, Massachusetts 02163

June 26, 1998

H G Lewis
COMMUNICOMP
340 N Fig Tree Ln
Ft Lauderdale, FL 33317-2561

Dear H G Lewis,

Your career isn't about money, is it?

I didn't think so. It's about something deeper.

Something so central to your core, to what makes you tick, that
you can't imagine living without it.

It's about leadership. Having your say. Making things happen.
Putting your stamp on the future.

For over 70 years, one publication has stood out from the crowd as
the indispensable resource for business achievers like you. The same
publication judged "most influential magazine in America" in the 1992
Erdos & Morgan/MPC survey of 1,700 opinion leaders.

The Harvard Business Review.

Only an elite corps of top managers get a chance to subscribe to
the Harvard Business Review. With this letter, I am pleased to extend
the invitation to you, along with a valuable free gift.

In Harvard Business Review, you will learn --

- Why decision-making power belongs at the lowest
  possible point in your organization
- The strategy that Wal-Mart, Canon, The Limited and
  Banc One use to outflank competitors
- The real boundaries of the 'boundaryless' organization
- How Nike designs emotion into its shoes
- Why you should watch what Europe's top managers are
  doing, not what its politicians are saying.

Harvard Business Review is unique. It comes to you from Harvard
Business School Publishing Corporation, the publishing arm of the world's premier
business research and management training institution. Yet it's not a
view from the ivory tower. It's a view from the board room, the corner

Figure 5-1: This letter opens with a self-answering question, to which the reader's
"No" might be agreement with the sales argument or rejection. (I'd like to hire a lot of
bright, knowledgeable, intelligent experts whose careers aren't about money. And try
asking that question of a professional basketball player.)

"Can you do it?" unquestionably has power you'll never find in "Can't you do it?"
Unquestionably, too, hurling down the gauntlet isn't a writing job for beginners. *Don't* do it when
you want the reader to be a partner: "Wouldn't you really rather have a Buick?" works; "Would
you really rather have a Buick?" suggests the opposite of the original intention.

In headlines and in confrontational broadcast commercials, don't ask questions to which the
reader or viewer can answer "No" unless you want a "No" (see Figure 5-2).

Figure 5-2: This question asks the reader to answer a question without knowing what the right answer might be. Some studies show that caffeine helps get rid of headaches. The phrase " . . . with that headache?" can confuse; why not " . . . to get rid of that headache?"

Questions have an implicit advantage: Their construction alone involves the targeted individual.

The "if" peril

An "if . . . " situation is always precarious for the copywriter. Sometimes you'll want the conditional "Wouldn't you . . . " and sometimes the circumstance demands the direct challenge of "Would you . . . ." For example: If you were on a desert island and could have only one book as your companion, (wouldn't) (would) you want the book to be *The Bedside Companion*?

Automatic indicators point to *wouldn't*. But the super pro sees possibilities in *would*. Apply two Rules of Question Asking:

1. Don't ask a question that risks rejection by your best potential buyers.
2. Don't be afraid to shake up borderline prospective buyers by challenging them to make up their minds.

The "if" peril extends beyond questions and *should/would*. Conditional statements are even more difficult to control than conditional questions. Some of the best uses I've seen lately are references to unpleasant situations over which the reader has no control: "If you're going to smoke, try Carltons"; "If you have to take a red-eye flight, make the best of it."

Would that last one be better as a question? "If you have to take a red-eye flight, why not make the best of it?" It's a toss-up; the question adds a little energy and the "why not" saps a little energy.

This use of "if" in a headline damaged the impact:

> If Mom Is Someone Special,
> Give Her Something Special

Why didn't this headline end with a period? Beats me.

Adding a condition to Mom's special place in our hearts adds a negative condition. Maybe she isn't so special. The writer has planted a doubt—almost subliminal, but why do it? The headline has better success without the "If":

> Mom Is Someone Special . . .
> So Give Her Something Special.

Dampening impact by using "if" phrases, in or out of a question frame, is a common mistake, even among professional writers. We can apply two rules to make the "ifs" work for us.

Here are two rules for using "if":

1. The Principle of "If" Control: An "if" condition should imply a "then" promise.
2. The "If" Subdecree: Logic stands behind the writer who makes an action conditional for the buyer, since buyer control is proper stroking, but to give this control to the seller through an "if" reference suggests seller superiority, which can provoke buyer antagonism.

If you regard these rules as obscure, condense them to this: "If you decide . . . " is permissible; "If we decide . . . " isn't, except under specialized "key club" circumstances in which you know the buyer is in awe of the seller.

DO STRANGERS WATCH YOU UNPACK YOUR LAPTOP ON THE AIRPLANE? From the way it integrates the latest technologies to the way it makes people look twice. There's something special about a ThinkPad® notebook. And the new ThinkPad 600 is no different. Thin, light, powerful. With a big, bright, high-resolution screen and CD-ROM capabilities. A tool you need. A tool you want. Visit **www.ibm.com/thinkpad600** or call 1 800 426 7255, ext. 4906.

Up to 266 MHz Pentium® II processor / Up to 4GB Hard Drive / Up to 13.3" display / About 5 lbs / 1.4" thin / From $2,799*

@ business tools

IBM.

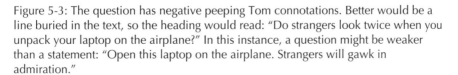

Figure 5-3: The question has negative peeping Tom connotations. Better would be a line buried in the text, so the heading would read: "Do strangers look twice when you unpack your laptop on the airplane?" In this instance, a question might be weaker than a statement: "Open this laptop on the airplane. Strangers will gawk in admiration."

Figure 5-4: This is a weak question, but it has the advantage all questions have: It automatically involves the reader, including one who has no interest in Spain's railroad.

"Can" and "will" questions

The difference between "can" and "will" is the difference between uncertain ability and uncertain decision. Use "can you" when you're questioning the reader's ability to follow through. Use "will you" when you're questioning the reader's voluntary agreement. You can see the difference in meaning between

> Can You Look 15 Years Younger?

and

> Will You Look 15 Years Younger?

When your copy refers to whatever you're selling, "will" is the better word. When your reference is to the prospective buyer, "can" might be the better word. Notice the qualifier—might be—which suggests you're usually safer with "will". (An example of the "can/will" difference is shown in Figure 5-5.)

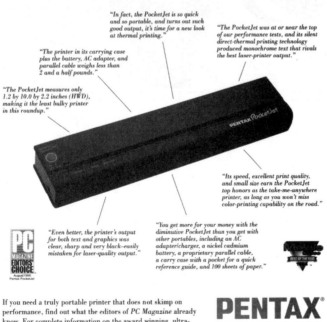

Figure 5-5: "When it comes to . . . " is a worn-out cliché (see Chapter 3). But this heading excellently exemplifies the difference between "can" and "will."

Turning Statement Into Question

The copywriter can turn any statement into a question. The question about this question-making technique: Why would you want to? Some writers claim they see greater strength in statement-turned-into-question than in straight question. The question

Won't you try this new taste experience?

becomes, as a statement-turned-into-question

You'll try this new taste experience . . . won't you?

The argument in favor of statement-turned-into-question is obvious: The writer has the benefit of the imperative without risking target antagonisms. The sales message is dynamic, but the reader still has a sense of control.

The argument against this format also has considerable merit: For some readers, the approach seems to take control of the reader's decision.

A thoughtful reservation is the danger of pomposity. Statement-turned-into-question has an overtone of superciliousness, the imposition of the writer's conclusion on the reader's.

If you can write statement-questions that avoid these seeds of unease, then sure, go ahead. It's an advanced procedure, though, and I suggest mastering basic question asking before running the rapids of statement-questions.

The Writer as Manipulator

A question is a challenge. That's the blessing in it . . . and that's the danger in it. Do you want your reader, listener, or viewer to be challenged? Part of the answer to this question is implicit in the form I just used to make a point. I wrote, "Do you want your reader . . . " Why didn't I write "You want your reader . . . "?

Playing the game? You may have glossed over the last couple of questions because you now accept the challenge. If you *did* recognize what I was doing—involving you not in one question but in a series of questions that I admit are a series of challenges—you probably aren't a good prospect for this kind of advertising.

But a lot of people are.

To the writer who's stumped for a copy approach, being able to ask a question can be as beneficial as a hip replacement. A mechanical technique that not only is respectable but has force in its very format is superior to almost any crutch.

So practice question asking. It's a technique you should know. After all, asking questions worked for Socrates. There's no reason it won't work for you . . . is there?

Chapter Six

THE PROS AND CONS OF COMPARATIVE COPY

Don't use unexplained comparatives. Here is the complete copy for a television commercial:

> Brown's Fried Chicken. It tastes better.

Give that writer a C minus. Brown's fried chicken tastes better than what? Other fried chicken? In that case, *which* other fried chicken? The thinness of this copy becomes apparent when (as an exercise) you complete the unexplained comparative:

> Brown's Fried Chicken. It tastes better than Kentucky Fried.

With this second version, the writer now gives us "desperation" copy, an unproved comparison showing neither imagination nor salesmanship. *How* does Brown's taste better than Kentucky Fried? Do research findings support taster preference? If Kentucky Fried sues us, what supporting evidence can we bring to court?

Still, the specific comparison with Kentucky Fried is better than "It tastes better," a line of copy of which no copywriter should be proud. If accompanied by evidence (a chart, a taste-test report, photographs, or videotapes of people tasting the two and saying, "This one!") within the ad, the comparison gets some muscles on its bony frame.

A detergent advertises itself with limp-wristed self-puffery:

> It gets clothes whiter.

Years ago, one detergent manufacturer advertised itself as getting clothes "whiter than white," which, however nonsensical the claim, still drew a word image. But "gets clothes whiter" draws none. Whiter than what? Whiter than green? If it's whiter than the white this same product used to get clothes, say so. It's a sales point, provided the product claims superiority in its previous incarnation. If it's whiter than specific competitors, say so. It's an even better sales point, but be prepared to back up your claim with evidence.

The Power of Comparative Advertising

Comparative advertising can bring a weak advertising campaign to life. It can make a product that's just one of the pack an instant contender.

Figure 6-1: Any claim beginning "The only . . . " is an absolute claim of superiority. Whatever follows should be a recognizable statement of benefit . . . which this claim isn't. "The only radar detector designed for travelers" is muddy and weak because the word "travelers" conjures up those who aren't driving. That isn't the intention here. Better: "The only radar detector you can 'pack and plug' for use in your rental car."

We all like to buy art.
And when we do, we want the whole picture, not just part of it.

But when buying systems, some people settle for just half the picture.
Why?

PAGE Systems provides a full spectrum of advanced yellow and white pages directory pre-press automation software. Our modules can function independently or be incorporated into your current legacy system environment. Together they provide smoothly integrated support for your print product needs. Whether you start with just one module or get the complete set, our open client/server architecture empowers your staff with flexible, adaptable technology to provide the Best-in-Class solutions you need. And PAGE systems are designed and configured with technologies which support the interactive advertising products that are part of your future.

Contact us for more information ...

Telephone: 416-695-2288   Fax: 416-695-2290   E-Mail: info@pageint.com

developers of automated publishing software solutions for today's directories ... and tomorrow's advertising revolution!

Figure 6-2: As dynamic as comparatives are, some seem to lack punch. This one writes around the benefit instead of attacking it head-on.

The comparative imperative

A challenger can leap to the attack; the leader, by joining the battle, acknowledges the challenge—and in doing so tarnishes his leadership.

From that conclusion, we formulate the Comparative Imperative: Good marketing strategy calls for Brand No. 2 to shout superiority over Brand No. 1; good marketing strategy calls for Brand No. 1 to shout superiority over all others without singling out any one of them.

The best demonstration of the Comparative Imperative is politics. Usually the incumbent is favored; a head-to-head debate has to help the other candidate through increased visibility and—by the very nature of a one-on-one debate—the admission by the incumbent that another candidate exists.

Avis can attack Hertz, but Hertz, from its Olympian number one position, is better off ignoring the gauntlet thrown at its feet. It made sense for Toyota to join the competitive attack on Volkswagen when VW was the leading import car; once Toyota ascended the throne, however, the brickbats of competitors, now including Volkswagen, were aimed at the new leader. It makes sense for a challenging politician to attack the incumbent and militate for a debate, but the incumbent seldom can benefit from entering the debate arena.

Figure 6-3: Uhhh . . . well, "The best just got better" is one way of stating a comparative claim. What that has to do with the illustration is anybody's guess. "The naked truth" is that this is (to be charitable) a peculiar illustration for an ad based on a comparative claim. No wonder the model looks embarrassed.

How to attack with this mighty weapon

Comparative advertising, like eye makeup and lipstick, was once considered obscene, then an indication of being not-quite-nice, then a novelty, then an accepted practice, then essential.

Effective comparative advertising, like most effective advertising, is specific. Raw claims of superiority not only have little impact; they're what the consumer expects an advertiser to say in the Age of Skepticism.

Why specifics outpull generalities

Comparative advertising, to be effective, has to be based on facts. Facts can come from research, from product testing, or from a source the creative thinker can explore without technical help—the opinions of others who, originally undecided, bought what you're selling. Opinion becomes fact if it appears to be epidemic. A good copywriter can make it so.

Is it better to name the competitor or to cavil with "the number one brand" ("Zilch Beer has 20 percent fewer calories than the best-selling beer")? In my opinion (excluding another weakness in this example, the use of a percentage instead of actual numbers), it's no ball game. Attacking an anonymous competitor doesn't have any wallop; instead, the ad becomes a public admission that another beer is more popular, a better seller. No! "Zilch Beer has 20 percent fewer calories than Belch Beer!" If you really want to put steam into the argument, specify the number of calories.

Figure 6-4: What a hard-hitting ad! A direct comparison, handled with flat statements of comparative superiority, can get both attention and orders.

How to kill the competition when you don't have supporting facts

Let's approach the marketing problem through the eyes of a copywriter who doesn't have hard ammunition. Zilch Beer doesn't have 20 percent fewer calories. Obviously, it doesn't sell as well as Belch. What can the writer do?

Easy. He moves to Position B and creates a comparative ad in which opinion becomes fact because it seems to be epidemic:

Does Zilch Beer taste better than Belch Beer? These beer drinkers think so!

► "I used to drink Belch but no more. Not since I tasted Zilch, the New Brew!" (Larry Smith, Pottstown)
► "I've tried them both and I choose Zilch!" (Harry Jones, Springfield)
► "Zilch or Belch? My friends drink Zilch!" (Mary Brown, Center City)

If the ad has a dozen more of these, its space is crammed with endorsements of Zilch. In a broadcast campaign, it's just as uncomplicated.

ANNOUNCER: Here's praise for Zilch Beer number six hundred and sixty-two.
SMITH: I'm Larry Smith from Pottstown. I used to drink Belch Beer, but no more. Not since I tasted Zilch, the New Brew.

Caution: You'd better have an actual Larry Smith and have his signature verifying that he used to drink Belch. Fiction doesn't enhance the noble cause of advertising.

Want ultimate power? Whack the better-known competitor over the head with its own market position: "The Grunge power-press became a best-seller, and it has only two ball bearings; Sludge has four. Which one should you buy?"

The view from Olympus—call in the engineers

Often you do have technical ammunition you can aim at not only one competitor but many, or even all. The gap between technicians and marketers often bears the blame for the failure to use this ammunition, or even to know where it's buried.

Figure 6-5: This ad, by a retailer, is both a comparative and a touchstone (see Figures 6-14 to 6-17). It compares the product with Viagra on grounds favorable to itself—side effects and price. No mention is made of effectiveness, another way of keeping score. Nor need it be: The advertiser is in command of whatever claims he decides to make or bypass.

In a casual conversation with a technician working for the same company, a writer may hear, "I don't know why we can't bury them in the marketplace. Our computer makes every other IBM clone, including IBM itself, seem like a snail." It's the first time the writer has even heard that his company's computer is the fastest. When he pursues the point, the technician drags some test results out of his desk, surprised that anyone is even interested in the specifics of the claim. In major industries, availability of comparative statistical evidence is not only common; it's doggedly pursued. In a smaller or more local situation, somebody has to prime the comparative pump, as the advertiser in Figure 6-6 has done.

Playing the lottery? There's a more reliable way to prepare for the future. Ask your financial advisor about Alliance Capital — with its <u>outstanding research</u>, <u>investment expertise</u> and <u>global strength</u>. Alliance can help get you from where you are now to where you want to be.

Alliance Capital ®
Because Later Is Sooner Than You Think. ℠
1-888-AC FUNDS   www.alliancecapital.com

Call your financial advisor for a prospectus with more information about sales charges, expenses, and risks. Read it carefully before you invest or send money. Alliance Fund Distributors, Inc. is a member of the NASD.

Figure 6-6: This ad uses the phrase "a more reliable way" without telling the reader "more reliable than what." Obviously the lottery is used as a ridiculous example, so the comparison has little relevance.

How to replace blanks with cannonballs

Are you the copywriter whose gun seems to be loaded with blanks? If so, pushing for an answer to the question "Why is what we're selling better than any competitor's?" can make you a hero. Example: An ad for a computer dealer financing organization has this pedestrian heading:

> Only TechBuyer financing makes every deal "AAA" rated.

Okay, you're a computer dealer. What about this full-page ad might motivate you? "AAA"? Sorry. Nowhere in the unimaginative text is this conceit followed up. The first sentences of the copy block:

> At TechBuyer, we are as concerned about bolstering the profitability of your business as we are about supplying e-commerce tools to your sales force. We work with you as a team: You provide the sales knowledge and we provide IT inventory availability, configuration, pricing, and end-user financing options. . . .

On it goes. Question: How about that word *Only* in the headline, an absolute promise of superiority? Nothing in the text (see Figure 6-13 on page 91) justifies the promise.

Don't do that.

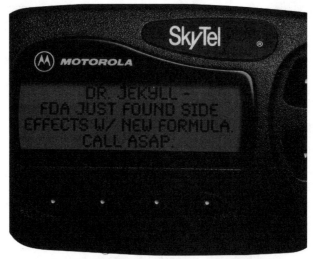

Figure 6-7: What an admirable way to sell a pager. This ad, part of a campaign with similar themes, accomplishes the difficult task of evoking a chuckle even as it makes a potent point.

Two Effective Techniques

Notice two techniques of effective comparative advertising:

1. The advertiser picks the elements he wants to compare. It's his ad, and even though the other word processing programs may be dominant in other areas, he theorizes, quite rightly, "I'm paying for this ad; if they want to tout their benefits, let them do it in their own ads."

Not all comparative ads are so absolute. An absolute claim can breed reader hostility and skepticism, so (especially in a list of comparatives) the advertiser feels safe as long as he has more yesses in his list than any competitor does. Showing an occasional Achilles' heel, in a feature no buyer would regard as important, helps overcome skepticism because it enhances verisimilitude . . . all without danger to salesmanship.

2. The advertiser picks the competitors with whom he wants to make a comparison. Does your word processing program compete with WordPerfect or Microsoft Word on better terms? Suppose yours has a single feature the others don't have, such as an ongoing on-screen word count or the ability to write over illustrations. Those become your edge. You are the company paying for the ad. You can make any comparisons you want to.

Damning all the competition doesn't require copywriting talent. Damning all the competition effectively does.

Figure 6-8: Even though television comedians might use this ad to say, "Oh, if nothing works better, then I'll use nothing," this is a classic example of parity advertising. The ad doesn't say the product works best; it says no other product works better. The reader interprets the claim as one of superiority.

An ad in an inflight magazine tries this approach:

We Apologize to Everyone
On This Plane Who Just Bought
A New Garment Bag.

Body copy begins:

Because your new bag just became obsolete. Now introducing the System 4 Valet
Garment Bag. . . .

I'd have preferred an approach that was more energetic, but just as effortless to write:

To Anyone on This Plane
Who Just Bought a New Garment Bag:
Too Bad.

If your magazine ad runs on anything less than coated paper, you may be forced to find other ways to create your image.

Advertisers have long recognized magazines as a great place to build brand image. That's because ads reproduce
so beautifully on coated magazine paper. You get a printed gloss, smoothness and opacity that imitations like
SC-A+ magazine paper just can't match. It's the kind of quality that assures you of an image words simply can't describe.
To find out more about the advantages of building a brand on coated magazine paper, call 203-358-6877.

Champion
Champion International Corporation

Coated paper. The place to build your brand.™

Figure 6-9: Copy and layout combine to make a point. As the reader slowly penetrates
the maze, the concept materializes in the comparative heading below the text. Hard
reading? Yes. Effective? Yes, because it makes a specific point.

My body copy would have put the sales argument in a more direct line with the ad's intention. As written, the copy loses impact because it says the other new bag just became obsolete. My replacement:

> If you'd waited until you read this magazine, you wouldn't have bought a garment bag that was obsolete the moment you bought it.

Comparative advertising can rescue a flat or unconvincing ad. In capable hands, it can be a grenade, not only shattering or at least damaging a competitor but, more to the point, gathering benefit from the damage. How do you fight back if you're number one?

What can the top dog, under constant attack, do to counterattack? Easy. The most powerful battering ram in the communications universe is lying at his feet, ready for use when he feels that statesmanship has run its course: Ridicule.

If you use this potent club, don't swing it wildly at individual competitors; that drops you onto the dusty floor of the comparative arena, where you don't belong. Instead, ridicule competitors as a group.

If you run a comparative features ad, the comparison should be with as many parallel products as you can cram into the space.

Singling out a single competitor is an admission you've been stung. So even if it's only one company whose sniping is eroding your share of total market, don't abandon your superior position to scrabble around in the dust. Your ridicule should remain generic, and this is one of the few aspects of advertising in which specificity (at least, the specificity of your target) may not be the best course.

How to Write Parity Advertising

If you write comparative ads, stick to the subject—the superiority of what you're selling, *not* the inferiority of your competitor.

Parity advertising is copy that seems to claim superiority but actually states only parity—"We're as good as they are." The hopeless cliché, "If you can find a better [WHATEVER], buy it," is inverted parity advertising, challenging a competitor to prove superiority but claiming only equivalence. True parity advertising usually begins with the word *No*:

> No bank pays higher interest.
> No other cereal has more vitamin C.
> No detergent, dry or liquid, gets clothes whiter.

Analyze these claims. Each one claims equivalence, not superiority. A knowledgeable copywriter won't strut and preen over parity advertising, but the technique is serviceable when you're advertising against competitors whose offers vary only fractionally from yours (see Figure 6-10).

Lumping a group of parities results in a realistic image of superiority:

> No other bank pays higher interest. No other bank gives you more free services, such as traveler's checks and free foreign currency exchange. No bank is open longer hours. Ask yourself: Shouldn't I bank at the First National?

Add even one genuine claim of superiority, however minor, and the whole message becomes an unrivaled claim:

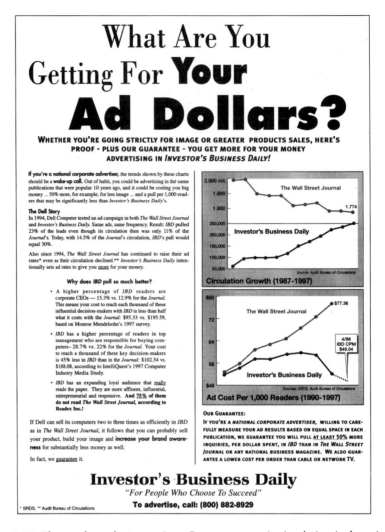

Figure 6-10: The graphs make two points: One newspaper's circulation is dropping while the other's is climbing; one newspaper's cost-per-thousand is rising while the other's is dropping. Altogether, a credible and effective ad by the number two player in the financial newspaper business. (See Figure 6-11.)

No other bank pays higher interest. No other bank gives you more free services, such as traveler's checks and free foreign currency exchange. No bank is open longer hours. And—get this—no other bank gives you an hour's free downtown parking every time you come in. Ask yourself: Shouldn't I bank at the First National?

In this type of mix, the benefit of putting the single absolute, unrivaled claim at the end is its reflection on the whole statement. Placing "free parking" first can trivialize the whole claim; placing it last reflects superiority back through the rest of the message.

What if your single absolute, unrivaled claim isn't "free parking" but a higher rate of interest? Easy! Then you don't need parity advertising at all. You have a major competitive advantage to exploit, and instead of starting your claim with the parity revealing "No . . . ," you'd begin with:

Where's the highest interest rate in Jonesville? Only one bank has it: First National. Don't bother looking anywhere else.

HOW TO LOSE YOUR POSITION AS A #1 COMPANY

1. **Keep telling yourself how good you are.**

2. **Build a plush new corporate headquarters downtown.**

3. **Raise your prices every year...**
   after all, you're the leader...they'll pay it.

4. **Keep making your product the same way...**
   same sizes...same styles...and keep selling it in the same old distribution channels.

5. **Continue to explain to your CEO why 1 – 4 above are so critical.**

6. **Ignore history...its lessons don't apply to you:**
   • Zenith's stock sold for over $300 a share.
   • Sears' sales used to be larger than its next two competitors' combined.
   • Schlitz was the best selling premium beer.
   • Korvette was the leading discount store.
   • Dow Jones' *Journal* used to have 2.1 million circulation and was a monopoly.
   • Chevrolet was the #1 car in America.

7. **Follow the herd.**
   Blow your budget on an expensive image campaign in the same old publications showing declining readership. Go only for mass reach even when it costs you 200% to 300% more, in terms of effectiveness, and when more efficient new choices are available. Since few companies accurately measure image campaigns or test them in competing media, you'll never know exactly how much money you blew... or why your sales and earnings are slipping.

8. **Explain all of the above to the new CEO...and the new ad agency.**

───────── *IBD'S GUARANTEE:* ─────────

If you're a national corporate image advertiser, willing to carefully measure your ad results based on equal space in each publication, we guarantee you will pull <u>at least 100% more inquiries</u> with *Investor's Business Daily*, per dollar spent, than in *The Wall Street Journal*, any national business magazine or regional newspaper. *IBD* also guarantees a lower cost per order than cable or network TV.

83% of *IBD*'s audience do not read *The Wall Street Journal*, according to Readex Inc., June 1998.

Investor's Business Daily
"For People Who Choose To Succeed"

Figure 6-11: Which comparative ad by this newspaper is more effective, this one or Figure 6-10? To a space buyer, no contest 6-10, which has comparative specifics, is more to the point. Had this ad used as its headline a point made in the text, "We guarantee you will pull <u>at least 100% more inquiries</u> with *Investor's Business Daily*, per dollar spent, than in *The Wall Street Journal*," power would have skyrocketed.

If you've used up your parity, another approach might be a challenge:

Hey, First National Bank. What's your answer to this? The State Bank of Commerce challenges you to disprove this statement: No other bank in Jonesville pays higher interest than the State Bank of Commerce. Not one. Not the First National, not the Exchange Bank, not one. The State Bank of Commerce—that's where your money will grow and grow.

Parity advertising can be a bail-out on days when you stare at the keyboard, cursing the cruel fate that stuck you with a copywriting assignment for a company or product that doesn't seem to be worthy of any statement other than, "We're the same as all the rest."

If you decide to go the parity route, don't waver. An office products catalog has this line of copy:

Guaranteed to be the same quality as the more expensive brands.

Instead of this approach, which suggests inferiority even as it claims equality, why not present the information more dynamically:

Guaranteed identical to brands costing considerably more.

You and I wouldn't have used the neutral-gear word *quality*, would we?

Figure 6-12: This is the classic comparative ad. Clarity adds to its power. Were other features, favorable to competitors, ignored? That's the prerogative of any advertiser.

At TechBuyer, we are as concerned about bolstering the profitability of your business as we are about supplying e-commerce tools to your sales force. We work with you as a team: You provide the sales know-how and we provide IT inventory availability, configuration, pricing and end-user financing options. But beyond that, when your customer finances a deal, our **streamlined system pays your invoices** in time for you to take advantage of early payment terms from your distributors. That adds to the **increased margins** you can realize by selling a low monthly payment instead of one total price. And when your customer finances through TechBuyer, **we assume the credit risk**, so there's no need for you to do the footwork checking trade and bank references, and there's no risk to you that the customer won't pay fully or on time. With TechBuyer you're dealing with a **top rated credit** source that, as your e-commerce partner, is working as hard toward **your success** as you are. For more info, call 1-800-900-7436, ext. 154 or check out the demo online.

1 - 8 0 0 . 9 0 0 - 7 4 3 6 e x t . 1 5 4   w w w . T e c h B u y e r . c o m / t b / 1 5 4

Figure 6-13: This ad makes an "Only" claim. About what? What is an "'AAA' rated" deal? Obviously, this is a self-imposed superiority, and the text makes no direct comparison with any competitor. Another approach might be preferable when the writer is unable to follow up a headlined claim.

The Touchstone Technique

A different type of comparative is the touchstone technique. This isn't easy; in the hands of a beginner, it can seem ludicrous. But when approached with polish, a touchstone has the advantage of delivering a powerful comparative without actually comparing. Thus, the writer is free from any accusations that might attend direct comparisons.

Some of the more common touchstones are comparisons with prior success stories, whether what we're selling has any relationship or not:

What if you had bought land in Miami Beach in the 1920s?
What if you had splurged on Microsoft's initial stock offering?

Another touchstone is the use of photographs, art, or historic personages, tying them to your offer. Michelangelo's art on the ceiling of the Sistine Chapel has been the illustration for dozens of offers. The *Mona Lisa* has been one of the most popular touchstones. Unassailable giants such as Shakespeare and Beethoven repeatedly appear in ads. For example:

Figure 6-14: This is a tortured touchstone. The relationship between Beethoven and Synquest, as "great performances," is thin and contrived.

GREAT PERFORMANCES
Beethoven Composing Symphonies
Synquest Optimizing Supply Chains

This example isn't a good one because the tie between musical composition and supply chains is tortured. So we have the Touchstone Rule: A touchstone becomes effective when the reader, viewer, or listener recognizes the value of the original relative to the pretender.

Figure 6-15: What a strange touchstone! Using Mae West to tout a 21st-century refrigerator is at best an odd selection. Yes, we understand the "Come up and see me" parallel, but so what? It's far from any recognizable statement of product benefit.

Figure 6-16: This advertiser uses the parallel of betting on a donkey at the Kentucky Derby with gambling on data. Huh? The touchstone isn't as ridiculous as Figure 6-15, but it makes a point more weakly than a straight statement of "Why" would accomplish.

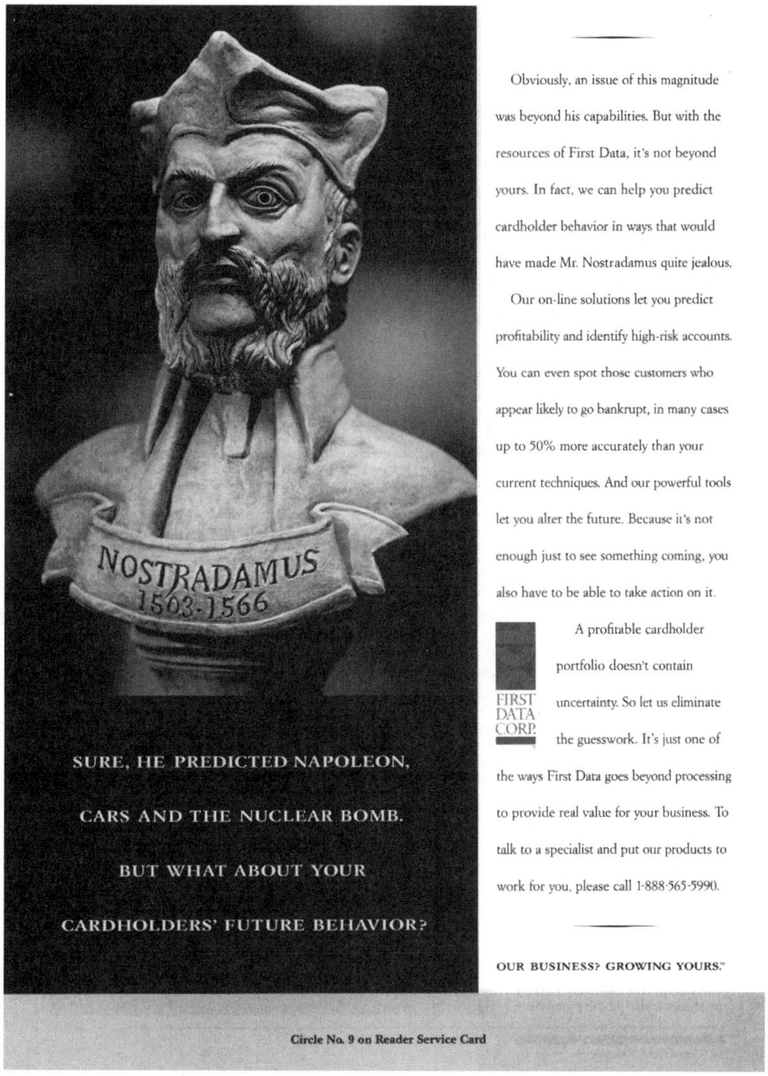
NOSTRADAMUS
1503-1566
SURE, HE PREDICTED NAPOLEON,
CARS AND THE NUCLEAR BOMB.
BUT WHAT ABOUT YOUR
CARDHOLDERS' FUTURE BEHAVIOR?
Obviously, an issue of this magnitude was beyond his capabilities. But with the resources of First Data, it's not beyond yours. In fact, we can help you predict cardholder behavior in ways that would have made Mr. Nostradamus quite jealous.
Our on-line solutions let you predict profitability and identify high-risk accounts. You can even spot those customers who appear likely to go bankrupt, in many cases up to 50% more accurately than your current techniques. And our powerful tools let you alter the future. Because it's not enough just to see something coming, you also have to be able to take action on it.
A profitable cardholder portfolio doesn't contain uncertainty. So let us eliminate the guesswork. It's just one of the ways First Data goes beyond processing to provide real value for your business. To talk to a specialist and put our products to work for you, please call 1-888-565-5990.
FIRST DATA CORP.
OUR BUSINESS? GROWING YOURS.
Circle No. 9 on Reader Service Card

Figure 6-17: This touchstone—Nostradamus as a predictor—would have worked if the second half of the equation were clearer. "What about your cardholders' future behavior?" generates a problem because of the word "behavior." "Decisions" or "card usage" might have made a more comprehensible point.

Handling 2,000-Volt Wires

Comparative advertising and its stepnephew, parity advertising, are hot wires with 2,000 volts running through them. Handle these ads the way you'd handle a live wire. You don't mind if they knock unconscious somebody you're jabbing with the end of the wire, but you don't want the uninsulated end to touch you.

When writing comparative ads, keep them sane. Keep them logical. And for the love of heaven, keep them truthful. Since you're in command and can pick and choose from a grab bag of facts, pick the ones that help you. If what you've picked seems stupid and trivial, maybe comparatives aren't the way to go.

Or maybe you, as copywriter, have the professional job of making the stupid and trivial seem bright and significant.

Chapter Seven

HOW TO WRITE A GUARANTEE

A Staple in the Word Store

The guarantee has become a staple in our word store. Copy looks naked without it. Some publications won't take mail-order space ads unless they offer a buy-back guarantee.

Assuming your copy isn't written with the deliberate intention of grabbing some orders and then going out of business, both the wording of your guarantee and the intention behind it should be less casual than the throwaway guarantees used by many local advertisers, who think they're safe from being nailed.

A marketing weapon

The legal difference between a guarantee and a warranty usually is the difference between a promise to take something back and a promise to fix or replace something. That's an oversimplification, but this book is for marketers, not lawyers, and for our purposes *guarantee* is the umbrella word covering our covenant with the buyer.

The Magnuson-Moss Warranty Act of some years back is a lemon law. It says if your product costs $15 or more, your warranty has to be available for inspection before purchase. (This refers only to written warranties to consumers.)

If you do it, why not advertise it?

I was discussing guarantees with some veteran direct marketers, a group whose advertising claims always are under close scrutiny. One of them made a comment worthy of answer in print: "If a customer sends something back, we don't even ask a question. We issue a refund. There isn't any right or wrong. So why bother using space in an ad or a mailing, when we're going to honor a refund claim regardless?"

My answer was one I hope you'll share: "Except for the last sentence, what you've just said is powerful copy. Why not use it?"

In my opinion, direct marketers have a far more statesmanlike attitude toward guarantees of satisfaction than do retailers. The vendor-by-mail doesn't force customers to go to an adjustment department and doesn't ask them to go to three different stations to get signatures. Someone sends something back or changes his or her mind; for most mailers and catalog houses, the response is knee-jerk quick.

We've come a long way from the "shifty hedge" guarantee we used to see—"During the fifth year in which you own the complete collection, we'll buy it back for the full purchase price . . . " —which in a three-year continuity program meant the buyer had to wait eight years before he could enforce his guarantee.

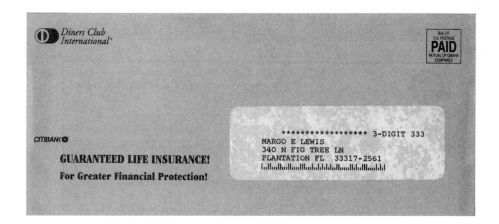

Dear Cardmember,

As a preferred Diners Club® or Carte Blanche® Cardmember, we are pleased to offer you the enclosed opportunity of security and protection from United of Omaha Life Insurance Company.

If you're between the ages of 45 and 75 (55 and 75 in Maryland), you can now enroll in Guaranteed Life Insurance – providing valuable graded benefit whole life insurance protection for you and your loved ones. This outstanding coverage is yours automatically when you return your completed application and charge your monthly premium payments to your Diners Club or Carte Blanche Account. (Each insured may own up to a combined maximum of $20,000 coverage of this type through United of Omaha.)

As a valued Cardmember, your satisfaction is important to us. Please take a moment now to read the enclosed materials. See how Diners Club and Carte Blanche make exceptional offers available to you – quality life insurance from United of Omaha Life Insurance Company.

Sincerely,

Lisa E. Rosenberg

Lisa E. Rosenberg
Vice President

LL1124 7-98

Policy Form 1469L-0889
(or state equivalent)

Figure 7-1: The word "guaranteed" is a sales weapon. In this instance, the word suggests this insurance offer is "guaranteed" to be accepted: "You can't be turned down for Guaranteed Life Insurance for any reason. . . . "

But don't rest too easily. I recently saw this guarantee:

> The (NAME OF COMPANY) pledges to redeem or repurchase your commemorative, upon demand, any time you desire within the next fifty years, for the full cash price you paid.

If you're still alive and that company is still in business fifty years from now, hobble over to the nearest window facing east so you can watch the sun rise.

The Four Standard Guarantees

The loose "We Guarantee Your Satisfaction!" doesn't hack it anymore because it's unspecific. We live in the Age of Skepticism, remember? If someone tells us he guarantees our satisfaction, we ask him *how* he guarantees it.

I offer the First Rule of Guarantees: Unless a guarantee specifically offers a refund, it probably is a cynically inspired sales gimmick, not a true guarantee.

I've identified four standard ways a copywriter can reach his target customer with a clear, easily understood guarantee. All four include a refund provision.

Guarantee 1:
We Guarantee Your Satisfaction. If for any reason you aren't happy with your purchase, bring or send it back for a 100% refund.

Guarantee 2:
We Guarantee the Quality of Everything We Sell. If you think something doesn't measure up to our description of it, bring or send it back for a 100% refund.

Guarantee 3:
We Guarantee Lowest Prices. If, within thirty days of your purchase, you find the identical item advertised for less, bring or send us the ad and we'll refund the difference.

Guarantee 4:
Unconditional Thirty-Day Guarantee. At any time within thirty days, if for any reason you decide you don't want to keep what you've bought, bring or send it back undamaged for a 100% refund.

Yes, it's possible to combine guarantees. Really, all these guarantees except the third one make the same promise: If you don't like it, return it, and we'll give you your money back.

One of the best, most honorable-seeming guarantees I've read was from a catalog by a company called Brookstone. It combines standard guarantees 1, 2, and 4:

> You must be delighted—or you get your money back. We sell only high-quality products, and we describe them truthfully. Each is carefully tested in actual use before acceptance for our catalog. We use these products ourselves.

A

YOU WILL
SAVE $5,000.00
Or More In
The Next Year!

You'll never pay those high prices in wholesale clubs, discount stores outlet malls again.

Secret real wholesale sources... never advertised... never available to the general public... now yours for savings up to 90% on everything you buy!

With these incredible savings you will live twice as good—enjoy double your current lifestyle––without earning a dollar more!

▶ $699 Sony 8mm Handyman camcorder $209

▶ Sunbeam 24,00 BTU gas grill $54

▶ Lifetime health club membership $25

▶ Speed queen washer and dryer set $147

▶ 1992 Winnebago motorhome–mint condition– $130,000

▶ Drapes, curtains, blinds up to 92% off

▶ $250 professional camera and lens $44

▶ $1,100 tool set and chest $199

▶ $143,000 eight unit apartment building $38,500

▶ $399 Deluxe patio set with table $94.

"THE WHOLESALE BARGAINS & FREE STUFF GUIDE is incredible. I have saved $7,432.80 already."
Dr Allen Johnston, New York

B

SAVINGS SO BIG YOU CAN DOUBLE YOUR STANDARD OF LIVING OVERNIGHT.

Dear Friend,

I know it's hard to believe now, but you can double your lifestyle without earning a dollar more. THOUSANDS OF EVERYDAY PEOPLE HAVE ALREADY DONE IT.

Frankly, it's very easy. You can, within 30 days, live as good as someone who makes twice your salary. The secret is having the insider sources in this incredible book.

You see, instead of buying the $199 gas grill your neighbor has, you can buy a $450 model for the same or less money. He will buy a $15,000 new car -- you will buy a $30,000 new car for the same or less.

Your family, friends, co-workers and neighbors will be impressed beyond belief. You'll be admired and respected for your money smarts.

IT'S ALMOST LIKE CUTTING YOUR BILLS IN HALF!

Times are tough these days. With prices constantly rising, you need a way to cut your expenses. Imagine, if you will, that suddenly all your bills got cut in half. You'd be on easy street. You could buy and do the things you want -- without money worries.

Well, that's exactly what is going to happen to you soon. Yes, this book makes it fast and easy to slash your expenses. It's almost like cutting all your bills in half. (That's what a reader in Hot Springs, Arkansas told us.)

Now you will have the money power to splurge . . . to really enjoy the lifestyle you deserve. Buy what you want. Do what you want. Go where you want. All without worry or concern over money.

YOUR $5,000.00 + SAVINGS GUARANTEE

You have nothing to lose during this special offer. THE WHOLESALE BARGAINS & FREE STUFF GUIDE has proven to save thousands of people a fortune. That's why I will take all the risk in sending it to you.

That's right! If you don't save $5,000.00 or more within the first year (or aren't happy with it for any reason), just send it back anytime within one year for a fast, full refund. You can soon double your standard of living. Prove it to yourself without risking a cent. Mail your no-risk order today.

To your new lifestyle,

Roger Conrad
Roger Conrad, Research Director

P.S. Please don't wait and lose out. You have too much at stake.

C

Figure 7-2A, 7-2B, 7-2C: A guarantee reinforces and repeats itself wherever logical. Here, the guarantee presented in a mailed brochure (7-2A) is echoed on the accompanying response device (7-2B). The promise also appears in the letter within the mailing as well as a separate enclosure (7-2C).

But you are always the final judge. If, for any reason or no reason, you want to return an article to us, please do so. We will gladly exchange it or return your money promptly.

This guarantee not only has the ring of truth but also builds an aura of confidence among those who don't even know the company. What an accomplishment!

The third guarantee is a specialty. Not every company wants to have the lowball-price image. For those that do, this becomes an absolute, and the very wording of the guarantee inspires confidence.

Question: Is this a guarantee?

We guarantee that your set of speakers will deliver pure, magnificent sound that will delight you.

Well . . . I wouldn't consider it a guarantee if for no reason other than that it doesn't guarantee anything. Take away the first three words and you have a standard piece of puff copy. (I'm not crazy about using the word "that" twice in the same sentence.) If this marketer wants to transform puff copy into a guarantee, he or she has to add some teeth, such as:

We guarantee that your set of speakers will deliver the purest, most magnificent sound you've ever enjoyed from a set of speakers. If you don't agree, just send them back for a 100% refund.

If the marketer doesn't want to implement the guarantee as a guarantee, then the copy stands as originally written. It's more effective—right now, at least—than a bald statement of puffery, but it adds another imperceptible amount of damage to real guarantees.

Some minor refinements

I believe in maximizing benefit, so I prefer "one full month" to "30 days." I prefer "send it back" to "return it" because ownership seems less conditional. I prefer "we'll send you our check or charge card credit for every cent you paid" to "we'll issue a 100% refund" because the action seems more positive and dynamic.

The Key Question: Does It Help Sales?

You may not prefer what I prefer, and these probably aren't major issues. If you sell by mail, three little words do become major issues if you decide to include them in your guarantee: Even including postage.

If you offer this golden guarantee, you have my admiration because I've seen the confusion, harsh words, and threats from never-do-well buyers who try to make a little profit from the transaction.

Some guarantees seem to be more truthful by seeming to be cold-blooded. This is a dangerous game, but if you know how to play it, you can have what few marketers have—an instant image of integrity. Here's an example:

We will exchange any factory-defective furniture if you pay the freight both ways. Any freight-damaged item can be returned to us at the carrier's expense for repair or replacement.

Damage must be noted on bill of lading at time of delivery if carrier is to pay for the damage.

Some vendors offer ninety-day guarantees because they think they appear three times better than a thirty-day guarantee. (Once again, I'd change it to three months.) Are they right?

In my opinion, they're safe, but they aren't right unless they add some seasoning to the stew. Safety comes from some recent testing showing that, regardless of guarantee length, returns usually come back within thirty days.

The extended guarantee becomes valuable only when it's promoted on a comparative basis. A ninety-day guarantee is just a word change unless the company makes a competitive issue of it. A lifetime guarantee, accompanied by the ring of truth, can boost an offer beyond the reach of a lower-priced competitor.

A catalog of data processing equipment has this headline on a page of computer disks:

BASF Qualimetric Disks are Certified 100%
Error-Free With a Lifetime Guarantee!

The descriptive copy repeats the "100% error-free" claim, but nowhere is the lifetime guarantee explained. So the reader, if he cares, has no answer to the questions: Do they mean it? Whose lifetime, mine or the computer's? Or is it a catch-22 guarantee, referring to the disk's own lifetime? And, oh, yeah—what does the word "qualimetric" refer to?

The hit-and-run guarantee shows up on another page of the same catalog, in which "IBM Diskettes are certified error-free." Certified by whom? What's my recourse? Does certification mean pretesting? Why leave us feeling you're just stroking us, not talking straight?

Too Good to Be True?

A carefully tailored guarantee can make an offer credible. The reader says, "This is just too good to be true." Then he reads the guarantee and is born again: "It's true, after all."

The Second Rule of Guarantees covers this contingency: When the buyer feels he is in total command, the offer becomes true regardless of its incredible nature.

That's a deep one, and the best way of illustrating it is this guarantee from a full-page newspaper ad by one of the more innovative—and controversial—mail-order companies:

Postdate Your Check for
30 Days—Free Inspection
In Your Home!

We are so certain that you'll be very pleased with a (NAME OF) diamond that we will let you examine them in your home without risking a dollar. If for any reason you don't like the (NAME OF) diamond, just mail it back to us within 30 days and we will return your postdated check uncashed.

Obviously the company takes a considerable risk, since these "diamonds" sell for as much as $60, and bad checks are epidemic. At least two of the following four factors have to be dictating this marketing decision:

1. The company is extraordinarily courageous.
2. The company has an enormous markup and feels credit card sales will more than cover any losses from bad checks.

3. The company feels the powerful guarantee will increase total sales far beyond any possible individual losses.
4. The company depends on buyer indolence to prevent complaints and returns from those whose dissatisfaction is based on buyer remorse rather than product deficiency.

The key is the postdated check. The company doesn't just offer to hold your check; they can't deposit it because you've postdated it. The buyer is in command, and the offer is true.

In the same ad is a product warranty:

> The (NAME OF) diamond will last many lifetimes without any worries. In fact, you will receive a Lifetime Warranty against any defects.

Clever, because any defects in a diamond, mined or synthetic, are apparent at once. Defects don't appear gradually, the way they would with a set of tires. Yes, it's a marketing ploy. Yes, it unquestionably helps sales volume. Ethical? I didn't order a diamond, so I haven't the foggiest notion.

But What If . . . ?

But what if the buyer returns merchandise *not* in the original condition? What if a shirt or dress has sweat marks under the sleeves? What if a toy is broken? What if the BASF Disk has a huge buyer-inflicted scratch on it?

That's a marketing problem, not a copy problem. But copy can set the right climate. A product enclosure, properly worded, can head off arguments. If, for example, you sell consumer electronics, you insert a neatly typed or printed piece of copy in each box:

> If you send it back . . . send it *all* back.
> We'll gladly refund your money if you decide you don't want to keep this precision electronic instrument. But don't make it impossible for us to send it back to the factory. If we included batteries, then please include batteries. Warranty, instructions, plugs, ear-jacks? We included them, so you include them. An incomplete return can cause a delay in your refund.

Depending on your company's attitude toward refunds, you can include an admonition against intentionally damaged or abused merchandise. You might even insist on an explanation of *why* the buyer is returning it. But good marketing strategy tells you not to include an automatic return form, encouraging the buyer to send the item back, unless you've made this factor a positive sales point in your original ad or literature.

And this brings us to the Third (and final) Rule of Guarantees: Deliver what you promise. This is another marketing circumstance that bleeds over into copywriting. If you regard your guarantee as an absolute personal promise and ask only that customers return your pledge to do business with honor, your guarantee will be the bird of paradise, not the albatross around your corporate neck.

I guarantee it.

Chapter Eight

THE IMPORTANCE OF SAYING "IMPORTANT"

If You Claim It, Prove It

In six words, I've just written this entire chapter.

If you claim it, prove it. That imperative includes the dynamics, the logic, and the morality of using the word *important* because if you can't prove it, you shouldn't use it.

How long has it been since you were able to write copy introducing a product, projecting a viewpoint, or trying to impale a buyer on the point of your message-saber without using the word *important*?

Overuse leads to abuse, and in my opinion *important* is about to join *quality* and *value* and *service* in the cemetery of killed-off words.

What's wrong is the thrust. The word has become a crutch copywriters use to prop up weak sales arguments. If we walk through a town and everyone we see uses crutches, we quit recruiting for our track and field team. (Figures 8-1 and 8-2 demonstrate this circumstance.)

The First Rule of Implied Importance

Everyone uses the word, but few know and follow the First Rule of Implied Importance: Importance should relate to the state of mind of the reader, not that of the writer.

It's a simple enough rule to understand: "Here's *why* this is important *to you*." The rule may not be so simple to execute because a sudden attack of writer's cramp can strike when the bewildered writer, having word-painted the promise into a corner, struggles to get out of his own trap.

The rhetorical aspirin

What called my attention to the rampant overuse of *important* was the accidental overlap of three pieces of direct mail.

One, from an insurance company, was headed:

IMPORTANT NOTICE TO ALL
U.S. VETERANS

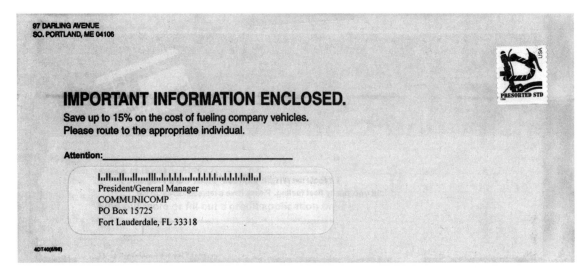

Figure 8-1: This envelope says, "Important information enclosed." Is a reduction in the cost of fueling company vehicles important? Maybe . . . but the "Important" reference certainly isn't the best way to get this envelope opened. A question might have been more effective.

Sure-Feed Engineering, Inc.
3340 Scherer Dr N Ste C
St Petersburg, FL 33716

Important Information Inside

MARGO LEWIS
COMMUNICOMP
PO BOX 15725
PLANTATION, FL 33318-572

Figure 8-2: Another envelope claims importance. Inside is an offer to see an inkjet system at a trade show. Uses such as this explain why the word *important* is losing its importance.

The second was a no-nonsense claim:

IMPORTANT NOTICE!

The third was in French, but the message was understandable on a universal level:

Communication importante —
OUVRIR IMMEDIATEMENT!

The last one was the catalyst. Struggling through the enclosures—all in French, from a Swiss company—I learned what was so important: The company wanted to sell me portfolios of tips and methods for speech making.

They'd had their way: I believed (partially because it was in French) their assertion that this was an important communication; I obeyed their demand to open it immediately. And, recognizing the tragic flaw, I damned them and their followers with the double-whammy they themselves had generated:

1. You lied to me, so I reject your total sales argument.
2. You've added a little more cynicism to my rejection mix.

Sure, what the writer is selling is important to *him*. But so what? I'm just as entitled to my own set of values as he is.

The writer who misuses, overuses, and abuses the word *important* is using it like aspirin: The word becomes the writer's instant solution to all marketing problems. Labeling the product or service *"Important!"* eliminates all the bother of having to organize a coherent, dynamic sales argument.

Aspirin reduces my fever, but you should be *building* my fever. Aspirin numbs my pain, but you should be *sharpening* my senses.

Important to whom?

The "Important Notice to All U.S. Veterans" suffered because of my reaction to the "Communication Importante." How many U.S. veterans are there? I wondered. Twenty million? Is this important to all of them?

Figure 8-3: The conditional word "If" saves this message because it puts the recipient in the proper position—deciding whether the proposition actually is important or not.

Actually, it may have been. The offer, well written and cleverly worded, was for term insurance. The offer began:

> This is to inform you of a BENEFIT OFFER (No. MP818) approved for all qualified Honorably Discharged United States Veterans . . . up to $50,000.00 Term Life Insurance based on the group-buying principle of G.I. Insurance.

Clever, huh? Official, isn't it? "MP818" just has to be a government regulation, doesn't it? "Approved" means approved by the government, doesn't it? And the "group-buying principle of G.I. Insurance" *is* G.I. insurance, isn't it? By carrying through on the "official notification" level, which this piece does for a while (later, subheads carry exclamation points, which give away the game, but by then the reader may be hooked), the word *important* actually becomes important.

Not so with the "IMPORTANT NOTICE!" The next three lines answered the question, "Important to whom?":

> CARPETS OF DISTINCTION WILL SELL
> 1/2 MILLION DOLLARS OF NAME BRAND CARPET
> TO YOU

Not since the demise of the St. Louis Browns has any news been so important.

The Second Rule of Implied Importance

The Second Rule of Implied Importance is the killer: If the copy message following the word *important* is a letdown to the reader, copy is more likely to breed rejection or contempt than to initiate a buying urge.

The curse isn't that dire. To avoid the penalty of this rule, all the writer has to do is tailor his message to avoid reader letdown.

What an easy charge that is! If, writing a piece of copy, you can't redeem the word *important* with a follow-up that keeps the power at 440 volts, all you do is restructure the opening to get rid of the claim you can't prove.

Figure 8-4: What a claim this is. If you can see the asterisked reference, the quote apparently is from *Newsweek*. (An enclosure validates by quoting many publications, including this one from *Newsweek*: "The Library of America can plausibly claim to be the most important book-publishing project in the nation's history.")

A cry of importance from the magazine published by the nation's most august museum lost me with this violation of the second rule. After a computer-personalized overline telling me I'm "one of a small group . . . invited to become national associates," the cover letter's first two paragraphs were:

> I know you receive many "personal" (i.e., computer-printed) invitations, but this is special.
>> By accepting this particular invitation, you will join a special group of Americans whose importance to our national culture I'll explain later.

The letter never does "explain later," but even if it did, I would resent being told "I'll explain later" by *anyone*. Why not explain *now*, which not only eliminates the waste of precious words used to hold me off and (if they'd done it) to reintroduce the subject later but also keeps the power white-hot at the reader's critical go/no-go interest point?

Even if the point were explained later, words such as *special*, used twice, and *importance* become nonmotivating clichés when, in the next paragraph, the writer lets his armor drop: It's a bald plea for a subscription.

Suppose, instead of this, the letter had opened:

> Let me tell you why I'm writing specifically to *you* and why you're so special to us:
>> You're one of the few people who (STROKE, STROKE) . . .

Why am I important to you?

A credit card company writes me:

> Dear Gold Cardmember:
> You will be receiving many communications from us in the coming months—but none, perhaps, as important as this one.

Okay, I'm an old weasel-word expert, and I know what that word "perhaps" is doing there. It's the copywriter's acknowledgment that this communication isn't the most important I'll be receiving (a weak, passive word) after all. As I read the letter and the accompanying brochure, I can't find any benefit of the Gold Card except that over having no card at all.

Probably the Gold Card does have a comparative benefit. But why make me fish for it? If this is, perhaps, the most important communication from the source, why don't they back up the claim of importance with some hard evidence of importance? This is their big chance because from now on any claim of importance will receive, to use their punchless word, a ho-hum.

Here's a double postcard—a *postcard*, for heaven's sake—with this legend on the face of the card:

> Important message inside.

Somehow it's suspect before we flip open the flap. Inside is a printed pitch in advertising language for a "High-Yield Tax-Free Income Fund." To those looking for tax-free income, this isn't really *un*important; the problem here is the mismatch between *important* and *message*. To some, it can be important information, but a message? Sorry.

A letter whose envelope has nonprofit indicia in the upper right corner has this envelope copy:

THE WALL STREET JOURNAL.

200 Burnett Road
Chicopee, MA 01020

Important Message
About Your Subscription To
THE WALL STREET JOURNAL.

MARGO LEWIS
340 N FIG TREE LN
FT LAUDERDALE FL 33317-2561-40

i. AUTO 33317   ‖‖‖‖‖‖‖‖‖‖‖‖‖‖‖‖‖‖‖‖‖‖‖‖‖‖

Figure 8-5: By specifying what the subject is, this envelope copy avoids the too-common practice of claiming importance for a subject the reader may reject as unimportant.

An important National Survey is enclosed.
Do you
☐ hike?
☐ bike?
☐ ski?
☐ run or walk?
☐ ride horses?
☐ or just plain enjoy the outdoors?

See the self-canceling nature of this envelope copy? Somehow I can't attach *any* importance to the bland questions on this envelope.

Inside are many pieces. There is also a five-page letter and a survey that would get a D in any class taught by Nielsen:

1. How do you (or would you) enjoy trails? (check all that apply)
   ___ bicycling
   ___ birding or other nature activity
   ___ commuting to work or school
   (and nine others including wheelchair)
2. Do you feel that your community needs more trails?
   ☐ Yes ☐ No ☐ Undecided

Should I apologize for my annoyance at the misuse of the word *survey*? It's about as scientific a survey as this dialog with a passerby:

"Does your brother like cheese?"
"I don't have a brother."
"If you had a brother, would he like cheese?"

At the end of the "survey" is a membership acceptance form. Also in the package is an en-

Please Deliver To: **HERSCHELL LEWIS**

Important Notice . . . Please Respond Immediately!

To: Marketing Colleagues Who Want to Dramatically Increase Their Attendance
at Upcoming Seminars and Conferences

From: **CLEMSON** UNIVERSITY   Conrad Stuntz
Marketing Director, Clemson University

Subject: Ralph Elliott's Two-Day Program on **"Effective Seminar/Conference Marketing"**

The North American Spine Society, National Association of Energy Service Company, Chemical Institute of Canada, Laser Institute of America, Indiana Chamber of Commerce, Central Missouri State University, Industrial Fabrics Association International, University of Texas at Austin, Greenville Memorial Hospital, SAE International, Rhode Island Society of CPA's, Medical College of Wisconsin, Johns Hopkins University, ASTM, The Institute of International Auditors, State Bar of Wisconsin, Harbor Branch Oceanographic, World Trade Institute ... these are just a sample of the organizations who registered for Ralph Elliott's two-day program on "Effective Seminar/Conference Marketing" to be held on January 7-8, 1999 in Key West, Florida.

Hear what some of your colleagues are saying about the value of Elliott's seminar:

"If you never spend another dime and never go to another workshop on seminar marketing, Elliott's program is the only one to attend. It will take you years to learn what you can learn in only two days from him."

Sally Chapralis
Sally Chapralis & Associates, Evanston, IL

"Brilliant . . . absolutely brilliant. I have heard Ralph Elliott speak on seminar/conference marketing on three occasions and I always leave with an incredible list of practical ideas to boost delegate bookings. I recommend his program to you without hesitation."

John Bodenham, Director
First Conferences, London, United Kingdom

"As a result of what I learned in your course, I increased the revenue from our major conference program from $400,000 to $1,000,000 in one year. I followed that with similar successes in our other conference programs."

Michale Critser, Director
Reed Exhibition Companies, Norwalk, CT

"We were considering canceling a program until we attended your conference; using the pointers on how to write effective copy along with broadcast fax, the phones began ringing off the hook the next day and we produced a 400% increase in attendance. In addition, the numbers at other seminars are up by more than 50%! I am very impressed with your program, and I strongly recommend the conference to others."

Stephanie Mensh, Director of Health Policy
American Urological Association, Inc., Baltimore, MD

You are invited to attend the Key West session to be held at the Marriott's Casa Marina Resort. Please book your room by December 9, 1998 to get the reduced room rate. Other sessions in '99 include presentations at Oxford, England March 16-17, Colorado Springs, CO April 15-16 and San Francisco, CA, August 26-27.

My colleague, Kay James, would like to mail you a copy of the full brochure, so please give her a call at (864) 656-2200; or for a quick response, fax this form to Clemson University at (864) 656-3997!

Or, see the brochure by clicking onto the "Sales and Marketing" hot link on our Web page at http://hubcap.clemson.edu/~elliot/

Name		Title	
Organization			
Address			
City		State	Zip
Business Phone		FAX	
E-mail			

☐ Check here to also receive information on Elliott's three day Advanced Marketing Conference to be held June 21-23, 1999 at the J.W. Marriott Hotel in Washington, DC.

RDE:jgo

> Your Priority Keycode is
> **M756.5**

Figure 8-6: Reading the offer, a copywriter charged with preparing an aggressive message probably could improve on the boilerplate "Important Notice . . . Please Respond Immediately!" (The exclamation point is out of key with the offer.)

closure offering a free booklet if you join this organization, a "lift" note from another interested person, a small bumper sticker, and a business reply envelope.

In defense of this mailing, it's professionally written and handled; but what made these people think "important" is the proper adjective? Why not envelope copy that doesn't generate a grimace when unmasked, such as "We need your opinion" or "Survey Documents Enclosed"? (Then include a survey that better masquerades as an actual survey.)

P.O. Box 9208
Framingham MA 01701

QUICKMAILER®

TO OPEN - TEAR ALONG PERFORATION
USE THUMB NOTCH TO SNAP OUT CONTENTS

```
*************** 3-DIGIT 333



LEW SAX
COMMUNICOMP
340 N FIG TREE LN
PLANTATION FL  33317-2561
```

Figure 8-7: A Snap-Pak often improves response because it has a semi-official look and opens so easily. This one, which says, "Important document enclosed—do not discard—" houses an offer to subscribe on-line to a publication called CIO (for "Chief Information Officer").

Semi-Important: *Urgent . . . Hurry . . . Rush*

Important is just one of a number of words that are supposed to convince without evidence.

Here's an envelope—a 9″×12″ jumbo—from a publication in the meetings and conventions field. In big stencil type on the envelope is the word "URGENT." But the postal indicia say "Bulk-Rate"? The recipient—your prospect—asks, "How is it that it's urgent for me but not for you?"

And what's inside? No letter. Right, *no letter*. Bulk-rate urgency without any semipersonal communication is semiprofessional.

What *was* enclosed was a beautifully printed brochure, on whose cover was the cryptic message:

Can You Imagine Having the Power to
Increase the Value of Gold?

Do you see the first two mismatches? It's too prettily laid out to be urgent, and it's also too lyrical. (The reference: Gold awards to visit the best hotels and resorts and golf courses.)

One of the simplest rules of communication applies here, the Rule of Implied Urgency: Stay in character.

Another attention-getter is "news flash." The latest news flash to reach my desk was an announcement of availability of a mailing list. Does this qualify as a news flash? Careful, now, before issuing a universal damnation: If the information is relevant to the recipient, within that recipient's experiential or professional background, "news flash" has merit because it grabs attention and doesn't do so capriciously.

Wolf, Fire, and Important

Labeling something "important" is an attention-getting device.

So is crying "Wolf!" So is yelling "Fire!" There's nothing wrong with crying "Wolf!"—if you show your readers, listeners, or viewers a wolf (see Tip 42, Chapter 13). There's nothing wrong with yelling "Fire!"—if you show them a fire. And there's nothing wrong with claiming your communication is "Important!"—if it really is important.

So the mailing to those on Social Security is right on target when it says on the face of the envelope:

URGENT! IMPORTANT SOCIAL SECURITY
AND MEDICARE INFORMATION ENCLOSED

It's on target because the claim of importance relates to the recipient's own background. And the letter, to "Dear Concerned American," doesn't let the reader down.

As you consider how the word can be used effectively, consider how it already has been weakened by casual or desperate use. Then join me in chiding the writer of the following copy selling books. This writer chips away at the strength of the word with:

And, importantly, these are books *fully bound in genuine, first-quality leather*.

I agree that the books are superior to paper-bound or cloth-bound books. But why the use of the inapt word *importantly*? Instead of using the word as an unexplained label, why not explain the superiority in terms of exclusivity, one of the great motivators of the late 20th century?

The brochure describing a limited edition plate cries "Wolf!" in a subhead:

The important back stamp in 24 karat gold

Why is "important" the wrong word here? Because it doesn't lead to the copy following it:

▲ Delta Air Lines
SkyMiles®

BULK RATE
U.S. POSTAGE
PAID
DOYLESTOWN, PA
PERMIT NO. 517

*************** ECRLOT ** C023
Mr. R. Keller
340 N. Fig Tree Ln.
Plantation, FL 33317-2561

Important Mileage Information Enclosed.

Figure 8-8: The qualifier "Mileage Information" saves this from being just another wild external claim of importance. By tying importance to the individual's own sense of what's important, this envelope gets itself opened, in accordance with the Cardinal Rule of Envelope Copy (Chapter 13). Had the envelope disclosed the actual proposition—miles for switching telephone service to MCI—the percentage of openings might have been considerably lower.

Dear Friend:

       This is a picture of YOU! There you are in
the mirror! YOU are a person, who is about to
order his new false teeth! Where will you get them?

       FROM THE FRIENDLY MEN AND WOMEN OF THE UNITED
STATES DENTAL COMPANY! WHY? Just read these three
good reasons:

  1. IT MEANS MONEY IN YOUR POCKET! You are dealing with the world's largest
mail order dental plate laboratory. You pay WAY LESS for beautiful, top-grade
materials BECAUSE we buy them in great lots. YOU DO SAVE!

  2. YOU HAVE OUR STRICT, MONEY-BACK GUARANTEE! If, during the 60 days after
you receive your new false teeth you are not pleased WE WILL REFUND YOUR MONEY.
WE WILL PAY BACK EVERY CENT YOU HAVE PAID TO US. OR, WE WILL MAKE YOUR TEETH
OVER WITHOUT CHARGE. Your word is absolutely final with us. We do as YOU say!

  3. YOU RECEIVE WORKMANSHIP THAT IS TRULY BEAUTIFUL! Your new false teeth -
handsome, pearly, natural-looking teeth - are set into our fine materials by
technicians who take real pride in their work!

       And now for the BEST NEWS...the most thrilling news of all! It's news to
take your breath away! Order your new false teeth TODAY and you may have them
at a special, REDUCED PRICE - a low price that is even lower than the money-
saving regular price!

       Just look at the check of miracle values attached! See how you can save
as much as $18.50 on two plates by ordering WITHIN THE NEXT SEVEN DAYS! Pick
out any style you like in our catalog folder. Fill in the 60 day trial blank.
Fill in the check. Enclose a deposit of $2.00 - or the full amount.

       Then hurry to the mail box! All the mirrors in your house will show your
face happy and smiling if you take advantage of this offer. Better do it now
because 7 days fly quickly! After that this offer will be void. We wouldn't
want you to miss out! Play safe -- WRITE US TODAY!

       You will be taking the first step toward a pleasant association with the
United States Dental Company who treats every customer in a way that makes
friends for always.

                             Sincerely,

MMJ:Ba   M. M. Johnson President

Figure 8-9: The wildness of this letter is underscored by the number of exclamation points. When a marketer yells, "Fire!" staying in character is mandatory . . . and whatever else you might think of this letter, you have to agree it does stay in character.

Betty Boop Stamp Causes Sensation!
Post Office Finally Honors Flapper

Charming, disarming and sassy as ever -
Betty Boop shows the world she's got "it."

Figure 8-10: After some of the commemorative stamp issues we've seen, it's unlikely that Betty Boop could cause a sensation. What makes this cry of "Fire!" fascinating is the implication that these stamps are issues of the U. S. post office. Their actual origin, Guinea, is neither masked nor emphasized.

112

Each Inaugural Day Plate in this Signature Edition will bear artist Jeffrey Matthews's full signature in 24-karat gold.

Maybe artist Jeffrey Matthews's full signature in 24-karat gold is important, especially if you compare it to his partial signature in black paint. But *why* is it important? If you can't tell me, don't abuse the word. While you're at it, why not look for another word to replace "bear"?

That goes for the cataloger of book remainders who heads a whole page of closeouts "Important Histories of W.W. II." And for the vendor of the "authentic" (but unofficial) Statue of Liberty Double Eagle, who invites me "to participate in a historic event—perhaps the most important collector's opportunity of the century." And for the fund-raiser who tells me, "Your check is more important now than ever," too terrified of language use to tell me straightforwardly, "Your check means more now than it ever did before."

See the key? Go ahead and yell "Urgent!" if your target will regard the information as urgent. Scream "Important!" if your target will actually regard it as important. Send a "News Flash" if your target will regard it as hot news.

So the next time you look at the screen or the paper and realize you've written, "It is important to remember that . . . ," either add the words "Here's why" to the front or quietly hit the delete key. You'll do yourself, and the person who gets your message, a favor.

Remember that, will you? It's important.

Chapter Nine

HOW TO TAKE CONTROL OF THE SELLER/SELLEE RELATIONSHIP

Understanding and Using the Rules of Positivism

An old song lyric suggests that we "accentuate the positive."

I'm not at all certain any song with inspirational lyrics, no matter how full of jargon it might be, could survive today. I *am* certain the message makes more sense for advertisers than it ever could to historians of song lyrics.

Obviously, where we have a *positive*, we also have a *negative*. As copywriters, we consciously choose one or the other; if we're uncertain, we skip both and write in-between copy. Ugh.

The pertinence of accentuating the positive is tied to a negative, a common advertising mistake—accepting description as *sell*.

Seller meets sellee: Bambi meets Godzilla?

The roles of the two parties in a marketing situation are neither parallel nor equal. We have the seller, who, usually uninvited, wants a transaction to occur. We have the sellee, whose skepticism has to metamorphose through three phases or the order form goes unheeded:

Phase One: I might benefit from this.
Phase Two: Yes, I'd benefit from this.
Phase Three: I'll get it, and I'll benefit from this.

Note the evolution of the sellee's attitude. It moves in a dynamic line, from consideration of a possibility to decision to act.

Some marketers (and many salespeople) are terrified of a confrontation that demands a decision from the sellee. They take comfort in description because it doesn't set up a circumstance in which the other person can state an aggressive "No!" Without leadership from the seller, the sellee makes up his own mind.

Isn't that the gentlemanly or ladylike way to sell? In my opinion, it's the gentlemanly or ladylike way to make one of two catastrophic admissions: 1) Your selling argument is weak; 2) you as a salesperson are weak.

That's why I suggest you examine copy that begins "Can you imagine . . . " and excise the first two words. "Imagine," without the weakeners, leaves you in control, with no possibility of generating the answer, "No, I can't."

Figure 9-1: A clear statement of benefit not only tells the reader what to do but explains, within that reader's experiential background, what the result will be. Hire that writer!

Figure 9-2: The typical writer might have headed the ad, "At last, the Blizzard System makes tenting for termites obsolete." This superior approach is likely to get the phone to ring.

More and more, as competition for attention on any level becomes ever heavier, the vendors who display wares in the back row of the market dooms himself to the quiet disregard of those who, pushed a little, might buy something. Remember the Fourth Great Law of force-communication? (Tell the reader/viewer/listener what to do.)

We conclude our selling argument—in person, in print, over the airwaves, or in the mail—by telling our target sellee what to do. The gentlemanly or ladylike way to sell doesn't enter into the mix. We didn't write the ad to impress Miss Manners; we wrote it to sell something.

The two Rules of Positivism

Fighting for power in our messages, we struggle to master our only weapon—the language.

The First Rule of Positivism becomes an easy guide to message strength: Stay out of the conditional and replace *can* with *will*.

The difference between *can* and *will* isn't subtle at all. *Can* puts the ability to decide or perform in limbo; *will* puts it in the hands of the message recipient.

Before giving examples, a caution: We're talking about buyer attitude, not product capability. If you're selling FDA-influenced products, your lawyer may advise using *can* instead of *will* for safety in product claims. Listen.

Couching the same message in each of five levels of strength will illustrate the point.

Level One:

Can you see the difference this would make in your life?

Level Two:

Can you see the difference this will make in your life?

Level Three:

You can see the difference this will make in your life.

Level Four:

You'll see the difference this will make in your life.

Level Five requires the Second Rule of Positivism, which is such a sharp verbal sword you dare not swing it wildly: After telling the reader you've presented a logical argument, take acceptance for granted.

So we have a Level Five sales argument:

What a difference this will make in your life!

Don't be misled. Contractions and exclamation points are parenthetical to what we're talking about. I stuck the exclamation point at the end of the Level Five argument because as we become more imperative, we become more exclamatory.

In fund-raising, "Can you help us?" is a weak plea combining an admission of weakness with the suggested possibility of reader weakness; "Will you help us?" tells the donor he has the capability; it's up to his sense of honor. That's guilt-creating copy with far greater strength.

Dear Julian,　　　　　　　*London*
So good to hear from you. I assume from your letter that you are referring to those hand-made socks my mum used to send me from Brown's. I was heartened to learn the Americans still appreciate some of the finer things we lent them. You and Henley are not the only chaps to appreciate the hand-linked toes and easy-care of Pantherella socks. The Empire lives on!
Cheers, – *Nigel*

PANTHERELLA
Fine English Socks
1.800.231.0775

Figure 9-3: Can you sell in a two-inch ad? Of course. Does this two-inch ad sell? Probably not, because it not only has no specifics but also masks any call to action in a device that avoids telling the reader what to do.

How to Use the Connotation Rule

Sure, we all know the Connotation Rule: Substitute words and phrases with a positive connotation for words and phrases with a neutral or negative connotation.

By now, we know how easy it is to spot words and phrases with negative connotations. They're the constructions that usually have a "don't" or "can't" or "no" or "not" in them, unrelated to the central selling argument. (If the negative *is* related to the central selling argument, such as "Won't stain your clothes," the rule doesn't apply.)

Figure 9-4: The simile couldn't be more bizarre: "It connects you to the road like a bug to your windshield." Does any driver want that kind of connection?

But knowing the rule doesn't mean we can recognize neutral words as painlessly as we recognize negative words. It's an exceptionally difficult problem because a word that might have power in one circumstance is weak in another.

That's why a beginning writer has no trouble replacing negatives but turns butcher by extending the scalpel to cut out the "good" negative words, while blithely bypassing neutral words.

Example? Here's a standard opening line:

I'm delighted to be able to send you this private notice.

Here's the same line, with one word changed:

I'm delighted to be able to send you this private offer.

When is *notice* stronger than *offer*?

The beginner leaps blindly into the fray, saying, "*Offer* is positive and *notice* is neutral, so *offer* is the better word."

Is it? Maybe. Maybe not. I changed "offer" *to* "notice" in a piece of copy I was writing for a public utility that didn't want to suggest it was pitching the reader. *Notice* becomes a more positive word than *offer* because we give the reader the impression that he or she is forming a positive reaction rather than that we are trying to sell something.

The picking of nits like this is what copy that sells is all about. Our targets are *individuals*, not people. They don't run on tracks, and as professionals, we're supposed to tailor our message to the circumstance.

The inversion technique: a shopworn challenge

In the 1930s and 1940s, some advertisers thought it was cute to invert a sales message so it was negative instead of positive: "Don't Read This Ad . . . "; "Why You Shouldn't Buy at Smith's"; "A Dozen Reasons Why Shoppers Avoid Us." The idea was to startle us into reading the ad by fashioning what appeared to be an outrageous ad.

Hold it! We've come hurtling through future shock and have bounced twice at the far end. This type of ad is about as startling as "Why does a chicken cross the road?"

But we still see it, as Figure 9-7 proves. A writer, slightly out of phase with today's seller-sellee relationships, uses the inversion technique. It's easy to write an inverted ad. All you have to do is, with whatever tongue-in-cheek talent you may have, suggest to the reader that he *not* buy from you.

The reader is supposed to say, "What a clever fellow that writer is."

You lose both ways. If the reader doesn't say it, your wit isn't as projectible as you thought it was. If he does say it, you've violated another Great Law: In this Age of Skepticism, cleverness for the sake of cleverness may well be a liability, not an asset.

So when I saw a coupon ad with an inverted headline, I was neither startled nor titillated. Instead, I was annoyed that the writer couldn't think of a less transparent gimmick. The headline:

Six reasons for *not* sending
for *absolutely free* details about
the Home Business Directory

Just what are you saying if your Web site doesn't accept cash, checks and credit cards?

www.cybercash.com

You don't want to alienate them – after all, on-line shopping is expected to be more than a six billion dollar business by the year 2000. Which means you'll lose out big if you're not using our CashRegister.™ Only the CyberCash CashRegister gives you an easy-to-implement solution, including a choice of Internet payment options – credit card (SSL and SET), checks...even cash. So if you're ready for your Web storefront to see some customers, get the system that's blazing the trail for electronic commerce worldwide. For more information on how to get the most secure Internet payment solution in existence, drop by our Web site today. Or call 1 888 860 6530, ext. 119.

Make Internet Commerce Pay

©1998 CyberCash Inc., Reston, VA   NASDAQ: CYCH

Figure 9-5: This ad may be misinterpreted because the intention—a sign in the window—could seem to be the headline. Greater safety and greater impact might have dictated bigger type for the actual headline.

Figure 9-6: Those three big "NO" headings at left dominate this furniture ad. Even though "No" is the strongest negative, in this instance the repetition makes a positive point.

After a listing of six cliché-generated "reasons" ("We have so much money now, we never want for anything"), the ad's body copy begins with my second-least-favorite line: "Be honest!" (This line is outranked in obnoxiousness only by "Let's face it!")

I'm beating this approach about the head and shoulders not because of a blind prejudice against the inversion technique, not because it isn't ever possible to use a negative effectively, but because whoever wrote this ad cheated whoever hired him or her by delivering a message that was much less effective than it could have been.

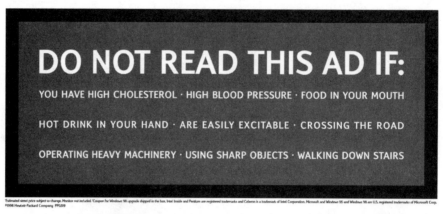

$799*
HP BRIO BUSINESS PC
Intel' Celeron' processor 266MHz, 32MB RAM,
2.1GB HDD, 16-bit sound,
10/100 Base-T LAN card, Windows 98, Model D6750T,
monitor sold separately

$1,218*
HP VECTRA VE BUSINESS PC
Intel Pentium' II processor 350MHz, 512KB cache,
32MB RAM, 3.2GB HDD, Matrox MGA G100 graphics
with 4MB SGRAM, Windows 95', Model D6570T,
monitor sold separately

For technology and manageability at prices you can't afford to pass up, check
out HP PCs for business at www.hp.com/go/vectra or call 1-800-322-HPPC x4083.

Figure 9-7: The ad is almost effective. Did the writer intend to create a wryly
humorous heading? Probably. Does reading the ad clarify or justify the heading, which
many will regard as a tired attempt at attention-getting? Probably not. The point isn't
whether the heading is clever or not; it's whether the writer had a better way to
suggest superiority for these computers.

Networking is a high stakes game –

You put both your reputation and your business on the line with every installation. SMC knows this and so does VARBusiness. They have rated SMC the easiest networking manufacturer to do business with three years running. That's because SMC offers everything you need to ensure your profitability – easy to install, quality products that work right everytime. Also, we've upped the ante with our toll free technical support, guaranteed compatibility and industry leading customer service.

And now, SMC has stacked the deck even more in your favor with our aggressive new Wild Card promotion! For a limited time only, we'll increase your take with two free 10/100 EZ Cards when you buy selected SMC switches, hubs and adapters. SMC's EZ Card 10/100 PCI adapter is one of the most affordable Fast Ethernet cards on the market today, and they couldn't be easier to use.

You don't have to bluff to make money with SMC. Take the gamble out of networking and play the sure hand. For more information on SMC products, services or our customer satisfaction guarantee, visit us at **www.smc.com** or call **1-800-553-7731**.

Buy These SMC Products...	Suggested Reseller Price	...Get Two Free Adapters
10 EZ Card 10/100's (SMC 1211TX) Fast Ethernet Adapter	$21⁰⁰ per unit	EZ Card 10/100's
1 EZ Stack 10/100 (SMC 5208DS) 8 Port Dual Speed Ethernet Hub	$279⁰⁰	EZ Card 10/100's
1 EZ Stack 10/100 (SMC 5216DS) 16 Port Dual Speed Ethernet Hub	$399⁰⁰	EZ Card 10/100's
1 EZ Switch 10/100 (SMC EZ108) 8 Port Ethernet Switch	$499⁰⁰	EZ Card 10/100's

SMC

1-800-SMC-4YOU
www.smc.com

Figure 9-8: This ad, and the two StarMedia ads that follow it, typify an approach that betrays creative desperation. The tortured tie between "Don't gamble . . . " and "Networking is a high stakes game" tries to show a relationship of elements that don't relate. The negative imperative "Don't" doesn't help because it doesn't tell the reader what to do; it tells the reader what not to do.

Don't let your boss find out you don't know about the Internet in Latin America.

With more than 10 million* Internet users in Latin America, the choices are clear: you either include Internet in your mix and enjoy the opportunities. Or, you ignore it, and face the consequences – see left.

StarMedia is the largest and fastest growing Internet community in the region. We offer our visitors a wide range of free choices – from chat to news, from email to shopping, personal homepages and more. All in Spanish and Portuguese.

Our users stay longer. They come back more often. And are among Latin America's most affluent consumers.

We will work with you to develop and maintain your program with precise targeting for greater efficiencies. You can have a number of different tailored messages. By country. By segment. By interest.

So don't wait! Target Latin America's Internet users. Contact us via email: **advertising@starmedia.net** Or call us at **(212) 548-9606.** By fax. **(212) 548-9688.**

www.starmedia.com

Latin America's #1 Internet Community

* Source: November 1997 Nazca Saatchi & Saatchi Study.

Figure 9-9: Another "Don't . . . " ad exemplifies the worst of a dangerous trend—the copywriter and layout artist trying to call attention to their talents instead of making a valid point. Succumbing to this wretched technique is a disservice to whoever is paying for the ad (although obviously somebody said, "Run it").

So, your boss found out you didn't know about the Internet in Latin America.

With more than 10 million* Internet users in Latin America, the choices are clear: you either include Internet in your mix and enjoy the opportunities, or, you ignore it and face the consequences — see left.

StarMedia is the largest and fastest growing Internet community in the region. We offer our visitors a wide range of free choices — from chat to news, from email to shopping, personal homepages and more. All in Spanish and Portuguese.

Our users stay longer. They come back more often. And are among Latin America's most affluent consumers.

We will work with you to develop and maintain your program with precise targeting for greater efficiencies. You can have a number of different tailored messages. By country. By segment. By interest.

So don't wait! Target Latin America's Internet users. Contact us via email:

advertising@starmedia.net

Or call us at **(212) 548-9606.**

By fax. **(212) 548-9688.**

www.starmedia.com
Latin America's #1 Internet Community.

TalkPlanet | StarMedia Noticias | StarMedia Mail | StarMedia Orbita | StarMedia Deportes | BuscaWeb | StarMedia Digital

* Source: November 1997 Nazca Saatchi & Saatchi Study

Figure 9-10: What is the point of an ad such as this? Will an irrelevant 1920s photograph enhance the image of a 21st-century Internet community? Inspecting this ad, consider how you might have formulated a credible and effective selling argument.

The difference between writers and "word-stringers"

Changing a negative to a positive can make a prosaic line exciting. Most readers wouldn't find fault with this line:

> That's a marvelously low price, but it isn't all I have for you today.

No, it isn't bad; the line transmits information clearly and efficiently. But would it have taken any longer to squeeze off a little shot of excitement, a tiny barb added to the bullet?

> That's a marvelously low price, but I have even better news for you today.

What's the difference in impact? 20 percent? 10 percent? 1 percent? I hope you see the point: However fractional it is, why not take advantage of it? That's why writers get paid.

How to Control the Play

When copy lapses into *could* and *would* and *should*, the writer cedes control to the target individual. In my opinion, we should never allow that to happen.

So how can we let the reins go slack? How can the pilot say to a passenger, "If you don't want to go to our scheduled destination, we can go somewhere else"?

We risk a "No" when we ask our reader, "Couldn't you . . . ?" or "Wouldn't you . . . ?" or "Shouldn't you . . . ?" The reader's "No" may be crushing. It may be flat. It may be thoughtful. It may be subliminal. The result is the same: No sale. Using a conditional approach requires a high degree of professionalism. (For an example of such professionalism, look at Figure 9-11.)

I say, *control the play*. Move into the subjunctive as part of your selling pattern, offering a glimmering of relief to your reader but sliding out of the subjunctive before any cataclysmic decision comes forth. Use *could* and *would* and *should* to lengthen the leash, creating an impression of reader independence, but never actually slip the leash off the reader's neck.

Is this procedure automatic, easy to do? Only on the crudest, most primitive level. A good ad, whether sales letter or space ad or commercial, flows smoothly, immersing the reader in a pleasant or energetic sea of words. The writer who fears the reader will surely drown in his own sea.

Don't let the prospect off the hook

An "if . . . " clause makes an action conditional; a "when . . . " clause makes it unconditional. If you write nonprofit institutional copy, this difference is etched into your mind because conditional wording ("If you decide to contribute, we'll be able to . . . ") usually won't bring in as many dollars as unconditional wording ("Your contribution makes it possible for us to . . . ").

Fund-raisers know how to close loopholes through which their targets might escape. Mightn't it be a good idea for those selling products or services to close such loopholes?

Now, a key point: Did that last paragraph leave you feeling a tad unconvinced? I'm counting on it because I slipped that word "mightn't" in there to torpedo the power. We can fuel the sentence with high octane with an easy change:

> It's a good idea for those selling products or services to close the same loopholes.

Or, if we want jet fuel, we take out all qualifiers:

> Those selling products or services have the same loopholes. Close them.

WOULDN'T IT BE GREAT TO
WATCH IT ON YOUR COMPUTER?

Video Highway Xtreme 98 (VHX 98) will turn your PC into a total entertainment center. This plug-and-play PCI card lets you watch TV on your desktop in movable, sizable windows up to full screen.

VHX 98 comes complete with an FM radio and easy-to-use software for video fun. Hook up your camcorder or CCD camera, get on the net and video conference. Leave video messages with *M@X* mail.

Movable, sizable windows up to full screen

Use *Intercast* and *WaveTop* to pull up stock quotes, sports statistics or even movie gossip while you watch your favorite shows. Whether you're running Windows® 95 or Windows 98 with WebTV, it just doesn't get any better than VHX 98.

VHX 98 is just $99 after rebate! The first 10,000 to buy VHX 98 will even get a *free* "Xtreme on my PC" T-shirt! Visit your local computer store or **www.aimslab.com** now. Get Xtreme today!

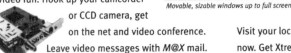

TV tuner • FM Radio • Composite and S-video in • Video mail • Video conference • More

© 1998 AIMS Lab. All rights reserved. Video Highway Xtreme and AIMS Lab logo are the property of AIMS labs, Inc. All other trademarks are the property of their respective holders. Rebate ends 12/31/98. T-shirts while supplies last.

Change the way you look @ computers!

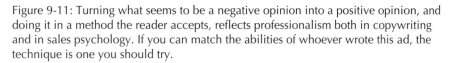

Figure 9-11: Turning what seems to be a negative opinion into a positive opinion, and doing it in a method the reader accepts, reflects professionalism both in copywriting and in sales psychology. If you can match the abilities of whoever wrote this ad, the technique is one you should try.

Contraindications

Oh, yes, we have contraindications for assuming the affirmative stance. Writing isn't yet an automated science; it's a learned art built atop a scientific base that's only gradually being excavated for professional examination. We know we have circumstances in which turning on the full force of our words can alienate half-sold readers.

Just what are those contraindications? I can think of three:

1. A sales argument written with finesse can shift from gear to gear. A good writer can begin in a low-key conditional vein and shift upward and upward with gathering speed until—wham!—the reader is transported into "copywriter's heaven," the state in which we lead and the reader follows like a captive dance partner.

If you can write accelerating copy, you're among the best and can disregard this admonition: Don't linger in low gear for one sentence longer than you have to. Readers will be peeling away.

2. When you want to project an I-don't-give-a-damn image, invert your forceful copy to mask the intent. Start with a dynamic statement of position; shift to a conditional statement of possible acceptance; then shift into a third stance—a difficult one for even the most accomplished wordsmith—supremely logical control, for the close.

This type of writing is tough to do well because the effectiveness of the third leg depends on the writer's ability to convince the reader of this message: "You'll be lucky if we open the door and let you in."

3. For specific marketplaces—art, for example—poetry might be better than hard sell.

Qualifiers all over the place! Note the word "might." A rule might be: The more exclusive the offering, the more valid is withdrawal from vigorous copy.

I suggest testing because schlock art often depends on the image of exclusivity to sell itself, while really fine art can be sold nonchalantly to someone who feels accepted into the in-group.

These variations don't skew the rule; they skew the classification of what belongs where, under the rule. If you write copy for fine art or "let's pretend it's fine" art, you already know what approach works, but if you're taking your first shot, test hard and soft copy against each other if you can.

Say What You Mean

I'm looking at a space ad for a chain of banks. The illustration—in full color, naturally—is a tropical fish. All the copy—naturally—is reversed out of black. This is the heading:

> So daring is the entrepreneurial spirit,
> it cannot survive rigid thinking.

Is this assertion true? Hard to tell, because in order to judge it we have to decode it. Go ahead, try: If the entrepreneurial spirit is daring, how can it be so fragile? So that isn't what the writer means.

If the writer and I were dinner companions, I've become enough of a curmudgeon to ask flat-out: "What are you trying to tell me?"

Whatever the answer to that question might be, it would be clearer and more to the point than the headline copy in the ad, an expensive but uncommunicative message.

If we're trying to lure readers into a house, we don't lock the gate so they can't even get into the yard. The Clarity Commandment, the overriding determinant for word choice, reminds us: When choosing words and phrases, clarity is paramount. Let no other component of the message mix interfere with it.

Might the commandment have suggested a less professorial tone for this next ad, which ran in an advertising publication? This was the promising headline:

HOW TO THINK CREATIVELY
ABOUT YOUR
BUSINESS PROBLEMS

Here's the entire text of the ad, except for name and address:

We've built a unique reputation as corporate growth and development consultants, with a track record of over $1 billion in incremental business for our consumer goods and industrial clients (not including acquisitions).

Our ability to develop innovative solutions to tough business problems is the result of:
- ▶ Structured creativity principles and practices developed by the firm over the last twelve years, which are proprietary to [NAME OF COMPANY].
- ▶ Performance-oriented professionals with individual track records in a broad array of disciplines including strategic growth planning, acquisition strategy, marketing, new product development, technology optimization and market research.

The lack of punctuation at the end is the advertiser's choice, not mine. (Again, the entire ad is a reverse. There has to be a relationship between reverse-type blocks and obfuscation. Maybe it's the desperate substitution of production techniques for communication.)

Okay, find one sentence—no, find one *phrase*—that keeps the promise of the headline. Chest-thumping ads aren't a novelty, but this one thumps with sterilized gloves.

A major financial institution built an entire campaign around this theme:

The latest
get-rich-slow
scheme.

It's hard to believe that someone in management, if not in the creative department of the institution or its advertising agency, didn't ask, "Hey, guys, isn't the combination of *slow* and *scheme* pretty sleazy copy for what we're selling?"

Why didn't they say what they meant? Probably because, in love with their own cleverness or position, they thought they *were* saying what they meant. It's the contemporary equivalent of the old "public-be-damned" arrogance.

Hurling Down the Gauntlet

The disadvantage of picking a fight with a random stranger is that you might get your head blown off for no reason. Why do it?

Somebody, somewhere, suggested in a writing class: "Challenge the reader." The result has been copy that swerves from the direct-to-sale path of *challenge + reward* to the rutted trench of *I dare you, you coward*. We have enough natural enemies without having to find a stranger to insult.

This is the opening of a form letter that came to me:

> Dear Mr. Lewis:
>   You consider yourself a hotshot direct-mail writer.
>   I consider myself the hottest investment writer in America.
>   I believe we can make big money together.

The letter has such Neanderthal motivators as "I'm offering creative types like you the opportunity to profit from their own performance" and "If you believe in yourself, and if you can *really produce*, you'll get rich." The deal is for me to mount and mail a direct-mail campaign for this man's investment newsletter at my own expense, and—benevolent despot that he is—he'll let me keep 90 percent of the $125-a-year subscription fee.

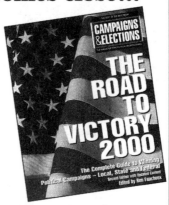

Figure 9-12: Aside from the weakness of any "There are . . ." openings, here we have an ad that admits deficiencies. Coming close isn't a way to sell books. The subhead would have been a better headline.

The letter ends, appropriately, with this warm expression of friendship:

If you're ready to put your wallet where your mouth is, now is the time.

Put yourself in this man's position. You want to convince copywriters to spend thousands of dollars promoting your newsletter. Would you launch into a blind diatribe, with the recipient of your message wondering, "Whose benefit is this, anyway?" or would you try to tailor an appeal to the recipient's ego, based on one of the Five Great Motivators—fear, exclusivity, guilt, greed, or need for approval?

Even if I were interested in working with someone whose whole approach is "I just don't think you can produce results," the opening—"You consider yourself a hotshot direct-mail writer"—would have me reaching for my gun before I even knew what the fight was about.

My reaction was a universal one, and we as writers (hotshots or not) need to remember the Say What You Mean Mandate: The reader inevitably will apply a negative interpretation to statements that violate the Clarity Commandment.

Too late to plead, "That isn't what I really meant," after your crumpled dispatch is lying in the wastebasket.

Compare the hottest investment writer's letter with this slick winner:

Dear Mr. Lewis:

    You and prize winners Rita Eickhoff, Marjorie Solberg, and Bob Thomas all have something special in common. Each of you were invited to participate in one of our national consumer programs with an opportunity to own an expensive new car without having to buy it . . . plus collect up to $10,000.

This letter is crammed with incentives such as "here's your opportunity to . . . ," "you can collect up to . . . ," and "you really can collect . . . " (Note the careful use of "can"; "will" would present a dangerous promise.) Even though this writer uses the plural verb "were" after the singular subject "each", I don't object because the writer strokes my dignity instead of shredding it.

A Not-So-Gentle Shove

Restrained terminology is a gentle shove, useful only in an *exclusivity* appeal that's genuinely exclusive. Neutral words take our hands off the semantic steering wheel: We might reach our destination or we might crash into a garbage can.

Copy selling limited-edition books has this curious phrase:

The paper used for this superb edition . . .

Of course you spotted the neutral word "used." (Neutral here but heroic compared with *utilized*.) Why didn't the writer give us *selected*, in key with what's being sold? *Used*, relative to paper, has no class—and, in fact, has a scatological overtone. We *use* Kleenex, but we *select* the fine paper for this volume.

Fund-raisers sometimes project their dedication onto the whole world. When they do, their copy goes flat because it assumes a base of common interests that doesn't yet exist. Here's the entire sales argument a mailer offers:

Dear Friend,

The American Institute for Cancer Research (AICR) is now conducting its Annual Fund Drive.

During this time, tens of thousands of Americans will make their annual contribution to fight cancer through AICR.

In the next several weeks, I will be meeting with several members of the AICR Board of Directors to plan our coming year's budget. During these meetings, it would be a big help to know what programs we will be able to afford next year.

So, if you could please use the enclosed postage-paid envelope to make your contribution to fight cancer, it would be greatly appreciated.

I want you to know that we look forward to counting you among our friends and supporters in the coming year.

Sincerely,

Dr. J. Dan Recer

President

P.S. If you make only one contribution to fight cancer every year, please use the enclosed postage-paid envelope to make your gift now during our Annual Fund Drive.

Just as *fear* is the natural motivator for insurance, *guilt* is the natural motivator for fund-raisers. But this copy shifts into neutral, shoving us sideways.

The second paragraph eliminates any possible exclusivity or sense of urgency: If tens of thousands of Americans will contribute, my contribution is a bucket of water in the Atlantic Ocean.

The next paragraph uses sand as a seasoning. Not only don't I care that Dr. Recer is meeting with his board of directors, I'm turned off by the image of malefactors of great wealth lounging around, deciding what to do with my money. The word "programs" is especially ill-chosen.

A nonprofit group I usually admire stumbled, I felt, in a mailing that included an ersatz cable from the organization's office in Sudan. A paragraph began with this sentence, highlighted in yellow:

AROUND 2.5 MILLION HUNGRY PEOPLE IN THE TWO WESTERN REGIONS OF SUDAN WILL SOON RUN OUT OF FOOD . . .

Why "around"? Why not *nearly* or *more than* or any word that doesn't seem vague and casual? *Around* lacks concern; it's an arm's-length word, an uninvolved word, a loose guess.

The writer forgot one of the rules of So-What Turnoff Control: Using a "so what" statement as a major selling point adds confusion in direct ratio to the reader/viewer/listener's own interest/knowledge.

We also employ Unassailable Loser Statute I, not only for "around" but for the statistician-accountant term "2.5 million": When seller and buyer both are uninvolved, the seller loses.

Why do so many sales arguments lean on neutral or negative words? It might be because some writers have difficulty projecting themselves inside the heads of their readers.

Can You Mesmerize Someone Who Doesn't Understand You?

What impresses a reader who has never heard of you before? Is one of your in-group going to grab him and shake him until he lifts his pen or phone or computer mouse?

Maybe a hundred years ago a mailer could bully his target by suggesting the reader knew less than the writer. No more. We're in the Age of Skepticism, and term throwing is out of fashion.

A mailing from what seemed to be a print shop came to me. Glancing through it, I saw sample prices for various quantities of printing. But the heading didn't match:

TAKE CONTROL OF YOUR FUTURE FINANCIAL SUCCESS!

I'm an old hand at unidentified quotations, so this imperative didn't bother me, although the thought itself is almost impenetrable: If I have future financial success, isn't control implicit? And if I'm successful without control, so what? I've beaten the system.

Anyway, the heading on this "Dear Friend" letter rated a "So what?" but the first paragraph dropped the reaction way down the scale to a "Huh?"

> Valley Distributing Company has recently introduced a fantastic FINANCIAL SUC-
> CESS PROGRAM. This program is a completely new and revolutionary WHOLE-
> SALE PRINTING MULTI-LEVEL MATRIX MARKETING PROGRAM . . .

I wonder how many recipients stopped right there. I didn't, sucker for puzzles that I am, and I was rewarded with this explanation:

> By limiting the number of distributors allowed on the first sales level of each member, and by paying sales commissions on each VDC CERTIFICATE purchased through seven complete sales levels, it is possible to build a very strong and profitable down-line.

Downline? What's a downline? For that matter, what's a VDC CERTIFICATE? I had the same frustrated feeling I sometimes have with *Time* and too many of the computer and Internet publications, thinking that if I go back to the beginning of the story, the initials will be explained.

All right. Let's suppose VDC stands for the company name, Valley Distributing Company. The company might have told me what it meant instead of saying, "Fish for it." It might have told me what the seven sales levels are and what they mean. Instead, the letter lapsed into "in-talk," and I'm left out.

Once again I invoke the Clarity Commandment: When choosing words and phrases for force-communication, clarity is paramount. Let no other component of the message mix interfere with it.

I'm not asking for oversimplification. I'm asking for adherence to a tenet of advertising copywriting that should be inviolable for anybody who wants to sell something: Write inside the reader's experiential background, not your own. That's one of the separators dividing professional writers from amateurs.

What Did He Say?

When a writer doesn't say what he or she means because of a grammatical lapse, justification usually comes swiftly: "Aw, they'll understand what I meant."

Maybe so, maybe not. How many sets of eyes saw this copy from a fine arts catalog before it hit the mailbags?

"Heavens! Can he really
do it?"...Martha whispered.

They Laughed When I
Sat Down At The Computer.
But When I Started to Use It! --

***"They didn't know I had taught
myself with the new IBM PC
MASTER™ from
Courseware, Inc.***

You can do it too!"

"Up until two weeks ago I had never
even touched a computer keyboard. I was
afraid I might accidentally ruin some expensive software, or look and feel foolish
trying to learn about bits, bauds and other
computer jargon. After all, I'm not a pro-
grammer; and math never was one of my
best subjects.

"So you can imagine my surprise and
relief when I started using PC MASTER!
In just a few interesting hours I was using
my PC with confidence. It guided me step-
by-step and at my own pace through the
different ways to use my PC.

***I learned the same way the Astronauts
do.***

"PC Master is the first tutorial software
package ever designed by Courseware,
Inc. for the general public. For more than
ten years, their staff of ninety instruc-
tional systems development experts only
designed custom training programs for
companies such as IBM, CDC, Bell &
Howell and Prudential. They know just
how clear and complete Courseware's
training methods are — so much so that
the special programs Courseware designed

for NASA space astronauts ten years ago
are still being used today!

Before releasing PC Master to the
public, Courseware tested it in real-life
situations with business executives, educators, students, professionals and senior
training directors. After using PC
MASTER their response was unanimous —
PC MASTER was the best introduction to
the IBM PC they had ever used. Their
comments typically went like this:

"Finally, someone did it right. Congratu-
lations!"
Dr. John Hughes, III/Los Angeles Baptist
College

"Help! I made the mistake of testing your
PC MASTER on my wife and 13-year-old
son. How do I get my computer back?"
John Meade, President/Hagan Associates

Here's What You Get

First, PC MASTER teaches you how to
take command of the keyboard and PC
DOS. And in less time than you would
spend watching a movie, you'll find yourself running actual applications software
programs!

The second diskette focuses on what
your PC can do for you, with a hands-on
guided tour through ten of your PC's most
useful applications.

Finally, you move on to learn *when* to
use your PC by participating in hands-on
practice sessions using the four most popular applications — Word Processing, Data
Management, Communications and
Spread Sheets. You even learn *how* and
when to choose the software that best
suits your needs!

Whether you're a novice or experienced
computer user you can profit from PC
MASTER. You can use it to introduce
business associates and your family
members to the exciting new world of
computers or if you're a new user who
doesn't want to waste valuable time in
long, often boring classes, then PC Master
is the perfect answer to your own needs.

***My second best computer buy amazed
even me!***

*I know my first smart buy was the IBM PC.
Now I know my second smart buy was PC
MASTER. Why not make it yours, too?*
Order your personal
copy of PC MASTER
today — and surprise
and amaze your
friends, family and
business associates
with your new-found
ability to use your
IBM PC.

Now Martha
does it, too!

Courseware, Inc.®

Figure 9-13: A valid technique for mail-order sales is writer-as-surrogate-for-reader.
This ad is an exact lift from one of the two most famous ads of all time, John Caples's
"They Laughed When I Sat Down at the Piano." (The other, which ran for 45 years:
"Do You Make These Mistakes in English?" for the Sherwin Cody School.) For those
who remember the Caples ad, this tribute is a winner. But is this group, many of
whom are well beyond their working years, a good prospect for what's being sold
here? Whether the reader smiles and responds . . . or considers the ad a stupid, out-of-
date cliché . . . depends on the reader's own background. Opinion: a dangerous crap
game.

Aphrodite by Erté
The late (died 1990) Erté's costume designs were as popular at 92 as they were in the 1920s. Aphrodite's dress was originally created for a 1914 show with the same name . . .

Now we have to sort out the dates. If I take the message literally, Erté's costume designs are over 90 years old; they're from the 1920s; this one was created in 1914. I say, "Huh?"

As an Erté fan, I know it's the artist who was 92 years old, not his costume designs. You and I would have clarified: "Even when the late Erté was in his 90s, his costume designs were as popular . . . " This writer has to rationalize: "Aw, they'll know what I meant."

Sorry, but we don't. Why bring in the 1920s if this design was executed in 1914? What kind of show was it? A musical? Or was it an art show? An art show named Aphrodite? We're asking even more questions because the writer was too cryptic.

How about this to begin a sales letter?

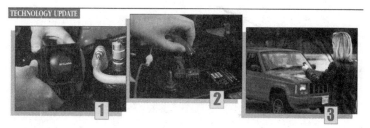

Figure 9-14: Here we have a more contemporary approach to "They laughed when . . . " The writer sells a difficult concept by simplifying the technique and defanging the typical skeptical reaction, "I can't do that."

Dear Executive:

Besides a rare mix of economic factors, another main force behind the coming super-boom in real estate is a new kind of *"factual* consensus."

For the facts from every quarter are all in agreement—consensus—that the American executive can make immensely more money in a single real estate deal than from decades of regular hard work.

And the growing awareness of this compelling point gives a further boost to natural demand, hence to prices, for real estate of all kinds. Coupled with the unusually favorable economic factors . . .

Opinion: a brutally uninviting opening. If an American executive (why "executive" I don't know, unless it's just everyday phony stroking) can make more money in one real estate deal than in ten years of hard work, why not put some *you* into the opening, together with a promise of what this company will do?

The point is obfuscated as it is. The writer doesn't say *ten years*; he uses the standoffish and nonspecific "decades"; he weakens "hard work" with the qualifier "regular."

Why use phraseology such as *"factual* consensus" and "decades"? Don't we want rapport with the reader?

Hara-Kiri and Other Keyboard Tricks

Stringing words together is easy. It becomes difficult when a writer wants to lead the reader by the hand through the mystic maze of potential misinterpretation.

Suppose you're selling a new vitamin supplement. You're in a minefield sown by regulatory agencies and years of claim-sameness. You can tinker with wording the way a racing-car mechanic tinkers with the engine, for maximum power:

1. WE MAKE NO CLAIMS AND MAKE NO PROMISES. BUT WE'LL TELL YOU WHAT OTHERS SAY . . .

2. WE CAN MAKE NO CLAIMS AND CAN MAKE NO PROMISES. ALL WE CAN DO IS TELL YOU WHAT OTHERS SAY . . .

3. WE WON'T MAKE ANY CLAIMS OR PROMISES. BUT READ WHAT OTHERS SAY . . .

4. THE LAWS WON'T LET US MAKE CLAIMS OR PROMISES. SO READ WHAT OTHERS SAY . . .

The differences aren't vast. But the sales arguments are *not* identical. No two have parallel impact. Each positions the marketer differently. Each tries to establish a buyer attitude toward the company.

If you see how word choice affects reader reaction, you also see that casual slopping through rhetorical alternatives can betray your message. Saying what you mean is implicit in effective copywriting.

Take a look at whatever piece of copy is sitting on your desk, ready to go. Does it really say what you mean to say?

All of Which Means What?

The writer's control of the communication relationship can dwarf every other facet of copywriting. Taking charge—with the reader becoming your willing follower, then your captive—is a formidable talent.

To me, the reward is that the talent can be developed, honed, sharpened, and perfected—an impressive credential, irresistible when your copy goes head-to-head against that of someone who hasn't polished the talent because he or she doesn't know it exists.

Chapter Ten

How to Warm Up Your Copy

Examples? Yes—Statistics? No

One reason I admire good fund-raising writers is because they know something lousy fund-raising writers don't know—the Rule of Statistical Deficiency: Readers respond less to cold-blooded statistics than they do to warm-blooded examples.

So instead of writing:

75% of the children affected might be saved

they'll write:

Of four afflicted children who died, we might have saved three of them.

Terrific, isn't it? If you agree, you're not yet ripe because the change has simply expanded on the statistic. What if, instead of numbers, the writer had used examples:

We lost Jimmy today. His parents knew his pitifully short days were numbered. They never lost hope . . . until the end. But Mary, Karen, and Billy are still alive. We're fighting for their lives.

Boy, that's easy. What isn't so easy is adding some *wham* to a journeyman line such as:

Save up to $81!

Nothing wrong, you say? You're right. It isn't *wrong;* it just isn't as exciting as it might be. Tinker with it for five seconds and you have:

Save as much as $81!

What's the difference? This: The hairline edge for excitement goes to "as much as" over "up to." Nitpicking does pay off in a business that measures effectiveness the right way—by fractions of a percent of response.

Hiring writers? How to separate wheat from chaff

I have long suggested an early-weeding procedure for employers and headhunters to separate the chaff from the real copywriters: Give the prospects—and they're all whizzes at writing re-

Nobody wants to be down during a critical print window. So, Xerox is dedicated to keeping uptime at 98%. But if downtime occurs, we'll get you up and running fast. Our over 10,000 trained service professionals average 18 years of experience. Virtually any part you need is available locally. And the reliability of our entire line of *DocuPrint Production Printers* is backed by our unique Total Satisfaction Guarantee. Because the only thing better than 98% uptime is 100% Xerox commitment. To learn more, visit our website at www.xerox.com/print.

THE DOCUMENT COMPANY
XEROX

Uptime based on actual service contract hours. XEROX,® The Document Company,® the digital X,® and DocuPrint® are trademarks of XEROX CORPORATION. 36 USC 380

Figure 10-1: This ad parallels Figure 9-12 in using not-quite-perfect as its sales base. It also has the tired "When it comes to . . . " headline. In today's era of precise engineering, would you want a document printer that was inoperable two days of each 100?

sumés—an opportunity to write some descriptive selling copy while sitting at a keyboard right there in front of you or your personnel manager. Lard the information sheet they're to use as background information with words such as *utilize*, *annual*, *requested*, and *commence*. While you're at it, use *for* when you mean *because* and insert a few clinkers such as *indeed* and *what's more* and *remember* (as a semi-command, followed by a comma).

If the sample copy regurgitates those words back at you, pass.

Remember Who Your Reader Is

We're selling books or records or videotapes or memberships. Staring at our merciless screens, we see what we've written:

> If you sign up for the program . . .

The writer who would have flunked the *utilize* test plows merrily ahead. What the heck—the reader will understand.

That's exactly what's wrong. Signing up for a program can seem to be too profound a commitment when blared from the keyboard halfway through a pitch. Instead:

> If you decide to go into the program . . .

Still too big a commitment? We have lots and lots of words to choose from:

> If you decide to try out this program . . .

The writer might have written "participate" instead of "go into" or "try out." It's a better description of the act we want them to perform—except for one aspect: *Participate* intellectualizes the sales argument, and we've known for years that emotion outsells intellect.

Let's look at another. Anything wrong with this?

> Please respond within the next 10 days.

Right! "Please respond," in the murky universe of unsolicited sales pitches, may seem to be too positive a commitment. So for the reader's ease, a minor word change:

> Please reply within the next 10 days.

If you're unusually jumpy about seeming too pushy, you can take yet another step backward without damaging the foundation:

> May I ask a favor? Please let me have your reaction within the next 10 days. Thanks.

While we're in this neighborhood, "Thanks" is considerably more convivial than "Thank you," which keep's the reader at arm's length. So choose carefully because a little distance has value when you don't want to seem brash.

The Peripheral Pussyfooting Weakener Rule

Writing around a point drains it of excitement.

That's the beginning of a valuable rule, the Peripheral Pussyfooting Weakener Rule. Let's look at the rest of the rule.

Visualize a setting: Into a sedate roomful of dinner guests bursts a breathless messenger. He gasps out: "A short distance down the road, our bellicose opponents can't go unnoticed. Within a short period of time, our defenses may be breached by hostile troops."

The message is dire, but the delivery is flat. How much more dramatic, as long as he's gasping anyway, to pant an exclamation: "The enemy is coming!"

So we form the rule to cover those thoughtless circumstances in which, dignity-driven, we forget why we're at the keyboard in the first place. The Peripheral Pussyfooting Weakener Rule can keep us from lapsing into punchless prose: Writing around a point drains it of excitement. Writing loses impact in direct ratio to the percentage of information given indirectly instead of directly.

Example? How about this line from a communication in, sadly, an advertising publication:

It hardly went unnoticed.

We all have written copy like that; but no more, not with knowledge of the Peripheral Pussyfooting Weakener Rule haunting our brains. If you have the time right now, analyze that four-word message. It's mushy. Rewrite it, transmitting its message directly instead of indirectly.

Why go through that exercise? Because you could have a parallel piece of copy sitting on your desk right now, that's why.

Maybe If We Tell Them We're Crazy

A loose deck card has this heading:

Market Test   Are we crazy?
Get a Full One-Year Subscription to These Famous $195 Financial Newsletters for
Just $19 Each . . . (as part of a daring 30-day marketing test we are doing).

Does the used-car dealer approach work for newsletters? Only the publisher knows for sure. We know, though, that this chap sacrificed his dignity without achieving martyrdom because he got nothing in exchange.

"Are we crazy?" doesn't work here because nothing in the copy suggests such a state of lack of mind. It's a straight discount deal; the headline might work if the publications were free, but at $19, the "famous" newsletters may or may not be a bargain; I had never heard of them, but maybe some folks who got this card had.

The word "daring" bothered me, too. When an adventurer tells me he's daring, it's less effective than if he tells me something that causes *me* to think he's daring. The word itself seems out of key, and because it's artificial in this context, it skews the message. I'm neither excited nor challenged.

Words Are Our Bullets

A peculiar mailing by the leading publisher of list data has a lift-letter inviting me to "Take this test, to see if you've made the correct decision."

Is this supposed to excite me? A test puts the mailer in a superior position, which I resent; a *quiz* would have taken the brutal edge off the implication that there's a requirement I might not meet; a *ballot* or *opinion* makes me superior, the most acceptable relationship of all.

Okay, what's the test, in that example?

There isn't any.

Instead, we have some testimonials, followed by this copy:

I ask you to do the most natural thing for any direct marketer: Test it.
It will cost you nothing, and the returns will be far greater than you think.
Remember the test is FREE! You try it in your home or office for 30 days, and if you're
still convinced it's not for you, simply return it, it will have cost you nothing.

Bizarre comma usage aside ("Remember the test . . ." without a comma suggests
"Remember the Alamo!"; in addition, the last two sentences are tied together with a comma),
here's an enclosure whose sole purpose is to excite. Instead, it annoys me twice—first by mis-
stating its content and second by lapsing into a tired "free test [trial]" pitch. It's aimed solely at
direct marketers—he says so himself—so this mailer should have known: Most of his targets have
used that same approach at least fifty times.

Words are our bullets. If we take gunpowder out, we're firing BB guns against the laser-
aimed rockets our competitors might use.

Roget's can't help you now

As often as not, delving into *Roget's* or the thesaurus on your word processor isn't the answer.
Would a thesaurus have helped the writer who referred to his company as "among the most respected publishers" instead of the equally simple-to-write "one of the most respected publishers"?

The difference is fractional, I agree; but "among" makes the company one of the mob while
"one of" suggests singularity. Why bother with neutral (ergo, denigrating) words?

Would a thesaurus have helped this hara-kiri line of copy glaring at us from the order form
of a consumer offer?

YES, please send me, right away, the referenced items I've selected.

"*Referenced* items"? Would a thesaurus have been of any value to the writer who generated
this deadly line of copy about art objects?

The manufacturer has told us the quantity we are to receive will be small.

Look at the mess here: "Manufacturer" (instead of, say, *producer*) for art? "Quantity" (instead of *allocation*) to suggest a limited number? "We are to receive" (instead of using *our* before
allocation) as a bumbling comprehension-delayer?

A thesaurus would have been helpful to the writer of the next example—but only as valuable as the writer's decision to use words that stimulate the reader to act. The writer's compe-
tence isn't in question; it's the dedication to reader excitement that flagged here:

SUBSCRIBE TODAY!
Here's what your peers have said about
The Office Professional.

What is it about that word *peer* that makes us think we're either being judged by a jury or
becoming part of a preteenage focus group?

Read it over one more time

Deadlines are the enemies of exquisite word selection. We all wish we had the time to polish and polish until every line shines like the hood of a Rolls-Royce.

Here's a test—no, a quiz—no, cast your ballot—no, offer your opinion on this suggestion: Just as you're ready to print out the words of your next piece of copy, run them back through your brain processor one last time, looking *only* for words you can goose up to the next level of excitement.

Maybe you'll be the only person consciously recognizing the difference. That's a majority, isn't it?

Chapter Eleven

THE COPYWRITER'S PRIVATE SHORT COURSE IN GRAMMAR AND USAGE

Clarity But Not Illiteracy

The Clarity Commandment overrides some of the traditional rules of grammar we learned when we studied English in grammar school.

Some, not all. The commandment doesn't give us an excuse for illiteracy. It doesn't let us form a plural "with's," and it doesn't let us string two sentences together separated only by a comma. But it does let us end sentences with a preposition. Why this exemption? Because contorting some sentences to force them into a purist mold impedes comprehension.

So we replace "This is the information you requested" with "This is the information you asked for." Even though we end the sentence with a preposition, we gain clarity and get a bonus besides: "requested" has a pompous overtone; "asked for" suggests positive action.

We use "like" instead of "such as" because, mirroring speech, it's clearer and cleaner. "They kept it for people like you" reads better than "They kept it for people such as you."

Subject and verb agreement

One rule of grammar we can't violate requires agreement between subject and verb. This sentence appears in a trade publication ad for a company named Arnart, selling miniature figurines based on Norman Rockwell's art:

> A true collector's item, Norman Rockwell is part of FIGURINE AMERICANA by
> Arnart . . . the most exciting and saleable collection of figurines in America today.

What happened here is simple misconstruction. The writer meant, "Each Norman Rockwell figurine is a true collector's item."

It's understandable that one copywriter, in a rush to meet a deadline, can make this kind of mistake. It isn't understandable that a four-color ad, which unquestionably went through many hands before appearing in the pages of a magazine, could escape from creative controls with the mistake intact.

A wordsmith shouldn't justify mistakes that skew the reader's comprehension. So the ad writer who referred to "Mr. Ziegler's last book" puzzles us. Does he mean Mr. Ziegler's most re-

The Platinum Card®

Alfred F. Kelly, Jr.
Executive Vice President and General Manager
Consumer Marketing

Margo E. Lewis
340 N. Fig Tree Lane
Plantation, FL 33317-2561

Dear Ms. Lewis:

As a Platinum Card® member, I cordially invite you to enroll in the Sign & Travel®
Account, the payment option from American Express® that gives you even more
flexibility with the Platinum Card.

• **Sign & Travel gives you the ability to defer travel charges, should you
 choose.**
With a Sign & Travel Account linked to the Platinum Card, you'll have additional
spending flexibility to vacation wherever and whenever you like. You'll enjoy the
option of extending payment on airline tickets, hotel and resort accommodations,
rental cars, cruises, and vacation packages you charge on the Platinum Card.

• **Of course, there's no pre-set spending limit.**
As always, your Card purchases are approved based on a variety of factors,
including your account history, credit record and personal resources.

• **We've made Sign & Travel so inviting by emphasizing convenience.**
You never have to request Sign & Travel when you make a travel charge with
the Platinum Card. Your eligible travel expenses will automatically appear in
a separate Sign & Travel portion of your monthly Platinum Card statement.

• **You maintain control—absolutely.**
You decide each month whether to pay your Sign & Travel balance in full, or
pay over time at a competitive interest rate. And as long as you continue to pay
your balance in full when new travel charges are placed on your Account, you
won't incur interest charges.

• **Please accept this invitation with our compliments.**
There is no fee to enroll. Simply sign and return the enclosed R.S.V.P. card by
September 28, 1998.

It is truly our pleasure to provide our most distinguished Platinum Card members
with even more spending flexibility. Please contact us at 1-800-525-3355, should
you need any further information or have any questions. I look forward to your
reply.

Sincerely,

[signature: Alfred F. Kelly Jr.]

Figure 11-1: Oops! A common but irritating grammatical error: "As a Platinum Card®
member, I cordially invite you . . . ". Of course you, the executive vice president,
would be a Platinum Card member. The "as" referral should be to the letter's
recipient.

cent book? Or is Mr. Ziegler no longer among us, in which case his most recent book is his last
book—in this life, at least?

A catalog description reads:

You'll either want red with white trim or navy with light blue trim.

Shifting the word "either" to its proper position, after the verb "want," not only clarifies the
meaning but enables the reader's eye to zip through the copy without having to go back for a clarifying look.

Word sequence

Clarity has to come first, no matter what you're writing or to whom. Throw out forever the "Throw Mama from the train a kiss" constructions in which out-of-position words result in confusion and, often, in unintentional humor. All the words are there, but sequence is helter-skelter. Here's the first line of copy from an ad for a self-help book:

As an infant, did your parents make you a partner?

Here's another, for a condominium development:

You'll live in a suite guarded by a security desk and a doorman you'll enter in complete safety.

The difference between "white man's shirt" and "man's white shirt" should be clear to a writer of department store copy, but I've seen proof to the contrary.

"We offer limousine service" has at least two meanings:

1. "We service limousines."
2. "We'll drive you there in one of our limousines."

Why force the reader to guess? Half the time you'll lose him to someone whose word constructions are clearer.

A magazine writer referred to the castle in which the prince of Liechtenstein lives. Said the writer, "One of its early inhabitants was Prince Joseph Wenzel, portrayed at right by Hyacinth Rigaud known for his artillery system that was adopted all over Europe."

Whose artillery system? Prince Joseph Wenzel's? Or Hyacinth Rigaud's? A grammarian would insist on Rigaud because that's the grammatical reference. Matching up the name Hyacinth and artillery, we say, "Nah, it had to be the prince." But why make us guess?

The headline in an advertising magazine article stated, "Black marketers push power to the people." Not good. A black marketer, as a distributor of goods obtained from an illicit source, isn't the same as a marketer whose racial background is black. We associate "Power to the people" with the latter, but this reference comes after the phrase "black marketers," which we comprehend one way and then have to go back and construe in another way.

A letter selling collectible art refers to "a time when people could walk about as fast as the cars could go." What does it mean? Are people walking about? Or are they walking as fast as automobiles can go? An easy word change saves us from having to go back over the sentence . . . or throwing out the letter.

The same letter has this curious description of the artist:

Acclaimed as one of the premier gallery artists of the Victorian Era, she has turned her great love of the period and her fascination with its young peddlers into a heart-warming collection to be cherished and enjoyed daily.

Yes, it's semipro writing. Yes, you'll find heartwarming on the list of no-no clichés in Chapter 3, and the word "peddlers" needs a qualifier when you're talking about art. But the major problem is calling this artist (described elsewhere as "bright-eyed," "born in California," and "fast becoming recognized") as belonging to the Victorian Era. That isn't what the writer meant . . . unless the artist is a time traveler.

Easy Clarifiers—How and When to Use Them

Sometimes, adding clarity to a muddy sentence is as easy as pouring a bottle of clarifier into a murky spa: Before your eyes, the water turns clear.

Hyphens can clarify

A catalog description:

> Decorator Lamp Cover

Is it a decorator lamp or a decorator cover? Only the catalog writer knows for sure. If it's a decorator cover (as it was), the description clarifies itself immediately when a hyphen appears:

> Decorator Lamp-Cover

When a noun becomes an adjective, the danger of confusion increases, and the advisability of hyphenation is more pronounced.

Put the qualifier near its noun

A grocery store crows:

> GIANT WATERMELON SALE

All right, what's giant—the watermelons or the sale? If it's the watermelons, why not word it:

> SALE! GIANT WATERMELONS

If it's a giant sale, why not word it:

> WATERMELONS—GIANT SALE!

On rare occasions you may deliberately muddle your point. But the technique suggests deception, and in the Age of Skepticism deception backfires as often as it works.

A woman's coat-and-trouser suit has this as part of the catalog writer's description:

> USA-MADE AND IMPORTED

We need qualifiers. We need explanations. A suit can't be both USA-made and imported. "USA-made (silk linings from Japan)" would clarify. Writing nothing would clarify. But this word sequence not only doesn't help; it hinders comprehension.

Puzzling copy is as inexcusable as cleverness-for-the-sake-of-cleverness copy. In my opinion, the principal cause of puzzling copy is desperation. A copywriter's imagination is on holiday, and out comes *Roget* or up goes the mouse to the thesaurus in the word processor. Rescue is temporary, like aspirin taken to mask the symptoms of arthritis.

How to Win the Dangerous Word Game

Overdependence on *Roget* can result in a word sequence that has color but doesn't have coherence. For example, how can we excuse the writer who thought up this catalog copy?

> Catalytic Caftan. Who says a stay-at-home caftan should be shy and retiring? This one's all glamour and gleam from shirt collar to hem . . .

What percentage of caftan wearers know the word *catalytic*? The copywriter is sunk. If they don't know the word, they guess its meaning (probably unsuccessfully); if they do know it, they puzzle over what the copywriter meant.

A travel brochure has this line:

> The beautiful, spectacular Japanese Alps, with their outrageous vistas and tranquil winding roads, call you to come explore.

I like the word "outrageous." It has color and vivacity; for the less adventuresome reader, however, it may be a total misfit here, destroying the tranquility of "tranquil" and suggesting an effect far from the one intended. If the writer had clarified the deliberate misuse of the word with a qualifier (" . . . outrageously gorgeous vistas . . ."), we'd have understood that "outrageous" wasn't supposed to have a pejorative overtone.

Usually a qualifier damages impact, but deliberately out-of-key qualifiers add impact—if the reader understands what you're doing. When you're using a word to startle or shake up the reader, be sure you don't mislead.

A Christmas catalog has this heading splashed across the first two pages:

> The Season of QUINTESSENCE

Not one word of copy explains this show-off line, which is repeated, themelike, throughout the catalog.

Merriam-Webster isn't much help: "The fifth or last and highest essence or power in a natural body." Huh? The adjectival form, *quintessential*, means the ultimate example of something. But so what? How many people know *quintessential*? Of those, how many can squeeze any sense out of *quintessence*?

One of the major news magazines changed its format. In a direct-mail letter to potential subscribers is this curious sentence, following the cliché question, "What more could you ask for?"

> You'll discover the answer to that in our Premier Double Issue—one of the most extraordinary single issues of *U.S. News* we've ever published!

Why, oh, why is the word "single" in there? It suggests the issue is extraordinary, all right: It's both double and single. This isn't what the writer meant, and dropping "single" not only would clarify the sentence; it would prevent the laughter that kills subscriptions.

Underline, capitalize, italicize

Look at an unintentionally obscure message component you've written. What if you underlined the word you want emphasized? What if you capitalized it? What if you put it in italics?

A "free" offer had this harmless copy:

An Extra Free Surprise for You

We don't have a major problem here. Some readers will read it as "Extra-Free," then recognize the intended message. But why put them to the test? Capitalizing or italicizing clarifies on the first reading:

An Extra FREE Surprise for You

You get an extra burst of promotional benefit—*free*.

The Rule of Copy Misdirection

The Rule of Copy Misdirection is firmly rooted in the Age of Skepticism. Its application reemphasizes the professional copywriter's insistence that substance is superior to form. The rule: Words that puzzle can't motivate.

Easy Suggestions for Copywriting Grammar

Don't drag out your junior high school English grammar textbook for comparisons with what you read here. As I repeat a dozen times in this book, grammar is our weapon, not our god. Let's use it wisely.

Abbreviations. For states, use the two-letter code: "Chicago, IL," not "Chicago, Ill." Use Dr. or St. before a name, but spell out the words when used generically: "Dr. John Brown"; "The doctor is coming"; "St. Jude, help me"; "He's a saint." For coupons, abbreviate St. and Ave.; elsewhere, write them out—424 Main Street; 610 Third Avenue. Never abbreviate when the words don't refer to a specific street: "We walked down the boulevard," not "We walked down the blvd." (Extra tip: To glorify, spell out the abbreviation: "Mount Olympus" has greater panache than "Mt. Olympus.")

Affect/effect. Affect is a verb. That's all it is. There's no such construction as "It had an affect on me." A less obvious example: "We effected the change," which means "We brought about the change"; "We affected the change," which means "We influenced the change."

Ain't. Use with care. If the reader won't be sure you mean to be colloquial, don't take a chance.

Alright. No such word. The proper phrase is *all right*.

Among/between. Use *between* for two, *among* for three or more.

An. Use only before words starting with a vowel sound. It's an honor, but it's a historic occasion and a humble man.

Anxious. Suggests worry. "We're anxious to have your reaction" has a Prozac-in-hand connotation. Use *eager*.

Appraise/apprise. Appraise means "to evaluate"; *apprise* means "to inform." The words aren't synonyms, so you can't appraise someone of something; you can only apprise him.

As/like. See *Like/as*.

As far as (SOMETHING) is concerned. The construction is grammatically sound, but it's a cliché. *As far as (SOMETHING)*, without "is concerned," is unacceptable.

Figure 11-2: Note the second bullet: "All stones are indigenous to the country of origin." Of course they are. They couldn't be anything else.

At. One of our most frequently misused words. "This is where it's at" (ugh); "Where are we at?" (ugh). If you end a sentence with *at*, reread it; can the sentence stand without it? If so, delete it (see *Where it's at*).

Bad/badly. "I feel bad" is correct. (Would you say, "I feel goodly"?) "I feel badly" means the individual has lost some of the ability to find something with the hands; if you use it in place of "We feel bad," you're guilty of phony gentility. The correct use of badly: "We played badly."

Better/best. Better shows superiority over one item or group. *Best* shows superiority over more than one. "He was the better player of the two"; "He was the best player of the three."

Between. If you ever write "Between you and I," burn this book. I don't want anyone to think we ever had any kind of relationship. (Of course you know it's "Between you and me.")

Bi. Refers to "every other" [period of time]. A bimonthly publication is issued every two months—every other month. (See *Semi.*)

Can/may. Can means "is able to"; *may* means "might" and is more conditional.

Capital letters. In advertising writing, a name gains stature by capitalizing *The*: "An official issue of The United States Juristic Society."

Capitalize organizations or institutions when they're part of a name, but not when they substitute for a name: "He traveled to Plymouth College on American Airlines"; "He traveled to college on the airline."

Most grammarians suggest not capitalizing seasons (summer, winter) and directions (south, north), but for advertising writing, capital letters may add strength. It's the writer's option.

Collective nouns. Nouns such as group, family, people, or percent can be singular or plural. "The committee is . . . " emphasizes the homogenized nature of the committee, making decisions" and acting as one; "the committee are . . . " (standard in the United Kingdom) suggests individual actions, not in coordination.

Comma. Never use a comma between subject and verb. This is 100 percent wrong: "The author's attitude, causes us to use commas when we shouldn't."

Never use a comma to separate elements that belong together. A company advertised its computerized typesetting machine: "Introducing, a complete tabletop digital scanner and typesetting package for under $600 a month." What's the comma doing there?

For clarity, use a comma after each element in a series: "John, Mary, and I." The comma after Mary is optional from a grammatical point of view, but we're copywriters, not grammarians. Clarity is always paramount.

Separate two complete thoughts with a period or a semicolon, not a comma. "We pioneered home satellite systems, come to us for lowest prices." This construction is inexcusable because it joins two sentences with a comma.

Company names. Singular, not plural. Smith & Co. is moving to new headquarters; the Jones Corp. is lowering its prices.

Compared with. The construction the copywriter uses for direct comparison; you'll compare a Ford with a Toyota. Save *compared to* for comparison of unlikes: you'll compare a Ford to a cheetah.

Complement/compliment. As a noun, *compliment* means "praise" or "flattery," while *complement* is a supplement to something. Each word can also be used as a verb.

Could of/should of/would of. Illiterate constructions. Replace *of* with *have*, and you're in business.

Dash. Stronger, more dynamic, more exciting than a comma. It's a good copywriting tool if you don't overuse it.

A dash is also stronger than an ellipsis (three dots), but each can be useful. Sometimes you want the raw strength of a dash, and sometimes you want the softer interruption of an ellipsis. Example: "The difference between a dash—a power stop—and an ellipsis . . . a soft interrupter . . . is clear."

Use the dash when you want hair-on-the-chest copy and the ellipsis when you want to draw less attention to the effect.

Different than. As a direct comparison, there's no such construction; it's *different from.* In the United Kingdom, it's *different to.* One exception: *Different than* is acceptable if the comparison uses a verb: "The dessert tasted different than we had anticipated."

Disinterested. Not a parallel for uninterested. *Disinterested* means "impartial," not having formed a prior interest or opinion; *uninterested* means without interest.

Distance. Should be a noun, not a verb, but times change. In today's jargon society, in which just about every noun is used as a verb, the old rules are out the window. We've seen the word *architect* used as a verb, so we're beyond surprise.

Each. A singular noun, to be followed by a singular verb. It's "each is" or "each was," not "each are" or "each were."

Each other/one another. I prefer *each other* when referring to two, and *one another* for three or more, but this rule is considerably looser than it was even a few years ago.

Easy/easily. Not interchangeable. *Easy* is an adjective: "It's an easy ride." *Easily* is an adverb: "He finished it easily." Advertese such as "We don't give up easy" is ghastly.

Either is, neither is/either are, neither are. No such construction as "either are" or "neither are." *Either* and *neither* always take a singular verb. *Neither* demands a negative: "Neither he nor I," not "neither he or I."

Exclamation point. Never use more than one.

Farther/further. *Farther* refers only to distance ("I threw the javelin farther than you did"); *further* refers to degree ("Let's pursue this grammatical discussion a little further").

Good/well. *Good* is the adjective, *well* the adverb. Correct usage: "I feel good"; "I did well on this piece of copy."

Had ought. Illiterate. Don't use it.

Has got/have got. No such construction. Never use either one. Use *has* or *have.* "He has his manuscript completed," not "He has got his manuscript completed." This isn't parallel to "I've got" or "he's got" or "we've got," which may be preferable to "I have" or "he has" or "we have" when you want to emphasize the convivial nature of the relationship.

Here is. Follow this only with a singular noun. "Here is several of the answers" betrays grammatical ignorance.

Historic. Preceded by *a,* not *an.* It's "a historic occasion," not "an historic occasion." Would you say, "an history book"?

Hopefully. Unless you're Rebecca of Sunnybrook Farm, don't use this word. If you've been using it to mean "I hope," stop within the next ten seconds.

Hyphen. When the first of two successive adjectives is also a noun, link the two words with a hyphen: "grammar-improving techniques"; "management-oriented writers"; "terror-stricken viewers."

I, me/he, him/she, her. *I* and *he* are subjects and predicate nominatives. "This is he" and "It was I" are correct; "This is him" and "It was me" are wrong.

We quickly see what's wrong with "Everything comes to he who waits" when we strip away the "who waits." "Everything comes to he" is just as ridiculous as "Are you calling I?" Only our phony sense of gentility changes an object (*him, her, us*) into a subject (*he, she, we*).

If you're uncertain about the case of a pronoun, take away what follows. (Purists know we can't do this with *who* because what follows determines whether the *who* stays or gives way to the consistently misused *whom*.) If nothing follows, but a noun or pronoun precedes, eliminate what precedes and often the case will come clear: "He gave it to Jim and I" shows itself to be patently wrong when we get rid of Jim: "He gave it to I." No. It's "He gave it to Jim and me."

I could care less. Corruption of "I couldn't care less." Don't use it.

. . . ics (politics, statistics, athletics, physics). Use either a singular or a plural verb, depending on the meaning: "Athletics is difficult for me"; "Athletics are available to all the students."

If. The best writing calls for *whether* instead of *if* after verbs such as *learn, know, doubt,* or *tell.*

. . . ing. When it is the suffix of the first word of a sentence, that word must refer grammatically to the person it describes. It's "Walking down the street, I saw her" if I'm the one walking down the street; otherwise, it would be "I saw her walking down the street" or, for greater clarity, "I saw her as she was walking down the street."

Irregardless. No such word.

Its/it's. A good literacy test. *Its* is possessive: "The ship lost its rudder"; *it's* means "it is": "If you're looking for the ship's rudder, it's at the bottom of the ocean."

Kind. This word is singular: "This kind of writing" is correct; "these kinds" is correct; "these kind" is wrong.

Lastly. A nonword. Don't use it.

Lay. A transitive verb. *Lie* is an intransitive verb. "Lay the book on the table" is correct because "book" is the object of "lay." "Lie the book on the table" is wrong because *lie,* an intransitive verb, can't take an object. What complicates the relationship between these two words is that *lay* is also the past tense of *lie.* So "Last night when I lay down to sleep, I lay awake" is correct; but *lay,* meaning *lie,* shouldn't be used to describe the present: "I'll lay down and think it over."

Lend/loan. Lend is a verb; *loan* is a noun. "Loan me your car" is not the best way to word it. Although a surprising number of critics still voice objections, loan is entirely standard as a verb.

Less. Not a synonym for *fewer. Fewer* refers to discrete objects, *less* refers to amorphous amounts. Correct: "He has less money than I have." Correct: "He has fewer dollars than I have." Incorrect: "He has less dollars than I have." As an adjective, *less* is the comparative form of *little.* As adverbial preposition, it means "without." ("He arrived less his luggage.")

Liable. Not a synonym for *likely.* One may be liable for something–that is, responsible for it but one is never liable to perform an act.

Like/as. Since the introduction of the advertising phrase, "Winston tastes good, like a cigarette should," the once-clear difference between these words has been clouded. Good usage would be: "Winston tastes good, as a cigarette should," but today's usage often makes this distinction an artifice.

Loose/lose. As an adjective, *loose* means "unfastened," but it's also a verb, meaning "to let loose"; to *lose* means "to miss from one's possession."

ly. This suffix on an adverb may be optional in some cases. In colloquial use, we might say either "Speak loudly" or "Speak loud." Highway signs economize on character count with "Drive slow." Opinion: We aren't that colloquial yet, so use *ly.*

Masculine/feminine. In a state of flux. References to mankind in general used to have a masculine reference ("Everybody had his book"), but awkwardness has hit us ("Everybody had his or her book"). Many writers have given up and use the still-jarring "Everyone took their seats." The ultimate solution will be a sexless word, but until such a word filters into common usage, the best procedure is to intersperse *his, hers,* and *his and hers*—or to write around the problem ("Those in the room took their seats"). In this book, as the reader will see to his or her pleasure or chagrin, I've practiced what I preach.

May be/maybe. The two words *may be* form a verb, interchangeable with *might be. Maybe* means "perhaps."

Muchly. An illiterate version of *much.* Don't use it.

Nowhere. One word. Don't write "no where."

Numbers. Most stylebooks suggest spelling out numbers from one to nine, using numerals for 10 or larger. For parallels, don't intermix in a single line of numbers. Write "He owns either 3 or 13 buildings" or "He owns either three or thirteen buildings."

In a direct quotation, spelling out the word seems to read better: "John said, 'I sent it July third.' "

Over. Not a good substitute for *more than.* Starting a piece of copy with "Over 40 countries . . ." can have two different meanings; "More than 40 countries . . ." has just one.

Plurals. Never formed by adding *'s.* Two or more people named Smith are "The Smiths," not "The Smith's." If the noun ends in *s,* the plural is "The Joneses," not "The Jones' " or "The Jones's." This is also true when referring to a certain time period. Write "90s," not "90's," and "1800s" not "1800's."

Words such as *each, no one, everybody,* and *someone* take a singular verb: "Everybody takes his best hold"; "Each of us knows the rules." (See also S*ingular and plural.*)

Possessives. In most cases, use "*s.*" It's "Lewis's Laws," not "Lewis' Laws." However, it would be "Moses' Laws" not "Moses's Laws." When dignity is paramount, use "of" instead: "The Laws of Lewis." However, when using plural possessives, it's best to write "the editors' laws" not "the editors's laws."

Prepositions. In my opinion, there's nothing wrong with writing the way people speak, and that means sometimes ending a sentence with a preposition. As the saying goes, "Ending a sentence with a preposition is an idea I don't approve of." The Emotion/Intellect Rule prefers "This is the information you asked for" to "This is the information you requested."

Principal/principle. Principal can be either an adjective or a noun, meaning "first" or "primary"; *principle* is a noun only, meaning "a rule" or "a code of conduct."

Proven. This tends to be a weak version of *proved* but is effective when using it as an adjective.

Quotation marks. American usage generally calls for quotation marks to be outside commas and periods. The exception is when referring to terms that are used when speaking of philosophy and theology, single quotation marks are used and the punctuation is traditionally placed preceding the quotation mark. For example: Our philosophy teacher often refers to 'the divine'.

British usage calls for quotation marks to follow commas and periods in quoted statements but to precede them when quoting a title. Other punctuation falls outside unless related to the quote.

For quotes within quotes, use single quotation marks. Examples: (American) Last night I went to a reading of Shakespeare's "Like as the Wave." (British) Last night I went to a reading of Shakespeare's "Like as the Wave". (American or British) I said to John, "I went to a reading of 'Like as the Wave'." (American or British) I said to John, "Did you go to the reading of 'Like as the Wave'?" Did John say, "Yes, I went to the reading of 'Like as the Wave' "? Or did he say, "I didn't go to the reading of 'Like as the Wave' "? Whether you've gone or not," I told John, "we're going tonight"; John didn't seem pleased.

One other point about quotations: When a quote runs for several paragraphs, don't put a quotation mark at the end of any paragraph except the last one, but put quotation marks at the beginning of each paragraph of the ongoing quote.

Real/really. *Real* is the adjective, *really* the adverb. Correct usage: "It's the real thing"; "I was really annoyed." Illiterate: "I was real annoyed."

Receive. A passive word. Don't be afraid to use *get.*

Semi. Means half. A publication issued twice a week (or once each half-week) is a semi-weekly (see *Bi*).

Shall/will. *Shall* is more formal; today's copywriter is usually safe with *will* except for emphasis. ("We shall do it!")

Singular and plural. Two or more subjects take a plural verb: "The ship and the airplane are here." Two subjects linked by *or* or *nor* take a singular verb: "Neither the ship nor the airplane is here." If one of the two subjects linked by *or* or *nor* is plural and the other is singular, the verb agrees with the subject nearest it: "Neither the ship nor the airplanes are here"; "Neither the ships nor the airplane is here."

None is singular or plural depending on the particular usage; collective nouns such as *council, scissors, politics, family,* or *news* are singular (in England, council takes a plural verb).

That. See *Who/that.*

Those kind. Illiterate. It's either "this kind" or "those kinds."

Toward/towards. Surprise! Either one is correct. Don't ask me why. (I use *toward*.)

Try and. Corruption of *try to*. It should be "I'll try to be there," not "I'll try and be there."

Unique. An absolute word. *Unique* is like pregnant—either you are or you aren't. It accepts no qualifiers. There's no such construction as "most unique" or "more unique" or "totally unique." (If Unassailable Loser Statute IV is valid, the phrase "totally unique" is a total rhetorical failure.) Instead of using weakening qualifiers, ask yourself: What makes it unique? This information is better than a nondescript, unimaginative word label pasted onto it.

Verb mood. Active is more dynamic than passive. "We'll always remember her" has power that "She will always be remembered" can never equal.

We/us. After any form of the verb *to be* (*are, were*), use *we*; avoid the awkwardness that can result from slavishly proper grammar. "The only source of these mint-condition silver dollars is we." Should be *us*? No, it shouldn't. But awkward, isn't it? You bet it is, and it isn't professional copywriting. Invert the construction: "We're the only source of these mint-condition silver dollars."

Where it's at. Colloquial, too forced and cutesy-pie for writing; use *Where it is.* (See *At.*)

Who/that. People are *who*, not *that*. "I'm the one that said it" is a hundred years out-of-date, and it wasn't an attractive construction then. It's "I'm the one who said it." A company can be a that. "We're the company that originated the flavor."

Sometimes *that* and *which* can be eliminated. Do it if you aren't sacrificing clarity: "Sometimes I think that we overuse the word *that*" isn't as crisp as "Sometimes I think we overuse the word *that*."

Who/whom. *Whom* or *whomever* is correct only as an object; if the word is the object of one clause and the subject of another, it's *who*: "Whoever I called returned the call." But it's "To whom am I speaking?" Complex but accurate: "Who was that whom I saw?" Seems wrong but is right: "Who you know is what you get." (*Who* is the subject of the verb *is*; you wouldn't say "Whom is.") Some uses aren't clear-cut. If you're uncertain, use *who* and don't worry about it.

Whose. Possessive; *who's* means "who is."

See? I told you it was short. It's also painless. Best of all, it's a floor under verbalized writing and a bridge between grammarian-martinets and casual speech.

As a linoleum laid on that floor, here are some chuckles, picked up from the on-line "A Joke a Day":

The rules of writing

1. Verbs *has* to agree with their subjects.
2. Prepositions are not words to end sentences with.
3. And don't start a sentence with a conjunction.
4. It is wrong to ever split an infinitive.
5. Avoid clichés like the plague. (They're old hat.)
6. Also, always avoid annoying alliteration.
7. Be more or less specific.
8. Parenthetical remarks (however relevant) are (usually) unnecessary.
9. Also too, never, ever use repetitive redundancies.
10. No sentence fragments.
11. Contractions aren't necessary and shouldn't be used.
12. Foreign words and phrases are not apropos.
13. Do not be redundant; do not use more words than necessary; it's highly superfluous.
14. One should NEVER generalize.
15. Comparisons are as bad as clichés.
16. Don't use no double negatives.
17. Eschew ampersands & abbreviations, etc.
18. One-word sentences? Eliminate.
19. Analogies in writing are like feathers on a snake.
20. The passive voice is to be ignored.
21. Eliminate commas, that are, not necessary. Parenthetical words however should be enclosed in commas.
22. Never use a big word when a diminutive one would suffice.
23. Kill all exclamation points!!!
24. Use words correctly, irregardless of how others use them.
25. Understatement is always the absolute best way to put forth earthshaking ideas.
26. Use the apostrophe in it's proper place and omit it when its not needed.
27. Eliminate quotations. As Ralph Waldo Emerson said, "I hate quotations. Tell me what you know."
28. If you've heard it once, you've heard it a thousand times: Resist hyperbole; not one writer in a million can use it correctly.
29. Puns are for children, not groan readers.
30. Go around the barn at high noon to avoid colloquialisms.
31. Even if a mixed metaphor sings, it should be derailed.
32. Who needs rhetorical questions?
33. Exaggeration is a billion times worse than understatement.

And finally . . .

34. Proofread carefully to see if you any words out.

Chapter Twelve

HOW TO WRITE DIRECT-MAIL LETTERS

Everybody Writes Letters

From the day you write your first job-hunting letter to the day you write your retirement valedictory, you create letters, letters, letters.

Ads may be written in committee; various sets of hands tinker and alter, so a finished ad or brochure may be a hybrid product unrecognizable by the writer who started it.

Not so with letters. They're one person's statement.

This tends to be true not only of two-paragraph notes but of four-page and eight-page direct-mail epics. Why? Because a letter is—or at least should be—a single, coherent statement. A copy chief might say, "Rewrite this section," but the starting writer usually is the finisher.

Are you a student of letter writing? If so, you ask yourself as you read: What about this sentence or paragraph bothers me? Your analysis leads to procedural rules; since you formulate them from others' mistakes, you're unlikely to make them yourself.

Ten Easy Rules for Letter Writing

Here are some rules, the easiest canons for letter writing you'll ever read. I say this with confidence because they aren't abstruse philosophical notions; they're *mechanical* rules a reasonably bright twelve-year-old can implement.

See for yourself.

Canon 1: *Keep your first sentence short.*

The first sentence is your indicator to the reader. From this early warning, your target forms a quick impression: The letter is going to be easy to read or is going to be hard slogging.

The short first sentence isn't an absolute, invariable law. It's just a good idea most of the time, and because it's a good idea most of the time as well as an easy idea to implement, it's on this list.

Canon 2: *Write no paragraphs longer than seven lines.*

When I suggested this tip to the assemblage of copywriters, I got the question, "But what if a paragraph has to be longer than seven lines?" The question brought several assenting nods.

My answer: No paragraph has to be longer than seven lines. Here's an example, from my own mailbox:

THE BUSINESS SOURCE

THE NEWSLETTER OF THE BUSINESS DEVELOPMENT BOARD OF MARTIN COUNTY

Volume 1-Number 10   October

Stuart Revitalized

Stuart Mr. and Mrs. Business Owner, if you're looking for a relocation or expansion site, Stuart on Florida's east coast is the place for you. A progressive city with a commission that wants to be your business partner is ready and willing to help you move in. The Business Development Board would like to invite you to drive by and look us over and perhaps stop at one of our many excellent downtown restaurants for lunch.

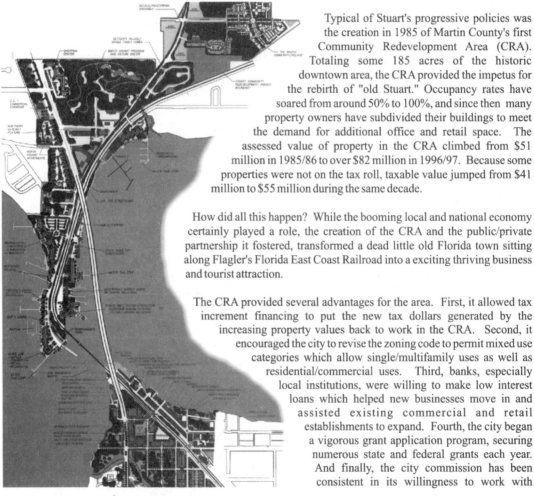

Typical of Stuart's progressive policies was the creation in 1985 of Martin County's first Community Redevelopment Area (CRA). Totaling some 185 acres of the historic downtown area, the CRA provided the impetus for the rebirth of "old Stuart." Occupancy rates have soared from around 50% to 100%, and since then many property owners have subdivided their buildings to meet the demand for additional office and retail space. The assessed value of property in the CRA climbed from $51 million in 1985/86 to over $82 million in 1996/97. Because some properties were not on the tax roll, taxable value jumped from $41 million to $55 million during the same decade.

How did all this happen? While the booming local and national economy certainly played a role, the creation of the CRA and the public/private partnership it fostered, transformed a dead little old Florida town sitting along Flagler's Florida East Coast Railroad into a exciting thriving business and tourist attraction.

The CRA provided several advantages for the area. First, it allowed tax increment financing to put the new tax dollars generated by the increasing property values back to work in the CRA. Second, it encouraged the city to revise the zoning code to permit mixed use categories which allow single/multifamily uses as well as residential/commercial uses. Third, banks, especially local institutions, were willing to make low interest loans which helped new businesses move in and assisted existing commercial and retail establishments to expand. Fourth, the city began a vigorous grant application program, securing numerous state and federal grants each year. And finally, the city commission has been consistent in its willingness to work with

Provided By: Business Development Board of Martin County
P.O. Box 2471, Stuart, FL 34995 (561) 221-1380 Fax: (561)221-1381

Figure 12-1: Should a letter look like a letter? Most often, the answer is yes. This hybrid has a headline—not an overline—and then addresses "Mr. and Mrs. Business Owner." Subordinating message to layout and using long, long paragraphs impede easy reading. As an official document, this mailing might have achieved greater impact . . . and certainly greater clarity . . . by separating itself into two units, an imperative (letter) and a descriptive (brochure).

Dear Friend:

It may surprise you, as it surprised me, to learn that even though we have high-powered, knowledgeable accountants, we still wind up paying too much income tax . . . although we don't know it at the time. We pay too much tax because our accountants can only work with the figures we give them; they can't "invent" deductions for us, they can't create unassailable tax shelters out of thin air, and they can't find productive uses for money that just isn't there to start with. But, what if you could . . .

NATIONAL GEOGRAPHIC SOCIETY

1145 17th Street N.W., Washington, D.C. 20036-4688 U.S.A.

```
       You've heard of the Seven Wonders of the World,
     and perhaps you can name one or two. But did you
   know that over the years people have compiled several
    "seven wonders" lists of magnificent sights, from
     ancient civilizations, the medieval world, nature,
            underwater worlds, and the modern age?

        Now for the first time, you can visit 35
      great wonders -- all in one incredible new book,
                 THE WONDERS OF THE WORLD.


Dear Member,

      For all of the glorious destinations that beckon us, only a few have
enticed and enchanted travelers through the ages. These include the "Seven
Wonders of the World," a phrase coined by travel promoters of ancient
times -- based on lists prepared by Greeks in the second century B.C.

      Tourists of the past crossed the deserts of Egypt to see the
pyramids, the only structures among the seven original wonders to survive
the ravages of time. Through the centuries, scholars, writers, and
travelers made new lists of wondrous sights to be seen -- masterpieces
of both humankind and nature that captivate us to this day.

      Now you too can marvel at 35 of the world's greatest sights, past and
present, in National Geographic's new volume...

                   THE WONDERS OF THE WORLD

      This journey of a lifetime unfolds in 232 pages of spellbinding
stories and breathtaking photography -- a showcase of history, culture,
art, architecture, nature, and adventure.

               Travel to five worlds of wonder,
            each one illuminating seven marvels.

      Your personal WONDERS OF THE WORLD tour takes you on five exciting
itineraries:

Ancient Wonders:  Experience the drama of long-lost wonders through
authentic, detailed reconstructions and fascinating facts and stories....

         • Explore the hidden chambers and twisting tunnels of the Great
           Pyramids, which remain the largest stone structures in the
```

Figure 12-2: Nine lines of type above the "Dear Member" greeting may be too many. Is that second group of three lines, beginning "Now for the first time," necessary before the sales argument begins?

That's a double whammy because this is the first paragraph. The writing isn't bad, but the impression is deadly.

I won't rewrite as radically as I would for pay, but here's how I'd have started this letter with the same ammunition:

> Dear Friend:
>   Does this surprise you? It surprised me.
>   Like you, I have a high-powered accountant. My surprise came when I found out that even with his hand joining mine on the tiller, I was paying too much income tax.
>   I was paying too much tax, and you may be paying too much tax because . . .

One paragraph becomes three or four, and reader fatigue vanishes.

Canon 3: *Single-space the letter; double-space between paragraphs.*

This tip is even easier to implement than the first two. It's founded on ease of readership. Manuscript and news releases traditionally are double-spaced, but that's because an editor needs the space between the lines to write in his blue-pencil chicken-scratch.

A letter should set itself up for easy reading; not only is a double-spaced letter harder to read, but double-spacing balloons every aspect fatly outward. A two-page letter becomes four pages, and an eight-page letter—well, don't even think about it. Worse, the page has an overall gray look because the space between paragraphs is identical to the space within paragraphs. Emphasis is far harder to achieve.

A suggestion, if you disagree on grounds of tradition rather than reader attention: Set your next letter both ways. Ask fifty people which one is easier to read. If you're really scientific, ask questions based on reader comprehension.

Canon 4: *In a multipage letter, don't end a paragraph at the bottom of any page except the last; break in the middle of a sentence.*

Newspapers have known this for decades. Readers demand completeness. Don't give it to them until you're ready. If you've ended a paragraph at the bottom of the page, the reader has a reason to read on only if he or she has developed a firm interest in what you're selling. But if you leave the reader in mid-sentence, you're in command. That person is your captive until the end of the sentence—which is on the next page.

This is the direct-marketing parallel to the movie on the Late Show. The show doesn't open with credits and titles; it opens with action. Once you've seen the first five minutes, it's too late to switch channels because you've already missed the opening of the film on the competing channel; it started with action, too.

Canon 5: *Don't sneak up on the reader.*

An inverse wording of this tip might be, "Fire a big gun to start the battle." We're in the Age of Skepticism, and letter openings such as this one betray a 1930s selling attitude:

> This story begins around the turn of the century, when times were peaceful and big fortunes could be made.
>
> Way back then, someone took a look at a contraption a lot of people still called a horse-less carriage, and they said, "Gee, wouldn't it be great if we could start these vehicles

1221 Avenue of the Americas
New York, NY 10020

Most Read. Best Read. Worldwide.

BONUS
www.businessweek.com
unlimited access
FREE
with your paid
subscription.

***************** 3-DIGIT 333
H G Lewis
Communicomp
340N Fig Tree Ln
Plantation, FL 33317

Dear H G Lewis,

Two brothers went off to work...

"Knowledge is power," said the older one and he'd study a business
plan to death, analyze stacks of internal memos and "run every
scenario" before he'd present his ideas to the client.

The younger one...well, he used to say that business was like a
jungle where "...you have to carry a club or join one." He decided
to carry a lot of clubs under his arm - that is, some of the best
business resources he could find to help fight his corporate
battles. More often than not he says he makes his big decisions from
the insight he's gained. He's up for Executive Vice President.

The older one...he's out on his own now - tinkering with global
strategies and new product ideas and sometimes "...panning the Net
for golden opportunities" as he puts it.

Two very different ways of succeeding, yes. But one very interesting
and insightful thing in common: both of them have been reading - and
arguing over - the same weekly business magazine for years. Business
Week.

Older: "They have *the business smarts* it takes to understand the
marketplace..."

Younger: "Because, more often than not, *I find out about it
first* in Business Week!"

                    **Try the next 8 issues
                of Business Week risk-free
                   and see who's right!**

I have 8 issues of Business Week for you - <u>8 weeks in a row - for
free</u>. It's to give you a good taste of the most widely-read and only
weekly business publication in the world.

It's to give you access to the same intelligence that a couple of
business-savvy brothers have depended on for so long (and more
chairmen, presidents and vice presidents than any other business
source).

With it in your hands you'll be able to top-line the critical areas
you want to know about...not just for information but for solid
insight into the financial thickets and marketing opportunities, the
nation's quirky economy and vital global issues.

Figure 12-3: A narrative letter has to walk carefully on the third rail. This one is more
cerebral than most, justifying its intellectual approach with the logical answer that the
publication is aimed at executives. Indenting the paragraphs would have helped
readability.

without cranking them by hand?" Old Silas broke his arm cranking his machine, and the danged thing never would go.

OK, it isn't dull. As this type of opening goes, it's more intriguing than most. I agree. Now read the next paragraph.

Half a century later, a guy named Al Shepard climbed into a different contraption, and a lot of smoke came out of the bottom end. Wham! Within a couple of minutes our first astronaut was not only out of sight, he'd made history.

Now I'm not so pleased. It's obvious at last—we aren't talking about starters or storage batteries, and we aren't talking about outer space. We still don't know what we *are* supposed to be talking about, and we're deep into the letter.

Just for the sake of history, I'll tell you. This writer is selling acreage (land). It could have been any of 10,000 other possibilities, including aardvarks and Zoroastrian texts.

Firing your biggest gun first is a good idea because you can't miss. As the letter opens, you're at point-blank range, and you may never have this advantage over your prospect again.

Canon 6: *Don't open with "Dear Sir" or "Gentlemen."*

Why not? Because they suggest stiff-necked, old-fashioned pomposity. Warming up the reader, establishing rapport with him, is one of the great hurdles we face. A greeting such as "Dear Sir" or "Gentlemen" adds sandbags to the obstacle when we should be shoveling sand away.

In a unisex age, I still occasionally see "Dear Sir or Madam." This is the kind of opening we might expect from a bill collector but not from our friendly mail-order vendor.

For years, the mail-order industry pretty much settled on "Dear Friend" as a neutral substitute when we couldn't personalize the opening. More recently, especially in business communications, we've used "Dear Colleague," which helps bind the recipient to the sender.

Depending on the list, you can thrust your rhetorical blade closer to the heart:

"Dear Fellow Member"
"Dear Executive"
"Dear World Traveler"
"Dear Collector"
"Dear Tennis Nut" (you can see the benefit of *equivalence* in greetings when you add a word—"Dear Fellow Tennis Nut")

Do we need the "Dear" at all?

I used to attack it on the grounds that it's a cliché, it's worn out, and the reader isn't really dear to us at all, which makes it hypocritical. I don't point a bony finger any longer because some of the substitutes I've seen are so contrived they make me long for good old "Dear."

Some strong usable substitutes for the old-fashioned opening gain their strength from suggesting the communication is limited to a special-interest group:

"Good Morning!"
"To the Relative Handful of Homeowners Who Demand Pure Water:"
"This Private Notification Is Limited to Executives Earning More Than $50,000 a Year."
"Information for Experienced Collectors Only."

In actual practice, don't let the greeting run over one line.

A nitpicking question: Should we put a comma or a colon after the greeting?

Business letter-writing classes teach colon, not comma, and I agree, conditionally. The colon suggests a respect for the reader. It's a subtle point, and it isn't absolute—especially since it's hard to stroke the reader at arm's length. But mastery of letter writing comes from exalting the reader, *then* sliding in next to him when defenses are down.

I often make the comma/colon decision based on whether or not I'll indent each paragraph. Indenting is less formal, which makes the comma more logical.

Canon 7: *Don't close with "Yours truly."*

"Yours truly" isn't as stiffly formal as "Dear Sir" or "Gentlemen," but it reeks of antiquity without polish.

Antiquity *with* polish is a standard and often elegant selling technique. "Your servant, sir" is an example of this writing style—which had better be consistent in *all* components or you look foolish.

You'll find "Sincerely" (*not* "Sincerely yours") as the close on most letters; business-to-business letters often use "Cordially," on the theory that "Sincerely" is more emotional a close than the text justifies. I used to rely on "Cordially." I don't any longer because I'd just as soon add warmth wherever I can. The *assumption* of a relationship can generate a relationship, and warmth is a key element in that bit of primitive psychology.

Attacking "Sincerely" is like breaking a butterfly on the rack: Why do it? If, though, you're doggedly determined to improve the close of your letter, try adding another pinch of salesmanship:

"Yours for more vigorous health"
"For the Board of Directors"
"Bless you, my dear friend" (fund-raising only, please)

Canon 8: *Use an overline and a P.S., if they aren't stupid.*

An overline is a preletter message at the top of the page. You can type it or handwrite it. You can position it toward the right edge, or, if you have a neatness complex, you can center it.

What you shouldn't do is give away your message in the overline. I read this overline on the letter in a fat, heavily produced mailing:

If you've driven accident-free for the past three years, you can save 10 percent to 20 percent on your automobile insurance.

I'd have said, " . . . let me show you how to save . . . " rather than " . . . you can save." My objection to this overline isn't based on this one small refinement; it's based on the notion that instead of accelerating reading, comprehension, and preacceptance, this one blunted my interest and lost me as a reader. Too much too soon.

The purpose of the overline parallels the purpose of envelope copy. Envelope copy is like a kamikaze dive, with one purpose only—to get the reader into the letter, with more enthusiasm or anticipation than one could generate without the overline.

In my opinion, "This is a private offer" and "Do you qualify?" are stronger overlines than the "accident-free" wording. Years ago, college courses in advertising passed over outdoor advertis-

World Library, Inc.
12914 Haster St.
Garden Grove, CA 92640

Time is Running out
Order - Now !

RE: An Out-of-This World CD-ROM Upgrade Offer

The Most Incredible CD-ROM Product Ever Created is Here!

<u>LIBRARY OF THE FUTURE®</u>
<u>THIRD EDITION</u>

Over <u>3,500</u> Books, Plays, Poems, Children's Stories,
Historical And Religious Documents
<u>Plus,</u>
Over 15 Minutes Of Full-Motion Video
On One CD-ROM!

Your One-Time Upgrade Price.....
Only $69.95

Plus Get A <u>FREE</u> Gift
(A $295.00 Value)

Dear World Library Registered Owner:

When my brother Bob and I founded World Library in 1989, our goal was to place thousands of literary works on CD-ROM at an affordable price.

But we never dreamed that in a few short years we would be able to offer our customers over **3,500** books, plays, poems, children's stories, historical and religious documents from over 1,750 titles, **and** include full-motion video clips from movies based on some of the literary works **on one CD-ROM!**

Well, with the help of many dedicated people here at World Library, we have been able to surpass our original goal, and we are proud to make this fantastic product available to our registered owners for only **$69.95!**

You know, when we started World Library we didn't have software to search for words, names, phrases, dates, etc., and it took us over a year and a half to find it. (We later developed our own Instant Access™ software with a whole list of great features).

And in the early days, we didn't know how hard it really would be to convert printed text to digital text, and we weren't sure that once

(Next page, please)...

Figure 12-4: The handwritten overline (blue, in the original, as befits a letter signed in blue—which for some reason this letter isn't) says, "Time is running out . . . ORDER Now!" Then a description takes over, before the letter itself begins halfway down the page. Pro: The offer is clear and unmistakable. Con: The exhortation of the handwritten overline is too generalized to carry much of a jolt.

ing with a single direction: No message longer than eleven words. We might resuscitate this suggestion today, for overlines.

A P.S. has easier rules. It should reinforce one of the key selling motivators or mention an extra benefit that doesn't require explanation.

Those who study such arcane matters tell us the overline is the most read part of a letter, and the P.S. is next. The format itself automatically gives us thunderbolts to hurl. Let's not take the electricity out of them.

Canon 9: *Experiment with marginal notes.*

Marginal notes are a specialty. Not every letter benefits from them, and this suggests determining from the tone of the letter whether or not they'll be beneficial.

When you do use them, the rules for marginal notes are even more stringent than they are for overlines. Two of them, in my opinion, are inviolable:

1. Handwrite everything.
2. Never use more than five words for each marginal note.

I'll explain. Marginal notes draw their power from the appearance of a spontaneous outburst of enthusiasm. The writer is so excited, so enthusiastic, that he or she bubbles over.

Handwritten bubbling over has verisimilitude, the appearance of truth. Typed bubbling over looks contrived. We struggle to avoid a contrived look, so why take the risk?

The five-word maximum is a good idea mechanically as well as creatively. Imposing this limit means you can write big enough to grab the reader's eye the way you should. There's no handwritten marginal message that can't be transmitted in five words, *maximum*. Some examples of marginal notes:

"Here's your FREE bonus!"
"Read this extra-carefully."
"Save 50 percent."

Don't be afraid to use hand-drawn arrows, lines, brackets, or even stars for emphasis. You're creating the impression of spontaneous enthusiasm.

Marginal notes, along with handwritten overlines, should be in a second color. What color? Don't consider any color other than the one in which you print the signature, usually process blue. If the whole letter, including signature, is printed in one color, you have no decision to make.

For heaven's sake, don't have an overline and marginal comments in beautiful writing, a showcase of fine feminine calligraphy, and then have an illegible scrawl for a signature at the end of the letter. The writing should match. (Incidentally, there *never* is an excuse for an illegible signature on a direct-mail letter. It may give ego satisfaction to an executive, but it drains intimacy out of the communication.)

Canon 10: *Use letters to test.*

The letter is the most logical testing instrument in a direct-mail package.

Testing one brochure against another is expensive, even if all the changes are in the black plate. Testing response devices such as order forms often gives muddy results because such tests

CNA PERSONAL INSURANCE

Your Membership in Senior Friends makes it possible for me to extend this offer to you.

Dear Fellow Senior Friends Member,

A bright good morning to you!

Like you, I joined the National Association of Senior Friends because it offers a rewarding group of benefits to those of us who have passed the age-50 mark.

Now it's my turn, as Senior Vice President of CNA Personal Insurance, to "bring something to the table" - the kind of auto insurance everyone in our age and economic bracket has wished for.

In one sentence: *You probably qualify for a number of discounts.* So...

Because you're a Member of the National Association of Senior Friends, I'm authorized to offer you automobile insurance from CNA, one of the nation's most respected insurance companies, at a very competitive rate.

Some folks, no matter how much evidence you show them, will lean on the tired cliché, "All insurance companies are the same." I hope you aren't one of those people, because <u>NO, THEY'RE NOT</u>. Those who make this statement usually are those who don't qualify for special rates. I have every reason to believe you do.

And benefits make sense. You and I have driven carefully for more years than a lot of drivers have been alive. So I'm pleased that at last, here is a highly respected major company - one with a history that goes back more than 100 years - that is eager to give you the pricing and service you certainly have earned. We are ready, willing, and able to justify your choosing us.

A few examples of possible discounts:

Well, let's see. You undoubtedly qualify for a discount if you insure more than one vehicle with CNA Personal Insurance (and that includes a van or a truck) More: If you have an anti-theft device you may get yet another discount. And others may apply.

Fig. 12-5: The overline is in a handwritten-effect font. The greeting is "Dear Fellow Senior Friends Member." These touches, plus phrases such as "Like you" and "Now it's my turn," build an easy rapport.

aren't always logical; a writer testing response device formats often throws one to the wolves because the offer doesn't suggest a second approach.

But letters! The writer becomes a hero because his four-page letter outpulled the one-page letter—or vice versa. The letter can test the five great motivators of our era (fear, exclusivity, guilt, greed, and need for approval) against one another.

The letter can test masculine wording against feminine. It can test a harrumphing executive against a hay-chawin' good ol' boy. It can test the validity of some of the tips in this chapter.

Best of all, letter tests are cheap. It costs next to nothing to print copies of two letters instead of one.

The freshest flowers in the world
1650 S. Dixie Highway • Boca Raton, FL 33432 • fax: 561-567-1160

Red carnations and holiday greens..."

I have a special offer for you, my friend...

...the colors of the season in a brilliant floral display, yours to send to a loved one, or to an associate. And by using the special Discount Order Form at the bottom of this page or calling **toll-free 1-877-357-3276,** you can enjoy a substantial discount. (Few, very few sources of flowers, offer a discount at this time of year.)

No symbol of this season of love and affection can match a bouquet of perfect flowers. And at this holiday season, I propose to make it possible for you to send a gorgeous, perfectly fresh floral bouquet or centerpiece to any loved one, to any close friend, to any business associate ... anywhere in the United States, at a remarkably low <u>direct</u> price.

Think for a moment:

Think of the delight you will be able to create, as someone opens the handsome designer box, delivered by air courier ... and discovers the symbol of fondness you have so thoughtfully sent.

Think of the marvelous difference between beautiful fresh flowers and ordinary, mundane gifts that lack the meaning and sensitivity only flowers can represent.

Think of the good taste holiday flowers symbolize ... at once personal, at once tasteful, at once elegant, always proper. You can't make a mistake, sending lovely flowers.

Think, too, of the pleasure and delight as someone you love and respect places these delicate blooms where all can see and admire them. What other gift can mean so much?

Now, please understand another crucial difference:

You will be sending your holiday flowers direct. That means they will stay fresh considerably longer than any flowers you might buy at a local store. I'll explain:

Typically, a local florist gets flowers from a wholesaler. The wholesaler gets flowers from a grower. And who knows how long the flowers sit at the florist before someone buys them? Much time - sometimes <u>days</u> - can elapse with each step.

Your flowers from Flower Farms Direct are shipped by air courier, usually the same day the flowers arrive. There simply is

---

Detach and mail ... or call **toll-free 1-877-357-3276.**
Flower Farm Direct • 1650 S. Dixie Highway • Boca Raton, FL 33432
SPECIAL HOLIDAY DISCOUNT ORDER FORM
sure to use <u>both sides</u> of this Order Form. Orders will be delivered on any weekday you specify, by air courier. Guaranteed fresh or 100% money back.
Please make any necessary corrections in your name and address as they appear here.

FF119810

John Q. Sample
123 Any Street
Richmond, VA 99999
llɪlɪlɪlɪlɪlɪlɪlɪlɪlɪlɪl

CS-449 Colors of Season Bouquet: should be $18.95, **special $12.95**
CM-956 Noel Bouquet: should be $26.95, **special $19.95**
AC-470 Holiday Centerpiece: should be $54.95, **special $39.95**
(plus air courier delivery; FL residents add 6% sales tax)

Send item no. _____ to: _____
Name _____
Address _____
City _____ State _____ Zip _____
phone number: _____
Date delivery desired: _____
Indicate personal message: _____

Indicate payment method: ❑ Check or money order enclosed for $_____
Bill to ❑ VISA ❑ MasterCard ❑ AmEx ❑ Discover
Card no.: _____ expires: _____
Signature _____
Daytime phone number: (___) _____

Mail this Special Order Form or call toll-free 1-877-357-3276.
Delivery is 100% *guaranteed fresh* and on time.
Use reverse side for additional orders. Don't forget your own home and office!

Figure 12-6: Note the rubber-stamp effect at top left. Rubber stamps have a unique value: They imply immediacy no matter what the wording may be.

While you're at it, consider testing a tinted paper stock against white. The text has to be identical, or you destroy the purity of results. This isn't a copy test, I know, but color psychology is itself one of the creative aspects of mass communications.

Easy rules to implement? You bet they are. What isn't so easy is establishing and maintaining rapport with the reader. How do you do it? Just adapt the rules from the next chapter to the rules in this chapter.

Chapter Thirteen

DIRECT MAIL/DIRECT RESPONSE: FIFTY PROFITABLE RULES AND TIPS

Writers Are Writers? Says Who?

Accumulating rules and principles is logical for direct response. More than any other medium, direct response gives us an absolute count of how we did in the competitive marketplace. Testing one writer's approach against another writer's approach is malarkey-proof because "nth-name" sampling is the ultimate equalizer.

If you've never written direct-response copy and never intend to, please read this chapter anyway. You never know when your keyboard will be thrust into the breach by an employer or a client who thinks, "Writers are writers." More significant to you as wordsmith: Many of these tips can be valuable to the person who writes *any* form of force-communication. The tips aren't parallel in content, but they share this in common: Every one is easy to implement.

The Five Unassailable Loser Statutes

The fifty tips are refinements of five Unassailable Loser Statutes that govern direct-response writing. Keep these statutes in mind and you'll be writing your own direct-mail copy tips. Want to be an unassailable loser? Nothing easier. Ignore the statutes, and it'll happen.

Unassailable Loser Statute I:

When seller and buyer both are uninvolved, the seller loses.

Unassailable Loser Statute II:

Readers are more likely to pick holes in transparent shouts of importance than in projection of benefits.

Unassailable Loser Statute III (the Illustration Agreement Rule):

Illustration should agree with what you're selling, not with headline copy. (See Figures 13-1 through 13-4.)

Figure 13-1: The Illustration Agreement Rule says that illustration should agree with what you're selling, not with headline copy. The rule is a close parallel to Hucksterism avoidance (see Chapter 4). Here the headline uses the word "breeze" . . . and the illustration is an electric fan, intending to show how old-fashioned the competition is. Execrable.

Figure 13-2: A handshake is one of the most hackneyed, least inventive, least imaginative, and least creativity-indicative devices anyone can use as a main illustration. Over the next week, count the number of ads that use a handshake as the illustration . . . and vow never to descend to this unimaginative creative cellar.

"One of the most impressive systems available today"
DOCULABS

"Identitech has created a new software genre"
GIGA

"Their business partnering program is the benchmark for this industry"
DOCULABS

The Guts To Compete.

Some call it "oomph." Others call it "chutzpah." We call it guts. And you need it to compete. You see, FYI is the guts of the best enterprise-wide applications on the market. We partner with leading software developers like you and fortify your product with workflow and document management functionality. That's FYI. The guts of good business software. So, do you have what it takes? **Call 1.800.883.9503** and find out how quickly you can integrate FYI into your solution.

Identitech
www.identitech.com

Advertiser/Product Info – www.kmworld.com/readerservice

Figure 13-3: Okay, it's eye-catching. With that recognition out of the way, if you didn't know in advance what the advertiser is selling, would the photograph and the three subheads give you a clue? Attention is one component of the force-communications mix, not its entirety.

Figure 13-4: This not only is not a violation of the Illustration Agreement Rule; it's an example of one proper way to use it. When an illustration has the reader nodding, "Yes, I get the point," the job is well done.

Unassailable Loser Statute IV:

Adding qualifying words to a statement of superiority is an admission of inability to claim superiority.

Unassailable Loser Statute V:

Use only as much of the language as you know. Your dictionary is your verifier, not your originator.

Here's a happy little self-quiz: Dig out the last piece of direct-mail copy you wrote. It might be a letter, a brochure, a catalog page, even an order form. Check it for violations of the five Unassailable Loser Statutes. Rewrite it. Then read on.

Fifty rules and tips you may or may not have known instinctively

1. *Tying two statements together with* and *adds coherent flow and subtracts impact.*

Unless you believe in the super-modern "staccato" school of writing, the word *and* is similar to a huggy blanket.

I suggest you take your most recent piece of copy and test it for strength by cold-bloodedly taking out the "ands" when they link two complete thoughts. To retest, insert "and" somewhere else, where you didn't have it.

For example: Which of these do you prefer?

1. We have our own toll-free phone number, and if you plan to charge your amplifier to your credit card, call that number—1-800-555-5555—at any hour.
2. We have our own toll-free phone number. If you plan to charge your amplifier to your credit card, call that number—1-800-555-5555—at any hour.

You can see the benefit and the detriment of each. Tying the statements together with "and" helps reading flow but saps a little strength from each side of the word; separating the statements loses their interrelationship momentarily but prevents the loss of narrative power.

Your choice. I offer this tiny nugget only as proof that, to a wordsmith, every word counts.

2. *If your mailing asks the reader to do something, such as placing tab A into slot B, be sure the reader recognizes a benefit in the action.*

Although tests still validate the "Place sticker here" instruction for free-issue subscription promotions, I no longer feel that having the reader complete the job is a universally successful technique. It seems to work when we want the reader to think we're doing him or her a favor; its performance is spotty when we are trying to achieve an open sale.

Specialty print shops love tabs and stamps because the job costs a lot more to print; some writers love tabs and stamps because 1) they grew up with them, and 2) they can charge more for what seems to be a more complex job.

Contests and award-potentials justify task performance per se; a straight selling job doesn't.

I impose the Workmen's Noncompensation Provisions:

▶ The reader's pleasure from absorbing your "Do this!" message diminishes in exact ratio to the amount of work he thinks he'll have to do. (An example: An unnecessary P.S. on a letter selling a calculator/memory-telephone: "When you get this remarkable electronic instrument, I suggest you find a comfortable spot and spend an evening familiarizing yourself with its features.")

▶ Excluding contests, asking the reader to perform a task that requires talent, prior knowledge, or problem-solving ability will lose that reader if he or she resents, feels inferior to, or is annoyed by the unsought challenge.

▶ In a contest or sweepstakes whose reward is geared to apparent talent, prior knowledge, or problem-solving ability, the reward justifies the challenge.

Reciprocity is the key to have-the-reader-do-something strategies.

3. *Words suggesting the reader has a choice are less subliminally irritating than words suggesting you, the communicator, are issuing edicts.*

Which of these is more likely to generate reader empathy?

I'm very pleased to ask you to read this reprint.

or

I'm very pleased to ask you to take a look at this reprint.

Subtle, isn't it? "Read" is 1) unemotional and 2) a demand. "Take a look at" is 1) convivial and 2) a request. In this particular instance, an even more profound difference influences the recipient's reaction: "Read" asks for completeness, a beginning-to-end scrutiny. "Take a look at" asks for a casual once-over, just enough to verify the content.

In the Age of Skepticism, I less and less often dare throw an obvious gauntlet down before the person who reads my direct-mail message.

4. *Including the message recipient in a statistical recitation enhances the probability of response.*

A piece of copy made this claim of exclusivity, once-removed from reader involvement because of the copy's inability to warm its own blood:

Only 1,500 individuals in all the world . . .
. . . can own this splendid symbol of gallantry.

The revised version ran far hotter:

You . . .
and only 1,499 others in all the world . . .
can own this splendid symbol of gallantry.

The first message is a raw statistic, apparently unrelated to the reader. Sure, she knows you want her to be one of the 1,500. But since you're standing off on the sidelines, uninvolved, it's all too easy for her to stand on the other sideline, equally uninvolved. You run afoul of Unassailable Loser Statute I: When seller and buyer both are uninvolved, the seller loses.

5. *When you're out of ideas for envelope copy, say anything with the word "you" in it.*

You'll seldom have a total flop if your envelope copy has a "you" in it and doesn't start selling too soon (see Tip 6). When such sure-fire old-timers as "Private Invitation Enclosed" and "Your Nomination to the Board of Advisors" don't fit, try a "you." (See   )

But be careful. "Now you can . . . " is fine for space ads, but on the envelope it suggests you're about to spill out too many of your guts. Tie the "you" to exclusivity and you're safe.

Another caution: Don't put on the envelope a message that might have the recipient say, "I hope the postman didn't see this." If your envelope proclaims, in twenty-four-point type, "Explicit sex information you asked for," expect some complaints.

6. *The purpose of a message on the outer envelope is to get that envelope opened. Saying more, or synopsizing your selling argument, can land your mailing in the round file.*

Overselling was a problem curse long before Shakespeare had Hamlet say, "The lady doth protest too much, methinks." If you agree that a good sales presentation builds to a logical close, then you automatically agree that you can't close on the outer envelope. If you could, why put anything inside?

This envelope message emasculates what might be a logical selling argument within its walls:

Inside!
Favorable terms on term insurance (which experts *term* the best kind of insurance for someone in your circumstances to buy).

Okay, we give the copywriter a D for the play on words, the inadvertently negative word "circumstances," and the betrayal word "buy." But lack of writing skill doesn't hurt this envelope copy as much as blurting out undigested sludge to the reader. If your postman brought you an envelope with this message on it plus ten other pieces of third-class mail, and you could open only three of them, would this be one of the three—unless the others were equally inept?

A remarkable new book
is about to be published-
and <u>you</u>, Herschell Lewis,
are in it!
— *Stanley T. Lewis*

Mr. Herschell G. Lewis
340 N Fig Tree Ln
Fort Lauderdale, FL 33317-2561

AUTO

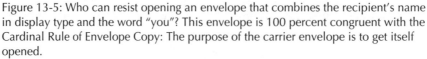

Figure 13-5: Who can resist opening an envelope that combines the recipient's name in display type and the word "you"? This envelope is 100 percent congruent with the Cardinal Rule of Envelope Copy: The purpose of the carrier envelope is to get itself opened.

ARE YOU A WINNER? SEE HOW YOU COMPARE...

BULK RATE
U.S. POSTAGE
PAID
NUMA CORP.

**The Amazing Book of Lewis Family
Facts & Favorites**

WHO was the first Lewis to come to America?

WHAT kind of cars do Lewises drive?

WHAT'S the Lewises' total annual income?

WHAT do Lewises do for a living?

HOW many children in a Lewis family?

Mr. Herschell G. Lewis
340 N Fig Tree Ln
Plantation, FL 33317-2561

ORDER YOUR VERY OWN FUN FACT BOOK TODAY

Figure 13-6: Compare this envelope with Figure 13-5. Which has greater impact? (Both were sent by the same source.) "Fun Fact" seems out of key, but questions are, as we know, automatically reader-involving. The two mailings may have been a response test.

7. *Specifics have greater verisimilitude than nonspecifics.*

A full-service direct-mail company sent me a mailing whose envelope had the somewhat overused legend "Check Enclosed." Pretty good use of the gimmick, I thought, until I looked at the check.

The format was impeccable, with my name (mildly misspelled), the usual computer code numbers, a bank identification, and a check number. I didn't mind the word "Nonnegotiable" printed in the signature area because I knew it couldn't be a real check. I *did* mind what was printed in the "Amount" area—"Free Service."

The sixth paragraph of the letter explained it (I'd have led off with it). I had my choice of free lettershop services, personalization, tipping of close-faced envelopes, or live wax seals, provided my mailing was 50,000 pieces or more.

The check, which is a powerful weapon in mailings despite repeated abuse of the technique, actually weakened this one because "Free Service" isn't a bank-related concept. I'd have reacted more favorably if the check had been for a specific amount, payable to the company against a job I might place there. Had the check been for $500, perceived value would have been immediate and the sense of gimmickry would have been less pronounced.

8. *Exploit the uniqueness of the direct-response medium.*

I have a mailing from the U.S. division of a European automobile manufacturer. The brochure is slick and colorful, obviously designed for showrooms instead of mailings. The selling job, then, is left to the letter, which begins:

Dear Mr. Lewis:

Car and Driver called it "a vision of the future."

They were referring to the new Audi—and I'd like to invite you to come test drive it yourself.

When you do, you will immediately discover what has the automotive world sitting up and taking notice—the revolutionary all-wheel drive, which delivers superbly refined performance, handling and steering . . .

By the time I read this far—and it was as far as I was going to read—I had already come to the conclusion that the writer was not of the direct-marketing world. Read the first sentence again. Isn't it typical of *radio commercials*?

A direct-response writer would have hit me in the solar plexus with his opening, using an approach something like this:

Dear Mr. Lewis:

I have the keys to a new Audi in my hand, and I want you to take them, put them in the car parked outside your local dealership, and take a 20-mile ride—*on us.*

What's the difference? Direct response is one-on-one, and writers who don't know how to communicate "only you" aren't going to have much luck in our medium. A direct-response letter that begins "It Happened on Wall Street!" might grab our attention, but head-to-head against a sales argument starting with solid reader benefit such as "Want inside information your broker doesn't have?" this approach is no more likely to win than "It was a dark and stormy night."

9. *Underlining (for letters; italics for typeset) can force the reader to emphasize the proper words and phrases.*

Is there a difference between these two statements?

1. If only one member uses it, the program has paid for itself.
2. If only *one* member uses it, the program has paid for itself.

Words are identical. In the second example, the reader has to emphasize the word *one* because the writer forces her to.

10. *Examples should match what you're selling.*

I'm looking at a mailing from a publication, reminding me to tell my clients to buy space in a particular issue. The entire message is printed on a small blue card, with this heading:

PLAY AGGRESSIVELY in MAY
with *National Thrift News*
The illustration? A golfer.

I'd understand this approach if the publication were *Golf Digest*, and I'd accept the cliché because typical readers would accept it. But what does a golfer have to do with *National Thrift News*?

I see the tie with "play aggressively," but can you really defend this high school–level concept? What makes it worse is that the magazine sent the Cheshire-labeled envelope carrying this nonmessage by first-class mail.

So let's justify Unassailable Loser Statute III, the Illustration Agreement Rule: Illustration should agree with what you're selling, not with headline copy.

Observing this statute will help keep you out of the cleverness-for-the-sake-of-cleverness abyss that gapes wide, waiting for writers who want readers to notice their wit before they notice what's being sold.

11. *Opening a sentence with a parenthetical phrase slows down reading, impedes comprehension, and muffles impact. Use the device sparingly.*

A friend who calls these "backward constructions" sent me, as an example, a product mailing from a major credit card company that opened with a parenthetical phrase:

> Revered and admired for its graceful flight and its powerful command of the heavens, the falcon has long been associated with majesty, lordliness and elegance.

The opening was no accident. More than half the copy used the same device! I'll quote enough to show the pattern:

> One of history's most persistent images, the winged falcon has captured the imagination of some of the world's greatest minds. . . .
>
> A masterpiece of fine design and workmanship, the Winged Stemware Collection has been created in the same tradition that has produced exquisite objects for generations. Crafted of fine solid brass with silver plated bowl, each piece has been carefully cast and then, as a final touch, finished by hand to produce the finely detailed images, dramatic textures and bold shapes that make stemware objects of enduring beauty. Of high quality, the Winged Stemware is both solid and elegant. . . .
>
> Especially created to appeal to both eye and hand, every aspect of these very special drinking vessels has been carefully considered to ensure that they are not only beautiful but functional as well. . . .

The sentence beginning "One of history's . . . " has enough creative problems without suffering from the oppressive weight of a backward construction; the paragraph beginning "A masterpiece . . . " sets an indoor record—three backward constructions in a deadly row; the sentence beginning "Especially created to . . . " is vaguely unsettling grammatically.

The biggest problem lies in the technique itself—throwaway, unexplained puffery.

12. *Don't ask the reader to provide your sales argument.*

Which would you rather have someone say to you: "I remember your name" or "I have your mailer; let's get together"?

The following copy (set in twenty-four-point type) is the total sales message in a brochure someone paid money to mail to me:

> At Sir Speedy we're always geared up to give fast service on all your printing needs. Our shelves are well-stocked . . . our gears are well-oiled and our people are always eager to help.
>
> Just give us a call or stop in and Sir Speedy will get in gear for you.

How can this printer hope to compete against the printer who sends me price lists, paper samples, and solid competitive sales arguments?

One more example of this tip. Suppose you're dissatisfied with your direct-marketing lettershop and might consider a replacement. You get a brochure in the mail, and this is the copy:

Recommend the Direct-Mail Professionals

At Pronto Post, we make it our business to meet your customer's mailing date. We're flexible enough to accommodate delays or other unforseen problems that might throw a schedule off course. We keep in constant communication with our clients every step of the way.

At Pronto Post, you'll get the benefit of our broad range of capabilities and a total of 60 years' experience . . . .

No, it isn't terrible. But I didn't call these people even though I was looking for a lettershop at the time because as resident curmudgeon I objected to the misspelling of the word *unforeseen*.

But suppose I *had* called. I'd have asked questions they should have answered in the brochure. They're asking for my commitment without giving me the information I need.

13. *When you're supposedly acting as a friend, don't betray your real role as impatient vendor by lapsing into hard sell.*

The evil genie is always at our elbow, prodding us to slip in just one more adjective. If we don't push the genie back into his dusty bottle, he runs amok and we wind up with copy such as this:

Just in case you misplaced the complete, beautiful fall catalog I enclosed with [your order from the space ad], here's another gorgeous, value-packed copy.

Take out the obvious sell and the recipient doesn't feel he's being pitched:

Just in case you misplaced the fall catalog I enclosed with [your order from the space ad], here's another copy.

I don't always favor restraint. I always favor consistency of position.

14. *In "cold list" mailings, don't assume the reader is preconditioned to know how lucky he is to be able to buy what you have to sell.*

A mailer from a supplier to advertisers and their agencies has this sixty-point headline on its descriptive folder:

How to track
successful advertising
for $395

The next two sentences aren't the body copy; they're the subhead:

The mission of *AdWatch* is to provide ongoing measurement of one empirical element of advertising awareness. Through ongoing measurement, using a strong methodology, *AdWatch* renders explainable this basic and critical advertising attribute—the degree that advertising can be remembered and recalled by the American consumer.

If you say, "David Ogilvy said people do read long headlines," my answer is, "Yeah, but this ain't what he meant." I submit, *"Adwatch* renders explainable this basic and critical advertising attribute" is *not* motivational, and if you think it is, please don't sit next to me at the next dinner party.

Think in terms of message targeting: This company sells a tracking service for $395. Who are their best prospects? If those who don't have prior knowledge of tracking are their targets, the headline is misaimed. But if the mailer is aimed at those who already know what this company is selling, the subhead is deadly—following but not following up on the promise made in the headline.

15. *Tell the reader what he wants to read, not what you want to sell.*

A computer-personalized mailing tells me:

H.G. LEWIS'
BRAND NEW FORTUNE
ANALOG DRESS WATCH IS WAITING TO BE
DELIVERED—AND IT'S FREE WITH
YOUR FORTUNE SUBSCRIPTION

The emphasis could just as easily have been on what they want to sell. Suppose the personalized heading had read —

FREE WITH YOUR FORTUNE SUBSCRIPTION,
H.G. LEWIS —
A BRAND NEW FORTUNE ANALOG DRESS WATCH!

The folks (people? individuals?) at *Fortune* are astute marketers. By subordinating the subscription to the free watch, they delicately stimulate my greed instead of showcasing their own. Incidentally, a "dress watch" is infinitely more desirable than just a "watch," isn't it? "Dress" adds value without pitching—a good word.

16. *If you have to make a choice about offending someone, choose anyone except your best buyers.*

I don't think many magazine circulation departments understand this. When I'm a subscriber to a magazine, a nonsubscriber invariably gets a better deal than I do.

Figure 13-7: This envelope presents a powerful combination of grabbers—the word "Warning," set as one might see it on a vat of poison, plus the word "You" repeated three times.

The reason I didn't renew my subscription to *Skin Diver* was a note from the magazine telling me, "Your subscription to *Skin Diver* is about to expire. Unless you act now . . . "

The words "act now" should be a tip-off that we're dealing with semipros, but that may be an unduly harsh criticism. I wasn't bothered by the "act now" or by the self-serving P.S.—"Renew today and avoid the risk of losing even one issue of *Skin Diver*."

What burned me was the offer—"only" $13.94 for 12 issues, "Regular newsstand $30." I save more than 50 percent off the regular newsstand price. What could be better?

I'll tell you what's better: An offer—in a blown-in card in the current issue of the magazine—of 12 issues for $6.97 (in six-point type: "New subscribers only!"),—a saving of exactly 50 percent of the amount they want from me, their loyal subscriber.

You bet I understand the logic behind pulling out all the stops to get a new subscriber. But what *they* don't understand is that they have 1,001 ways to do that without penalizing existing subscribers. Oh, and did you catch that exclamation point after "New subscribers only"? That really pours salt on the wound.

17. *If you introduce a notion foreign to the experiential background of the reader, a question may be less likely to generate rejection than a flat, imperious statement.*

A direct-mail service company sent me a mailing, printed in full color on eighty-pound enamel. The headline:

Profitable Direct Marketing
Starts With
Profitable Fulfillment Systems

I don't agree. Until you've sold something, you don't need a fulfillment system. But, sure, fulfillment is a key component of the direct-marketing mix. What I don't like is the "voice of god" pronouncement here.

Suppose the heading were . . .

Just How Important Is Fulfillment
To Direct-Marketing Success?

I wouldn't think I'm being pressured by an arrogant, insensitive salesperson. I feel the same way about a space ad headed:

List Segmentation
Is a Myth!

In my opinion, rephrasing the same words as a question—"Is List Segmentation a Myth?"—defangs the hostility flat pronouncements breed.

A space ad for a "Wealth Seminar" seems to walk the tightrope between hurled gauntlet and provocative question and does it very well:

A Challenge:
Do You Have
"The Courage to Be Rich?"

Obviously, it would take more courage to be deliberately poor than to be deliberately rich. The reason I embrace this headline as a valid example of tip 17 is that *within the experiential background of those who might attend* ("$395 Wealth Seminar for Only $39.95 for Motivated People Who Can Act Within 48 Hours"), the "challenge" is both dynamic and logical. A seminar really aimed at rich people would have thin attendance if promoted with a headline such as this one.

18. *"We" is no substitute for "You."*

Are you nodding smugly, with an I've-known-that-all-my-life reaction? Great! It really isn't aimed at you. It's aimed at those other guys who use the mails so seldom that they're afraid the reader won't look at their offer if they don't try to cast a giant shadow.

Here's a typical example from my mailbox:

> Dear Sir,
>
> I would like to introduce you to The Creative Network, Inc. We are an exciting new creative art company specializing in screen print art for T-shirts, hats, sportswear and illustration for fashion, logos, ad layouts and catalogs.
>
> Never before has a company been so direct and creative by offering our services to advertising agencies that specialize in "Ad Specialty" merchandise for their clients. . . .

Don't you grind your molars, reading all this self-love? And "Dear Sir" is as out-of-date as a Nehru jacket.

19. *Get to the point.*

Sometimes I enjoy the leisurely pace of a down-home letter. But I never do enjoy hunting through a high-powered letter for its point.

The difference is one of writing technique. In my opinion, writing a "jes' plain folks" letter is easy; writing an *effective* "jes' plain folks" letter is a test of the writer's talent. The infrequent letter writer is on rocky shoals there. Go with percentages, I say, and pull out the dynamite.

But unless you're writing a down-home letter, don't you dare let half a page slip by without telling me what you're selling me. That's a kamikaze letter, and your text and my interest both perish in the flames.

An example is a letter that might have succeeded if, anywhere in the first three paragraphs, it had told me what they were selling:

> Dear Mr. Lewis,
>
> I'm writing to you to tell you why Computer Communications, Inc., can do a faster, more accurate and less costly job for you.
>
> The proof is in the 300 satisfied clients we now have, more than half of whom have been with us since our company began.
>
> Last month, for instance, we ran 498 separate jobs, ranging in size from 2,000 to over a million donor names.

There's a weak clue: "donor names." But I'm not in the mood to play detective. Suppose the letter had opened —

Dear Mr. Lewis,
  I'm writing to tell you why Computer Communications, Inc., can update your master name-file with greater speed and accuracy than any system you've ever used before. And we'll do it at less cost.

I'm assuming this is what the company does. Why? The last paragraph of the letter says, "I believe we can make a difference in the quality of your file maintenance."

20. *Assume acceptance, not antagonism.*

The theory behind "lift" letters ("Open this only if you have decided not to take advantage of this offer . . . ") is that an extra push, by another person and from another direction, can re-track an undecided skeptic. You'll never retrack someone who has already decided against you.

  That's why it amazes me when someone who wants to be a supplier comes out swinging and starts Round 1 by hitting the referee—as this mailing from a producer of personalized letters does:

Dear Mr. Lewis:
  It always amazes me that less than 25 percent of the executives who receive this letter respond.
  Because, we turn executives into heroes. You see, every executive has to be interested in increasing profits . . . lowering marketing costs . . . and enhancing company image. And that's what Letterex Communications can help you do. . . .

What this company *has* done is 180 degrees from what they've just said they do—enhance company image. How easy it would have been to write a pleasant letter, perhaps opening with the nonaggressive question, "How'd you like to be even more of a hero than you are?" instead of pronouncing judgment on 75 percent of the executives who get the letter. They're stupid because they, the majority, don't respond and therefore have no interest in increasing corporate profits.
  What can anyone with any ego of his own do but reject both the claim and the person who makes it?
  Taking the position of the Last Angry Man is dangerous. It's like spray-painting your car when it's parked between two other cars.

21. *Format can't mask dullness.*

An overweight woman thinks fashions from Bloomingdale's will work magic she wouldn't need if she had any willpower. An unimaginative copywriter thinks a format that labels itself "exciting" will work magic with his dull message.
  Opinion: Both are wrong. Both deserve failure because they expect others to create a transformation in attitude that they themselves can't accomplish.
  I rescued this mailgram from an office wastebasket:

DEAR MARGO:
  SOFTWARE MERCHANDISING CELEBRATES ITS SECOND ANNIVERSARY NEXT MONTH. WE'RE PROGRAMMING IN SOME EXCITING CHANGES THAT YOU'LL WANT TO KNOW ABOUT. THE NEW SOFTWARE MERCHANDISING IS YOUR KEY TO THE ENTIRE HOME COMPUTING AND SOFTWARE MERCHANDISING MARKETPLACE. DETAILS TO FOLLOW . . .

That's the entire message. Someone wrote this, for pay.

Suppose you, as an acknowledged expert, address a high school class. After your speech, one of the students comes up to you and asks your opinion of the mailgram copy, written not for a trade publication but for the high school yearbook. Could you suppress your conscience and lie, "Use it; it's fine"?

Or would you explain, patiently or impatiently, that labeling a nonevent "exciting" doesn't make it exciting and that the mailgram format doesn't add a thing except harder-to-read all caps?

This may not be a fair example because I think the mailgram format is implicitly dull (see "Speed Formats," Chapter 14) unless it stays in sync with its carrier envelope. The way to overcome that dullness isn't a one-paragraph tribute to self-importance, but, rather, individual words spaced to overcome the limitations of the format, using as their foundation the solid rock of reader benefit instead of the eroding sands of self-interest.

22. *Timeliness is second only to verisimilitude in its ability to bring dollars through the mail.*

I still remember, years after the event, the massive fund-raising campaign for the Statue of Liberty restoration. One of the best examples of using time as a fear motivator was a mailing two years before the completion date, from the Statue of Liberty Ellis Island Foundation, Inc., which extended its sense of urgency even to the date on the letter—"Wednesday." Clever, for a third-class nonprofit mailing that otherwise defied dating, wasn't it? (Many people thought so because this has become a standard dating technique.)

The letter is a potent classic. It started out in high gear, as a fear/time appeal should:

The most powerful symbol of our nation's liberty is in a serious state of disrepair.

A few paragraphs beyond, another signal of timeliness crashed into our psyches. Doom isn't impending, it's here now.

But right now the Statue of Liberty faces its most serious danger since it was officially dedicated in 1886. . . .

It is an alarming situation. . . .

I've enclosed two dramatic pictures that show just what has happened and why we must preserve it now. . . .

In order to continue this work, we have to raise a minimum of $1.8 million of the total budget within the next 45 days. Time is crucial since there is real danger that if. . . .

Think for a moment. If you had to create a "right now" demand for a project whose fruition isn't scheduled for another two years, could you have written this any better? The letter was unrelenting; proof of its effectiveness now stands proudly renewed in the New York harbor.

23. *Be sure they know what you're talking about.*

You work for a company selling fingernockles by mail. You spend your entire day saturated with fingernockles. You can assemble one blindfolded, with your toes. You're steeped in fingernockle lore.

Don't make that same assumption about the persons to whom you're selling fingernockles. He doesn't spend his days in your office and he's made enough money to be considered a good prospect . . . without ever owning a fingernockle. Telling him how your fingernockle is better than anyone else's fingernockle isn't going to move him. First, you have to tell him why he needs a fingernockle.

This point came home to me a few years ago when I was trying to find a way to sell collector's plates by mail, to people who weren't collectors. The list broker was sourly unhelpful: "You can't sell collectibles to anyone but a collector."

I didn't like this catch-22 approach. Why wouldn't lists other than lists of collectors respond on a better-than-break-even level? I staggered into a Eureka! discovery while reading a mailing from a company selling something to do with Dolby noise reduction in hi-fi sets.

Like many, I had heard of Dolby for years. This mailing, for the first time, told me what it is.

The next opportunity I had, I tested an additional enclosure that explained in a nonpatronizing way what collector's plates are. The enclosure made little difference in the response from collector lists, but previously unresponsive lists of art book buyers suddenly came to life.

My conclusion: Previously I had treated them as though they knew what fingernockles were; they didn't. They not only wouldn't order; they couldn't because I'd sent them "in-group" mailings and they knew they weren't members of the in-group.

24. *Truth doesn't justify an exclamation point unless the statement excites the reader.*

A savings and loan institution, referring to mortgage payments, says:

Save a big 1%!

Put this way, the reason for the exclamation point doesn't register on the reader's emotional/exclamatory computer. "Big" and "1%" just don't logically go together. The same information can lay claim to the exclamation point by dropping the obvious mismatch:

You'll save a full percent!

But laying claim to an exclamation point and justifying that claim aren't quite the same thing. If the writer can relate the 1 percent mortgage differential to actual dollars, he has every reason to exclaim:

If you have a 30-year mortgage, you'll save *thousands* of dollars!

25. *Beware of words with two meanings. They can bite.*

The English language has an astounding number of words with more than one meaning. Sometimes a direct-marketing wordsmith deliberately uses a word that his lawful prey can interpret in several ways. But the writer should never use a word that, if misinterpreted, can generate a negative reaction.

Innocently, a writer let this construction escape:

It was handled right in our office.

A writer might get away with this in broadcast media, by instructing the announcer how to read it to achieve proper word emphasis. The direct-mail writer doesn't have an intermediary; "direct" is his first name, and message interpretation is squarely in the reader's hands. Unless the reader attaches *right* to *in our office*, as a single phrase, *right* gets hooked to *handled—handled right*, which suggests it might *not* have been handled right on other occasions.

The sentence illustrates the reason for having a disinterested (not *un*interested) party proofread the copy, which casts off the possibility of misinterpretation when put this way:

We handled it—right in our office.

Now the writer forces the reader to group the words as intended.

Apparently harmless constructions such as "simple child psychology" prove that the writer, who reads the words one way only, isn't the best proofreader of those words.

26. *Test in, and test out.*

A risky approach to direct marketing is discarding a profitable copy approach and replacing it with a new ad or mailer because "we're tired of it" or "it's worn out."

When your ads or mailings are profitable, test changes in copy gingerly; even if they're wildly profitable, keep testing. And keep records.

Replacing a good old control mailing or ad is a trauma for many companies. They see it dipping, dipping, but they won't initiate a quiet series of component tests to learn what might add some fresh steam. When the power finally runs out, they're left marooned with no tracks to guide them back to profitability.

In direct response, refusing to test turns you into a bull elephant crashing through the veldt with a bullet in your brain. You're dead but don't know it yet.

27. *If you aren't sure of buyer gender, don't polarize it.*

An extravagant mailing, addressed to me, has this overline beginning the letter:

You can now acquire the doll collection
that every little girl has dreamed about

I don't understand the lack of punctuation at the end of the thought, but I'm bewildered by a sentence that implicitly eliminates half the readers without improving sales appeal to the other half.

By now, logical targets of collectible doll mailings have been circularized often enough to take an asexual product view. See the problem here? They can't, when the writer eliminates them from the pod of prospects.

Laura David
CONSUMER RESEARCH CENTER

#088

BULK RATE
U.S. POSTAGE PAID
SHOPPER'S VOICE

I think the enclosed survey will interest you.
Please complete and return it within
the next couple of days.

Thank you,
Laura

Field Survey Project # ECRWSSCO23**

The Main Grocery Shopper
340 N Fig Tree Ln
Ft Lauderdale FL 33317-2561

Figure 13-8: This envelope wants to imply officialdom and succeeds because of several devices—the typewritten legend at upper left, the handwritten "#088," and the words "Field Survey Project # ECRWSS**CO23." Note to whom the envelope is addressed: "The Main Grocery Shopper."

28. *Opening with benefit is an insurance policy. No matter how unprofessional the writing, you'll be floating in the warm sea of the reader's self-interest.*

My apologies for reprinting so much of the opening of a four-page letter, sent to cold-list names. I want to illustrate Tip 28.

> YOU are personally invited
> to examine for 15 days FREE
> THE NEW "Red Books"
> and SAVE $117.00 NOW —
> if you decide to order them.
>
> These remarkable guides can save you
> many valuable hours of work and
> perhaps help you discover your most
> profitable breakthrough of the year!
> Please read on . . .
>
> Dear Executive:
> Imagine how much easier, more rewarding and more satisfying your job would be if you had powerful information like this at your fingertips right now:
>> —the names and phone numbers of those key decision makers *who* control the big advertising money today . . .
>> —exactly *how much* they're spending . . .
>> —the media *where* it's being spent . . .
>> —current, reliable reports on *what* is really new and important on the client *and* agency sides . . .
>> —*how to reach* the creative, production, and other people responsible for that new ad campaign everyone is raving about . . .
>> —*which* accounts your competition is likely to go after this year . . .
>
> Well, you can feel good knowing that all this exciting information—*all accurate, complete, reliable, and current*—can be yours *at a glance* when you have THE NEW RED BOOKS on your desk.
>
> And right now, because I think you're a leader who needs these essential business facts *fast* to work more effectively and more efficiently, I am making you this RED BOOK FREE TRIAL and SPECIAL SAVINGS OFFER. More on this exciting offer in a minute.
>
> First of all, I'm pleased and proud to announce the publication of THE NEW RED BOOKS. And *new* they are!
>
> As you know very well, the advertising and marketing business changes rapidly and frequently. It has changed so dramatically that *up to 80% of the listings are different* than the information in last year's editions.

That's the entire first page of the letter. Let's first eliminate from consideration (relative to Tip 28) the grammatically incorrect "different than," the apparent lack of familiarity with the company's own statistics (" . . . *up to 80% of the listings are different* . . . "), and the almost random underlining and capitalization. We're concentrating on *benefit*. Where is it?

What the writer did here was throw down a gauntlet many readers don't recognize as a gauntlet. Yes, we understand what they're selling—information. What we don't understand is the benefit. "These remarkable guides can save you many valuable hours of work and perhaps help you discover your most profitable breakthrough of the year!" isn't even tantalizing because *every* business mailing promises to save hours of work, and we can't quite penetrate "profitable breakthrough."

How *do* we project benefit from information? I can think of two ways: 1) specific examples of benefits RED BOOK readers have had from owning the publications and 2) a no-risk trial, which changes the reader's "I don't know what this will do for me" to "What do I have to lose while I see whether their *features* become my *benefits*?"

The no-risk trial does appear, on the fourth page of the letter. Opinion: Too late for many readers.

29. *The wording of information-seeking questions in a coupon or order form can have a negative effect.*

Suppose you aren't a scuba diver but would like to be. From an ad for scuba gear, you fill out a coupon that has a question emphasizing your second-class status:

    __I am   __I am not a certified scuba diver.

Someone who scraped through Child Psychology 101 would know how easy it is to avoid the negative effect:

    __I am not   __I am a certified scuba diver.

Reversing the two won't bother the already-certified divers and will make the nondivers feel their position is the most common one.

30. *Bullet copy forces specificity.*

Bullet copy, by its very terseness, prevents those rhapsodic lapses into puffery that throw sand into the gears of a dynamic selling argument.

Which of these copy blocks transmits the most information, the most credible information, and the most action-inducing information?

Now you can have all the quality features you've wanted in a 25″ color TV and you can have it at *an outstanding value*. With this Sharp TV you have the convenience of 6-function wireless infrared remote control plus exceptional performance. There's a 105-channel cable-ready tuner, the reliable Sigma 8000 chassis with 100% solid-state circuitry and the exclusive Linytron Plus one-gun picture tube for bright, clear color.

Or

The Sharp 25″ Remote Color TV
▶ infrared wireless remote control
▶ cable-ready to 105 channels
▶ LED channel display and 1-button picture balance control
▶ one-year in-home parts and labor limited manufacturer's warranty

The bullets separate the selling points that, in a block of prose, sap impact from one another. To me, though, the biggest benefit of bullets is their implicit culling of puffery from the factual core.

31. *If you're unsure of a word's use and no one in your office is qualified to judge your vocabulary, pick another word.*

Whether you're a writer or nonwriter, it's a good idea to learn a fresh word every day. But don't treat words like new toys that you grab and play with until you break them.

I had bad vibes when I first spotted a headline for a soft drink: "A curious lugubrious brightness." Huh?

Yup. Body copy was overblown, always an indication of land mines. This one had to explode all over the writer:

> You'd think "lugubrious" and "brightness" don't go together. Well, as a matter of fact, they don't. What we're suggesting is that you drink it slowly. YOU'RE the one who will brighten. Curious, isn't it?

Damned right it's curious. What's even more curious is that anyone thought this would sell a soft drink—or *anything*, for that matter. And of all the words one might choose in a selling ambience, "lugubrious" has to rank in the lower $1/100$ of 1 percent. What's most curious is the image of a writer, struggling to convert a useless fact to a "Hey, look at me!" effect, using more of the language than he or she knew—and needlessly exposing this deficiency in print.

32. *Nonsense parallels have become popular as writers' crutches. They're noncommunicative attempts at cleverness for the sake of cleverness. Don't use this device.*

A laundry product called Gain started a flood of these nonsense parallels in a television commercial. The husband, obviously in need of psychiatric help because he becomes orgasmic over his wife's clean dress, nuzzles the dress and murmurs lovingly:

> "Do you think it's so clean because it smells so good?"

His wife, carried away by the passion of the moment, responds:

> "Or does it smell so good because it's clean?"

I'm not attacking the nonsense parallel because it's grade-school easy to write or because of its format; in fact, I like parallels. My objection is to the ridiculous premise. Invariably, at least half a nonsense parallel is impenetrable. Example: "Do you think it's so clean because it smells so good?" I defy you to make sense out of that.

More than half a century ago, a Harold Lloyd movie had this line: "Clothes don't make the man. Man makes the clothes." Did this start it all? We now have nonsense parallels springing up like dandelions:

> "My backyard turned into the PGA–Sheraton Resort?"
> "No, the PGA–Sheraton Resort turned into your backyard."

Now: Are you proud because you figured this out? Or did you figure this out because you're proud?

33. *If half a parallel is negative, the parallel itself is probably weak.*

This tip isn't (pardon the term) parallel to tip 32. A nonsense parallel is ridiculous; a negative parallel isn't. Rather, it's logical but not helpful.

A sample will clarify:

Kendall Drive used to be a road to nowhere. Now it's the road to everywhere.

Another:

People used to say the taste wasn't exciting. They don't say that anymore.

Still not convinced that a negative parallel probably isn't your best-selling copy? Let's look at one more:

Who says this computer has a poor service record? Not the users who get their Winchester hard disk drives from us.

The negative parallel plants a negative seed. Everybody who sells . . . whether head-to-head, in print, on the World Wide Web, or through a broadcast signal, knows negative seeds sprout at ten times the speed of positive seeds. In the Age of Skepticism, our readers look for negatives. Let's not feed them.

34. *Don't assume that a mildly favorable fact is a selling weapon.*

Somehow, researchers have superimposed on marketers the notion that a majority—51 percent or more—is ammunition. My opinion differs. I suggest the existence of a major difference between the voting majority at a stockholders' meeting and a powerful sales argument in an ad or mailer aimed at somebody who doesn't know you.

Here's an example of a fact-based copy platform:

Fact! 93.7% of those who already have bought these self-adjusting trousers say they're satisfied.
Fact! 72% say they plan to buy more.
Fact! This low price can't be available forever.

My reaction to the first "Fact!" was negative. Aside from the weakness of the word *satisfied*, I was troubled by the existence of 6.3% who *weren't* satisfied. "Planning to buy more" isn't the same as actually buying more—a common problem with attitude research. Had the copy been able to claim, "Three out of four buyers came back and bought another pair!" we'd have a *salesworthy* fact—not just a naked piece of information floating in the Dead Sea of description.

35. *The components of a direct-mail package should reinforce one another, not parallel one another.*

I say "One another," not "each other," because sometimes a letter, a brochure, a lift letter, and a third-party endorsement will all project the same message. Uh-uh.

The most common violation of this tip is writing a letter and a brochure whose sales messages are nearly identical. When copy in a sales letter and a brochure is the same (perhaps reorganized but not presenting different dimensions of thought on the subject being sold), someone has gone back thirty years and followed the old saw: "Tell 'em what you're going to tell 'em. Then tell 'em. Then tell 'em what you've told 'em."

That still works, when you do it within a single component. It becomes boringly repetitious when you use a letter, a brochure, and maybe a third enclosure to restate your approach.

FREE SUBSCRIPTION VOUCHER FOR:

..uge it, enjoy it, use it for 8
weeks at no cost or obligation
and discover its unique
perspective on business today.
If you decide to continue,
you'll receive 51 issues of
Business Week (including
your eight free trial issues)
for the low rate of just
$37.95... that's 81% off the
cover price.

H G Lewis
Communicomp
340N Fig Tre
Plantation,

33317>2561 ||.||...||...||...||....|||....|.|.|.|.|.|.||.....||.|.||....||.|

Figure 13-9: This is what can happen when a response device doesn't fit the window
on the envelope: Even though envelope copy says "Free subscription voucher," the
recipient can see "$37.95 . . . that's 81% off" through the misdesigned window.

Instead, the letter should point out reasons to "look over the brochure I've enclosed," and
the brochure might quote an excerpt from a magazine article—a reprint of which is another enclosure. When the pieces reinforce one another, the effect is synergistic: Each gains power, validity, and the appearance of truth.

36. *When you sign a letter, type your name below the signature unless you're positive the
reader will recognize the signature. And if you want to be cordial, type the full name and handwrite the personalized version (e.g., you'd sign "Dave Smith" and type below it "David I. Smith").*

The first half of this tip is mechanical rather than creative. It's based on the increasing number of idiot-scrawls masquerading as signatures. Since John Hancock put his beautiful, clear John
Hancock on the Declaration of Independence, we've suffered a gradual deterioration in pen-
manship. Some executives think it's executive-ish to have an unintelligible signature.

The reader wants to deal with a person, not a company. Clear signatures are reassuring.

The second half is based on the increasing informality of 21st-century communications. In
courtship, pomposity is out.

37. *Before turning a piece of copy loose, check paragraphs beginning with the word* as *and
replace the word—and the phrase following it—if you spot limpness.*

A paragraph starting with "as" is especially vulnerable because the word so often begins a
refer-back: "As mentioned above . . . " or "As previously stated. . . . "

I don't know the percentage of *as* refer-backs that can be strengthened, but I'd guess it's at
least half. We all do it; we shouldn't, since *as* refer-backs are holding actions at best. Even in the
active tense, an *as* phrase probably is weaker than the same phrase without it: "As I told you,
we'll . . . " has far less impact than "I told you we'll. . . . "

38. *Don't suggest on the outer envelope that the reader has to do something that might be
considered work to get a benefit.*

If the purpose of the message on an envelope is to get the envelope opened, suggesting the reader has to work in order to enjoy benefits can be the reason your envelope gets the old heave-ho.

I'm looking at an envelope I never did open. This legend is on its face:

FREE REPORT!
You Can Save
Thousands of Dollars a Year
By Correcting
These Common Tax Mistakes

Heck, I think this mailer can save thousands of dollars a year by correcting this common tactical mistake. "Do You Make These 5 Tax Mistakes?" might have teased me into opening the envelope ("5" instead of "Five" for impact); the word "correcting" killed off my interest in whatever they were selling.

An envelope preaches at me:

Luck is no substitute for Knowledge.
And Knowledge doesn't come easy.

Maybe the writer was thinking of knowledge of grammar. Whatever might be inside this envelope, couldn't the writer have promised me something instead of adding more creases to my forehead?

39. *A dash is harder and stronger than an ellipsis.*

I've lifted this tip from Chapter 11 (where the information refers to grammar and usage) to this position (where it refers to impact) because . . .

Figure 13-10: The envelope describes just about everything it contains. Usually this isn't good salesmanship, but for a computer program such as this one it can entice the recipient to look inside.

Careful! You may not want hardness and strength. This is a subtle tip. The difference between a dash—a power-stop—and an ellipsis . . . a soft interrupter . . . is clear. What isn't so clear is when to use which.

Generally, use the dash when you're writing dynamic copy. Use the ellipsis when you want to draw less attention to the effect.

Don't apply this tip to the grammatical use of the ellipsis. When you want to show an incomplete quotation, use dots, not dash: "I was saying. . . ."

40. *Consider perceived value when describing product use or inventing a product name.*

Which one probably will sell more merchandise?

—Protects your lower arms

or

—Protects your arms far above the wrist

The typical reader doesn't regard "lower arms" as a vital area; wrists are damage-prone. I favor the second approach.

A company trying to sell children's videotapes refers to "Annie, a Pigtailed 10-Year-Old." "Annie, a Little Girl in Pigtails" changes the emphasis from the pigtails to the girl, replacing clinical description with charm.

This tip can apply to product names and descriptions, from steak to shoes. Which is a better shoe, the "Ensign" or the "Commodore"?

What's in a name? Plenty, if you're selling by mail.

41. *You usually can strengthen a weak headline beginning with the word* if *by making it a question.*

A list company sent an enclosure with the *Direct Mail List Bulletin*. On both flaps was this provocative copy:

TELEPHONE
NUMBERS?
62,861,427

Had the list company used standard "if" copy—If you need telephone number appending"—the effect would have been fractional compared to the impact of this powerhouse copy.

Try it. Find an old piece of copy starting with *if* and play with it. Converting an opening "if . . . " phrase to a question, especially a terse question, can start off your message in high gear.

42. *If you cry "Wolf!" be sure your readers can see a wolf.*

Fear sometimes is too powerful a motivator. If you use it, be certain your words generate fear in the reader's heart. A fear approach that falls short is a disappointment to the message recipient; from your early warnings, he anticipates being rocked by your words.

An example is a fund-raising mailing whose key component is a note typed in all caps on colored stock. Look what happens here:

URGENT URGENT URGENT

RECENT REPORTS FROM ETHIOPIA AND EAST AFRICA INDICATE THAT THE SITUATION CONTINUES TO BE VERY SERIOUS. THOUSANDS OF DESPERATE REFUGEES ARE STILL TRAVELING FROM ONE COUNTRY TO ANOTHER IN SEARCH OF FOOD.

ALTHOUGH RECENT SHIPMENTS HAVE PROVIDED SOME RELIEF, MUCH MORE IS NEEDED. . . .

The words "Although recent shipments have provided some relief" sap impact from the three "URGENT" headers that demand copy power. Suppose the phrase were dropped; the sentence would read, "Much more relief is needed." The sense of urgency would continue unadulterated.

If you suggest a hunter has shot out the wolf's canine teeth and trimmed its claws, you make the wolf far less dangerous. It's *your* wolf. He's as fierce or as tame, as dangerous or as remote, as you make it.

43. *Mysterious forces may terrify the reader, but they won't have much luck selling him or her something.*

A company that for some insane reason wants to handle my investment portfolio sent me a brochure describing its services:

We Give SoundAdvice
on the Best Electronics
Mailing Division
7571 N.W. 78th Street
Medley, FL 33166-7530

First-Class
Pre-Sort
U.S. Postage
PAID
Miami, FL
Permit #3157

HERSCHELL LEWIS

340 N FIG TREE LN
PLANTATION   FL 33317-2561

I.II..II..II....IIII..I.I.I.I.I..II....II.I.III....I.I.I

Please open in private.

Figure 13-11: The word "private" still has some impact. Even though this communication obviously has no personal element, the envelope copy helps it get attention. The four words would have had greater verisimilitude if they had been handwritten.

ADVANTAGE # 1
   Your portfolio will be reviewed and analyzed, and appropriate suggestions will be made.

Big Brother is watching me! Apparently he's in the publishing business, too, because his magazine starts its sales pitch this way:

This NEWS
Is SIGNIFICANT
To YOU
Dear Sometime Reader:
The decision has been made. You'll be allowed to join us.

Check your own copy. If it uses the passive voice—"something will be done," not "I'll do something"—it could suffer from the Mysterious Forces Terror. "They," whoever they are, are taking over. The decisions are out of our hands.
   No! By taking responsibility, you build rapport. Although I hate the premise, I'd have been a reader/participant and not an adversary had the communication begun:

I'd like to believe
this news
is significant to you.
To a Special Friend:
We've decided you're one of us.

Dispelling implicit hostility can be as easy as taking responsibility for the words you're writing.

44. *Whenever you can add the word* you *to a benefit, you clarify it as a benefit.*

A letter offering a money-back guarantee says, "There are no risks involved." The writer could have injected potency into the same information by wording it, "You take no risk whatever," or "Examine it at our risk—not yours."
   Copy selling a medical reference book says, "This book supplies information about . . ."; you or I would have worded it, "This book gives you information about . . . " because our revised sales argument narrows itself to reader benefit.

45. *The difference between* can't *and* won't *is the difference of whether or not you're able to control what you're selling.*

Usually *won't* is preferable, but *can't* is better when you want to emphasize that all the forces of creation are unable to influence the result.
   Two examples might clear up any confusion hovering over this tip. The first is a piece of catalog copy that in my opinion grossly misstated the value of a shampoo:

A gentle shampoo that can't dry even the most delicate hair . . .

I've quoted it as it was, with the word *out* missing after "dry." But assume it reads the way the writer must have intended it to read—"can't dry out." See how the words make the product seem to fail at a job it means to do?

We replace *can't* with *won't*, and voila!

A gentle shampoo that won't dry out even the most delicate hair . . .

The second is copy for a ball-point pen:

Bang it. Knock it. Scrape it against a concrete wall. Rasp it with a file. You won't damage it.

The writer has given us factual accuracy, not inspiration. This situation is the reverse of the one before it because we're supposed to think that no matter what we do, this pen can take it and come up smiling. So we change one word:

Bang it. Knock it. Scrape it against a concrete wall. Rasp it with a file. You can't damage it.

In this tip, we have one of the tiny keys to copy-power we sometimes overlook because using one word instead of another isn't a ghastly error but only a thinning of the magic paste.

46. *Emphasize the right point.*

This tip means extrapolating benefit from factual information. Copy for a fax machine crows:

Uses thermal paper (included).

As a plain-paper fax user, I don't regard thermal paper as a benefit. In fact, the word *thermal* implies something combustible, likely to burst into flame as I stare at it. How easy it is for the copywriter to answer my "So what?" with a benefit aimed squarely at me:

Special "thermal" paper means you never have to add toner.

See how the emphasis changes? Copy now focuses where it should—on what the paper does for the user, not on the structure of the paper itself.

A parenthetical point: I oppose indiscriminate use of quotation marks, but I embrace the notion of putting "thermal" in quotes here. Why? Because this device tells the reader the paper isn't really hot and fiery. The quotation marks don't help our direct comprehension, but they indirectly help our acceptance of the unknown. (See the Quotation Mark Rule under "Punctuation and Grammar," Chapter 26.)

47. *Comparative copy should specify areas of superiority. Damning the competition without giving the reader solid meat leaves your reader chewing air—and burping out your sales argument undigested.*

You want me to switch from an existing supplier to you. What do you tell me?

I'll wager that an apprentice insurance salesman, armed with little more than the realities of competition, could mount a more realistic selling argument than this letter from an insurance agency, which starts off in just the wrong key:

Dear President:

I have contacted you in regard to your pension assets being managed by someone other than the best. We have been ranked the **#**1 manager of pension funds for years and manage in excess of $50 billion dollars of assets . . .

The letter goes on to bury with unflagging success its core—the actual percentages of asset increases—in lines such as "I believe that you are a wise and successful business person" (Urp!) and words such as "utilizing," which we'd expect in a communication such as this. The writer signs his name "Edward H. Maass, EQA," as though I had even the foggiest notion what "EQA" means.

The capper is the P.S.:

WHY MANAGE WITH THE REST WHEN YOU CAN HAVE IT MANAGED BY THE BEST!!!

Tell you what, Mr. Maass. Drop your initials. Take the spats off your copy. Use only one punctuation mark at a time. Write in complete sentences. Open with benefit to me. Then we'll talk.

(You'll find a complete discussion of comparative advertising in Chapter 6.)

48. *If you want to use testimonials but don't have any, offer a prize for the best ones. You'll get a lifetime supply.*

I can't show you examples of testimonials obtained this way because in print a testimonial is a testimonial. You'll have to take my word for it. The procedure does work.

A caution, though: Don't ask for testimonials; ask for *opinions*. Results will be just as good and your ethics will remain intact.

49. *The word* needs *as a noun is never as explicit nor as effective as another noun you already know.*

Yellow Pages copy is shot through with headlines such as "For All Your Insurance Needs!" or "For Your Office Supply Needs." Don't use that reference as an excuse to use "Needs." Yellow Pages copy isn't a treasure-house of brilliant copywriting; your direct-mail piece should be.

What set me off was a mailing from someone *within* our industry whose letter was headed:

WE CAN SERVE *YOUR* DIRECT MAIL NEEDS . . .

The heading itself wasn't peculiar. What *was* peculiar was that much of the letter that followed was bright, thoughtful, and pointed. Dullness, in the first two paragraphs, was the direct result of having to lean on the broken crutch "Needs."

If the writer of this letter had reasoned, "What *are* this guy's direct-mail needs? They'll be the focus of my headline," then the letter might have resulted in an inquiry from me instead of inclusion in my "What Not to Do" file.

Try to program an automatic red flag. When the word *needs* goes in, the red flag goes up and the writer backspaces until every evidence of this dulling malady is eradicated.

50. *Plate your word-faucets with gold.*

Without getting flowery or labored, use words with magic in them. They're there, not only in your dictionary or thesaurus but in your imagination. Fertilize your imagination, nurture it, prune it, turn its face to the radiant sun of reader involvement, and it will sprout.

A writer whose imagination had some weeds in it wrote this:

J.R.R. Tolkien's masterful epic tale of wizards, orcs, and heroic hobbits was printed as a three-volume set.

Are you bewildered by an attack on what seems to be a good piece of copy? Weeds choked one key word. We have "printed," a plumber's word, instead of *published*, a wordsmith's word.

The difference between motivational copy and bulk description lies in the fraction of a degree separating the reader's almost unconscious reaction to *printed* from the reaction to *published*. It's the difference in fund-raising copy between "Now we want your help" and "Today we want your help." It's the difference between the flat "This is to notify you that . . . " and the attention-grabbing "This is to alert you to . . . "

The Inevitable Conclusion

To the copywriter, sensitivity to words is just as much a key to professionalism as the ability to put those words onto a sheet of paper. Your viewpoint is closer to the target individual's than to the writer's. You're the filter, the border guard, the last stop before mistakes are immortalized.

To all who write direct-mail copy, the last bastion of copywriter control: Good luck. Your competitors want to drink your blood. Let them starve.

Chapter Fourteen

HOW TO WRITE SPEED-FORMAT COPY

Speed Formats Don't Have to Be Ho-Hum Formats

If you're old enough to remember World War II, you probably also remember the excitement a telegram could engender.

A clean-cut young man rode his bicycle to your door, and when he handed you the yellow window envelope, the surge of emotion was almost overpowering. What was in that envelope? An order? A job offer? The possibility that it might be bad news heightened the suspense.

I remember the telegram that came a few days after I had gotten an advanced degree. It offered me a teaching job at a college I had no intention of considering. So powerful was the *medium* that I heeded the *message* and taught there for two years.

Where are the joys of yesteryear? Western Union drained the magic out of telegrams by phoning them to the recipient and asking, "Do you want a printed copy of this?"—an anticlimactic record, like watching an instant replay. Clean-cut young men don't ride their bikes anymore; the occasional cyclist is either a ten-year-old, veering into your path on his deadly trail bike, or, if he's older than ten, chances are he isn't clean-cut. And try finding a Western Union office.

Can bulk mail be "rush—instant!"?

One of the inevitable results of novelty is early burnout.

The mailgram was a novelty when business mailers first started using it. In my opinion, its cool blue color damaged the emotional impact, but that's just an opinion.

Another opinion: The proliferation of speed formats has brought the whole technique close to the deadened land of ineffectiveness, where no response grows.

The original mailgrams weren't to be bulk-mailed. They were designed for first-class postage, they had to be "handled," and they added so much expense that it was completely logical for alternative formats to appear. The ideal format would have impact stemming from the appearance of immediacy, "Open me now!" screaming from the envelope, and not too severe a letdown once trembling fingers had pried the message out of its garish womb. (The Western Union "Priority Letter" is now yellow and orange. See Figure 14-1.)

Hundreds of speed-message formats have appeared. Some are far more cleverly conceived than the messages they carry. All suffer from the overpopulation within their ranks.

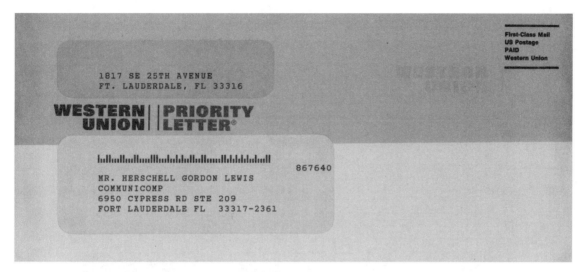

Figure 14-1: Western Union has refined its "Priority Letter" to make it seem hotter and more immediate. Competition has dramatically reduced both impact and share of market, even though this competitor is first-class mail.

Some iconoclastic notions

If you're in business, check your mail for the next few weeks. You may find, to your surprise, a dozen or more speed-format mailings. The phrase "to your surprise" validates the claim I'm about to make:

> If these formats have become so commonplace that they no longer have a singular impact, their very purpose has become self-defeating.

Only when I sorted through my files, gathering documentation for this book, did I realize that one of the samples actually *was* a genuine piece of first-class mail with an honest-to-goodness urgent message.

Hah! The joke is on the sender. I've become so jaded that I treat all speed formats as third-class mail. My resistance seems to grow in direct ratio to the frenzy behind them.

From this, I've formulated the First Law of Speed Formats: If the recipient becomes annoyed by discovering your ploy, the speed format has worked against you, not for you, because more conventional formats wouldn't have generated a negative reaction.

The Second Law implements the philosophy of the First Law: The message must project timeliness, personalization, and possible loss of benefit, or it falls out of key with the format and violates the First Law.

Consider those first two laws before you throw them out, saying, "The speed format gives excitement to my dull message." Here's an example of how mailers misuse speed formats through their ignorance of the laws. Even as I was at the keyboard attacking speed formats, the postman delivered a Federal Express look-alike. On the flap, in a red reverse, was this legend:

EXTREMELY URGENT LETTER ENCLOSED

Figure 14-2: Mailed at bulk rate, this speed format is an obvious . . . and sometimes successful . . . attempt to have the recipient think it's Priority Mail, a two- to three-day delivery service of the U.S. Post Office.

Figure 14-3: Because most people associate the eagle with standard mail, the bird is a common choice for speed formats. This is one of many available from Allpro Printing, Clearwater, Florida.

Burned by my earlier ignoring of a genuine urgent letter, I opened the thing. Inside was a printed message, the urgency of which could apply only to the sender. He wanted to sell advertising space.

Nothing in the message said "You." Nothing in the message said "You'll lose this benefit unless . . ."

My reaction: Since the message was fraudulently couched, the medium was fraudulent.

The Rule of Pseudo-Lying

The Rule of Pseudo-Lying is the control, the governor on what might be a disgusting runaway throttle. If enough mailers recognize this rule, matching medium to message, then "Urgent" will mean urgent and "Hurry!" will relate to reader benefit as well as sender benefit. The rule: When the reader thinks you are not telling the truth about one point, he extends that opinion to your entire sales argument. He rejects even the statements that *are* true.

So let's suppose I really could use the advertising space pitched in the "Extremely Urgent Letter." My decision on the space is still "Forget it"—not because the sender misstates the facts, but because he cloaks them in duplicity.

When emotion and intellect come into conflict, emotion always wins. I reject the factual (intellectual) core of the message because I must; emotionally, I'm wounded by deceit. Under the Rule of Pseudo-Lying, if fact is 1 percent contaminated with deceit, the whole rhetorical meal is full of maggots.

Four More Laws of Speed Formats

To those who value form more than substance, I offer a venerable comment by David Ogilvy: "What you say is more important than how you say it."

We're in the Age of Skepticism, remember? The validity of Ogilvy's notion (published in 1963) may be blurred by whole generations of television glitz, but for direct marketers its focus couldn't be sharper.

So if you're hung up in speed formats, I beg you: Don't drive your message recipients deeper into skepticism, where the rest of us copywriters won't be able to get at them. Keep the message sane and apparently true. We'll all benefit.

Four more laws can prevent the siren song of format from drowning out the victory march of message:

▶ The Third Law of Speed Formats: Open the message with compelling benefit.
▶ The Fourth Law of Speed Formats: Don't let any distraction soften the "bulletin" copy approach.
▶ The Fifth Law of Speed Formats: If your message is supposed to be one-to-one, keep excitement high by keeping adjectives down; your message will match the medium if its entire structure demands imperative action that produces benefit.
▶ The Sixth Law of Speed Formats: Slash away mercilessly at hard-selling copy that leans toward the verbose. It destroys speed-format credibility.

Nothing difficult here, is there? Let's see how the laws work under battle conditions. A computer-personalized yellow-and-black speed format, with the word "International" in its name, had this heading:

Figure 14-4: Not exactly a speed format, this envelope mirrors many of the devices such formats employ.

ONE MORE REASON TO
VISIT BOOTH 423
AT [NAME OF TRADE SHOW]

See the violations of the Third Law? "One more reason" means other reasons, more compelling than this one, exist. Visiting a conference exhibit isn't exciting unless benefit to me transcends the simple notion of the visit itself. The "International" band circling the envelope misinterprets the relationship between the states: The message came from Chicago.

The Fourth Law is probably the most abused of all the protective controls. An example is a speed format using the words *HIGH PRIORITY COMMUNICATION* in the standard reverse-band that girdles most of the envelopes of this genre. What's the high-priority communication? Here's the first sentence:

WE HOPE YOU ENJOYED THE DIRECT MARKETING ASSOCIATION CON-
FERENCE AS MUCH AS WE AT [NAME OF COMPANY] DID.

What may have gone awry here is that the hapless copywriter was instructed, "Write a sales letter to those who attended the conference." The writer didn't know the company would use a speed format. If the writer *did* know, the blame is clear. His message didn't match the medium because the opening denied the urgency the envelope and format proposed.

The Fifth and Sixth Laws are tied together and are the most subtle of the list. Even moderate attention to the discipline of force-communication would have prevented this copy from being superimposed onto a structure that implicitly rejects it:

GET READY FOR THE BIGGEST TRUCK SELL-A-THON OF THE CENTURY!
MORE THAN 2,000 FORD & GM TRUCKS "BY INVITATION ONLY," VANS
TOO! AT FANTASTIC PRICES! EVERY LETTER HOLDER WILL RECEIVE A

LOVELY 10 PC WOK COOKING SET, 35MM CAMERA, OR OTHER SENSATIONAL GIFT!

As purists, we're jarred by the feminine adjective "lovely" in truck-selling copy, and as creative types we're annoyed by dependence on exclamation points for artificial excitement. While we're on the attack, 2,000 trucks is quite a number for an exclusive "by invitation only" sale.

After this Barnum and Bailey opening, the copy settles down but never justifies the format housing it. My question: Why use a speed format for a standard hard sell?

A Speedy Conclusion

Like the hippies of the 1960s, speed formats try so hard to be different that they begin to look the same.

The format has logic, but logic is transgressed when the message doesn't deliver. If you mail your offer in an envelope whose face is a breathless "Here's hot news only for you!" then justify the envelope by matching the components.

You can practice by writing fifteen-word telegrams in the old, exciting style; before long you'll revitalize an otherwise ho-hum use of a medium that threatens to become overused. The format does work—if the writer puts on his telegram-delivery hat and envisions the young man on the bicycle, scurrying with a message the recipient knows will be hot news.

Sometimes I think American history would have been changed if Paul Revere had had access to speed formats. Instead of charging through the countryside yelling, "The British are coming!" he'd have mailed an envelope, red white and blue or yellow and black, with copy such as this:

Dear Friend,

We hope you enjoyed watching for the British as much as we did. Now it's our pleasure to tell you their soldiers are available for a limited time only, in their lovely red coats.

This information is by invitation only. Please respond within the next fifteen days. You may indicate your acceptance of this offer by loading and firing your musket. As a prize you will receive a signed DECLARATION of INDEPENDENCE.

For more details, call George at 1-800-555-1212 during normal business hours eastern time.

So we have the Ultimate Rule of Speed Formats, which also governs any communications that have any hope of verisimilitude: Stay in sync with yourself.

Chapter Fifteen

WRITING TELEVISION COPY

A Different World

Ask ten beginning copywriters what kind of copy they'd prefer to write. Eight of them will answer, "Television!" (The other two will answer, "Online copy.")

It's no surprise. Television is the glamor medium, all right. And in years past, it had another advantage for the beginning writer: A charlatan could survive well in its oily waters.

So television writers who hadn't the slightest idea of how to use the most powerful and influential medium ever made available to wordsmiths filled their scripts and storyboards with spins and wipes and optical effects . . . and they got away with it because a television commercial that called attention to itself *as a commercial* was a marvelous sample for the writer and the producer. What do you mean, did it sell? That isn't how we keep score.

Those days of golden brass are going into eclipse. Advertising agencies win awards for their television spots—then lose the account because the award is given for artistry, not for salesmanship. When this happens enough times, sanity reappears in the screening room.

Until sanity returns, the journeyman writer is penalized by a harsh reality: The commercials that win awards, that are glorified, and whose key scenes appear in trade magazines have high visibility because of big budgets, celebrities, and expensive effects. Quiet successes get their cheers in limited intraoffice reports.

How to Structure a Television Spot

In a controversial recommendation, Video Storyboard Tests suggested you *not* mention product name in the first five seconds of a TV spot. Why? Because, they say, viewers will tune you out before you've established rapport with them; they recognize too early they're looking at a commercial. (A qualifier, says Video Storyboard Tests: This limitation doesn't apply to brands the viewer already uses.)

Thus, Saturn automobiles produced a "wraparound" commercial. A small boy struggles to play "When the Saints Come Marchin' In" on a tuba as big as he is. After 15 seconds, the station runs other commercials. At the end of the "pod," we're back to the small boy with the tuba. A Saturn pulls up, and he and the tuba are able to enter the semi-backseat of Saturn's three-door car.

Subsequently, the second half ran as a single 15-second spot.

I'm skeptical about the whole notion of holding off identification, so I'd add another qualifier: With so many commercials having a total airtime of 15 seconds or less, and with advertisers

Bozell

CLIENT: JEEP
PRODUCT: Grand Cherokee
COMM'L NO.: CRJE-6433
TITLE: "Gates"

1995 Model Yea
LENGTH: :3(

(MUSIC UNDER THROUGHOUT) . . .

. . .

. . .

. . .

. . .

. . .

. . .

. . .

. . .

. . .

(SFX: BOY TOSSES NEWSPAPER OVER BOULDERS)

Figure 15-1: Jeep has mastered the technique of making a point without using a single spoken word. This commercial shows cars driving through upscale entrances; then a Jeep climbs over a huge pile of boulders, its entrance. The payoff: A boy on a bicycle tosses a newspaper over the boulders.

Figure 15-2: This storyboard of a Jeep commercial emphasizes the SUV's ability to go anywhere, under any conditions. The final frame, not as visible on the storyboard as it is in actual production, has the slogan: "There's Only One Jeep." A minor point: Why capitalize "Only" and "One" in a conversational sentence?

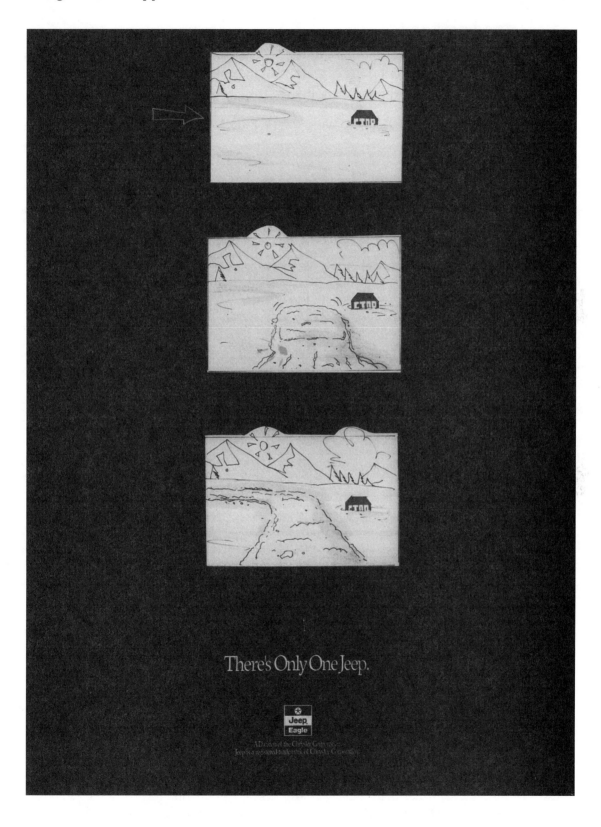

splitting 30-second spots between two separate and unrelated products, we can incorporate this suggestion into the First Rule of Television Impact: If you open with a five-second episode excluding product, close with five seconds of hard visual and auditory emphasis on product.

An Explanatory Subrule helps keep the First Rule of Television Impact on the rails: Validity of the First Rule of Television Impact increases with a decrease in spot length.

So the rule applies more profoundly to a 15-second spot than to a 60-second spot.

The viewer's perception

The viewer has no sense of television timing. An advertiser will air two versions of the same commercial, one 60 seconds long and one 30 seconds long; the viewer finds them indistinguishable from each other.

This has become common practice: During the introductory phase of a campaign, the advertiser runs a 60-second commercial or a 30-second commercial; once familiarity has been established, a condensed version—30 seconds or 15 seconds runs.

With the breakdown of the traditional 30-second spot into "split-30s," it was inevitable that networks and individual stations would begin selling 15-second spots to advertisers at large.

The argument, "Total commercial time hasn't increased," doesn't wash. If we're foot soldiers in the army and every enemy gun is aimed at us, it's inconsequential that the total war hasn't escalated. The number of bullets fired at us is what matters.

The 15-second flood

The challenge to any old-time television writer who broke into the business creating 60-second spots (or even two-minute spots for mail-order items) is a tough one. From 60 seconds, the preferred length shrank to 30 seconds. Then the preferred length became 15 seconds. The typical challenge: Write a spot with the same impact . . . using half the time.

If you analyze this challenge, you'll see it's a *geometric* increase in difficulty because the commercial faces twice as many competing spots in the same commercial break.

The commercial glut hasn't slacked off in the face of a plethora of competing cable channels and the World Wide Web. Sometimes frenzy replaces marketing logic in an advertiser's attempt to seize the viewer's attention.

And right there is one of the most common pits of quicksand: Seizing the viewer's attention is a means; some advertisers see it as an end. The result is attention without payoff.

An example is Miller Lite beer. Targeting a logical group of prospects—the twentysome-things—a batch of 1998 ads attempted to create a "hip" image with visuals described as "quirky"—such as people licking the beer bottle. Sales fell. Eventually, Miller's vice president of marketing told distributors the campaign would be scrapped.

Another example was a television commercial for Nike tennis attire. The spot had players dropping dead on the court. Nike withdrew the spot after complaints poured in, including one from a heart-attack victim's wife.

Is getting attention the alpha and omega of marketing? Those who want samples for their reels feel that straightforward presentations don't further their own image; but the purpose of effective advertising is *not* to further the image of the creative team, but of what's being sold.

Celebrities, overused, call attention to themselves more than to what they are selling. Sprint used Candice Bergen as a spokesperson. Some of the commercials emphasized where she was (e.g., in a space suit, unrelated to long-distance service) rather than what she was selling. Later Sprint spots centered on the company's competitive position rather than on a name spokesperson.

Figure 15-3: The talking Chihuahua of the Taco Bell commercials has been the most popular, most memorable, and most productive spots any fast-food restaurant has ever run. Many come into the restaurant just to repeat the little dog's slogan, "Yo quiero Taco Bell." But eventually the novelty wore out. Franchise complaints of flak sales brought back emphasis on what Taco Bell locations have for sale.

Kmart hired Rosie O'Donnell and Penny Marshall, deliberately bypassing glamor for customer prototypes as spokespeople. BellSouth used former MTV personality Daisy Fuentes to sell telephone service in areas that had a high percentage of Hispanic residents. In the surge of consumer advertising for prescription drugs, Claritin hired Joan Lunden as spokesperson. Taco Bell, meanwhile, used a "talking" Chihuahua as spokesperson . . . make that spokes*dog*. According to Taco Bell, the talking dog . . . or, more probably, the novelty of the talking dog . . . resulted in short-term increased business. The others? Reports were inconclusive.

Add to this the plethora of car dealers and other business owners who decide to present their own commercials, and you have the strong possibility of emphasis on the person instead of on what that person is selling. For every George Zimmer, CEO of Men's Wearhouse, who exudes camera-savvy confidence on camera, we see dozens of business owners—would-be self-financing celebrities—who struggle painfully to read the words on the TelePrompTer.

The 15-second spot: blessing for advertisers, curse for viewers

With the 15-second spot standard as this book is published, television advertisers show considerable hypocrisy as they coincidentally 1) say the multiplication of spots within an allocated time period won't damage effectiveness as long as *total* commercial time isn't increased, and 2) ask stations to put their commercials in the first position within a stack of spots.

Having six to ten spots in a single break is an extraordinary challenge to the writer. "Think like a poster" is a good yardstick when you write short spots whose share of the viewer's attention will be sapped by its podmates.

Can you emotionalize within a 15-second spot? It's a struggle because building rapport demands precious seconds; let's remember our ultimate goal and sadly conclude that if the viewer loves the situation we've built but doesn't get the notion to buy something, we're dramatists, not salespeople.

A study done by the J. Walter Thompson advertising agency and the ABC television network showed muddy conclusions: Informational ads for well-known brands should work well; consumer awareness of new products should increase; campaigns requiring emotion shouldn't use the shorter length; effectiveness can be as little as 30 percent or as high as 80 percent for the 30-second ads. (The study isn't new; it was conducted just as 15-second spots became a fact of life. A more recent study might show deterioration of overall effectiveness because of the typical result—an increase in bulk and density.)

Some advertising giants lean on what they call "testing" as a replacement for creative thinking. These advertisers pretest a whole group of ideas in front of a focus group, using semiproduced commercials. They then produce those with the best scores.

Better than no testing at all? Sure. Reliable? No. A self-conscious viewer looking at a semifinished commercial hardly parallels battle conditions.

For the advertiser whose 15-second spot is fifth or sixth in a pod stack of eight to twelve, life can be tough. Attention-getting devices wear out quickly; they subtract precious seconds from an already-short spot and they're a Band-Aid at best: If every 15-second advertiser opened his, spot with an attention-getting device, the whole medium would be laughable.

Commercial Zapping? You Ain't Seen Nothin' Yet

Recognizing and reacting to the inability of viewers to sort through piles of televised messages, and anticipating clamor added to the clutter, some advertisers and agencies have begun to explore ways to enable their commercials to crash through the dull barrier of viewer apathy.

Crashing through the apathy barrier

Take 30 seconds (lots of time, equivalent to two commercials) to think of ways for *any* advertiser to crash through the apathy barrier. Ready? Go.

Thirty seconds later. Chances are your solution (if any) involved noise or intensification of visual images. Either solution has a percentage of mechanical or morphing (one key item transforms itself into another, as the viewer watches) procedures at least as high as the percentage of creative wordsmithery.

Maybe that's as it should be. How long has it been since you saw a "stand-alone" commercial—one that wasn't preceded or followed by other commercials? It's naive to assume we can control the viewer environment or the attention ratio our commercials get from their televised environment.

Startling graphics are easy when you have any mastery of morphing or computer animation. Attention-getting sounds are easy, too. Ten years ago, a television writer who admitted sensual dependency would have been regarded as a dilettante or a beginner. No more. (Yet a commercial that employed none of the contemporary devices was the winner of a major award. See Figure 15-4.)

A by-product of intensity as a television technique is the downgrading of people in spots. Traditionally, a spot showed or suggested human participation. The intensity philosophy makes people optional—or even an intrusion into brilliantly colored abstract art.

What happens when sensory saturation cuts the relative attention ratio of televised messages to a 10 to 15 percent level? It's parallel to tasting many wines in succession without the palate-cleansing sip of water in between.

The writer might propose an experimental "limbo zone" of several seconds between spots. With a visual of clouds, trees, or the seashore, a quiet voice might say, "Take a breath." Total elapsed time: three seconds.

An impossible dream? Of course it is, unless an adventurous advertiser incorporates those three seconds into a paid commercial, and who would do that?

A more likely approach is to follow the procedure an underdog candidate for governor of Minnesota attempted in 1998 . . . and succeeded in getting himself elected. Jesse Ventura, a for-

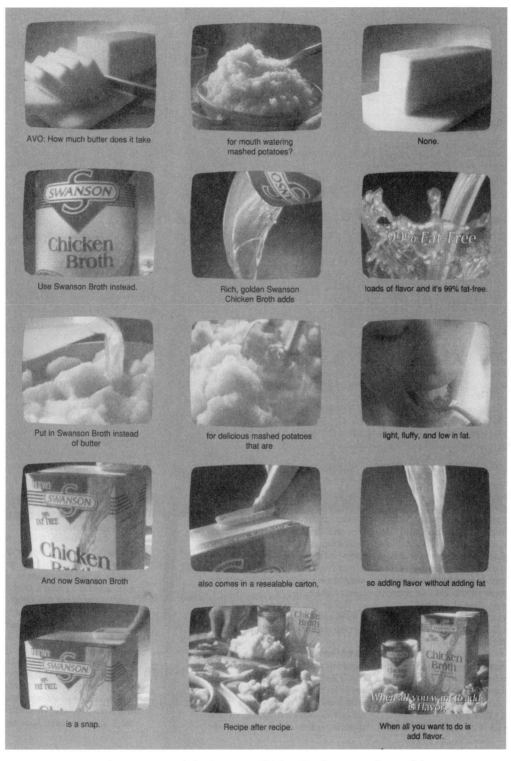

Figure 15-4: This commercial, for Swanson Chicken Broth, was a winner of the Advertising Research Foundation's David Ogilvy Research Award. According to reports from the brand, the approach resulted in a 34 percent sales increase, much of which was attributed to the advertising. Note that the commercial has no trickiness, no morphing, no dependence on effects. It is an exercise in straightforward exposition of comparative benefit.

Figure 15-5: Television has become the prime medium for political campaigns . . . and as personal attacks become vote-getters, campaign commercials become more and more offensive, in both connotations of the word. The text of this commercial: "Is Valerie Huttle qualified to be our senator? State law requires her to have lived in Bergen County for at least one year. She didn't. Last year, Huttle voted from her home in Long Beach Island. The truth? Valerie Huttle has never voted in a Bergen County general election. No wonder she told the *Bergen Record,* 'I don't know all the issues.' If Valerie Huttle can't tell the truth now, can we trust her as our senator? We need Senator Lou Kosco, a real fighter for our families." Typical of this type of attack commercial, it mentions the opponent's name four times and the attacker's name once.

mer professional wrestler known as "The Body," used television to parody his existing image. Playing off his nickname, "The Body" became Rodin's "The Thinker," abetted by toy action figures. One spot showed two children playing with action toys. One was Jesse Ventura; the other was a lobbyist attempting to buy favorable legislation. The child holding the Ventura doll had his figure emphatically reject the lobbyist. While competing candidates scoffed, the clear message took hold with Minnesota voters.

If, after 30 seconds of cogitation, you came up with "Make an offer the viewer regards as beneficial," congratulations. But you can spend an entire evening viewing various high-budget television commercials and not see even one that qualifies.

Zapping

Zapping is a television viewer's elimination of television spots by turning off the sound during a broadcast, stopping the videotape when recording a show, or fast-forwarding a prerecorded tape. The intention is simple: to avoid seeing commercials sponsors may have paid many hundreds of thousands of dollars to produce.

Zapping isn't a cry of outrage against any particular sponsor or any particular commercial. Rather, it's a reflection of boredom, of oversaturation, of annoyance with commercial clutter.

The natural conclusion of having four 15-second commercials instead of two 30-second commercials or one 60-second commercial has been a confusion of clutter. "Which car is it during this break?" has given way to "Which car commercial will follow the car commercial I'm looking at now?" Hey, there's Ford. Didn't we see a Chevy spot thirty seconds ago? Which toothpaste is this? Which detergent? Which fast-food restaurant?

The viewer, who doesn't time the spot but sees only a succession of tired situations—automobiles shrouded by smoke machines or driving on wet pavement, too-happy waitresses lecturing customers on the virtues of paper towels and detergents, athletes thinking of their residual pay as they mumble their lines endorsing all manner of items, and orgasmic dances glorifying soft drinks or perfumes.

It's zap time. Here's the latest electronic gadget to help the viewer escape the gnat pack. Ahhhh!

To avoid zapping

If you can't lick 'em, join 'em.

Stations aren't about to retreat from the 15-second income bonanza unless these clustered spots reach so low a point of effectiveness that television advertisers start retrenching. So we see a counter-minitrend: Advertisers who want to cut down zapping have begun to buy longer time periods—even old-fashioned 60-second spots—and turn them into condensed shows. The spot will open with a sports or entertainment quiz, or a news update, or a nostalgic trivia teaser. Then, with the viewer well hooked, the message pours through, like the castor oil mixed into a chocolate soda.

Isn't this an expensive alternative to zapping? You bet. Obviously, only a few advertisers can use it—one or two per station break—which means other alternatives have to be explored. Among the experiments are dynamic use of non-show-biz celebrities, electronic gimmickry, and the often self-defeating technique of using up to two-thirds of the spot to stroke and entertain the viewer, limiting actual *sell* to a quick flash.

One unhappy reality of television exposure for the smaller advertiser is the relationship between the advertiser's name recognition and spot length: The less recognizable the name, the longer the spot has to be to sell the same type of merchandise. Lower-budget advertisers, then, should look to 30-second and 60-second spots. The benefit is the greater dominance a longer spot might expect within a cluttered commercial ghetto. But look out: That word *might* puts the obligation right back onto the writer.

Can a Spokesperson Be Too Distinct or Too Vivid?

A few years ago, the creative team at the Leo Burnett advertising agency had an idea: To introduce a Pillsbury product called Crusty French Loaf, why not use an actor impersonating the late Peter Sellers as Inspector Clouseau (from the *Pink Panther* movies)?

Have you entered an automatic objection to the concept of impersonating an actor who himself is projecting an impersonation? Good for you.

The question is academic because the spot, as originally produced, never made it to the air. Why? Because research revealed a tragic flaw: The character was emphasized more than the product. In the words of Pillsbury's director of market research, as quoted in *Advertising Age*, "We determined that the commercial's ability to communicate and persuade was very good, but we needed to give the product more time. Also, we built in a little more exposure of the brand name."

When you consider celebrity or fad coattail riding, watch it! Don't fall in love with your device and don't forget the purpose of a commercial—to sell something.

Lee Iacocca, the sometime head of Chrysler, decided in the 1980s to go on camera as company spokesman. Iacocca had both a powerful personality and down-home credibility. His commercials succeeded.

By the mid-1990s, a cascade of CEOs were delivering their own commercials, with results best described as mixed. Dave Thomas, head of the fast-food chain Wendy's, achieved a sort of fatherly notoriety until the copywriters began emphasizing *him* instead of what he was selling. By the late 1990s he was reduced to the role of tired-looking bit player.

The head of an organization, whether a stock brokerage or a restaurant, has an automatic advantage: That individual can look the camera in the eye and say "I." A promise has more teeth. Just one caveat: The CEO has to have a credible personality. Many who have charisma in the boardroom look silly and ill-prepared as they recite from a TelePrompTer.

Trends in commercials shouldn't affect the approach of any writer who realizes:

1. Countertrends develop as quickly as trends.
2. Trends result in overuse of a technique.

Analysts who try to establish trends have to explain why many advertisers abandon slice-of-life advertising in favor of clinical demonstration while others begin to embrace the former technique and abandon clinical demonstration. As advertisers bite the bullet and pay their impactless celebrities for *not* appearing on camera, other advertisers seem to stand in line to sign up sports and entertainment figures to mouth on-camera messages for them. Result: For every likeable Michael Jordan, television seems to spawn a dozen Joe Mumbles. (A more complete exploration of celebrity use is in Chapter 16.)

A dangerous trend is the overproduced commercial with little impact on sales; after the fact, the company or its agency issues "Standard Explanation A-37": The commercial wasn't supposed to have any effect on sales; it was supposed to increase "awareness."

Think back, if you were actively in the marketplace in January 1985: Many thought the trend had peaked way, way back then, with a commercial for Apple's Macintosh computer showing an endless line of people in business suits singing "Hi ho, hi ho, it's off to work we go," following one another lemminglike off the edge of a cliff. This was one of two Macintosh commercials still revered in advertising classes. The other was a one-showing-only (Superbowl) spot in which a daring woman smashed an "Orwellian sameness" scenario.

Recall tests (an undependable method of judging, surely) showed that the public neither understood nor remembered the expensive Superbowl commercial. When SRI Research Center asked 300 viewers whether they recalled the spot, only 10.3 percent described the commercial correctly; 69 percent of those who said they had seen an Apple commercial said they didn't know what product was being advertised.

Apple might say: It was aimed only at the segment that is IBM-aware. The speciousness of the argument is doubled when one reexamines the commercial in this light: It neither suggested nor demonstrated a competitive benefit, and—if it really was aimed at IBM-conscious viewers—television was a hopelessly wasteful medium for this advertising message.

But anyone who thought this failure would end the trend had no grasp of the psychology of major advertisers and their agencies. Burger King, a division of Diageo (whose very corporate name seems peculiar to many), went through advertising agency after advertising agency before finally abandoning cuteness and esoteric messages and adopting a "Here's why you should eat at Burger King" posture. Oldsmobile and Saab somehow simultaneously created commercials in which an automobile became part of an oil painting. Infiniti produced some impenetrable spots. BMW concocted a spot in which the car careened down a street so awash with water that the car had to dodge oceangoing ships.

In late 1998, Home Box Office produced a peculiar and obviously expensive commercial in the Macintosh mode. The late actor George C. Scott, apparently chosen because of his role as World War II General George Patton, commanded a battalion of people dressed as germs, rising up against something or other on behalf of HBO.

A hard-boiled question, one that may seem strange to those whose primary thought is of their sample reels when they create television spots: Will this cause the phone or the cash register to ring?

Ten easy-to-write TV techniques

1. *The touchstone commercial.*

The touchstone commercial uses as a touchstone a monument, a person, or an event in which we have confidence. The American flag, the Rock of Gibraltar, the Statue of Liberty, and the Grand Canyon are examples. The viewer transfers his respect, admiration, and confidence to whatever is using the touchstone. Insurance companies use this approach constantly.

2. *The lovely payoff.*

We love romance, especially when a story turns out in a storybook way. The viewer's implicit hope that the story will turn out "right" turns the viewer to the item being sold. A version of this was a group of McDonald's commercials in which children's discomfort was eased when the parent drove into McDonald's.

3. *Benefit tied to technology.*

The claim of benefit doesn't overcome skepticism; benefit tied to technology dissolves skepticism because of our implicit trust in technology to overcome all mechanical problems.

4. *Problem solved.*

Nobody wants a portable generator; but if we can show a problem-solving situation in which the generator saves the day, we can establish buyer receptivity. So a portable generator spot, placed in hurricane-prone areas, would show how a generator keeps the refrigerator working and provides light when power is out, perhaps for days.

5. *Improvement over what was before.*

Advanced and relatively inexpensive morphing techniques make possible a clear image of the change from what was to what is. The 2001-model car morphs into the 2002 model as we watch. A man's paunch disappears. A woman's hair changes color and style. The viewer accepts the upgrade because he or she sees it happen.

6. *Lean on celebrities.*

In my opinion, this is the most crutchlike of techniques—the easiest to write because the selling message is buried inside celebrity worship, but the most dubious for effectiveness because viewers remember the celebrities and not the company responsible for their appearance on screen. (I won't ever forget a 1980s spot for defunct Western Airlines, featuring comedian Rodney Dangerfield. One commentator described the image as "a pop-eyed, semiliterate spokesperson with a too-tight collar, deserving no respect.")

7. *Nonsense.*

When all competitors in a product category seem to be the same, nonsense *might* be a way to gain exposure. A peanut butter makes the claim of being "Peanutty"; it's "made from the best peanuts in the world." A cereal has an animated tiger saying, "It's grrrrreat!" Neither has logical substance nor demonstrable product superiority. That isn't the purpose. A nonsensical spot is implicitly nonthreatening and might cause some children to lobby for a particular brand. When

Figure 15-6: Coca-Cola's animated polar bears have achieved huge popularity, but their effect on sales seems to be uncertain.

aimed at adults (what comes to mind is a long-distance service that uses dog heads on human bodies), the effect can be grotesque. (I know, I know . . . "but it's memorable.")

8. *P.O.C.B.*

The Plain Ol' Country Boy approach carried Bartles & Jaymes to a strong competitive position among the various wine coolers during the brief heyday of those drinks. The fictional Bartles & Jaymes characters (the latter character never saying anything) became folk celebrities through perfect underplaying. Motel 6 uses a P.O.C.B. voiceover to give the chain a good ol' boy image. Many local advertisers adopt this posture because the P.O.C.B. image is more likely to generate viewer rapport than a behind-the-desk authoritarian posture.

9. *Spokesperson.*

A spokesperson differs from raw celebrity use in that the spokesperson doesn't self-identify; instead, he or she discusses the product or service being sold. As mentioned earlier in this chapter, the actress Candice Bergen was for years the spokesperson for a long-distance phone carrier, basketball star Michael Jordan for another long-distance company, uneasy-looking actor John Lithgow for another, embarrassed-looking and sluggish James Garner for another, smug Dennis Miller for yet another, and actor Michael J. Fox for a soft drink. Regardless of when you might read these words, turn on your television set and certainly within half an hour you'll see spokespeople whose relationship with what they are selling is simply that they are being paid as spokespeople.

10. *Empathy.*

Spots with empathy are hard to write; successful empathetic spots reflect high professionalism. Some of the fast-food commercials solve a problem (technique 4) a segment of viewers recognize as generic to them. The result is a high degree of empathy: "I relate to that." So a spot shows a baby smearing his dinner all over the floor. The young mother isn't exasperated; she simply cleans it up quickly with a specific brand of paper towel. Effective TV empathy looks simple, but don't try to write a spot like this unless you know what you're doing, as this writer did.

Help! It's 2001 and I Can't Get Up

Mightn't we, to round out the list, add an eleventh technique—straightforward product sell, emphasizing why the viewer should buy?

We might turn the clock backward to the antediluvian days before noncommunicators seized control of the television-writing function. As the stranglehold of term throwers and effects-mad technicians begins to weaken, that eleventh category might be a factor again.

When will this happen? I once set the year 2001 as the millennium year for a lot of changes in communication. Oops. How about 2010? Is the time capsule scheduled for opening then?

Good. Let's climb in.

Chapter Sixteen

How and When to Use—and When Not to Use—Celebrities

Boorstin's Complaint

Would that more advertising agencies that lean on celebrities knew this magnificent comment by Daniel J. Boorstin (Vintage, 1992: *The Image: A Guide to Pseudo-Events in America*):

> A celebrity is someone who is well-known for his well-knownness.

A "Y'know" Habit With Legs

Much of the magical aura that seemed to surround celebrities in the 1970s through the early to mid-1990s seems to have dissipated.

The major reason for this disenchantment is the openly cold-blooded commercialism that lets the public in on an ugly nonsecret: "For Sale" signs hang around the necks of actors, former politicians, and professional athletes. Skepticism and cynicism seemed to peak when unsuccessful U.S. presidential candidate Bob Dole began appearing in television commercials (Pentax cameras). Later, Dole became a semispokesman for the impotence drug Viagra.

The comment "A celebrity is someone who is well-known for his well-knownness" has been enlarged by even more cynical shots at the celebrity syndrome:

- ▶ They ought to shoot fewer motion pictures and more actors.
- ▶ She lost the election but won the endorsement contract.
- ▶ A professional athlete is a "Y'know" habit with legs—hairy ones, probably in panty hose.

In the Age of Skepticism, even the most naive viewer knows celebrities are for sale. A young woman does well in the Olympic Games and suddenly becomes the spokesperson for products far removed from any conceivable area of her knowledge or expertise: Pay and I'll endorse your product.

Originally race-car drivers began adding patches to their garments, for Goodyear or Firestone, Autolite or Champion, Texaco or Mobilgas, STP or Wynn's, until the coveralls were themselves covered. The sponsor company trades merchandise for a greasy by-product appear-

Figure 16-1: An archetypical example of celebrities-for-hire is actor John Lithgow as spokesperson for a long-distance service. The theory of celebrity use is unchanged over the past two centuries: Trust and loyalty bleed over to whatever the celebrity is selling or recommending.

ance during television interviews or candid shots. Tennis players have begun to add patches to their shirts. Companies pay them because the television cameras pick up the patches—semifree advertising.

Is such a trade logical? On a retentive level, perhaps, because the dollar investment isn't extraordinary.

Cover Story

Chris Evert has long been a familiar name around Broward General Medical Center and the North Broward Hospital District. After all, the tennis legend was born at Broward General in 1954, and that's where she chose to deliver all three of her children. The youngest was born in 1996.

Now the District and Evert have made the association "official" with the formation of the Chris Evert Women and Children's Center, located at Broward General.

"I am pleased and excited about working with the North Broward Hospital District and Broward General," says Evert. "I am a great believer in the quality of care the hospital provides."

Christened "America's sweetheart" on the tennis circuit during the 1970s, Chris Evert has achieved worldwide recognition not only as a tennis star, but also as a devoted mother. She is a strong proponent of assisting children in need, and her Chris Evert Charities has raised millions to benefit abused and neglected children throughout Florida.

Evert will play an active role in the Women and Children's Center, specifically with programs relating to children. She will be Broward General's official spokeswoman for children's issues and will make annual appearances at and for the medical center.

The Chris Evert Women's and Children's Center will provide inpatient and outpatient diagnostic and treatment services and will also include Broward General's regional perinatal center, pediatric emergency/trauma center, pediatric intensive care unit and 50-bed pediatric unit. The new labor/delivery/recovery suites and an array of specialty services, including the Comprehensive Breast Center (featuring the ABBI breast biopsy system), will also be part of this exciting new center.

"We are delighted with this partnership. I can't think of anyone who better represents good health for women and their children."

Ruth Eldridge, regional vice president/ administration for Broward General.

Figure 16-2: Retired tennis pro Chris Evert is the "official spokeswoman for children's issues" of a medical center. Some logic pertains: She and her children all were born there. Giving a hospital some persona, when hospitals as a phylum have been under attack for overcharging and treating patients too impersonally, may be a good public relations move.

As individuals such as Wendy's Dave Thomas, the controversial hoteliere Leona Helmsley, and hundreds of car dealers have shown, a person who can afford a big advertising budget and features himself or herself in the ads becomes—voila!—a celebrity. He or she is stopped on the street and asked for autographs.

In no way is this parallel to Colonel Harlan Sanders appearing for Kentucky Fried Chicken . . . first in person, and then posthumously as a cartoon. The difference: Colonel Sanders *was* Kentucky Fried Chicken. Compare this to the disastrous Kenny Rogers Roasters, which simply used the singer's name.

The celebrity waste factor

Is hiring a celebrity, for thousands or even millions of dollars, logical? Only if the result doesn't violate the Celebrity Waste Factor: Having a celebrity move out of context is an artifice that exposes itself to the viewer or reader. A professional athlete may keep credibility while endorsing breakfast cereals or athletic equipment, but not alkaline batteries; an actress may keep credibility while endorsing fashion or beauty aids, but not machinery or automobile muffler installation.

If your analysis of potential celebrity-endorsers exposes this Waste Factor, consider scrapping the celebrity in favor of a hand-tailored personality whom you build and own—an individual whose celebrity status stems entirely from appearances in your television commercials (and in supplementary print advertising and point-of-purchase exhibits).

Figure 16-3: Do you really believe figure skater Michelle Kwan said that, unless the "challenge" was accompanied by dollars? Quotations such as this baldly typify commercial recruitment of celebrities.

An unknown can't violate the Celebrity Waste Factor. But occasionally, if your budget and exposure are heavy enough, you'll become a Dr. Frankenstein. Your unknown becomes a celebrity, begins to act like one, and kills the reason you chose that person in the first place.

If you're considering a celebrity-presenter

The Celebrity Matchup Principle will prevent some of the ridiculous misreadings of the Age of Skepticism some major advertisers have made lately. The principle: Matching your spokesperson

Figure 16-4: Rockport shoes initiated a campaign using semicelebrities (see also Figure 16-5). The relationship between its choice of celebrities and its product line isn't clear.

to what you're selling accelerates your target individuals' acceptance of what the celebrity is pitching.

Here's the copy somebody put into singer Barbara Mandrell's mouth:

> When I first put my band the Do-Rites together, we were small and our overhead seemed reasonable . . .

Okay, what was she selling? Sheet music? Uniforms? Fast food? All we see is the woman herself, no clue. Now we get the payoff:

> . . . but as we've grown, our costs seem to grow even bigger. The cost of health care has skyrocketed. It's a major concern to us all. If your business wants to provide employees the best health plan, you should consider . . .

I can't believe Barbara Mandrell knows more about group insurance than I do. Can you see the tortured copywriter with an impossible assignment? "We've signed up Barbara Mandrell. She's a country/western star. Write the ad."

This guileless reliance on a nonrelevant name is like leaning on a broken crutch: You probably have a better means of support. In no way is it parallel to the cold marketing logic of having a basketball player endorse Nike or Adidas or whichever brand of sports shoe is paying him.

Logic is out the window . . .

Some peculiar recent celebrity uses:

> ▶ comedian Bill Cosby, for almost anything
> ▶ Michael Jordan with cartoon character Tweety Pie for a phone company.

. . . And consumers are beginning to know it

Why would a viewer actually watch and respond to a celebrity-driven message? One study showed that only about a third of viewers said they watch commercials "that show their favorite celebrities." The conclusion reached by the survey's sponsors: Celebrities do *not* provide a compelling reason for paying attention.

Paying attention parallels deciding to buy in only a peripheral way. If the viewer doesn't attend the pitch, it's unlikely that a sale will result.

Celebrities tend to draw attention to themselves rather than to what they're selling. This is the fault of the copywriter, who concludes erroneously that having the celebrity "in character" is more important than sales argument. It ain't so.

An example: During its "frantic" period, Burger King hired television actor and sometime wrestler "Mr. T," who threatened the company for changing its Whopper, then tasted the revised hamburger and snarled, "Fool! I'll let you live." How far we've come from gentle Ronald McDonald. (*Advertising Age* reported that the campaign was a flop.)

Another example: A campaign (primarily on the radio) for Kronenbourg Beer starred British comedian John Cleese, known as a member of the classic Monty Python troupe. The campaign won a Clio award for Kronenbourg's advertising agency, but winning awards is only the alpha of advertising, not the omega. The campaign was abandoned in favor of a print campaign without Cleese because the radio campaign had increased awareness as planned but failed to boost sales.

Figure 16-5: Rockport chooses as one of its celebrities Rupaul, "drag superstar," in a very masculine pose. The photograph is skewed to give heavy emphasis to the shoes.

Figure 16-6: Imagine Al Capone as a celebrity. The Al Capone Collector Knife is a curious tribute to "the most notorious gangster of them all."

DRIVING LESSONS, WHARTON STYLE.

Wharton's George Day coined the term "market-driven strategy," used today by companies worldwide.

To successfully drive your business, you must be competitively focused and customer focused. It's a lesson too many people forget.

As the oldest business school in the world, Wharton has been at the frontier of finance, management, strategy and marketing. Driven by a faculty with unparalleled depth and breadth, Wharton continues to help organizations negotiate the tricky turns of our increasingly global environment.

This rich tradition of innovation is the foundation for our executive programs, which incorporate a unique blend of scholarly excellence and real-world pragmatism. These insightful, dynamic courses offer business people around the globe the opportunity to refocus and refuel.

Are you running low on new ideas to drive your business? Come to Wharton Executive Education. You'll put what you learn into action — and quickly pull away from the field.

- **Competitive Marketing Strategy**
  December 6–11, 1998 • May 23–28, 1999

- **Industrial Marketing Strategy**
  November 29–December 4, 1998 • November 28–December 3, 1999

- **Becoming Market Driven:**
  Prospering in a Newly Deregulated Environment
  December 6–11, 1998 • May 2–7, 1999

- **New Product Development and Launch**
  October 11–16, 1998 • April 11–16, 1999

Wharton
Executive Education

Aresty Institute of
Executive Education

The Wharton School
University of Pennsylvania

For a complete program catalog: **1.800.255-EXEC** ext. 2200 • 1.215.898.1776 ext. 2200
• FAX Attn: Dept. 2200 1.215.386.4304 • http://www.wharton.upenn.edu/execed

Figure 16-7: George Day isn't a celebrity as we understand the term. Nor does the setting, with a racing car, have much relevance to the prestigious Wharton School. The idea might have been to humanize an individual who is worthy of recognition within the world of finance and economics. On that level, the ad succeeds.

That is the most common danger of celebrity-driven campaigns—increasing awareness but not increasing sales.

Two-Way Cynicism

How much credibility do celebrities have? Those who market sports personalities claim a benefit anonymous presenters can't match—unquestioning loyalty from fans. If this is true, danger lurks on the two-way street of fan loyalty.

An indication of sponsor cynicism is the beer commercial in which two men appear. Realizing that their names might mean little to the typical viewer, the spot superimposes their names; below their names is this super:

Famous Ex-Basketball Players

You can see the logical gap. If they *were* famous, the super would be unnecessary. When we've dug so deeply into the celebrity barrel that we have to tell the viewer, "These people are famous," mightn't it be time to reevaluate?

Soon after a company named First Fidelity Financial Services was closed down by the state of Florida, leaving investors of $9.5 million without recourse, the president of the second-mortgage firm was sentenced to twenty five years for organized fraud and grand theft.

But investors who decided to sue, in America's litigious society, said they didn't care about the president of the company. He wasn't the reason they had put their money into his pocket. Instead, they blamed former football jock Johnny Unitas, who was advertising spokesman for First Fidelity. In radio and print, Unitas had said:

> When you're standing in a huddle with ten of the youngest, roughest players and you now have a big decision, knowing that if you call the wrong play, you'll be in a lot of trouble, you'd better make sure you have a lot of confidence in your game plan.
>
> My name is Johnny Unitas. I played football, made some key decisions, and won some important battles. I know what it's like to put your money on the line and make it count. That's where my friends at First Fidelity come in.

One of the plaintiffs commented on the ultimate irony attending so many celebrity endorsements: "He said they were his friends. He never met the people at First Fidelity until after he made the commercial."

Celebrity clutter and contagious cynicism tell the uncertain advertiser, hovering in limbo and trying to decide whether to spend money on a celebrity: Save your money.

An Unconcluded Conclusion

When a life-size sign in a supermarket attracts curious stares but no sales, when television viewers remember the pitchman and not the pitch, when a spokesperson commands a fee equivalent to a huge percentage of the whole advertising budget, when the purpose of a commercial appearance seems to be to enhance the celebrity's "This is what I'm known for" image instead of what the celebrity is selling—flashing red lights signal me: "Danger! Leave your wallet in the car!"

Figure 16-8: The relationship between venerable golfer Arnold Palmer and tires is basted together with the word "Drives." Such a combination of hucksterism and meaningless use of celebrities cannot generate a buying impulse as strong as a more dynamic offer to do business might achieve.

Figure 16-9: The ultimate celebrity is God. Michelangelo's Sistine Chapel art has been used and overused by every type of marketer from *Inc.* magazine to Walt Disney. One advantage the advertiser has: One can use God without having to deal with an agent (although many claim that mantle).

Ask yourself, when considering a celebrity-for-hire: If my target consumers were the hard-eyed jury in a court case, could I prepare evidence for this individual to recite that would convince them to find in my favor?

At the very least, don't be blinded by awe of those whom passersby ask for autographs. What will the autograph of a famous ex–basketball player be worth ten years from now, anyway?

Chapter Seventeen

HOW TO WRITE WINNING RADIO COPY

Subtlety Is Second-Best

Sneaking up on a target ignores the multiplicity of competing messages, which causes exasperation with communications that aren't instantly comprehensible and tuning out of messages that require effort to appreciate.

The First Rule of Radio Spot Writing explains this creative truism: Aggressiveness leaves a stronger residue than subtlety.

Without that residue—that spoor, leading the listener back to the message source—a radio spot hasn't succeeded. You're trying to convince, or at least educate, somebody who can't see or lay hands on what you're selling.

That in itself isn't extraordinary since whenever you sell services, your prospective customer doesn't have the comfort of being able to see or feel the end product. What *is* extraordinary is the size of the relative attention ratio fragment you can command.

Radio Words and Terms

"Look into a new gas oven." The thoughtlessness of this sentence suggests to the writer of radio commercials a logical procedure: Inspect each phrase for double meanings.

Watch out for word sounds too. The letter combination *sl* is slippery and difficult to pronounce: *Slapstick, sludge, slick, sloop*. Try *Louisiana Legislature* on your own tongue before asking some hapless announcer to spew saliva.

Pronunciations and the Big Word Syndrome

You can't make a mistake—and better yet, the announcer can't make a mistake—if you specify the pronunciation of specific words. Unless you want to risk the embarrassment of an announcer referring to *hyperbole* as HYPER-BOWL, indicate the pronunciation. You do this in capital letters within a set of parentheses, immediately after the word. Here's the way it should look:

If we told you this is the strongest rope in the world, you probably would accuse us of indulging in hyperbole (HY-PER-BUH-LEE). But . . .

I'd say you can't overuse this device. If there's any question, phoneticize the pronunciation. Resumé might be REE-ZOOM or RES-YOU-MAY. Don't count on the announcer seeing the acute accents, if they still exist after multiple retypings—or his understanding what the accent mark means. *Read* might be RED or REED. *Slough* might be SLEW or SLUFF (and this is a word you probably needn't *ever* use because so many of your listeners won't know what either pronunciation means).

Now, more to the point, relative to the hyperbolic example: What was "hyperbole" doing there in the first place? If you didn't ask this question about a radio commercial for rope, you probably used hyperbole to get your copywriting job.

Whenever you see the possibility of mispronunciation, ask yourself whether you've made the dangerous mistake of showing off your vocabulary. I'd never let a piece of radio copy out of the printer with words like *hyperbole* in the text. I wouldn't use *banal* or *insouciance*. I wouldn't use words whose pronunciation differs from their parent-word, like *technological* or *zealot*. But if you have to use questionable words, create an environment in which you won't wince. This makes sense even if you have the spot recorded and you're personally on hand when it's recorded because you'll save time.

Some local circumstances demand phoneticizing. If you were asking directions in Chicago, few would understand the question if you asked them how to get to Devon Avenue or Goethe Street, using the generally accepted pronunciations of those names. So for a radio spot aired in Chicago, you'd write:

> Two locations . . . at one-eleven East Goethe (<u>GO</u>-THEE) Street and two-twelve West Devon (DUH-<u>VONN</u>) Avenue.

If you're referring to Peru, the town in Indiana, it wouldn't be the South American PUH-ROO; it's the uniquely Indianan PEE-ROO. Chickasha, Oklahoma, isn't CHICK-A-SHAW; it's CHICK-A-SHAY.

And how do you assure yourself of the proper pronunciation of geographic locations? Call somebody who lives there, or at least the local telephone company.

Be careful when you use words with two types of spelling or two pronunciations. Examples:

> *complementary* (might also be *complimentary*)
> *herd* (might also be *heard*)
> *presence* (might also be *presents*)
> *read* (as already mentioned, might be pronounced *reed* or *red*,
>   might be interpreted as the word *red*)
> *too* (might also be *to* or *two*)

Words to avoid in radio copy

Descriptive words of more than three syllables are hard for the listener to take in. As the brain hears one word, half a dozen others pour through unheard.

Other words don't form images for the listener. Perfectly acceptable in print, they cause listener block on the radio.

When an uncommon word begins with a syllable that itself is a word—such as *in*, *an*, or *to*—the brain has to catch up as other words are spilling out. We don't have a problem with *information* because it's a common word; we might have a problem with *anachronism* because it's an uncommon word. (A stronger reason not to use *anachronism*: At least half your listeners won't know what it means even if you tell the announcer to take five seconds to pronounce it.)

Since lots of alternatives exist, why use words such as:

comprehension	facilities	portfolio
disbelieves	ill-fitting suit	reciprocate
enervate	inconsequential	repetitive
envision	innovative	tabulation

Why use words that don't sound like what they are? You have a dictionary and a thesaurus to replace words such as:

albeit	fatigued	sequence
awry	laughably	stoic
bitten	oblique	syndrome
carrion	opt	ware
equate	precept	wield
facile	ritual	wily
falter	seethe	

Some words are absolute homonyms. They present no problem in print advertising but have to be used in explanatory context for radio copy. Some examples:

beat (beet)	suite (sweet)	teem (team)
lead (led)	tale (tail)	

Avoid literary constructions the ear has to reevaluate. A straight noun-verb sequence is always safe.

Poor: "Long have we known that . . . "
Better: "We long have known that . . . "
Best: "We've known for a long time that . . . "

The Principles of Clear Radio Reception

From all these examples—and they're just a fraction of the possible snares in language use—we get the First Principle of Clear Radio Reception: Help the announcer's pronunciation and you'll help the listener's comprehension.

So what do you write? 1,001, ten-oh-one, or a thousand and one? Seeded into that last example is another radio copy must: Spell out numbers. You wouldn't write on the radio copy sheet, "This is our 22nd anniversary." You'd write: "This is our twenty-second anniversary."

If you want to be in command of the way your words sound, you wouldn't write "1001 Main Street." You'd write:

A-thousand-and-one Main Street

or

A-thousand-one Main Street

or

One-thousand-and-one Main Street

or

One-oh-oh-one Main Street

or

Ten-oh-one Main Street.

Don't leave pronunciation decisions to a producer or an announcer. You're the creator of those word sequences.

Put hyphens between digits so the announcer can read them more easily. Example:

Our bank has a capitalization of more than four-billion, three-hundred-million dollars.

Don't use ampersands or abbreviations. It isn't savings *&* loan, it's savings *and* loan. It isn't *Mt.* Olympus, it's *Mount* Olympus. It isn't *Ft.* Lauderdale, it's *Fort* Lauderdale. It isn't *1111 33rd Ct.*, it's *eleven-eleven thirty-third Court*. It isn't *$9,256*, it's *nine-thousand two-hundred and fifty-six dollars*.

This gives us the Second Principle of Clear Radio Reception: Spell out numbers, symbols, and abbreviations. The words will come out the way you want them to.

Possessives are tricky, too. A good procedure is to use *of the* instead of the possessive, for plurals. Example: "The boats' propellers" requires reinterpretation after the listener has heard the whole phrase. Better: "The propellers of the boats." (The problem doesn't exist for the singular possessive.)

It's the Way People Talk

Essay writers usually have a tough time when they try to write for radio.

They're used to changing word sequence to add color to their writing. It doesn't work for radio. An example of reversed word-sequence:

Says the typical teenager—Cap-Cola is the soft drink I love.

Aside from teenagers hating the term "teenager," starting the thought with "Says" is an out-of-sequence beginning. The listener can't absorb it as it goes but has to wait until he has the whole phrase. The second phrase, too, is inside-out because the word just before "Cap-Cola" is "teenager."

Grammar doesn't enter into it. All the writer has to remember is to write the way people talk.

Revision I, using the same phraseology:

The typical teenager says—the soft drink I love is Cap-Cola.

Revision II, getting rid of "teenager" and putting "drink" where it helps message absorption:

Young people know their soft drinks—and the one they love is Cap-Cola.

Revision III eliminates the weak phrase "soft drink" and hardens the message:

ANNC.: Here's the voice of somebody who knows.
VOICE: (TEENAGE EFFECT) I *love* Cap-Cola.

Let's try another. This construction causes no comprehension problem in print copy:

Says John Brown, of Pinehurst, North Carolina, "I use it."

When the same message is planned for radio copy, two changes help comprehension. First, we put the noun before the verb as we did with the previous example. Second, because commas don't appear in verbalisms, we replace the word "of" with "from," so listeners won't think John Brown is talking *about* Pinehurst. The copy now reads:

John Brown, from Pinehurst, North Carolina, says, "I use it."

Making an Easy Job Difficult

The radio writer's job is technically the easiest of any form of mass communication. Usually, the maximum length of a message is one minute, or about 150 words; the writer can concentrate on only one of the senses without considering appearance.

Another benefit: The negative reaction some viewers have to a television announcer's appearance doesn't apply to radio.

The challenge: The ear has to be the surrogate for the other four senses. The writer has to create an image in the mind without being able to demonstrate.

No question. But from a writer-technician's point of view, radio isn't a difficult medium to master. Maybe so many beginning writers either volunteer to write radio spots or are assigned to the job because radio requires less technical knowledge than print, on-line, or television. The result? Humor that more often than not falls flat.

If the masters of humorous radio commercials fall flat as often as they succeed, what, then, is the batting average of the beginner?

This problem is why the Second Rule of Radio Spot Writing exists:

If humor isn't directly related to what you're selling, scrap it.

The fact sheet

If you're running spots on talk shows, a little-used prop—the fact sheet—can mine gold for you. Instead of delivering a produced commercial, give the talk-show host a fact sheet about what you're selling. You enjoy two benefits:

copy for: Youth Again

description: radio commercial fact sheet, human growth hormone

POINTS TO BE MADE REGARDING HUMAN GROWTH HORMONE

1. As everybody — *everybody* — ages, the body's production of human growth hormone (known as hGH) declines. In fact, by age 30 you've typically experienced a fourteen percent decline in your production of hGH.
2. Replenishment of hGH has these possible benefits: less body fat and "love handles"; gray hair returns to its natural color; facial wrinkles begin to disappear; everyone, man or woman, has greater vitality and sexual energy; skin-age spots begin to disappear; memory and brain function get sharper.
3. I'm not making this up. One of the most distinguished medical publications, *The New England Journal of Medicine*, reported on a doctor's clinical tests. This is what the *Journal of Medicine* said: ""Within 6 months...his patients had become younger. Ten to twenty years of aging were peeled from their laboratory profiles. Their skin was thicker, muscles were bigger, age-related stomach fat was disappearing, and lost bone from the spine was restored."
4. Until now, only the very rich could afford this anti-aging miracle. It had to be by injection, at a cost of two-hundred-and-fifty to five-hundred dollars every week.
5. At last a laboratory has synthesized the formula and is making available powerful tablets that stimulate human growth hormone.
6. Don't compare hGH with aspirin or ibuproven or Aleve. It's as far beyond them as the seven-forty-seven airplane is from the Wright Brothers.
7. It isn't cheap, but it's just a fraction of what the injections would cost. A one-month supply of Pro-hGH tablets — that's one full month — is a hundred-and-twenty dollars.
8. You aren't risking one cent, because this is absolutely guaranteed. If even at the end of your first month you don't see and feel a noticeable improvement — if you aren't actually *younger* — send back the empty container for a one hundred percent refund of every cent you paid. You can't lose. You can only regain the vigor and power you had when you were younger.
9. This may be your chance to reverse the aging process ... to look and feel the way you did twenty years ago. This is the real thing. How much is getting younger worth to you?
10. The laboratory can't produce enough hGH tablets for everybody. Call Youth Again now. It's toll-free: One-eight-seven-seven ... New Youth. That's One-eight-seven-seven, six-three-nine, nine-six-eight-eight. Money back if it doesn't work for you. *[REPEAT PHONE NUMBER]*

#####

Figure 17-1: A radio advertiser may get better results from a fact sheet than from a formal script or a produced commercial. That is not only because the proposition can coattail-ride on the popularity of whoever delivers the spot, but also because some personalities, especially talk-show hosts, will allocate more than the amount of time bought. This fact sheet is for the same product described in Figures 17-2 and 17-3.

copy for: Youth Again

description: 120-second radio commercial, human growth hormone (production spot)

VOICE 1: Getting old is natural. Having your skin begin to wrinkle is natural. Adding body fat is natural. Losing strength and sexual vitality is natural. Developing age-spots is —

VOICE 2: (ECHO MIKE) Stop right there!

VOICE 1: What do you mean, "Stop"? Everything I've mentioned is the natural result of growing old.

VOICE 2: (REGULAR VOICE) That used to be true. But now everyone can enjoy the benefits of Human Growth Hormone. It's the hormone that actually reverses the aging process. Its power is confirmed in the New England Journal of Medicine.

VOICE 1: I thought Human Growth Hormone was only available from a few doctors, and only by injections.

VOICE 2: That used to be true. Now Youth Again has a Human Growth Hormone stimulating tablet. The tablets are available direct and without a prescription.

VOICE 1: Is this the real thing or a substitute?

VOICE 2: It's the real thing. This compound can peel ten to twenty years off your age, or your money back.

VOICE 1: What does it cost?

VOICE 2: These tablets are a fraction of what you'd pay a doctor for injections. A sample one month supply is a-hundred-and-twenty dollars. It's absolutely guaranteed or your money back. Typically, growth hormone declines fourteen percent each decade once you're over thirty. For the first time in history, you just might keep old age away from your door. If you're over sixty, you can feel young again. Guaranteed.

VOICE 1: How do I get to use Human Growth Hormone?

VOICE 2: Call Youth Again toll-free at one-eight-seven-seven ... New Youth. Write that down, because this may be your

Figure 17-2: Although two-minute commercials no longer are available on most television outlets, many radio stations offer them. This is the two-minute two-voice commercial for the same product described in Figures 17-1 and 17-3.

copy for: Youth Again

description: 60-second radio

Every day you're getting older. What do you have to look forward to? Wrinkles, gray hair, love handles, loss of vitality and sexual energy. Everyone ages and grows older, but now at last you can do something about it! Human Growth Hormone is the key to unlocking the door to youth. As we get older the body's production of human growth hormone, known as hGH, <u>declines</u>. Replenishing hGH has these possible benefits: Believe it or not! The respected New England Journal of Medicine reported less body fat and "love handles" ... gray hair begins to return to its natural color ... facial wrinkles and skin-age spots begin to disappear ... memory and brain function get sharper ... and you'll have greater vitality and sexual energy. The new growth hormone replenishing tablet isn't cheap but it's one hundred percent money-back guaranteed. A one-month supply of growth hormone tablets is a hundred-and-twenty dollars. That's a <u>no-risk</u> hundred-and-twenty dollars, and this is all-natural and safe, even if you're taking medications. If at the end of the first month you don't see and feel a noticeable improvement, just return the empty package for a one hundred percent refund of every cent you paid for it. Call Youth Again now, toll-free: one-eight-seven-seven, six-three-nine, nine-six-eight-eight. That's one-eight-seven-seven, six-three-nine, nine-six-eight-eight. Money back if it doesn't work for you.

#####

Figure 17-3: This is straight "continuity" for the same product described in Figures 17-1 and 17-2. Only direct tests can prove which version is the best buy.

1. The talk-show host will couch the pitch in his or her own words, capitalizing on whatever listener loyalty might exist.
2. You might get time exposure far beyond the amount of time you're paying for. It isn't unusual, especially on local stations, to buy a 60-second spot and actually get up to two minutes of airtime as the talk-show host works through the fact sheet.

You get another benefit, too: A fact sheet is considerably easier to compose than an actual commercial.

Specifics make them remember

What's wrong with this radio copy?

> ANNC.: Cars are moving at Lehmann (LAY-MAN) Motors, twenty-five-hundred Boise (BOY-ZEE) Avenue. Buicks, Oldsmobiles, Cadillacs—Lehmann has them all. Save thousands of dollars on a new Buick, Olds, or Cadillac. Isn't it time to get rid of that old clunker and move up to a beautiful new car from Lehmann Motors? There never was a better time because Lehmann is offering top trades right now! Why? Because Lehmann needs used cars, so drive in . . . then drive out in a new Lehmann car. Lehmann Motors, twenty-five-hundred Boise Avenue—where you'll find the biggest bargains in new or used cars. Open nine A.M. to nine P.M.

What's wrong? It's the same old commercial. Ten thousand car dealers could run this commercial, changing only the name and address.

In radio, even more than in print media, specifics sell; generalities don't motivate. What if Lehmann Motors had run a spot like this one?

> ANNC.: Are you driving a nineteen-ninety-eight car? Hold it! Listen carefully! If your nineteen-ninety-eight Buick Riviera is in reasonable condition, Lehmann (LAY-MAN) Motors will give you at least a fifteen-thousand-dollar trade-in on a brand-new two-thousand-and-one model Buick, Oldsmobile, or Cadillac. And how about this? If you're driving a nineteen-ninety seven Ford or Mercury, it's time to think about a new car. Your nineteen-ninety-seven Taurus or your Mercury Cougar is worth at least eight-thousand dollars on a new Oldsmobile. Whatever you're driving, stop at Lehmann to find out what it's worth in trade on a Lehmann new or used car. Lehmann Motors, twenty-five-hundred Boise (BOY-ZEE) Avenue. Open nine A.M. to nine P.M.

The difference between the two commercials is the specificity of the offer, which grabs the attention of the listener. The person who drives a 1997 or 1998 Chrysler will pay just as much attention, listening for his make and year; and it's easy to write a whole group of spots, each of which nails down a different *specific*.

How to write business-to-business radio spots

More than the business-to-consumer advertiser, the astute business-to-business advertiser constantly asks three questions:

1. What group am I trying to reach?
2. Why am I trying to reach them?
3. How will this particular message influence the individuals in the first question in order to accomplish the purpose of the second question?

For the business-to-business radio advertiser, the three questions come into sharp focus. Ads aren't running in comfortable trade publications that, by their very existence, support the excuse, "This is image advertising."

The business-to-business radio advertiser accepts as a given condition a tremendous amount of waste. Radio has come a long way in segmenting its audience, but its reach is general compared with any trade publication or even a mass business publication such as *Business Week*.

"Why are we running this spot?" The copywriter should ask this question before attacking the keyboard, during every moment the creative juices flow, and after the spot is written.

Necessarily, business-to-business radio spots do have an overtone of image. Advertisers such as temporary office staffing companies, office machine manufacturers and dealers, payroll services, and business phone systems say radio spots are a softener, making their name both recognizable and favorable when one of their sales representatives makes a call.

No argument. What this unanimity of intention tells the writer can be codified into the Mandate of Business-to-Business Radio Spot Writing: Break hard into the listener's usual apathy. Intrude on his easy-listening attitude. Grab his attention and then shake it so the listener knows what you want to sell him.

This mandate is congruent with the First Rule of Radio Spot Writing—Aggressiveness leaves a stronger residue than subtlety—so the writer needn't worry about violating one rule in order to satisfy another.

Cutting Through the Tune-Out Effect

A conversation can help cut through the tune-out effect many radio listeners develop. Drivers, especially, tune out without realizing it: Haven't you deliberately turned on the radio to hear the weather or traffic report, then realized, just as it was ending, that you tuned it out?

This spot, for Teleflora, is a light production that doesn't require a lot of concentration, but it might grab the listener who tunes out a straight-reading commercial:

SFX:	TELEPHONE RINGS
GIRL:	Hello?
GUY:	Hi, kid. Got any ideas about what I can get your sister for Valentine's Day?
GIRL:	Sure. A Bear.
GUY:	What?
GIRL:	The Cupid Bear Bouquet from Teleflora. It's a cuddly white teddy bear hugging a red heart filled with fresh flowers.
GUY:	Think she'd like that?
GIRL:	She loves the one Tom sent her.
GUY:	(ALARMED) Tom? Who's Tom?
GIRL:	(CALLS) San-dee—telephone!
(DEALER TAG)	

The spot runs twenty-five seconds, allowing five seconds for the dealer tag. Necessarily, the hard message is compressed into a single overcondensed line, but comprehensibility is immeasurably enhanced by the mild dramatic "frame."

Let Logic Prevail

Don't make an easy job difficult. A lot of radio spots fail because of overwriting. The writer shoots himself in the foot.

If you write the way people talk and sincerely try to convince the listener to buy, you can't make a major mistake in radio copywriting.

If you write production spots with complicated messages and intricate sentence construction, take off your shoe because you've increased enormously the possibility of having a bullet hole there—from your own word-gun.

Chapter Eighteen

WRITING COPY FOR THE INTERNET

The First Rule of Internet Advertising

The World Wide Web combines the persuasive capabilities of television with the one-to-one marketing benefit of telemarketing. Another part is the dynamically advertised dichotomy between those who create Web messages and the Webmasters who bring them to the screen.

Add to this the strange phenomenon that Web advertising and site maintenance consistently represent a greater expenditure than transactions from Web sites, and you see a complex medium that seems to evolve in multiple directions. (The last tabulatable year at press time, 1998, saw $2 billion spent on on-line advertising, according to Salomon Smith Barney, Inc.) More losers than winners exist. Advertiser drop-off and cutback rates are high . . . even as sites bloom, representing marketers from every country on the planet. Much of the copy is either primitive, nonmotivational, ego-driven, or pointless.

But no question about it, revenues are climbing at geometric rates. Forrester Research estimated, at the beginning of 1999, that by 2003 the Internet would represent 9.4 percent of total commerce, with computing/electronics accounting for nearly $400 billion of a total revenue of $1.33 trillion.

Other predictions for on-line sales: Health and beauty products, from $2 million in 1997 to $1.18 billion in 2002; travel, from $999 million in 1997 to $11.70 billion in 2002; groceries, from $63 million in 1997 to $3.53 billion in 2002. Valid predictions? By the time you read this, you'll be able to reach your own conclusions.

But regardless of *any* prediction, the Web parallels the media that preceded it in attracting a mix of talented and untalented communicators. Web sites flourish; Web sites fail. The medium endures, the hot 21st-century attraction for incoming copywriters.

So a surfer sees Web sites . . . by the hundreds and thousands . . . and subliminally concludes, "I can write stuff like that."

Probably.

But in this newest mass medium that is overtaking all others, rules of force-communication specific to the Web are coalescing. One overriding rule should dictate any creative approach to selling on the Net. This is the First Rule of Internet Advertising:

Stop the surfer in his or her tracks.

The ability to think in terms of salesmanship instead of technology separates the Internet marketer from the Internet advertiser. Surfers are like the waves they ride. They're here for an

> **Just to let you know ...** We're going to be doing some site maintenance here on Saturday starting at 8:00 a.m. and finishing up on Saturday afternoon. So if something looks different or you experience problems with the site, don't worry. We'll get it right by supper time.

For new Garage Sale shoppers, here's a big Garage "Howdy." My claim to fame is that I sell new stuff cheap. Dirt cheap. In fact the prices on my <u>Top 20 Products</u> of the week are always below cost and the prices on my <u>Big Deal of the Day</u> are way below dealer cost! I sell everything from boom boxes to bedspreads, toasters to computer games, kitchen gadgets to jackets. The products are brand spankin' new and many have brand names. Now, don't be a stranger. You're always welcome at my Garage. And one more thing, if you like shopping here in the Garage, please TELL YOUR FRIENDS about the deals, and how easy it is to shop from me!!

 Keep your eyes peeled for my <u>Big Deal of the Day</u> -- that's right, it changes every single day! **I guarantee that it will be a very BIG deal, in fact, the Big Deal of the Day is way below dealer cost!** A word of caution though, when the Big Deal of the Day is gone, it's as long gone as a homer knocked into orbit by Paul Molitor. By the way, it's such a good deal that I have to limit the Big Deal to 1 per customer. Of course if we do have anything left you can still order, even if they go off line.

 Or, just go on over to the <u>Top 20 Products</u> of the week to find the top products in the ol' Garage. **The prices will always be below cost and there will be new products added every week.** You never know what you'll find there. Quantities are limited. Gotta get 'em while the gettin's good, otherwise you'll be cryin' in your root beer. **IMPORTANT NOTE:** Like I said with the Big Deals, if we have any left over you can still get them even if they aren't posted (we may have to look behind some boxes or move the kids' bikes to find 'em but we'll dig 'em up for you).

 Check out <u>Andy Says</u> for a humorous look at what's happening with the Garage Sale Gang. Last week, I reported on some of the New Year's resolutions the gang here in South Branch are makin' and breakin' in **"Good Intentions Meet Stark Reality."** This week I'm gonna finish it up by tellin' you about how Happy Hooten, Jakob Billiger and the MacKenzie Brothers (among others) are doin on *their* quests for New Year's perfection. Read all about it in **New Year's Resolutions Around The Town ... Good Intentions Meet Stark Reality, Part II!** Catch this story and get caught up on all the news South Branch news right here in my **Andy Says** column -- just click on the gizmo above! <u>Ask Andy</u> is where you can find answers to your e-mails, opinions about garage salin'

Figure 18-1: This home page is copy-heavy but in sync with the heading—"New stuff, dirt cheap." Many "links" exist in the text (on screen in blue), such as "Top 20 Products" and "Big Deal of the Day" in the first paragraph. In keeping with the one-to-one image, scrolling down reveals jokes and other personal communications.

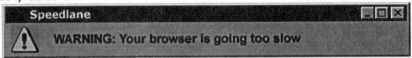

Figure 18-2: Count the banners and links on this page. Clicking on any one of them brings a home page, which itself opens a huge universe of more banners and links. (Note the ValuPage link at the bottom of the page. Clicking on this brings up Figure 18-3.)

instant and then disappear. If we fail to grab them and shake them, they are quickly gone to greener fields.

So the biggest problem an Internet advertiser faces . . . and the biggest key to successful Internet advertising . . . is the Web's elephantine size. Finding a specific site requires a cross-reference. One doesn't just stumble onto a site. In fact, we're beginning to see ads like this in trade magazines: "What good is a Web site if no one knows it's there?"

Banners attract passersby. But as few as one viewer in 2,500 clicks on a banner, and, according to *The Wall Street Journal*, a Web advertiser "could end up spending an astronomical $1,500 to recruit each new customer on-line."

The *Journal* reported on a shotgun campaign covering the entire DoubleClick network by BSC Inc., an on-line loan service: "Many of the sites turned out to be duds, generating click rates of 0.6% or less." A parallel report from research company Jupiter Communications pointed to overall falling click-through rates: Viewers click on banner ads at about a 1 percent rate.

Which means what?

Simple: It means we live on our wits, as we should in all media. It means the First Rule is inviolate. That's the copywriter's job.

Can you depend on accidental landings or directories? Some Web directories are gigantic, a thousand pages of sites. And they cover just a fraction of the millions and millions of sites. You can see the benefit of having somebody add your site to an automatic list of favorites or bookmarks so that they can call it up with one click of the mouse.

So the key to understanding the technique of copywriting for the Internet isn't knowing a batch of technical terms. It's the First Rule.

Writing in *InfoWorld*, columnist Dylan Tweney commented, "All this data has convinced a lot of industry experts that banner ads will soon be extinct, and with them, all forms of on-line advertising." Harsh words? Oh, yes. A valid prediction? Turn on your computer and look for banners.

Niche, Not Mass

The Internet has become known as a place to shop for bargains. (*The Wall Street Journal* called it a paradise for comparison shoppers.) But shoppers for discount vitamins aren't interested . . . at that moment, at least . . . in surge suppressors, the latest novel, or airline tickets unless their mind-set can be adapted, *fast*, to what seems to be a related bargain.

ValuPage sponsored by SuperMarkets Online Page 1 of 1

Help FAQ

Sunday, July 19.

To receive your coupon **savings**, rebates, samples and more, please **enter your zip code** and click on the button below.

Submit Your Zip Code

Just a few of the leading brands helping you save over $40.00 with this week's ValuPage.

Best Viewed Using

your thoughts
Tell us how we can
improve ValuPage!

© SuperMarkets Online®, Inc., 1997-1998 - All Rights Reserved
About The ValuPage Business

Figure 18-3: On-line couponing is a burgeoning marketing procedure. The shopper can choose the type of item for which he or she wants a discount. Because specials can be changed daily, on-line couponing has become a popular daily stop for many Web users.

Will the Internet replace television, radio, newspapers, direct mail, and skywriting? Hardly. Along with its advantage of multiple comparisons, the Web has the disadvantage of slowness in finding comparisons. Regarding the Internet as a mass market is a mistake. Rather, it's a colossal collection of niche markets.

An example of major marketer recognition was Procter & Gamble's decision to market Hugo Boss men's and women's fragrances through a Web site. The company explained that it would not be using its usual retail channels because, referring to the Hugo Boss lines, "their main channel is fine department stores." Apparently the move added another niche-marketing channel to existing niche-marketing channels.

ValuPage sponsored by SuperMarkets Online   Page 1 of 1

Click on the supermarket where you would like to use your ValuPage savings.

Don't see the supermarket you want?
Click here to find out why.

 This native Mediterranean marvel was used by the ancient Assyrians for medicinal purposes. Greeks and Romans used it to perfume their luxurious baths. Today it perfumes recipes the world over--Scandinavian cakes, rolls and pastries, as well as French, Spanish, and South American delights. (Today, it mostly comes from Spain.) What is the most expensive spice in the world?

your thoughts...
Tell us how we can
improve ValuPage!

Figure 18-4: Unlike coupons in newspaper freestanding inserts, on-line coupons are easily tailored to specific supermarkets. Clicking on "Winn-Dixie" brings up the screen shown in Figure 18-5.

The Internet has a mystique, just as television had fifty years ago. The medium has glamor. In the early days of television, people watched their television sets *because* they were watching television. Programming was secondary to novelty. The medium was the message.

So it is with the Internet in the early 21st-century. But a profound difference exists: The Net is heavily mired in *technology*. Television wasn't: One turned on the set and saw a picture. The surfer enters the world of cyberspace with or without computer adeptness . . . a problem? Certainly, in the antediluvian period from 1994 through 1997. By the year 2000, the main remaining obstacle was the necessity to bookmark an exact Web address.

Some Web sites get millions of hits (recorded visits to a site), and only a handful of actual buyers. Why? In my opinion, for two reasons:

1. The site makes no unique offer.
2. The site is not visitor-friendly.

Generating the thirst for business is a factor Web marketers should regard as mandatory. Instead, too many congratulate themselves based on the number of surfers who land. Please: If too many depart without having taken a positive action as the result of what they see, something is wrong with the structure of your message.

Early Web successes were primarily in computer-related products (an obvious match) and adult items (a unique medium opportunity). Publishers, too, recognized their unique position to cross-promote their sites within their own principal medium. The significance is greater for publications dependent on single-copy sales than for publications whose circulation is almost totally achieved by subscription. Obviously, this is because offering a site visit to existing subscribers is a gesture more tuned to public relations than to new circulation.

Actually, advertising a publication's site within the publication has to be done with finesse. If the subscriber feels others are getting something he or she cannot get, public relations and rapport are working in reverse.

How Do You Stop the Surfer in His or Her Tracks?

If your home page is dull and flat, forget it. If you substitute puffery and unbacked "We are the best!" claims in place of offering contagious excitement, forget it. If you use long sentences of text, forget it. In short, the Rule of Internet Ennui applies: If you state who and what you are instead of stating, quickly and dynamically, a recognizable benefit that will transform the surfer into a visitor, forget it.

Most important of all: If you use the Internet for image advertising or to transmit a generalized "A nice place to do business" or "Quality, Service, and Value" nonmessage, forget it. And I mean *forget it*. You've forgotten what medium you're in.

Avoiding this problem doesn't require a re-education. It's as easy and simple as this: Make an offer.

Being Digital, a book by Internet advocate and authority Nicholas Negroponte, claimed that by the year 2005 each of us will be spending more time poking around the Internet than watching television. By 1999, Negroponte's prediction had come true for many demographic groups. From a marketing point of view, Negroponte's prediction is less significant because being on the Net and being on the Web are not the same. Seniors, for example, spend many hours on the Net . . . in chat rooms. Pre-Generation X-ers spend many hours on the Web . . . but have little buying power.

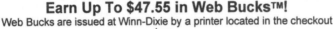

Help   FAQ   Join ValuPag E-mail   Win Free Groceries

Earn Up To $47.55 in Web Bucks™!
Web Bucks are issued at Winn-Dixie by a printer located in the checkout lane.

Below are the ValuPage savings available at Winn-Dixie. Click on the box next to the offer(s) you wish to use, then click the "Get My ValuPage" button at the bottom of the page.

When presented at Winn-Dixie, your ValuPage will produce coupons -- called Web Bucks -- from a printer located at checkout. Web Bucks are good **ON ANY ITEMS PURCHASED*** on your next trip to Winn-Dixie.

Offers For The Week Of July 13,   through July 19

Grocery Items

 ☒ Buy any 2 different boxes of **Wheaties®** Cereals (10 oz. or larger) and earn $1.50 in Web Bucks™ at Winn-Dixie

 ☒ Buy **McCormick® Lemon & Pepper** and earn $1.00 in Web Bucks™ at Winn-Dixie

 ☒ Buy one box of **Cinnamon Grahams** Cereal (10 oz. or larger) and earn $1.00 in Web Bucks™ at Winn-Dixie

 ☒ Buy any 2 different boxes of **Cheerios®** Cereals (10 oz. or larger) and earn $1.00 in Web Bucks™ at Winn-Dixie

 ☒ Buy two 12 oz. cans of **SPAM® Luncheon Meat** and earn 75¢ in Web Bucks™ at Winn-Dixie

 To help you stay Healthy, Active, & Energetic, ☒ Buy any box of **Ensure® Bars** and earn 50¢ in Web Bucks™ at Winn-Dixie

 ☒ Buy **Hellmanns® Mayonnaise** (32 oz. or larger) earn 50¢ in Web Bucks™ at Winn-Dixie

 Buy any **Ragú® Chunky Gardenstyle Pasta Sauce** ☒ (excluding Super Garlic or Tomato, Basil & Italian Cheese Pasta Sauce) and earn 50¢ in Web Bucks™ at Winn-Dixie

http://www.valupage.com/Form.pst?From=SMO&ZipCode=33317&Chain=31,Banner=1   7/19/98

Figure 18-5: This is just the first group of many on-line specials the shopper can redeem at his or her chosen retail store.

A Governor on the Throttle

Four logical conclusions can act as a governor when a copywriter assumes that the Internet parallels any previous advertising medium:

1. *Few ads are a single screen.* The viewer has to scroll down, and as new information comes into view, previous information disappears. If you assume this means you can take your time getting to the point, your thinking is inside-out. Time works against you on the Web, and *vertical* layouts—that is, layouts longer than the typical computer screen size—can result in a quick exit. A coherent screen is a logical sales weapon that seems to have eluded many early advertisers.

2. *Exploit the interactivity of the medium.* In conventional media, the customer feels powerless. If you let visitors to your site influence the buying decision, they draw a different conclusion—they're influencing the totality of the communication. Give them "What do you think about this?" easy questions . . . which also make it possible to capture their e-mail addresses.

3. *The Internet parallels phonograph recordings of forty years ago, with 78 rpm, 45 rpm, and 33 rpm.* Not all computers are tuned to pick up sound, motion, and the differentials among various browsers. Viewer comfort is a major factor. Don't let an evil Webmaster dictate electronic tricks that will either confound visitors or cause them to feel incompetent. (You know from the whole process of marketing that making a prospect feel uncomfortable also makes that prospect hate you.)

4. *"Edutainment"—a hybrid word combining "education" and "entertainment"—will cause people to return to your site.* It is easy to get a reputation for dullness: Just have one exposure of flat statistics, nonspecific descriptions, and joyless text, and you can be sure you won't be on the future hit list of anyone who has wandered by.

Generating international response

The Eurodollar and the low cost of international communication have made the Web a promising advertising medium for generating international response.

No longer do residents of other countries feel left out if text has "flavor" or "color" instead of "flavour" or "colour." They understand "different from" as well as "different to." They can translate ounces and miles to metric measurements (while U.S. residents struggle to convert).

For some products, Americanization of selling copy is a totally sound concept; for others, working within individual cultures and idioms is mandatory. The logical suggestion: On the home page, have a language selection. Yes, this means translating copy into whatever languages represent buying targets (usually Spanish, German, Japanese, and French). The major advantage isn't clarity because most who *deliberately* reach your Web site know it's U.S.-based; rather, it's the comfortable feeling that they're desired customers.

Mandatory procedures

The First Rule of Web Site Order Forms can be condensed into three words:

Make ordering easy.

We see order forms that are straight pickups from printed forms in catalogs or mailers. We see subscription renewal forms that are straight pickups from printed renewal forms.

Help   FAQ   Join ValuPage E-mail

This week at Winn-Dixie: 58 offers worth $47.55!

Get My ValuPage Now!

Click on the "Get My ValuPage" button to receive all **58** offers without further delay. If you don't want offers for baby or pet products, check the boxes that apply.

☐ No Baby Items on my ValuPage, please
☐ No Pet Items on my ValuPage, please

Edit My ValuPage

Click on the "Edit My ValuPage" button to review all the offers and select only the offers you want most.

How To Use ValuPage

1. Click on the "Get My ValuPage" button and wait for the next page to appear. The next page is your ValuPage.
2. Print ValuPage by choosing the print option from the file menu of your browser.
3. Present your printed ValuPage to the cashier at Winn-Dixie for scanning along with the items you've purchased.
4. The combination of your purchases and the scanning of the barcode on your ValuPage will prompt coupons -- called Web Bucks -- to be printed at checkout. Web Bucks are good **ON ANY ITEMS PURCHASED*** on your next trip to Winn-Dixie.

*Good on all products except as prohibited by law.

This native Mediterranean marvel was used by the ancient Assyrians for medicinal purposes. Greeks and Romans used it to perfume their luxurious baths. Today it perfumes recipes the world over--Scandinavian cakes, rolls and pastries, as well as French, Spanish, and South American delights. (Today, it mostly comes from Spain.) What is the most expensive spice in the world?

Helpful Hints About ValuPage & Web Bucks

It's a New Service and You're a Pioneer

ValuPageSM, a shopping list of money saving offers that you print off of your home/work PC and present at your local supermarket, first hit the online world in January of 1998. Every supermarket listed on the site has been approved for participation by its corporate headquarters. When you take the ValuPage shopping list to the store, the cashier must scan the bar code at the top of the page along with the products you've purchased. This will prompt coupons called Web Bucks™ to be printed at the end of your order. Web Bucks are good **ON ANY ITEMS PURCHASED*** on your next trip to Winn-Dixie.

If a cashier looks at you and your ValuPage with a bit of skepticism, please understand that it is part of his/her job to be on watch for counterfeited coupons.

http://www.valupage.com/ValuPage3.pst?From=SMO&ZipCode=33317&Chain=31,Banner=1 7/19/98

Figure 18-6: The technique of redeeming "Web Bucks" is described clearly on this page. Any computer printer can generate redeemable coupons, tying the Web and retailers as marketing partners.

ValuPage sponsored by SuperMarkets Online   Page 2 of 2

Please be patient with the cashier since you may be one of the first customers to use this new money-saving program in the store. Thank you for your support and patience -- before long, everyone will know about it!

We've put instructions and pictures on the ValuPage to help both you and the supermarket cashier do what is necessary to receive the Web Bucks.

What's a Web Buck -- It's Money at Your Supermarket

Consumer packaged goods companies have long wanted to issue coupons online, but were very reluctant to do so because coupons delivered online and printed on home PC's could be easily replicated or altered compared to the glossy, color coupons found in the newspaper. ValuPage solves this problem because it rewards you with a secure coupon (a Web Buck) only when you have actually purchased one or more of the products promoted on ValuPage. To help you feel good about this "delayed gratification," the Web Bucks you earn are good on ANY products you buy on your next visit to the store from which they were issued. Plus, Web Bucks tend to be of higher value than the coupons from the newspaper or in direct mail. And, if you've earned $5, or $10 or even $50 in Web Bucks you're free to use all of them on your next visit to the store. Think of Web Bucks as money at your local supermarket.

Tell Us About Your ValuPage Experience

As a new service nothing is more important to ValuPage than your feedback. Good or bad, happy or sad we want to hear about your ValuPage experience. Feel free to contact us at 1-888-SHOP123 or at helpdesk@supermarkets.com.

*Good on all products except as prohibited by law. Not all items carried in all stores.

your thoughts
Tell us how we can improve ValuPage!

ValuPage E-mail
Save Time AND Money, Sign Up Now!

http://207.245.142.19/dev/   7/18/98

Fig. 18-6 *Continued.*

Error 404   Page 1 of 1

HTTP Error 404

404 Not Found

The Web server cannot find the file or script you asked for. Please check the URL to ensure that the path is correct.

Please contact the server's administrator if this problem persists.

Figure 18-7: One of the drawbacks of on-line shopping is the too-common appearance of this message, after having spent considerable time trying to find a site.

So what's wrong with that? Such lengthy forms, expected and therefore unnoticeable in print, are annoying to the Web visitor whose finger is on the mouse. Make ordering easy.

That automatically brings into play the Second Rule of Web Site Order Forms:

Have an order form or "shopping basket" visible at all times.

The Giant Stepchild: E-Mail

E-mail is cheaper, faster, more controllable, and easier to target than any other medium of our time.

Subj: **MOVE YOUR BUSINESS ALONG!!!**
Date: 12/29/98 7:29:53 AM Pacific Standard Time
From: msn.com@server1.mich.com
To: lowcost1@earthlink.net

Super Low
Cost Advertising!

Do you need bulk e-mailing services?

If so, we've got some extremely good news for you. As a way of getting the word out about our new company, we are offering guaranteed reliable bulk e-mail services at rock bottom prices.

So lets cut to the chase. Here's our SUPER LOW Prices:

E-mail Your Offer to 50,000 Fresh AOL Addresses For Only $69.00!

E-mail Your Offer to 100,000 Fresh AOL Addresses For Only $89.00!

E-mail Your Offer to 200,000 Fresh AOL Addresses For Only $119.00!

E-mail Your Offer to 500,000 Fresh AOL Addresses For Only $219.00!

Best Buy Anywhere:

E-mail Your Offer to 1,000,000 Fresh AOL Addresses For Only $405.00!

We can only offer these prices for a limited time so reserve your spot right away. Mail is sent out on a first come first serve basis. Normal turnaround time is 48 hours. Our quick and reliable service is unmatched by any in the industry.

We Dare You To Compare!

Simply pick up the phone and dial...

1-423-625-8787 Ask for Ron
Anytime 5 days a Week!

Explode your business - starting today. We unlike all of our competitors take all forms of payment both credit cards and YES we even take personal checks!
All personal checks are a 3 to 5 day waiting period for check to clear.
Special Limited Offer 1 Million Emails A Week For A Month $1295.00
We Allso offer to submit your web site to over 700 search engines for $39.00

CLICK HERE FOR REMOVE

Tuesday, December 29, 1998   America Online: HGLEWIS1   Page: 1

Figure 18-8: E-mail has two huge advantages–close-to-zero cost and quick exposure–and two disadvantages–a sour image caused by misuse and inability to penetrate true identity of individuals' on-line names. Aside from using e-mail to dip a toe into on-line marketing, certainly the medium makes sense for ongoing contact with existing customers and clients.

Subj: **LOW LOW RATES, Free info!!!!**
Date: 7/17/98 5:12:35 PM Pacific Daylight Time
From: nJ5e52bvh@msn.com
Reply-to: poy31@msn.com
To: memow15@earthlink.net

Hello:

Let me ask you a question. **Are you in debt? Please go to our site, even if you are thinking about getting a home, the information that we provide is free!! Yes free!!! You will not be disappointed!!**
Think about that for a moment while I introduce our company.

We are **American Capital Mortgage Services,** we specialize
in helping homeowners establish **ONE easy LOW** monthly
payment with the added benefit of not needing any equity in your
home. American Capital is constantly working with other lenders
throughout the U.S. to provide you with the best interest rate
possible. We have a number of different companies that we work
with and this is at **NO** cost to you **EVER.** We are
simply a referral agency.

If you answered **yes** to the above question, please
read on as I am sure American Capital can save you a huge amount
of money on monthly payments as well as in taxes..

Consider This.....Did you know that:

~78% of Americans are in debt...
~$5,000.00 is the average Credit Card balance...
**~8 Million plus people will file Bankruptcy in
1998 alone...**

Are you aware that banks throughout the United States are
pressuring Congress that people in a high tax bracket can only
file Chapter 13 so that the banks have some kind of recourse.

Let me assure you these statistics are not to scare you
but rather to inform you that you may or may not be alone.

The goal of American Capital is to provide homeowners
with lenders that fit your needs. We can provide you with
lenders that will loan you up to **125%** of the value of your
home and there is **NO** equity needed.. In any case there
are **NO upfront fees or advances of ANY KIND on your part.**
What do you have to lose, why not give it a shot and see if you
can better your situation.

Utilize the loan for whatever purpose you may need:

~ A new car

Saturday, July 18, 1998   America Online: HOTSHOT949   Page: 1

Figure 18-9: A typical e-mail offer invites the individual to visit a Web site for more comprehensive information. Once there, a "cookie" may capture the name; but even if cookies aren't allowed, the very act of clicking to a site or typing in the address is an indicator of interest.

~ College tuition
~ Taxes
~ Credit Cards
~ Vacation
~ Home improvements

and the list goes on.......

You can have the cash in your pocket usually within 7-14 days. Did you also know that your loan is tax deductible?

All we simply ask for is your name, address, phone number and e-mail address. The rest is optional. This way a representative can personally call you so he or she can answer all your detailed questions.

For a **FREE** loan evaluation please,
visit our website by
CLICKING HERE
or type: **www.magicsolution.com/patb/insurance/138.html** in your browser

Thank you for your time and I know that we can help you in getting the money you deserve and in some cases need.

TO BE REMOVED FROM OUR MAIL LIST CLICK HERE NOW..

***   The mailing list for this message has
                                                                    been
                                    preprocessed by an independent service to remove
                                      the addresses of those who are not interested in
                                           unsolicited email. Free registration for this
                                         mailer-independent removal service is at
                                                  http://www.ctct.com
                                    ****

Figure 18-9 (*Continued.*)

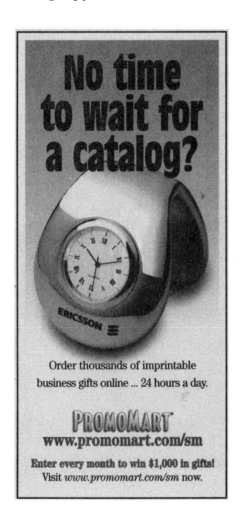

Figure 18-10: Although a Web catalog usually requires more time than printed catalogs to find and buy an item, ads such as this reflect the competitive nature of the medium.

Example of targeting ease: One can isolate specific telephone area codes, to reach only those prospects who are geographically desirable; "cookies" attach themselves to user addresses, enabling a marketer to follow up by e-mail; packaged products such as Ilux make it possible to send targeted follow-up messages to site visitors.

So, naturally, e-mail is ridiculed and attacked by advertising and marketing professionals. Some of the criticism is well justified. Unsolicited e-mail can be both obtrusive and intrusive. Even e-mail one recognizes as relevant can be overwritten, disgustingly misleading, and self-important.

These deficiencies don't eliminate the value of e-mail: It is, flat out, faster, more controllable, and easier to target than any other medium of our time.

To generate effective e-mail, the writer has to observe three key rules:

The First Rule of E-Mail: Promise benefit in the heading and justify the promise in the first two sentences.

The Second Rule of E-Mail: Once you have justified the promise and specified a quick and easy means of response, end the message. Figure 18-8 is an example of e-mail that exasperates. How is this possible, when the message is almost 100 percent either factual or fact-justifying? Oh, it's possible . . . because the message should offer links for information many recipients would regard as peripheral.

The process is exactly parallel to a direct-mail package: Elements are separated, not combined into one huge chunk of reading matter.

So we have the Third Rule of E-Mail: Give the recipient an option for additional information. Don't force-feed that information.

For an extended analysis of Web and e-mail copy, see other books by this author, *Selling on the 'Net* and *Cybertalk That Sells*, both published by NTC Contemporary Books.

Chapter Nineteen

WRITING EFFECTIVE FUND-RAISING COPY

"It Worked Then." "Yes, But It Won't Work Now."

Using the mails and media to raise funds isn't the simple, straightforward "He ain't heavy, he's my brother" or celebrity endorsement or "We need your help" that worked before the Age of Skepticism became entrenched.

The year 2001 is so far removed from the year 1971 that we might as well compare it with 1871. In the 1970s, that friendly monster, the computer, opened a Pandora's box of available donors; in the 1990s, the Internet spread the contents of that box all over the world. And the old dependable, "snail mail," delivers hundreds of millions of fund-raising messages. Yes, the last item out of the box is "Hope," but hope exists not just for us. Thousands of equally worthy causes compete for fund-raising dollars . . . from the same people. How does one survive in this brutal marketplace? Adherence to four rules gives you a strong start.

The Four Rules of Fund-Raising

The First Rule of Fund-Raising

The first of these rules states: Effective fund-raising reaches the most people who might contribute and avoids those who never would or could contribute.

Simple, isn't it? A truism, isn't it? Then tell me why so many organizations mail blindly into zip codes, on the wild assumption that a zip code gives a homogenized universe. For example, Chicago has a zip code, 60610, which includes a group of lakefront high-rise buildings with high-income people. It also includes the Cabrini Green housing project, a slum.

The arrival of the nine-digit zip code brings hope to blind zip sorting. But except for local charities, zip-sorts are undependable criteria for fund-raising effectiveness.

The Second Rule of Fund-Raising

The second rule is the fund-raising version of the "Whose Message Is It?" Rule: Operate inside the experiential background of the person you're contacting, not inside your own background.

This is the most useful of the four fund-raising rules because it's the core of contemporary copywriting.

THE OFFICES OF

Records of Sweepstakes/Disbursements Division

Please Read Official Letter Below

<u>Personal and Confidential</u>   **REGISTERED DOCUMENTS**

Herschel Lewis   DESIGNEE: Herschel Lewis
340 N. Fig Tree Ln.   SELECTED PRIZE: $3,000
Plantation, FL 33317-2561   Entry Number: #0183802
┃ıllıılIıııIlıııIllıılılılılılıılIııılılılIlıııılılıl

Dear Herschel,

    This is an official letter of notification from the Records of
Sweepstakes/Disbursements Division of National Cancer Center.

    Please accept our heartfelt warm wishes on this announcement.

    You have been identified and confirmed by the national sweepstakes
computer as eligible for a cash prize in the amount of $3,000. A certified
check in the amount of $3,000 will be cut and mailed via first class mail.
All that is required from you to receive this cash prize is to meet the three
legal requirements of this letter. The requirements are as follows:

    LEGAL REQUIREMENT NUMBER ONE: You must complete and sign **Form W-855.**
This is a necessary step so that our advisors can evaluate your entry number
and verify your standing. On or about August 10, 1998, your entry number was
assigned to you, and a pre-selected winner was chosen. Only upon receipt of
this document will we determine if you are the holder of the pre-selected
winning entry number.

    LEGAL REQUIREMENT NUMBER TWO: You must notify us on the attached
Donation/Entry Form if you intend to make a donation to help us fight cancer.
Since 1953, the National Cancer Center has been a leader in early detection
and elimination of cancer. Though great strides have been made, cancer is
still America's #2 killer, claiming another life nearly every minute of every
day! Your gift of $7 ... $10 ... even $25 would help us intensify our search
for a cure! No gift is required to win ... but every gift is greatly
appreciated. See Official Rules for complete details.

    LEGAL REQUIREMENT NUMBER THREE: You must return both the **Form W-855**
and the **Donation/Entry Form** in the envelope provided. Do not separate.
Both forms are required to be returned by the deadline of Midnight,
October 10, 1998.

    Once again, accept our heartfelt warm wishes on this announcement. We
look forward to receiving the documents and processing your entry upon your
compliance.

                                   Sincerely,

                                   Regina English
                                   Regina English
                                   Executive Director

P.S. Please note the signatory authorization of your legal identity on the
Form W-855. It is mandatory that this be signed by the winner before any
winnings can be released. Failure to return and complete the Form W-855 will
mean any and all rights you may have to the $3,000 prize will be permanently
terminated. Thank you for your prompt attention!

                                                      A 1251 34065 0287038 V01

Figure 19-1: Here we have a thoroughly professional sweepstakes offer. What might
have seemed unusual a few years ago is the sponsor: the National Cancer Center.
Disclaimer copy on the reverse side says, "This Sweepstakes may be presented in
different creative presentations by various non-profit organizations," which simply
means that like many commercial sweepstakes, it is syndicated.

The assumption that your mailing will work because your cause is worthy, you're a good fellow, and you personally are emotionally involved with a cause is a big mistake. It's a *zero-base* motivator to someone who doesn't know you. This is why a museum doesn't ask you to send a donation; it asks you to become a sustaining member of the advisory board.

It's why the mailing asking for money to fight kidney disease doesn't say, "Have a Heart"; it says, "Enter the Have-a-Heart Sweepstakes." The thrust of the message is as greed-oriented as a mailing from Publishers Clearing House (with a dollop of obfuscation, since the charity is for *liver* disease and the pitch uses *heart* repeatedly).

It's why the Audubon Society, asking for money to "achieve a clean, healthy planet that's safe for all living things," uses a sweepstakes featuring a Honda instead of a passenger pigeon.

It's why a local public television station does what television stations are supposed to do. It uses some showmanship. On the face of the envelope is this legend:

INSIDE:
YOUR TICKET
TO WIN!
LIMITED EDITION
COLLECTOR'S GIFT OFFER
INSIDE

Sure enough, inside is a card headed:

How would you like to have
this great TV in your home?

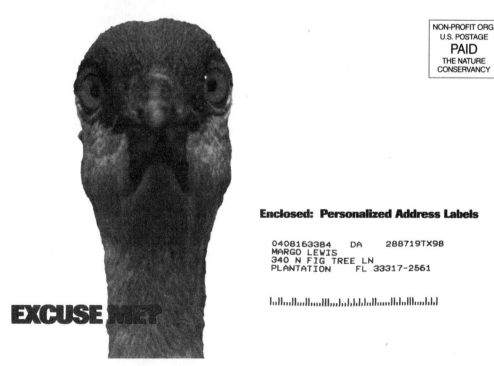

Figure 19-2: This famous envelope treatment has resulted in many thousands of contributions to The Nature Conservancy. Note the additional incentive to open the envelope—"Enclosed: Personalized Address Labels."

Fund-raising advertising and the Consistency Command

If we were grading this mailing, we'd note: The word "great" isn't the greatest, but the approach is reasonably professional except for one mistake: The writer forgot the Consistency Command, which is as critical to fund-raising impact as it is to product/service force-communication impact. Remember it? Components of an ad or mailing must reinforce and validate one another, or reader response to ALL components is lessened.

EXCUSE ME?

The Nature Conservancy®
Saving the Last Great Places

<u>Friday Morning</u>

Dear Investor,

Please let me quickly explain why I am forwarding the enclosed mailing labels to you — personalized in your name.

You see, I want to introduce you to a certain bug-eyed bird who's ogling you with undisguised bad temper.

He has a point. He's a native American sandhill crane and you may be sitting on top of one of his nesting sites.

From his point of view, every time our human species has drained, plowed or built a city on a marsh, since 1492 or so — there went the neighborhood. It's enough to make you both edgy.

So give us $10 for his nest egg, and we'll see that a nice, soggy spot — just the kind he and his mate need to fashion a nest and put an egg in — is reserved for the two of them, undisturbed, for keeps. Only $10. (Watch those cranes come in to land, just once, and you're paid back. Catches at your throat.) Then the crane can relax and so can you. A bit.

But how will we reserve that incubator with your $10? Not by campaigning or picketing or suing. Instead:

We'll just BUY the nesting ground.

That's the unique and <u>effective</u> way The Nature Conservancy goes about its business. We're as dead serious about hanging on to nature's balance as are the more visible and vocal conservation groups. But our thing is to let money do our talking.

We buy a whopping lot of land.

It all started with 60 acres of New York's Mianus River Gorge in 1955 (now

Figure 19-3: Here is the first page of a four-page letter enclosed in the envelope shown as Figure 19-2. Note the convivial, conversational tone, a copywriting technique that seems to bring far greater results than the more formal appeals of earlier times.

Apparently, by the time he or she came to the letter, the writer was gnashing teeth over the ignominy of having to use a TV set giveaway to get members for the station. One can almost see the writer *erroneously* concluding that the communication had too much Uriah Heep in it. Result? A pompous letter totally out of key with the rest of the mailing.

Here, for example, is the opening of the letter, whose "we" approach ignores the Consistency Command and drenches the "you" approach with softener:

> Excellence is a standard of measurement. It is not a title that can be won or assigned. The only way to achieve it is to earn it.

While we envision the writer emptying his basket of rhetorical frustration in this outburst, we can also see the reader, who may have been about to write a check (figuring, "What the heck, I might win a TV set"), recapping his pen with a bewildered "Huh?" (Incidentally, the word *earn* is one of the least useful words in reader motivation. It doesn't matter at whom it's aimed; it suggests work.)

It may strike you as a paradox to have to appeal to human greed to raise funds for a community program. No, it isn't a paradox at all. Greed is one of the most potent motivators of our time, regardless of subject.

The Third Rule of Fund-Raising

The third rule says: Since you're operating inside the reader's experiential background, select and shape a selling argument you think will grab his or her emotional handles.

So a mailing that begins, "144 Reasons Why You Should Support the United Way" or a public service ad headed "Your Dollars Help 17 Ways" loses me before it begins. A laundry list might have some historical or archival value, but it has the impact of a wet dishrag when it's trying to pry some dollars out of someone who ignores any message that doesn't appeal to his or her self-interest.

The Fourth Rule of Fund-Raising

The fourth rule is another adaptation of a universal communications law: Tell the reader how much to give.

A subrule, the Fund-Raising Reminder Rule, says: When writing prior donors, remind them how much they gave last time and ask for a little more.

It takes a certain amount of guts to tell the reader to contribute $25 or $100 or $1,000. I suggest we all develop our guts, or we aren't going to maximize our dollars.

On the other hand, let's not let the Fourth Rule of Fund-Raising of elbow all the others out of the appeal. A Muscular Dystrophy Association mailing comes right to a hard point, concentrating on the fourth rule while ignoring the second rule. This approach is a game of Russian roulette, in my opinion. It doesn't say, "We need your help," or "Won't you give what you can?" Flat out, it says:

> Dear Mr. Lewis:
>   Can you give $15 or more to support MDA's worldwide research effort and help achieve final victory over deadly muscle diseases?
>
>   Thanks, Jerry

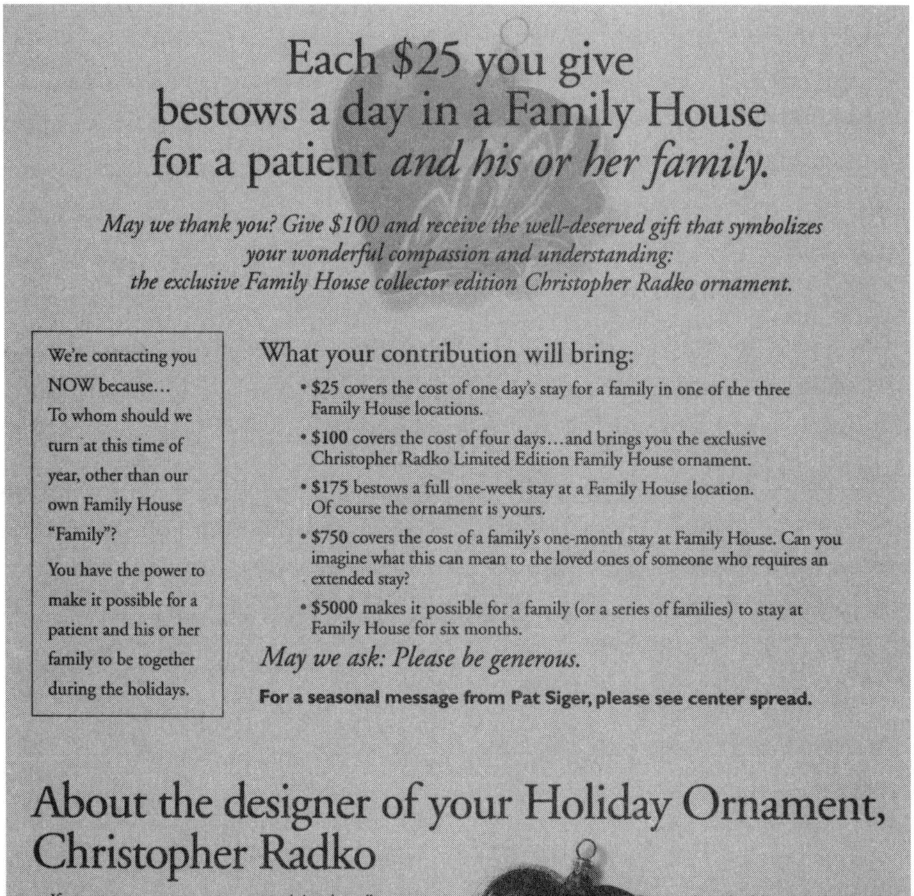

Each $25 you give bestows a day in a Family House for a patient *and his or her family.*

May we thank you? Give $100 and receive the well-deserved gift that symbolizes your wonderful compassion and understanding: the exclusive Family House collector edition Christopher Radko ornament.

We're contacting you NOW because…

To whom should we turn at this time of year, other than our own Family House "Family"?

You have the power to make it possible for a patient and his or her family to be together during the holidays.

What your contribution will bring:

- **$25** covers the cost of one day's stay for a family in one of the three Family House locations.
- **$100** covers the cost of four days…and brings you the exclusive Christopher Radko Limited Edition Family House ornament.
- **$175** bestows a full one-week stay at a Family House location. Of course the ornament is yours.
- **$750** covers the cost of a family's one-month stay at Family House. Can you imagine what this can mean to the loved ones of someone who requires an extended stay?
- **$5000** makes it possible for a family (or a series of families) to stay at Family House for six months.

May we ask: Please be generous.

For a seasonal message from Pat Siger, please see center spread.

About the designer of your Holiday Ornament, Christopher Radko

If you were to enter "Christopher Radko" as an "online" e-mail computer quest, you might be astonished at the hundreds and hundreds of entries associated with this famous designer name.

Or perhaps you wouldn't. Everyone knows the value of Christopher Radko's name on a work of collectible art.

Did you know that a Radko Collector's Club is enjoying a constant flow of new members? (Box 745, Ardsley, NY 10502).

Radko newsletters, ornament trading groups, and fan clubs are everywhere. The most exclusive gift and department stores give Radko creations special treatment. The posh Tamsen Munger Art Gallery features Christopher Radko ornaments next to fabled Fabergé eggs.

Just in case you decide to visit Radko's own Web site, the online address is: http://

www.christopherradko.com
There, you'll find new and vintage Radko ornaments. **But you won't find the exclusive 1998 Radko Family House Ornament.** You can acquire it only from Family House.

What many, including even the most enthusiastic Radko collectors, may not know is that although this artistic genius is just 37 years old, he is celebrating thirteen years of adulation as the most creative ornament designer of our time.

How did Radko decide to begin designing ornaments? As Shakespeare said, "Sweet are the uses of adversity": In 1983 he had replaced his family's rusty tree stand with a shiny new one, to hold their collection of some 2,000 hand-made, mouth-blown ornaments.

Crash!

The entire assembly — tree and fragile glass ornaments — was in pieces.

This exclusive Limited Edition Collector Ornament by famed artist/designer Christopher Radko will grace YOUR home this Holiday Season: It is yours for a contribution of $100 or more.

For the next year Christopher searched, without luck, for ornaments that might

have the delicacy and beauty of those that were lost. But he did find a craftsman who still used the traditional mouth-blown technique. Christopher sketched ornaments and the glass-blower made them.

But Christopher Radko never was able to deliver those first ornaments to his family. Friends and acquaintances quickly bought them all. Thus was born, literally, an industry which now represents many millions of dollars…and a reputation without peer in the world of design. This year's Radko ornaments are priced up to $100 at famous stores such as Bloomingdale's, Marshall Field, Neiman Marcus, and Saks Fifth Avenue.

Your Christopher Radko ornament is more than a symbol of your own great heart. It is a collector's treasure, destined to become a significant part of your personal estate.

Figure 19-4: Fund-raising is competitive. Recognizing that fact, many not-for-profit organizations spice their appeals with the offer of a gift.

Well, he certainly told me how much to give. Yes, he followed the Fourth Rule of Fund-Raising, but what about the second one? He ignores my experiential background, and the rules work only in combination.

Look at the difference between this approach and the Muscular Dystrophy Association's annual telethon. That event is about 80 percent aimed at our experiential background because about 80 percent of it is entertainment-oriented. The demand is integrated into a palatable mixture.

Might it be that a misguided list broker said, in renting my name to the association, "This is a list of knee-jerk donors who will give to anything. You don't have to waste pieces of paper for why-to-give arguments"? Might it be that the association drew too broad a distinction between the mass appeal of television and the selective appeal of direct mail? Whatever the rationale, it's faulty.

Another fund-raising organization includes in its mailing for a project called "Women in Development Campaign" a response device whose approach is as baldly direct as the muscular dystrophy mailing: "$150" is circled, with the words "Please consider a gift of this amount."

In my opinion, the only circumstance in which a fund-raiser can unwrap the heavy cannons and aim them openly, asking for money without justifying the demand, is when that demand is congruent with the first rule—when the organization is writing to its own in-group of captive donors.

So, those are the Four Rules of Fund-Raising, with subrules to grip an appeal and hold it in the center of the track.

Don't Get Pedantic

"Emotion over intellect" not only is just as valid for fund-raising copy as it is for other types of advertising, it's critical because showing benefit to donors isn't automatic . . . as it might be when you're advertising an automobile or a weight-loss program or a beauty aid.

Just as a quick test, if your letters use "pass away" instead of "die," and "We need your aid" instead of "You have to help us," and "Combat kidney disease" instead of "Fight kidney disease," and "Did you overlook our previous mailing?" instead of "Did you let Jimmy down?" you'd better warm up your prose because you're firing blanks. The words make noise, but they don't hit anybody. ("Anybody," not *anyone*, while we're on that subject. Why? Because *anybody* is a more emotion-laden word than *anyone*, and we might as well practice. The same principle applies to *somebody* and *someone*, and, yes, it's so mild a difference that about half the time *anyone* and *someone* are preferable, depending on how high up the emotional tree you're aiming.)

Statistics Don't Sell

The American Cancer Society sent out a mailing that said:

> The facts about cancer are startling. One cancer-related death every 78 seconds. Nearly 1,100 deaths a day from cancer. As the second leading cause of death in this country, cancer will touch the lives of 1 person in every 4.

Is this copy good or bad? My personal opinion: neither. It's terrible. Before you start throwing tomatoes at me, ask yourself: How much impact is there to the word "touch"? What if, instead of writing "cancer will touch the lives of 1 person in every 4," this copy changed one word: "If yours is the average family, cancer will try to snuff out the life of one of you"?

All right, that's a minor change. We've added a little emotion to the mix. We haven't attacked the bigger problem of using statistics instead of examples.

I didn't say this was bad; I said it was terrible, and I'll justify my outrageous opinion with one clear sentence—three little words that form the Rule of Statistical Failure: Statistics don't sell.

It's a puzzlement. You can't put together a sweepstakes because your board would never stand for it, and you don't have the budget for it, and anyway, a sweepstakes is a genuine 100 percent headache. Now here's this chap telling you not to use statistics either, and statistics always have been a safe and true crutch. So what can you do?

I offer this option: Replace your statistics with episodes and victims, and your mailings will come to life. If you use broadcast media, the comparative impact isn't even measurable.

Figure 19-5: When a publication agrees to make a page available to a not-for-profit organization, a hard-hitting "ad" competes with commercial offers. Here we have a "stopper," although the call to action isn't a contribution but rather a toll-free number "for information."

One easy example: Instead of saying, "Nearly 1,110 deaths a day from cancer," we say something like this:

> We lost Tommy today. All the love his little brother gave him, all the prayers his father said for him, all the tears his mother tried to wipe away so he wouldn't see them, and all the determination of a dedicated medical staff—none of these helped Tommy. We lost him.
>
> But we might save Mary Lou. She's a scrapper at the age of eight, and . . .

I offer for your consideration the Rule of Bulk Negation: Bulk doesn't create an emotional reaction. Episode does.

With this rule in mind, I rejected a fund-raising plea that concluded, "We have so many millions of tiny lives to save." "Millions" is too many. It's a depersonalized number, changing the challenge to a mob scene.

I rejected, too, a plea to "expand upon the 164,036 acres already rescued. . . ." They have lots of acres; they don't need me. This validates the Rule of Claimed Fund-Raising Success: Claiming success works if you credit that success to the prior donors you're contacting; it's a turnoff in contacts with those with whom you have no previous connection.

Fact is the cornerstone, but cornerstones don't sell houses; emotional appeals do. If you still think the typical citizen is altruistic and has a genuine compassion for his fellow beings, you won't agree with me that the letter that begins this way, although flawed, is better than a statistical opening:

> A lady should never get this dirty, she said.
>
> She stood there with a quiet, proud dignity. She was *incomparably* dirty—her face and hands smeared, her clothes torn and soiled. The lady was 11.
>
> My brothers are hungry, she said. The two little boys she hugged protectively were 8 and 9. . . .

This letter emphasizes *victims* and *episodes*. I opine it's infinitely superior to the letter we dissected before it. Cold-bloodedly, let's define *superior* as "having more pulling power," but don't you agree it has more poetry, too? (I said it was flawed: The word "lady" has a patronizing, down-the-nose overtone that could infect the reader's attitude toward the seriousness of the little girl's situation.)

We see more and more dependence on *victims* rather than *statistics* in space ads. Victims are superior to statistics, if they're shown with verisimilitude and clarity. An example is an ad showing a small girl with the legend, "Marta goes to bed hungry every night."

But this is where verisimilitude has to enter the mix. The photograph of Marta shows us a winsome child—but one not particularly hungry-looking. Emotion outpulls intellect, so with the pictures that have to be available, why not use one that adds visual impact to the words?

The opening sentence of the ad's copy is thin:

> When Marta goes to bed hungry, there's not much hope she can forget all the bad things that have happened to her.

The ad never does tell us what those "bad things" are. Why not have some copy with power: "What did *you* have for dinner last night? Marta had a handful of cold rice and some water."

Figure 19-6: The ad appeared in a publication circulated to advertising professionals. Asking for an organ donation is a tricky request that too easily can degenerate into a maudlin or gory tone. This appeal handles the matter with dignity yet retains an emotional overtone.

One of our best-known fund-raisers mailed me a computer letter illustrated with a picture of a little boy. The opening of the letter:

> Dear Mr. Lewis:
>   This little boy is lucky. Your Red Cross got there in time.

At the risk of attacking God and motherhood, I'll offer another iconoclastic opinion, congruent with the Rule of Claimed Fund-Raising Success: This letter would have been stronger if we showed a little boy who *wasn't* lucky instead of a little boy who was. One of the great motivators is guilt, and I don't feel guilty over a lucky child.

I mentioned *episodes* along with *victims*. For some organizations, such as libraries, victims are hard to find. But episodes are universal and have power potential. Here's a sample, not from a library but from a U.S.O.:

> It's Saturday night—late.
>   Normally I wouldn't sit composing a letter at this hour. I'd be watching TV, or sleeping the happy sleep of someone who knows he doesn't have to get up early Sunday morning. But tonight, I have to write this letter. I have to.

Can't you feel the sincerity? Whatever follows is true because we accept the opening—an episode—as true. You can see why a properly constructed episode works: It personalizes the communication, establishes rapport through the ring of truth, and involves the reader.

"It's Important Because I Say It Is"

Ah, you say, but my particular venture doesn't fit that mold. I'm not lucky enough to be involved with a war or a famine or a loathsome disease or even a U.S.O. All I have to work with is a library or a museum or a college. Does this rule of reader involvement apply to me, too?

You bet it does. In fact, if you're an institution dedicated to education or culture, it's more dangerous for you to position yourself above the reader's orbit than it is for a fund-raiser who has a war or a famine or a loathsome disease as his *raison d'etre*.

Here's why: No matter how poorly a fund-raising campaign represents a highly emotional issue, that campaign will gather in some dollars. Some people will respond because they have a Pavlov's dog reaction to crippled or starving children. But the library or the college or the museum isn't on the emotional main line.

I needn't tell you how difficult it is to raise money from people who already have a tie to you—college alumni, those with library cards, or people who have signed the register in the museum. If getting them to respond is such a Herculean labor, what chance do we have with outsiders?

In my opinion, if we approach them with ads such as this one, which ran as a full page in a consumer magazine, the answer is *none*:

First, the headline:

> Society is changing . . . and so are museums.

Suppose you're in this field. If you don't greet this nonsense with a yawn, then you're as far away from contemporary society as the writer of this headline was. What about this headline forces the reader to stop and say, "I'd better read this"?

I'm quite convinced that any reader of this book can think of a better headline in thirty seconds, even if it's only a thin holding action such as "How long has it been since you've been in a museum?" or "Ben Franklin would be stunned!" You wouldn't put the reader to sleep the way this writer did—I hope.

These are the first three of the five paragraphs of copy in the ad:

> Museums are no longer musty, dusty corridors filled to the brim with odd curiosities. Today, they are open, lively places attracting over 500 million visitors each year.

> Museums provide a context for understanding the present and anticipating the future—an increasingly important responsibility in our world of enormous and accelerating change.

> In 1982 the American Association of Museums assembled a blue-ribbon commission of distinguished museum directors, trustees and foundation and business leaders to examine the place of museums in our changing society. Over three years the Commission on Museums for a New Century engaged thousands of museum professionals, futurists, educators, businessmen, civic leaders, scientists, supporters of the arts and humanities and members of the general public in activities that focus on the role of the museum in society.

The coupon in the ad asked for $17.95 plus $1.50 postage for a book titled *Museums for a New Century.* I want to know: Why should I buy and read this book? Certainly I wouldn't buy it for the nonreason this group gives me:

> The report is a blueprint for the future of our nation's museums—complete with recommendations, an assessment of the issues, concerns, achievements and aspirations for American museums and examples of innovative and successful museum programs.

This "It's important because I say it is" copy—in a *consumer* magazine! As a communication to museum donors, it has logic. As a communication to the world at large, it doesn't.

In mitigation: This isn't the worst use of space for fund-raising I've ever seen; it just happened to be one that infuriated me at the moment, and I clipped it out.

I really hope you're infuriated, too, at the decision so many fund-raisers make, a decision that costs literally billions of dollars in gifts and donations that don't come in because the person who reads the mail or sees the notice in the paper or reads a slick ad in a magazine or gets e-mail or watches a television spot is left outside the orbit.

That decision is: "This is important because I say it is. If you question my decision, you don't deserve to give us money."

Some Yardsticks for Fund-Raising Copy Length

Does long copy outpull short copy? Maybe. Results of copy tests point in both directions.

One preconceived notion we can't budge: Copy length has a specified maximum in broadcast media, a logical maximum in print media, a "short attention span" maximum on the Web, and no maximum in direct mail.

Long copy seems to work best for religion, politics, and other areas in which prejudice can be polarized.

Short copy seems to work just as well for education, health, welfare, and culture—areas in which the writer needn't build a massive head of steam. If short copy works just as well, it actually works better because its production costs are lower.

Let's form the Rule of Fund-Raising Copy Length: The need for long copy is tied to the need to feed an implicit or expressed reader prejudice or belief.

A dangerous rule and a fluid one! I offer an opinion—and it's only an opinion, which is why you won't see it as a rule: If you don't know who your target is, write your message without paying attention to length. If it still is long after you've trimmed the fat, if it still is long, leave it alone. Obviously this can't apply to computer letters with predetermined length or to short broadcast spots.

For fund-raising mailings, do you need a descriptive brochure? The answer is tied to letter length. Results of tests seem to indicate that if you need a long letter, you also need a descriptive brochure. In practice, it means that if the reader knows who you are, a brochure won't justify its cost in increased contributions; if the reader doesn't know who you are, the brochure helps establish credentials, integrity of purpose, and correlation to the reader's own philosophy.

How to Reach Outsiders

Some fund-raisers just go through the motions. They depend on a couple of big donors to keep the enterprise afloat, and everyone else is the victim of the fund-raiser's overblown dignity. Why send that mail? Why pay for typesetting an ad? Why spend money on a videotape session? The Second Rule of Fund-Raising is clear and invariable. Remember it? It's the rule that says: To reach an outsider, you have to communicate on his level of experience, not your own.

Ignoring that rule or being unprepared to implement it when you contact outsiders will cost you plenty, as it has cost thousands of fund-raisers billions of dollars.

I think some of the problem stems from technology. A printer calls on us. He has a novel way of computer-personalizing a communication, and we fall for it. So we become one of 4,000 organizations mailing a stack of fifty address labels or a cold-blooded unjustified invoice to unwitting recipients.

We've joined the depersonalization movement. Instead of being an oasis, in an era when so many copywriters downgrade the people they're approaching to zip codes and digits, we're absorbed into the ghastly trend. We say to the reader: "We don't know who you are. We don't care who you are. We don't know what you want or like. We don't care what you want or like. This is our address. Send us money." Sometimes we don't even say, "Please." Then we wonder why our mailings pull so miserably.

Ask yourself: If a store sent you a commercial mailing with no more motivation than "Can you give $15 or more" in it, would you order whatever they're selling?

The Two Magic Words

Of the five great motivators (fear, exclusivity, guilt, greed, and need for approval) exclusivity is the easiest to use because we know that during the Age of Skepticism—which may last for another decade or more, or even forever—the two magic words *Only you* still work.

Remember the basis for this? I care about me, not you. If you want my money, what's in it for me?

That's why a mailing from the American Film Institute starts off in a classic way. I open the envelope, and the first piece I see is a formal-looking card with an ornate border:

> OFFICIAL
> Membership Nomination Certificate
> The Board of Trustees hereby certify that
> H.G. Lewis
> has been nominated to participate as a
> National Member
> of
> The American Film Institute
> entitled to all privileges and recognitions
> of membership.

I overlook the British use of words, laughable for the American Film Institute: "The Board *certify*" instead of *certifies*.

I also have a "Dear Member-Elect" letter from Francis Ford Coppola, and the letter's third paragraph invites me to join a "very select number of people." Right on target for exclusivity.

But now we have to be careful. To combine exclusivity with heavy selling in the same document is not only an art, in most cases it's a mistake. And that's exactly what has happened here. On the last page of this letter—page 8, by the way, which in my opinion is far too long for an invitation letter to run—I read:

> . . . but when you remember, you'll also get a full year's subscription to *American Film*—10 colorful and informative issues—as well as many additional member benefits—all for *25% off* the regular member dues of $20—*a full year of AFI membership for only $15.*
>
> . . . then you have the best reason yet to accept your nomination for membership. All you need do is send in your Membership Acceptance Form to begin enjoying *American Film* and the other benefits of membership.

See what they're doing? They're *pitching* me. They've gone over the edge. I don't believe them anymore because if this were really an exclusive invitation, they wouldn't spit saliva all over the page to get my $15. They've lost credibility, and it's just another fund-raising letter. I no longer feel specially chosen.

The Copywriter's Insurance Policy

As postal rates climb, as printing costs skyrocket, and as public apathy enshrouds us, adherence to the rules of logical force-communication is our insurance policy.

If we reach the most people who might contribute and avoid those who never would or could contribute; if we operate inside the experiential background of the people we're contacting, not ourselves; if we increase impact by emphasizing one or two key arguments and subordinating the rest; if we tell the reader how much to give—we have the "accident" portion of our policy.

The "life" portion of our policy comes from adherence to the Consistency Command (Components of a mailing must reinforce and validate one another, or reader response to ALL components is lessened) for our ads and mailings, and the use of one of the five great motivators—fear, exclusivity, guilt, greed, and need for approval—for any medium, whether mail, print, or broadcast.

One other portion of our policy, "endowment," we inherit because we've included the three magic ingredients in our selling mix–verisimilitude, clarity, and benefit—and we've coated them with emotional terms, not intellectual terms.

Does it bother you to codify rules and procedures for fund-raising? If it does, think how bothered you'd be if the rules and procedures didn't exist and every mailing, every space ad, every broadcast appeal were a new game of Russian roulette.

Chapter Twenty

WRITING FOR SPECIAL-INTEREST GROUPS

The Key: The "Whose Message Is It?" Rule

The key to success in writing for special-interest targets—children, senior citizens, disabled persons, ethnic groups—is the "Whose Message Is It?" Rule. Remember the rule? (Your message should operate within the experiential background of the message recipient, not within your own experiential background.)

You might think: If my experiential background is exactly like that of those for whom I'm writing, I can't miss. Not so. The difference between sharing a background and using it to sell is in the communicative power you can muster.

It's common today for advertising agencies to have separate creative staffs for Hispanic and black consumers. Some agencies specialize in just one area, and a client (such as a beer or soft drink company, an automobile manufacturer, or a packaged goods processor) may split the account, assigning marketing segments to specialists.

Buying patterns aren't profoundly different. Language use aside, ethnic differences are a smaller creative problem than the differences attending target groups whose product choice differs. Let's take a look.

Writing for Children

The television writer usually has creative license not granted to writers for print media; but that license is loaded with restrictions when one writes for children.

In recent years, as the entire world of communication has become hypersensitive to nuances, advertising that might be aimed at children, or even seen by them, has come under tighter scrutiny. For example, Camel cigarettes withdrew its popular Joe Camel campaign after numerous parent and watchdog groups complained that the Joe Camel image appealed to children, regardless of its direct aim at adult smokers.

The Writing for Children Rule is simple and absolute: Don't exaggerate, either in picture or in verbiage.

Where the simplicity gets complicated is in the interpretation of the word "exaggerate." For example, the Franklin Mint ran some television spots for a coin continuity program. In the spots was the line, "Each month we'll send you two issues, each only $13.95, a price that covers it all—reference materials, mint-fresh coins, cachets, stamp, foreign postmark, and all customs charges."

Figure 20-1: How does a cruise ship say, "Children welcome"? A big cartoon of "Tweetie Pie" transmits the message instantly . . . and more effectively than "Bring the kids" could accomplish.

No one objected until the spot ran in a children's program. Then the complaints came in thick and fast. Why?

The Children's Advertising Review Unit of the Council of Better Business Bureau's National Advertising Division objects to what it calls "minimization." In this case, the offending word was "only." The logic: This word blurs the cost and makes the ad an exaggeration in that it fails to convey the true cost to children.

In advertising aimed at any other group, the word *only* is an accepted bit of mild puffery, about as dangerous as *at last* or *new and improved*. But watchdog groups abound in the children's advertising arena, and effectiveness has to come from child actors seeming to have a good time, not from puff words.

The Franklin Mint said the ad wasn't aimed at children (although the spot did run at a time dedicated to children's programming) and agreed to avoid scheduling the spot during children's programs.

Figure 20-2: The products advertised aren't for children. The premiums are. The obvious intention is to gain a competitive edge by inducing the parent to choose these household items.

In this instance, the spot could survive by changing the time period. But what about those spots for toys?

Hasbro's Milton Bradley division made a commercial for its WWF Wrestling Superstars Game. Interspersed with shots of the game were scenes of live wrestling—actual matches in which the contestants were "executing kicks, throws, holds, and punches." Hasbro told the Children's Advertising Review Unit that the footage was a depiction of children's fantasies while they were playing the Wrestling Superstars Game.

A logical explanation? The Children's Advertising Review Unit didn't think so, and Hasbro agreed to change the spot.

A television spot that used a wide-angle lens to exaggerate the apparent size of a toy was denied airtime, as was a spot that suggested self-movement in a toy whose motion had to come from the owner's hand.

Disclosure copy

You can see the challenge in writing television ads for children: Generate a fantasy without having it "pay off" visually. Or tell the media department to keep the spot out of child-dedicated viewing time. Or use media other than television. (As of this writing, on-line advertising is practically unregulated, and children swarm onto the Web.)

In regulated media, an advertiser usually can avoid a challenge by including disclosure copy. Television spots use audio only for this copy, which satisfies regulatory situations while de-emphasizing the point.

Cynical? Some of the rules themselves are cynical. For the writer, embarrassment comes not so much from having copy challenged but from having to reshoot a commercial.

So stringent is the rein on overdemonstration that Coleco was called to task by the National Advertising Division for television spots advertising its "Sentaurs" action figures. The Children's Advertising Review Unit questioned whether the figures, manipulated by a child, could perform all the movements shown on the screen.

Then, after testing, the unit decided most—but not all—the movements could be duplicated by children. Coleco agreed to add disclosure copy to cover this suggested discrepancy as well as lack of information about purchase requirements.

Matchbox Toys also agreed to add disclosure copy to cover its failure to mention whether its Robotech figures were sold together or separately.

The plastic years: ages two to six

Researchers tell us that by age six a child has solidified many of the "buying" habits that will last a lifetime. Messages imprinted during the plastic period—ages two to six—can be hard to overcome later. So not only do marketers have their best shot between these ages; it's when the most protection against chicanery is necessary.

If you're trying to plant a seed, don't just keep your message uncomplicated. Keep your product name uncomplicated. Children have a hard time remembering product names that have three or more words. One-syllable product names are best; two syllables are fine. More than two words put you in peril, even if what you're selling is infinitely superior to the competition.

This explains the success of Cheerios cereal, instantly mnemonic to children. A cereal with a name such as Super Bran Crunchy Flakes would have too many words and too generic an image to ignite a child's desire; it couldn't compete with Tony the Tiger, who sells cereal based on his image rather than on the benefits of the cereal. Awareness of words and image helps explain the delight children take in being able to ask for Smurfs.

What's in a name? If it's the name of something aimed at toddlers, don't put too many words or syllables in it, or you'll lose them.

Writing for Senior Citizens

Whatever euphemisms we use, senior citizens are the elderly. They're a huge buyer group, the fastest-growing buyer group, and if we want to sell them something, we can benefit from our knowledge of some of the common denominators of this group. Generally, compared with younger age groups, they are:

- ▶ less flexible in attitude
- ▶ more loyal to brands and procedures with which they've become comfortable (because they're less flexible)
- ▶ less willing to change just because you tell them to change
- ▶ more skeptical and sensitive to being patronized
- ▶ more impatient

Knowing these traits, you as a writer can exploit them. Four of your procedures are mechanical:

1. no sentences longer than twenty words, and never two consecutive sentences longer than fifteen words
2. no paragraphs longer than seven lines
3. no more than 200 syllables per 100 words
4. no type smaller than 10-point (if you're writing for print), no more than 100 words per minute (if you're writing for broadcast), and no more than seven paragraphs with a maximum of seven lines per paragraph (if you're writing an e-mail message)

Eight creative procedures tend to work:

1. Instead of shouting "New!" tie newness to an established base—an improvement that does not discard the security of something they recognize.
2. "Bargain!" is an exceptionally valid sales argument to those whose incomes have peaked or declined or who are on a fixed income.

When It Comes to Health-Care Coverage for Your Medicare Years...

AARP Wants You to Know You Have Choices.

Figure 20-3: The American Association of Retired Persons dedicates itself 100 percent to the 50-plus age group. So its health care coverage specifies a situation unique to that group. ("When It comes to" is a mildly clichéd opening.)

3. Don't be overly familiar or convivial. Keep your dignity, and let the readers or listeners know you respect theirs.
4. Stress ease of acquisition, ease of operation, ease of results.
5. Recapitulate your key selling argument, for clarity as well as emphasis.
6. Peer-group testimonials help dispel skepticism.
7. Refer to age in positive terms. It's "But you must be at least sixty" or "Sixty years or over," not "Sixty years or older."
8. Never suggest you're compromising the individual's independence or ability to care for himself or herself unless you have a specialty product designed to enhance the ability to be self-reliant.

That's the tightrope we walk when writing for this group, which has enormous buying power and political power.

Every one of the Fifteen Ways to Thwart the Age of Skepticism, listed in Chapter 26, applies to writing for senior citizens. Take a look. (One of the author's earlier books, *Silver Linings*, deals entirely with the creative and mechanical aspects of marketing to seniors.)

Writing to Disabled Persons

Don't use the word *disabled* as a noun. Use it as an adjective and it seems less harsh. So you won't write "the disabled," you'll write "people who are disabled" or "disabled people." You won't write "the deaf," you'll write "those who are deaf." You won't write "the arthritic," you'll write "people with arthritis."

Or you might use the current buzzword for negative conditions, *challenged*. Example, for those with poor eyesight: "People who are visually challenged."

Don't use words that might be misinterpreted; this group is far more sensitive than others, and copy should never have phrases such as "victim of" or "afflicted with." Never use "deaf and dumb" or "diseased" or "confined to a wheelchair." If you're referring to someone who has multiple sclerosis, don't be afraid to write, "a person who has multiple sclerosis." (Incidentally, use "deaf" only when an individual is totally deaf. Otherwise it's "hearing impaired" or someone "with a partial hearing loss.")

And don't patronize. It's easy, so easy, to start writing "You're a hero" copy. Disabled people want reality, not fantasy. So don't write copy that reads as though you're afraid to acknowledge reality.

We're discussing writing *to* this group, not writing *about* this group. If we're creating fundraising copy, these rules don't apply because we're after a different target group altogether. (See Chapter 19.)

Advertising to Ethnic Groups

A single rule applies when advertising to ethnic groups; The Ethic Rule advises: Keep your dignity.

This means writing in conventional English, not slang. Even if you hire a member of the group at whom you aim your message, as test reader or even as writer, you run the horrible risk: The reader may think you're being patronizing. The risk doesn't exist if you write as you would for any mass medium.

Figure 20-4: Ethnic advertising has become a major factor as Hispanics and African-Americans have become the fastest-growing discrete consumer groups. Aimed at the advertising community, this ad points out that Hispanics, as a percentage of the U.S. population, grew from 7 percent to 11 percent between 1985 and 1998.

If the ad is to be translated into another language, you lose some control. Certainly you should have at least two outsiders read the translated copy; they never should read it together and you always should consider changing any copy they both question.

Some advertisers who make regular forays into foreign-language media use language-school teachers as their bellwethers; some use employees of foreign embassies, who are more likely to be conversant with current usage, and some leave the whole job to the media, all of whom offer a translation service from copy written in English.

If you're a careful writer, you want your translated copy examined twice: once when it's re-typed, for usage; and again when it's typeset, for typos.

Most advertisers try to reshoot posed photographs, using individuals representative of their target group. The setting should be logical and not jarring, but the original Ethic Rule applies: Keep your dignity.

A suggestion: If you have the opportunity, test your original mass-media photograph against an ethnic-slanted photograph. You just might have a surprise because a deliberately aimed photograph can generate a "Who the hell do you think you are?" reaction.

A Job for Specialists?

Should the advertising community develop a cadre of specialists to write this kind of copy? I don't think so. I'd rather work with experienced communicators, their hand on the throttle tempered by a governing device that prevents a case of foot-in-mouth disease.

What happens when a writer becomes too hung up on sensitivity to a group is a gradually evolving negative attitude: "You can't say this." "We can't write that."

The happy middle ground: A writer who's alert to what can and can't be said and who doesn't regard the logic behind the few rules as unfair restrictions.

Chapter Twenty-One

SPECIALTY AD WRITING: LOTS AND LOTS OF MEDIA AND TECHNIQUES

A Valid Technique for Each Medium

The number of advertising media seems to be growing geometrically. We have ads on taxicabs. We have ads projected onto the sides of buildings. We have ads inside fortune cookies. We have ads on grocery carts.

If you, as a writer, have the assignment of preparing copy for a medium for which you've never written before, this educational step is in order: Ask the representative of the medium for any information about how to write for that medium, especially samples of what others have written and found effective.

The difference in fixed-position media between copy for a card on the outside of a bus and copy for a card on the inside of the bus isn't major, but there *is* a difference, and knowing what it is will result in more effective copywriting.

One other area for exploration: the news release. A news release is, generally, a public relations function, not an advertising function. But so what? You never know when you'll be pushed into the breach with the instruction: "While you're writing the ad, give us a news release, too."

Let's take a quick look at some of the specialized media.

Outdoor Advertising

A generation or two ago, in the days of the 24-sheet poster, a standard rule was: no more than eleven words on an outdoor sign. Signs have doubled, trebled, quadrupled in size, and the rule is more pertinent than ever before.

Some of the best signs with the highest impact have almost no text. They'll show the product and (if the name isn't on the product) its identity, plus a single descriptive line.

More dramatic and far more dangerous are signs that, instead of playing up product, show an implied *result* of product use. A huge illuminated sign will show a basketball player leaping to the hoop; in a corner of the illustration is the product name.

These "total experience" signs are much in vogue, and no one doubts their ability to win art directors' awards. More questionable is their ability to generate sales.

A Nike billboard, placed in a high-traffic area in Atlanta during the Olympic Games held there, had this message: "You don't win silver. You lose gold." The negative psychology resulted in widespread complaints about lack of sportsmanship.

Is controversy a positive feature for outdoor signs? Possibly, since outdoor ads often are a subliminal medium. The line between "controversial" and "outrageous" being thin, the writer of outdoor copy who wants to startle the passerby out of passivity has to be psychologically aware.

This is the most "mass" of all media . . . with the restriction that, like all advertising messages, one placed here appeals to a specific group of targets. Creating effective outdoor copy isn't as easy as the casual viewer may think.

Graphics sí, copy no

The copywriter creating a billboard has to consider total visual effect. Impact comes from the graphics; unless graphics copy are one—a murderously difficult achievement—the copywriter can't hit and run with a few words of copy left to an artist's interpretation.

Color is a major factor. The Outdoor Advertising Association of America ranked these colors in order of effectiveness: black on yellow, black on white, blue on white, white on blue. Least effective: brown on yellow, yellow on brown, red on white, white on red, red on yellow, and yellow on red.

Accept these rankings with some skepticism. The ranking of black on yellow, the combination offering the greatest contrast, is many decades old. The other limitation to these suggestions is the assumption that your board will have only two colors. On a multicolor billboard, yellow on red might work if surrounded by blacks and blues.

For what it's worth: Color psychologists say orange is the most irritating color to the eye, which is why so many fire extinguishers are painted orange.

Technology to the rescue?

Outdoor parallels television in that, being a visual medium, it offers the writer a host of mechanical tricks to cover a lack of ideas.

Motion, dimension, and sound are becoming commonplace. Outdoor differs from television and even the World Wide Web in the significance of technological help because a mechanical trick that calls attention to a billboard can result in the viewer remembering the board he otherwise might not have noticed.

So Kodak's "Kodarama" may be one of the pillars of outdoor expansion. The backlit transparency achieves detail and visual impact that a painted sign never could.

Some years ago, a company named Modern Graphics began producing heat-sealed PVC panels to make molded dimensional signs. A number of companies are experimenting with highly reflective materials, multi-image eye-foolers, and signs whose image is geared to a low-power radio station (a legend on the sign asks motorists to tune to that frequency to hear the sign's message).

Many state lotteries have quick-change signs. The drawing is on Saturday night; by Sunday noon, hundreds of outdoor signs have been changed to show the new jackpot.

Logic tells us to write an attention-grabbing message tied to visual impact because this medium, more than any other, is also the message.

Rhymes and Reverses

Quick: Can you remember an effective rhymed ad?

I can remember a couple, but they aren't true rhymes; they're radio jingles of a bygone era:

Pepsi-Cola hits the spot,
Twelve full ounces, that's a lot.
Twice as much for a nickel, too:
Pepsi-Cola is the drink for you!

What ever happened to jingles that deliver a hard message? They've been swamped by tightly orchestrated and often unrhymed jingles prepared by latter-day specialists—"jingle writers"—whose attention (like so much expensive, mediocre advertisers) is on form, not substance.

Rhymed copy implicitly calls attention to form, not substance. As a contrivance, it's less noticeable when spoken than when written.

When might you take the dusty rhyming dictionary off the shelf? In my opinion, rhymes are worth exploring in two circumstances:

1. when your company or product has an obvious rhyme with a complementary word
2. when your message is implicitly unexciting and needs external massaging

If you rhyme copy for a print medium, be sure the production artist sets it up as a rhyme. Initial letters help. Capitalizing the first word of each line helps. Whatever you do, don't run the rhyme as text with a backslash indicating a new line. It doesn't work:

Roses are red/
your face will be, too/
if you miss the kangaroo/
at the Metrozoo!

Set in type that way, it's just text. Don't go halfway with a rhyme. If you use it, exploit it:

Roses are red.
Your face will be, too . . .
If you miss the kangaroo
At the Metrozoo!

Comic Strips and Comic Books

Don't laugh. Or maybe, do laugh. Comic books can solve a complex marketing-information problem if they aren't merely clever for the sake of cleverness.

Ever since Mickey Mouse helped train World War II bomber crews, educators have known the value of comics. Except for a handful of marketers of children's items, advertisers have been slow to test comic strips and comic books as serious message carriers. With the onslaught of computer and Internet periodicals, comic strip drawings have emerged as a way to break out of the clutter. Why? It's obvious: The very nature of this type of drawing says the message will be quick and easy to comprehend.

Comics and cartoons have this advantage going in: They aren't threatening. The reader doesn't fear them. The reader doesn't have the slightest feeling of inferiority or inadequacy. The immediate impression is entertainment, not instruction. What better medium to uncomplicate a complicated message?

Figure 21-1: The theory underlying the use of comic strip characters is that they are 1) disarming; 2) familiar; 3) easy to understand; 4) highly visual. Readers of publications in which these ads appear may chuckle over the cartoon and ignore the selling message . . . unless the cartoon itself includes a selling message.

Figure 21-2: Like Dilbert, the Jetsons have represented many products and services, usually those related to advanced technology such as videoconferencing and cellular phones. Unlike the Dilbert ad (in Figure 21-1), this one has the cartoon characters actively participating in product sale.

The theory underlying the use of comic strip characters is that they are disarming, familiar, easy to understand, and highly visual. Cartoon characters such as Dilbert (see Figure 21-1) and the Jetsons have been used by so many advertisers that their appearance in advertising has little novelty. Readers may chuckle over the cartoon and ignore the selling message . . . *unless* the cartoon includes a selling message. If the syndicator or other source of the cartoon refuses to have the cartoon character participate in the selling argument, an advertiser might do well to look elsewhere.

Figure 21-3: Readers of technical and trade publications may welcome a cartoon ad as an easy-to-read alternative to text-heavy or pompous product advertising. Undoubtedly this ad scored high in readership; only the advertiser knows whether it increased response.

Whether it's a comic strip in print media or a full-blown comic book for mailing or point-of-purchase distribution, copywriter and artist should work together to ensure congruence of copy and art. Keep the art simple and double-check every facial expression.

If the artist says, "I need more space for word-balloons," you have a danger signal. No more than ten words in any one balloon, please, or you get preachy. You can add nonballoon explanatory text at the bottom of any panel.

After you've roughed out a comic strip or comic book approach, ask yourself: What do I have here I wouldn't have with a conventional brochure or ad? If the answer doesn't hit you right in the eye, you haven't used the medium to best advantage . . . or it's the wrong medium for the message.

Single cartoons are far more dangerous because one cartoon probably is a replacement for a realistic graphic. Careful! Are you being clever for the sake of cleverness? Are you violating Unassailable Loser Statute III (The illustration should agree with what we're selling, not with the headline copy)?

Consider single cartoons under these four conditions:

1. You're selling a concept that defies illustration.
2. You fear the reader will be embarrassed if you draw too close a tie to what you're selling.
3. You're trying (ugh!) to establish a corporate character.
4. You want to ridicule someone or something or create a grotesque or ugly image (primarily in political advertising).

The Three Master Rules for Writing News Releases

Three master rules, or canons, cover both technique and content for news release writing.

The First Canon of News Release Writing: The reader, viewer, or listener should be unaware that the message is sponsored.

The Second Canon of News Release Writing: Put puffery in quotes.

The Third Canon of News Release Writing: Replace or eliminate descriptive adjectives that suggest editorial viewpoint.

Information, not raw exposure

Some practitioners of "contact" publicity function on a different level. They deal in exposure, not information. The intended result of their professional activity is mention, not persuasion. Rules of writing are superfluous.

This rock-'em-sock-'em variation of public relations is on the wane, not only because their outlets (gossip columnists and broadcast personalities) are fewer than they once were but also because little benefit accrues (except for the show-biz personality) from raw mentions.

For the rest of us, adherence to the three canons is not only an insurance policy covering our own dignity and that of our message but also a direct road to editorial acceptance of messages any publication has to regard as optional. A writer should be constantly on guard against sliding into ad copy.

A news release shouldn't crow; it should have the aura of dispassionate reporting. So you wouldn't write:

LILLIAN VERNON CORPORATION
CORPORATE HEADQUARTERS

ONE THEALL ROAD
RYE, NEW YORK 10580-1450
TEL: (914) 925-1200
FAX: (914) 925-1444
www.lillianvernon.com

FOR IMMEDIATE RELEASE   **CONTACT: DAVID C. HOCHBERG**
WEDNESDAY, DECEMBER 2, 1998   dch@lillianvernon.com
                                                              (914) 925-1300

LILLIAN VERNON LAUNCHES NEW INTERACTIVE ONLINE CATALOG

Rye, New York, December 2, 1998 -- Lillian Vernon Corporation (AMEX:LVC), a leading national mail order catalog company, has launched a new Internet site, www.lillianvernon.com. The site is also accessible on America Online, keyword: Lillian Vernon.

The new World Wide Web store integrates upgraded shopping capabilities and graphic enhancements to offer customers a user-friendly site featuring over 400 of the Company's most popular items in nine categories. All of Lillian Vernon's 6,000-plus products from its nine catalog titles can be ordered online using an electronic order form.

"Internet sales will play an increasingly important role in our business. Our state-of-the-art site is easy to use and offers our customers a fast and convenient shopping experience from the comfort of their homes or offices," said Lillian Vernon, Chief Executive Officer. "Our online catalog provides another opportunity to offer unique merchandise at exceptional values. During this busy holiday season, why stand in line when you can shop online?"

Features of the new online catalog include a Gift Registry and Gift Reminder which allow customers to add items to a wish list, automatically sent via email to family and friends as a reminder three weeks before special occasions such as birthdays, anniversaries and holidays. Gift Search makes shopping easy by providing gift suggestions by specific age, gender and price range. Special sales available only to online shoppers, and featured products are updated weekly. Encryption software ensures the security of all transactions.

OVER

Figure 21-4: An effective news release convincingly walks the tightrope lifting information above obvious puffery. This one accomplishes that. Although some editors may question the word "leading" in the first sentence, publications serving the catalog industry know the company and accept its claim of position.

LILLIAN VERNON CORPORATION
CORPORATE HEADQUARTERS

ONE THEALL ROAD
RYE, NEW YORK 10580-1450
TEL: (914) 925-1200
FAX: (914) 925-1444
www.lillianvernon.com

The site also features a directory of the 16 Lillian Vernon Outlet Stores, an Investor Relations section, press releases, Company history, email link directly to Company founder Lillian Vernon, a quarterly email newsletter featuring Lillian's shopping, entertaining and decorating tips, information on the Company's Special Markets wholesale division, and Company-wide employment opportunities. The Company first went online in 1995 with both an Internet site and an America Online store.

Lillian Vernon Corporation is a 47-year-old specialty catalog company that markets gift, household, gardening, kitchen, Christmas, and children's products. The Company, founded in 1951, is one of the largest specialty catalog companies in the United States. Lillian Vernon Corporation publishes nine catalog titles: Lillian Vernon, Favorites, Lilly's Kids, Christmas Memories, Neat Ideas, Personalized Gift, Lillian Vernon Kitchen, Lillian Vernon Gardening and Private Sale.

###########################

Figure 21-4 *(Continued.)*

These are the biggest bargains in fur coats Mason Fur Company has ever offered. It will be years before another furrier can equal these prices.

Instead, you'd write:

"These are the biggest bargains in fur coats Mason Fur Company has ever offered," said John Mason, president of the company. "In my opinion, it will be years before another furrier can equal these prices."

After you've written your news release, ask yourself the ultimate question: Does this release tell the reader how the information relates to him or her?

Keep in your forebrain the temper of the times: We're in the Age of Skepticism. The reader doesn't ask, "What is it?" The reader asks, "What will it do *for me*?"

Don't skimp on information

Does your news release leave questions unanswered?

Suppose, for example, you're writing about a personnel appointment. Is it a new position? Is the new appointee succeeding someone? If so, whom? What happened to the person who previously held the job?

If titles seem similar, explain the job a little: If John Jones is the new director of advertising, reporting to John Smith, vice president of advertising, what responsibilities does Jones actually

NEWS FROM INTERACTIVE HEALTH SYSTEMS
1337 OCEAN AVENUE
SANTA MONICA, CA 90401

contact: Ms. Anne Stanton
    phone: 310-451-8111
    fax: 310-656-1806

FOR IMMEDIATE RELEASE

New "Mastering Stress CD-ROM
Now Available to HR Departments

Until now, relieving stress meant visits to a professional counselor.

It still does ... except that the "counselor" is a new CD-ROM developed by one of the nation's best known practicing psychoanalysts.

"Mastering Stress" is being distributed by Interactive Health Systems of Santa Monica, California. A breakthrough interactive procedure, the program closely parallels actual sessions with a professional counselor.

Author of "Mastering Stress" is Roger Gould, M.D., a well-known and highly respected psychiatrist. Dr. Gould is Associate Clinical Professor of Psychiatry at the University of California at Los Angeles and is widely regarded as a key expert on stress and its prevention. He is the author of *Transformations: Growth and Change in Adult Life* (Simon & Schuster) and many professional publications. His paper, "The Uses of Computers in Therapy," is widely quoted.

Human resources executives are especially logical purchasers of "Mastering Stress." The program has proved to dramatically reduce poor work quality and absenteeism.

Depression is, according to many health experts, a misunderstood and too often ignored problem in the workplace. The New York Business Group on Health has reported that depression, anxiety, and stress accounts for 47 percent of reduced productivity, 40 percent of morale problems, forty percent of absenteeism, 30 percent of substance abuse, and 19 percent of poor work quality.

How does "Mastering Stress" work? The program asks questions, just as a professional would ask questions. Each

Figure 21-5: Inclusion of a photograph usually helps the chances of an editor using a news release. This one also has a note to the editor, explaining the new concept the release describes.

question provides a "menu" of answers, or the individual may choose to provide his or her own answer.

In response to each answer, the program asks another question. The questions are increasingly targeted and pointed, so that focus becomes clearer and clearer. The individual literally leads himself or herself to the solutions.

According to Dr. Gould, "Mastering Stress" quietly shows you any inconsistencies. It shows you how to consider the implications and effects of your attitudes and involvement. And it does all this with complete privacy. Only you have access to your comments and answers." The benefit of privacy, plus the capability of handling multiple users, makes the program a logical adjunct to human resources assistance to employees.

The market price of "Mastering Stress" is $89.95. During its initial marketing period, the CD-ROM is available to human resources directors at the direct price of $49.95. The program is also available in disk format.

Requests for additional information and direct orders should be addressed to Interactive Health Systems, 1337 Ocean Avenue, Santa Monica, CA 90401. Phone is 310-451-8111; fax is 310-656-1806.

Interactive Health Systems of Santa Monica, California, has released the CD-ROM "Mastering Stress." Authored by noted psychiatrist Roger Gould, M.D., the program parallels a private session with a professional counselor. Also available in disk format, "Mastering Stress" is priced at $49.95 for human resources executives.

Dear Editor,

The enclosed news release describes a major breakthrough in the field of professional psychoanalytic counseling.

Roger Gould, MD, is one of the foremost analysts in the United States. His remarkable "Mastering Stress" CD-ROM makes it possible — for the first time — for an individual to have many of the benefits of professional guidance, solving personal problems as though a trained analyst were on hand. Developing the program required more than two years of research and testing.

Because this is a totally new concept ... and because we are much aware that you may regard the effectiveness of the program with some skepticism ... we'd be delighted to send you a CD-ROM for your personal evaluation.

Phone or fax me if you'd like to have a copy of "Mastering Stress."

Sincerely,
[SIGNATURE]

Seminar Schedule page 2   **Directions to Expo page 3**   **Registration Form page 3**

TECH DATA TIMES

VOLUME 1 ISSUE 1   BRINGING RESELLERS THE NEWEST TECHNOLOGICAL ADVANCES TODAY AND EVERY DAY   SPECIAL EXPO EDITION

EXPO COMING TO TAMPA!

Says one reseller:

"It's not just insightful, informative and inspiring — it's FREE!"

Complete the form on page 3 and fax it to: 813-571-9250 TODAY!

TAMPA - Computer distributor Tech Data will host its Tech Expo '98 — the annual event that offers resellers sneak previews of new technology and seminars offering solutions to beat the competition — from 7:30 a.m. to 5 p.m. August 14 and 15 at the Tampa Convention Center.

Free to all resellers, Tech Expo is the ideal place for getting the best information on product offerings from the industry's premier vendors. You will be able to gain new product information, take in a variety of business-building seminars and foster strong business relationships.

Small to Midsize Business Solutions, Building Your Own PC, Networking, and Peripheral Sales Strategies are some of the areas covered by the 2-day seminar program.

Plus, tips on how to increase your profitability using Tech Data's Electronic Commerce Solutions, managing your cashflow through Tech Data credit options, and an introduction to the full scope of services offered exclusively to resellers purchasing through Tech Data.

The product area open on Saturday will have representatives from among the 900 Tech Data vendor partners to demonstrate new products or answer your questions about the use of their products.

The Tech Data Services Consultation Area open on Saturday will have representatives on hand to discuss the unique value-added opportunities available to you as a Tech Data reseller, including:

■ integration and assembly

■ technical support services

■ online services (cutting your proposal preparation time dramatically)

■ online ordering with a free freight bonus

■ software licensing

■ floorplanning

■ leasing options and other credit arrangements

■ training and certification for you and your employees or to resell to your customers

To attend this free event, resellers should register in advance by completing and faxing the registration form found on page 3. Resellers can also register online at www.techdata.com.

Resellers are encouraged to bring their customers or their employees to this event so they can see hands on demos of products or talk directly to vendor representatives. Only guests accompanied by a reseller host will be allowed to register.

EVENT SCHEDULE

FRIDAY: AUGUST 14

7:30 a.m.	Registration Opens
7:30 - 8:30 a.m.	Continental Breakfast
8:30 a.m. - 12:15 p.m.	Seminar Sessions
12:15 - 1:45 p.m.	Lunch
2 - 5 p.m.	Seminar Sessions

SATURDAY: AUGUST 15

7:30 a.m.	Registration Opens
7:30 - 8:30 a.m.	Continental Breakfast
8:30 - 11:15 a.m.	Seminar Sessions
11:30 a.m. - 4:30 p.m.	Exhibit Hall Opens
12:30 - 2 p.m.	Lunch served in Exhibit Hall
2 - 4 p.m.	Seminar Sessions
4 - 4:30 p.m.	Door Prize Drawings
4:30 p.m.	Exhibit/Expo Closes

New Features In Tech Expo '98

Small to Midsize Business Pavilion   *Tech Data — Your Home Field Advantage!*
Hit a home run with the Small to Midsize Business Pavilion. Join the fun and don't be left in the outfield when it comes to selling into this major league market. Batter-up to our vendor partners and get more information on specialized products, programs and promotions geared toward the 7.2 million businesses in the United States, defined as small to midsize businesses.

Peripherals Pavilion   Have an enchanting experience in the Peripherals Pavilion. Only Peripherals knows the delightful deals and offers in store for you! Thousands of dollars await you along with many exciting mystical, magical treats. From large panel monitors to magnificent mice - we have all your Peripheral needs.

Computer Telephony (CT) Pavilion   Computer Telephony, it's not just talk anymore... Are you interested in expanding your product offerings? Tired of selling low margin solutions to your customer base? Then visit Tech Data's Computer Telephony (CT) Pavilion and find out how you can make high dollar margins selling CT solutions. Make your business be the talk of the town.

Software Demo Suite   Visit this suite on Friday from 8:30 a.m. to 5:00 p.m. We will have 40 of our software vendors available to demonstrate their products in a hands-on setting. Take advantage of reseller specials and free demo software.

Software Pavilion   Join us at the Software Pavilion while we celebrate Software Month. Stop by early and check our Software presentation schedule to discover when our vendors will be presenting demonstrations in either of our two mini theaters. It's all here at the Software Pavilion!

Figure 21-6: A mailing that looks like a newspaper suggests timeliness. It may get attention when a conventional mailing won't. In this instance, separating the center portion into more standard newspaper columns might have added to readability.

have? If a vice president is promoted to senior vice president, what's the significance of the move?

If someone wins an award, explain the award. If you're moving to a new building, specify that you're "streamlining" (a euphemism for cutting back) or "expanding" (in which case you emphasize the amount of space). The Rule of News Release Information: Don't leave obvious questions unanswered.

The fact sheet

Television interviewers, personalities, and newspeople often regard their own on-camera position as paramount and whatever they're saying or showing as subordinate. Many of these people prefer a fact sheet to a news release. For safety, send both to broadcast media. The fact sheet should list in an orderly and organized way why your subject is worthy of airtime. Be sure your first point is a bell ringer.

If someone from your organization will be on hand as spokesperson, include half a dozen questions the reporter might ask that individual. The questions should be those the station's viewership or audience regards as logical; don't lapse into questions whose answers would be transparently self-congratulatory. (See further explanation of fact sheets in Chapter 17.)

Writing cutlines and captions

If you send out a news release without a photograph, you not only damage the possibility of your words winding up in print; you're leaving out what can be the best-read component—the cutline. (Generally, cutlines are words below a picture; captions are words above a picture. In the news world, cutline is the most common term.

Here are the Five Rules of Cutline Writing:

1. Repeat pertinent information even though it also appears in the news release. (That way, a publication that runs the photograph but not the news story won't leave out something you think is important.)

2. Don't be afraid to write long cutlines. (The worst that can happen is the publication will edit them down.)

3. Write complete sentences, not bullets. (If a publication has stylistic idiosyncrasies, an editor will change your copy to conform, but most publications prefer full sentences.)

4. Set a limit of twenty words per sentence.

5. If you include several pictures, write a separate cutline for each one, even if they're similar. (Assume that only one will be used—and you don't know which one.)

How to handle negative news

It seldom pays to write a direct answer to an accusation or a negative circumstance. Instead, have a "library" release of achievements ready. Tie it to one of these nonresponses to an accusation, built around the temporizing words *appropriate* and *inappropriate*:

▶ We haven't yet had an opportunity to study and discuss the matter and will have an appropriate comment once this has been accomplished.

▶ The matter is in litigation, and it would be inappropriate for us to comment at this time.

▶ We have undertaken an internal investigation of the issue and are compiling information for analysis.

A news release or prepared statement should never be worded like this:

We regard the report as biased and unfair, and we are discussing with our attorneys the possibility of strong legal action.

Instead, a reply might be worded something like this:

We haven't yet read the report, and of course we'll have a comment at the appropriate time. We do call your attention to our positive record of achievement in affirmative action hiring and civic service.

A Hard Look at Remails

Remails—mailing a second message to someone who didn't buy from you but should have—weren't discussed in Chapter 13 because remails are becoming their own medium.

Why are remails a hot media concept now? A major advantage direct marketers have over their brethren in media advertising is the ability to pinpoint market segments. The computer, one of the two principal bases for the renaissance of direct response (zip codes are the other), tells us just about everything we might want to know about our buyers. We're almost able to predict who will buy what.

Tantalizing, isn't it, that word *almost*. It's the word that keeps us off-balance, no matter how big a pile of data we accumulate.

Here's Mary Jones: age 46, married, two children, exurban, zip code starts with 6, works part-time, household income $65,000–$70,000, husband an engineer. She bought from us three times before and she bought this offer, too.

Here's Mary Smith: age 46, married, two children, exurban, zip code starts with 6, works part-time, household income $65,000–$70,000, husband an engineer. She bought from us three times before and she *didn't* buy this offer.

Why?

The "random intrusion" factor

In my opinion, taking the time to ferret out a psychographic differential between Mary Jones and Mary Smith is a less efficient use of time than remailing Mary Smith.

Why? Because if Mary Smith didn't buy, the reason might be a subtle difference between the two women, but it's just as likely that Mary Smith simply didn't see the offer.

Please don't limit "see" to the standard explanations (she wasn't home that day or missed this one piece of mail or was the victim of a post office peccadillo). Include the possibility that the most uncontrollable circumstance changed the mix. We can call that circumstance "random intrusion."

Mary Smith may not have "seen" our mailing or ad as Mary Jones did because of her mood, buying position, family attitude, personal exhilaration or disgruntlement, or momentary aberration. These circumstances are beyond the reach of any marketer. But—happy day!—they're subject to immediate change.

So what do we do? We remail Mary Smith. We give her a second chance because no matter how black her mood, how disgusted she is with us as vendors, how wasteful she felt after her last buying spree, or how changed her demographics or psychographics might be, she still is a buying prospect of far greater value than any cold-list name. We give her a second chance.

Don't insult the blind

We all have seen so many "You fool!" follow-up mailings that our attitude toward this approach probably has polarized. We love it or we hate it.

The insult lovers do have a point. Mary Smith hasn't bought. As a member of the prime target group, she should have. What's wrong with a little shock therapy?

Nothing, really. I just think it's too soon. If Mary Smith didn't have proper exposure to our message, which of these approaches will bring in her order?

> Your subscription has officially expired. Here is one last opportunity to renew your subscription at the preferred rate.
>
> Please send us your renewal immediately, as otherwise no further issues can be sent to you.

Or

> Oops!
>
> We know our subscribers get more mail than most people. So it's possible you missed the renewal notice we sent you a few weeks ago.
>
> Not to worry. I've enclosed a duplicate. Please send it back right away because technically your subscription has run out.

I lean—mildly—toward the second approach not only because it's more likely to slide under the barrier the recipient may have erected (what if, yes, the first notice did get through, was considered and rejected, and went the way of all flush?), but also because it's too soon to connect the electrodes.

Sure, in a series of four follow-up letters, the fourth is loaded with explosives. Three strikes and we're out, so what do we have to lose?

What if budget or corporate philosophy dictates only one follow-up? My suggestion: Test. Test friendship against hard-boiled "You're the loser" copy.

We are, after all, in the Age of Skepticism. I, for one, am increasingly antsy about a reaction I'd have regarded as strange a dozen years ago . . . contemptuous rejection of copy we intend as friendly. The reader concludes, "He's trying to sell me something," and this conclusion is grounds for refusal.

Subscriber turnover being what it is, it's a rare and courageous publication that gives up after only one subscription reminder. Magazine subscriptions aren't typical of our total cosmos anyway because a subscriber may go his way and return to the fold a year or two later when the ninth follow-up offers a calculator or a camera.

We're selling merchandise here

Suppose, instead of a subscription offer, we've mailed a merchandise offer. How do we offer the target individual a second chance?

Do we just remail, with no changes? After all, the "no see" theory suggests we might as well, since the recipient probably didn't get a good look at what we're selling.

I don't agree, and I'll tell you why: This book is based on the Five Great Motivators that work during the Age of Skepticism—fear, exclusivity, guilt, greed, and need for approval. Here's a painless way to add guilt to the blend. (It can't hurt, especially since the "no see" theory might not be the reason the original mailing didn't pull a response.)

On the outer envelope, put a legend—something such as:

Did you overlook it?
Here's another copy.

Inside, add a single enclosure to the mailing. This would be a small sheet of paper, either a "From the desk of . . ." sheet or a small piece of notepaper with no heading. The message on this sheet:

I sent you this information a few weeks ago. I haven't seen a reply from you, which suggests my original message didn't reach you. So here's another copy. You still have time.

Two rules form themselves when we consider remailing. We might call them the Remail Determinants. Here's the First Remail Determinant: If the mailing has been successful, the only content change for a single remail to someone whose characteristics match those who bought from your first mailing is the information that this *is* a remail.

The Second Remail Determinant: For prospect groups other than proven names—the "Mary Smiths"—it probably will be more productive to send additional mailings to cold lists.

If you haven't tried second-chance mailings of offers that have pulled fairly well, consider them. They can be a road to increased profit, and the additional creative and mechanical costs are nil.

Learn Your Craft

Whatever you're writing—outdoor signs, comic strip advertising, news releases, remails, or copy for an ever-changing kiosk sign in a bus station—learn your craft.

Too many writers look down on what they do: "This kind of copy is beneath me." Uh-uh. It's impossible to know too much. And it's a lot easier to write potent copy for *any* medium if you know how that medium works.

Chapter Twenty-Two

SOMETIMES A HOT MEDIUM, SOMETIMES COLD: HOW TO WRITE CARD DECK COPY THAT SELLS

Unique Problems for the Writer

What a nasty shock loose deck cards are for the writer who usually settles in comfortably to grind out a four-page letter, an eight-page brochure, or a full-page ad.

Except for oversize "end cards," the whole sales argument has to squeeze itself into one side of a 3½- by 5½-inch card!

That isn't the worst of it. The card is embedded in the center of a deck, with 59 competing cards elbowing it out of the way, clamoring for attention on their own.

The ambience is the contemporary equivalent of the huge classified section of *Popular Mechanics* in the 1930s—page after page of classified ads. What hope could a little advertiser have?

Somehow that hidden classified ad did pull. And somehow that buried card does pull. But the differences between 1932 and 2002 aren't just improved technology and degraded mail delivery. They're more profound than that.

The biggest difference is the tremendous onslaught of advertising messages. The 1932 reader may have subscribed to *Popular Mechanics* and no other publication; that could be why the tiny classified ads pulled. Do you know anyone who subscribes to just one magazine?

With an average of at least fifty hours a week of television viewing, plus all that time spent on-line, plus home and car radios, plus metropolitan and community newspapers, plus catalogs and mailers, plus an endless sea of signs, plus telemarketing, it isn't surprising that we have become more and more desensitized to all advertising.

But we bear a nastier cross: The typical card deck is business-to-business, so we have to add to the attention-grabbing mix all the trade publications competing for attention. Question: What chance does one card have?

Grab 'em or lose 'em

Experts agree on what chance one card *might* have. Opinions are that the typical recipient of a sixty-card deck spends from one to three minutes riffling through it. You have *one to three sec-*

Figure 22-1: A card has to grab and shake attention fast. This one does, with a specific—binders as low as $1.56 each. The reverse of the card has the usual postal indicia, plus a place for the responder's name and address, although, cleverly, the card gives an option of taping a business card to it. Note inclusion of a Web address as another option.

onds to grab your prospect's attention, hold it, and impel him or her to put the card aside for action. Not much time, is it?

That's why the headline on a card is crucial. Your powerful brief headline has to clearly state a definite benefit to the buyer.

Many experts suggest using full color on the cards. Others don't, theorizing that color can be a distraction. The deck riffler is looking for personal benefit, not artistry.

So in the middle of a deck of four-color cards, wouldn't a dynamic two-color card stand out? "No," says one deck publisher. "If you're in the middle of the deck, color is even more important. We've tested it in split-runs, and color invariably pulls at least 20% better." Suggestion: Test it for yourself, possibly as a split-run within a single deck.

For card headlines, terms such as "New," "At last!" and "You've been waiting for this" seem to work. Description of benefits is crucial, and the writer's focus should be on the prospect, with copy that can be read and understood quickly. An expiration date, prominently displayed, helps force that card out of the desk and onto the desk.

Six Principles for Card Deck Copy

Those who have used card decks successfully agree unanimously on one point: The recipient wastes no time dawdling over cards. Whether one second or three seconds, selling time is perilously short. So I've codified six principles for card deck copy.

The six principles of card deck copy

1. *Your offer must be instantly identifiable.* Flash a photocopy of your card's camera-ready art at half a dozen people who don't already know what you're selling. Give them the longest estimated digestion time—three seconds. Then have them tell you, minus refinements they'd have to probe the body copy to find, what it is you want them to do.

2. *Sell, coherently, what the headline promises, not a secondary service or product down the road.* If you're offering free details, emphasize the free details, not what you might sell later on. In my opinion, this is the principal problem in unsuccessful cards.

3. *Stress benefits. You don't have room to write poetry about features, and the reader has neither the patience nor the interest to read your poetry. Use a bulleted format, to save space and hold attention.* Contents aren't automatic. Place yourself in the position of your best prospect. What does he or she regard as a benefit?

4. *Assume your card is buried in a deck of offers, all of which are as good as yours or better.* I suggest this principle because seldom will a direct-response writer face as murderously competitive a medium as card decks. This is doubly true if your card isn't one of the first six. The response rate falls as the reader shuffles toward the bottom of the pile. Many decks charge a premium for position within the first six; others use the top card to offer some sort of prize, which can be claimed only by digging through the deck.

Another penalty: Making the offer isn't good enough. You know a deck riffler won't scribble his name on sixty cards or even ten. Why should yours be among the chosen few? Because your words burst with power and the other guy's words don't.

5. *Tell the reader what to do.* You know this principle doesn't apply only to card decks. It's one of the great laws of direct mail. I include it here because this is the most obvious and most common deficiency in copy for cards.

Now you can tell Pitney Bowes to... stuff it!

CONQUEST T-1000 PUTS INNOVATIVE BIG-METER FEATURES WELL WITHIN YOUR BUDGET.

The Conquest T-1000 is the first totally electronic postage meter that provides:

- Smudge-free, no-ink, non-impact printing
- Departmental accounting
- A money-saving scale interface
- TELESET resetting through a built-in self-dialing modem

FRANCOTYP-POSTALIA BRINGS YOU ALL THIS FOR AS LITTLE AS **$33.50 per month!**

So why keep paying extra to be treated like a small fry? Now you can afford to tell them to stuff it!

For the dealer nearest you call (800) 95-NO INK

Call (800) 956-6465, or complete the information on the reverse side for more info.

Figure 22-2: The heading stops the eye and promises a benefit. Good copywriting! Body copy specifies comparative benefit. The company's name appears in small type, possibly because of the supposition that a little-known name is less likely to sell than an exposition of competitive advantages.

Invariably the least successful cards ignore this principle. Peculiar, isn't it, since it's the easiest one to apply?

6. *Force the reader to respond immediately because delay will cost money, reduce benefits, or lose business to a competitor.* Time can work for us as well as against us. The recipient is flipping through the cards, but he or she did open the deck. Why is this person allocating one to three minutes to turn a neatly packaged deck into a jumbled mess of discards—and a few precious cards to mail back?

Decisions are instant, and keeping this in mind can benefit the canny card advertiser. Create urgency. Give your readers a reason to act now.

Why Should I Mail Back This Card?

I'm looking at a card for, of all things, a card deck. The heading on the card:

OUR CUSTOMERS MEAN BUSINESS

What a ghastly cliché! Sometimes, in speeches, I'll show about sixty ads for various companies, headed "[Name of Company] Means Business." I've seen this tired line so often I've quit collecting samples.

But cliché or not, where's the clarion call to action? Having read it, what am I supposed to do? Remember the first principle: Your offer must be identifiable instantly. Remember the cosmic great law that has become the fifth principle: Tell the reader what to do.

FREE **Office Supplies Catalog!**

Quill has a large inventory of office supplies at unbelievable savings. Thousands of businesses depend on QUILL for their basic supplies because we cater to the needs of Office Managers.
• Outstanding Everyday Low Prices. Save As Much As 68% Off List!
• Call as Late as 6pm and In-Stock Orders are Shipped the Same Day!
• Most Orders Over $45 Are Shipped Free! Satisfaction Guaranteed.
• 11,000 quality products in stock!

Complete this coupon or
Call 1-800-789-1331
Fax to 1-800-789-5364
Refer to Code 68311
YES! *Send me Quill's FREE Catalog.*

Name: _____ Title/Mail Stop: _____

Company: _____ Phone #: ( ) _____

Address: _____ # of Employees _____ **QUILL**®

City/State/Zip: _____ Type of Company _____

Figure 22-3: Every business office has office supply catalogs on hand; so why would someone want another? "Large inventory" and "unbelievable savings" aren't as potent as an example of what might be in that inventory (such as obsolete computer printer ribbons) and an example of unbelievable savings. A card has to kill with a quick, hard blow.

Here's the unconvincing nonargument following "OUR CUSTOMERS MEAN BUSINESS":

> And that means business for you when you offer your product or service to 100,000+ proven mail-order buyers with MEETING POWER CARDS.

This was the first card in the deck. I suggest a separate principle to the publishers of card decks: Those first few cards should be barn burners. If the first few cards are boring, we throw the deck into the wastebasket.

What a disservice to the advertiser whose brilliantly written, perfectly produced card is number fifty-eight in the deck!

An advantage of writing copy that doesn't violate the six principles is clarity. In cards, clarity and the first principle are Siamese twins.

Here is all the display copy on a card:

> Look
> $ Trade Commodities with a Professional
> before Investing a Dime $

Okay, you have one second. Aw, make it three seconds. Tell me what they're selling. A more leisurely inspection of the card tells us the advertiser is pitching a "unique commodity program, designed for the beginner as well as the experienced investor." Yawn. Copy ends with the suggestion that we "send now for a free booklet." Why? What's in that booklet?

See the point? The card violates the first principle, and implicitly it's unclear. What if the writer had pitched the free booklet, finding a benefit in it? Impact would be centered, and clarity would justify holding the card for a few more seconds.

Compare that card with this super-clear offer:

Figure 22-4: What kinds of products organize a business or home office? Naming a few might result in higher response than a generalized pitch.

INTRODUCTORY 1/2 PRICE OFFER
(Expires in 30 Days)
18 rolls of PCS
SUPER-STICK
SHIPPING TAPE
+ PLUS +
a heavy-duty
SWEDISH STEEL
DISPENSER
only $29.98 (a $63.01 value)
* SAVE $32.03 *

Not one clever word. Not one slip toward subtlety, the enemy of clarity. Sparing use of adjectives. It's an effective card, proof that, yes, you can sell directly off the card.

One-Step, Two-Step, and Misstep

The card-selling shipping tape is one of many successful one-step cards—cards making a direct offer to sell, not an offer to send information.

There are three requirements for one-step conversion:

1. Means of ordering and billing should be simplified.
2. Product use should already be known.
3. Bargain should be apparent.

The free details two-step conversion is usually less troublesome than going for the order direct from the card, but when the possibility of getting the order exists, it's a tantalizing prospect.

Examining previous issues of the deck and testing inquiry cards against go-for-the-jugular cards will start a card education that becomes increasingly worthwhile as loose deck cards become, for some marketers who have neither the budget nor the inclination to use publications or direct mail, major direct-response media.

Chapter Twenty-Three

LOTS OF TIPS FOR WRITING CATALOG COPY

Adding Motivators

Catalog copywriters spend their days struggling to answer the toughest question in our business: Why should I buy from you?

Raw product description depends on luck to get that target customer to lift the phone or fill out the order form. Luck won't hack it for us. Safety lies in giving the catalog reader a reason to order. Remember the magic formula?

Only you.
Only from us.

Sometimes one word makes the difference. A specific word can motivate. Another specific word can be a turnoff.

Words do and words don't

What qualifies as a motivator? Headlines projecting benefit qualify. Here's one:

It's not a *copy* of the famous $185 European shoe.
It *is* the $185 shoe. Yet you pay only $89.99!

Here's another:

Exclusive Country Clothes Collection
Designed by us, made by us,
Available only from us.

A bonus is an automatic motivator because a bonus is a pure appeal to greed, one of the great motivators.

On the inside cover of a flower catalog, we find *two* bonus offers, one atop the other:

FREE BONUS
OFFER
If your order is received by September 25 . . . we will send you FREE, with your or-

der, 6 top size Red Riding Hood tulips. These bright red Greigii hybrids flower in early April on sturdy 12″ stems. Their foliage is a rich green with purplish stripes. Excellent for beds, borders, and background in the rock garden. A $2.95 regular value.
ADDITIONAL FREE
BONUS OFFER
12 Dwarf Daffodils Hawera
This dainty Triandus hybrid is extremely free flowering. The flowers are usually 3 to 4 on a stem with bell-shaped cup and recurved petals. The soft creamy yellow flowers are only 8″ tall making them ideal for borders and rockgardens. They will naturalize well and come back year after year. A $4.00 value free with orders over $40.00.

Assuming the typical reader scans the two free offers in sequence, a proofreader should have demanded consistency—one word or two words for rock gardens. What's good here is the motivational descriptions; I might not be interested in tulips or daffodils, but the descriptions give them a universal appeal.

A minor copy note: I'd prefer the colorful word *purple* to the cardiac-arrest color "purplish." Color *can* be a motivator. A suede skirt in another catalog gains elegance by the copywriter's touch; it might have been *red* or *vermilion*, but this writer adds value by calling it *ruby*.

Even the lowly phone number can be a motivator:

24 HOURS
7 DAYS A WEEK
CALL TOLL-FREE
1-800-225-8200
We'll answer your call by the third ring!

Adding the standard line "Have your VISA, MasterCard, or American Express card ready" won't hurt the motivation and will speed up the order-taking process.

Another catalog adds the motivator of timeliness to the phone number:

Call 1-800-543-8633
For Same-Day Shipping

Customizing, extraordinary wording of guarantees, direct-quotation testimonials—all are motivators. Like the others, their potency depends on the copywriter's mastery of the craft of force-communication.

A sales expert doesn't just describe

What's wrong with this copy?

THE PERFECT DRESS
Wear it anywhere and enjoy being seen
in this stylish and flattering timeless classic.
Midnight Black or Champagne White, sizes 6-12.

No, it isn't terrible. No, it isn't professional. It hangs in that limbo separating those two universes.

It isn't terrible because it *does* describe what the catalog is selling—a dress. The photograph shows it, relieving the copywriter of some of the burden. Colors and sizes are covered.

What prevents the copy from entering the hallowed halls of professionalism is the decision—conscious or unconscious, by writer or employer—that description is equivalent to salesmanship.

What if, instead of the pitifully uninspired "Wear it anywhere," the writer had written:

Wear it to the tennis matches.
Then go directly to your dressy banquet.
It's in perfect taste for both.

The writer now transmits a message the reader can pick up through eyeballs. It's visual, as good catalog selling copy should be.

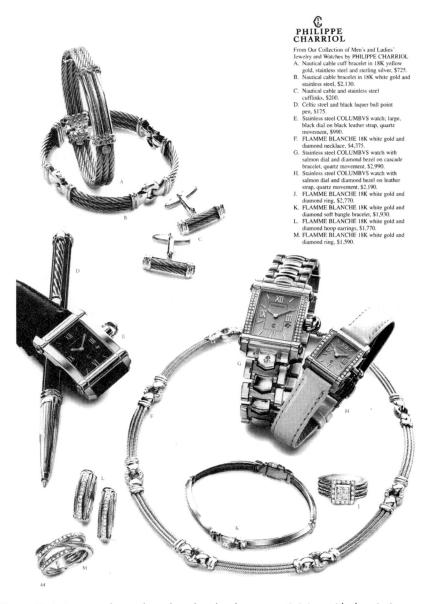

PHILIPPE CHARRIOL

From Our Collection of Men's and Ladies'
Jewelry and Watches by PHILIPPE CHARRIOL
A. Nautical cable cuff bracelet in 18K yellow
   gold, stainless steel and sterling silver, $725.
B. Nautical cable bracelet in 18K white gold and
   stainless steel, $2,130.
C. Nautical cable and stainless steel
   cufflinks, $200.
D. Celtic steel and black laquer ball point
   pen, $175.
E. Stainless steel COLUMBVS watch; large,
   black dial on black leather strap, quartz
   movement, $990.
F. FLAMME BLANCHE 18K white gold and
   diamond necklace, $4,375.
G. Stainless steel COLUMBVS watch with
   salmon dial and diamond bezel on cascade
   bracelet, quartz movement, $2,990.
H. Stainless steel COLUMBVS watch with
   salmon dial and diamond bezel on leather
   strap, quartz movement, $2,190.
J. FLAMME BLANCHE 18K white gold and
   diamond ring, $2,770.
K. FLAMME BLANCHE 18K white gold and
   diamond soft bangle bracelet, $1,930.
L. FLAMME BLANCHE 18K white gold and
   diamond hoop earrings, $1,770.
M. FLAMME BLANCHE 18K white gold and
   diamond ring, $1,590.

Figure 23-1: An upscale catalog often decides that romanticizing with descriptive copy can damage the image. A rule seems to be: The higher the price, the less the amount of descriptive copy. Note, too, that prices are run in, not set in boldface.

The curse of parochial isolation

The curse of parochial isolation is the gradual widening of the distance between you as seller and "those people" as possible buyers. What's parochial isolation? It's the well-intended but self-defeating practice of becoming so *over* knowledgeable about what you're selling that you lose touch with the marketplace.

The friendly neighborhood grocer of pre-supermarket days never had this problem. He saturated himself in the open marketplace. He knew his demographics inside out: Who bought what, and why. He knew, within the limited sphere of his own marketing area, the survival potential of a new product. His customers kept him aware of his competition.

Early catalogers had this same advantage. They knew, whether instinctively or aggressively, that isolation stifles communication. And what, after all, is a catalog if it isn't a profit-seeking maneuver in force-communication?

How to Prevent Copy Anemia

Isolation can make copy so anemic that it becomes too weak to compete. Why? Because as the gap between seller and buyer widens, the words in the catalog mean less and less to the prospect.

Let the writer scrabble around in the open marketplace to get those batteries recharged! Let him spend a week behind the counter at a retail store! Let her spend a week either selling door-to-door or over the phone or wandering slowly through a shopping mall making notes of comments and conversations!

The Buyer/Seller Equivalence Equation explains why inbred copy keeps seller and buyer apart: The Seller's Concern = What it is. The Buyer's Concern = What it will do for me.

Can you see the logic behind a plea for catalog writers to immerse themselves in the marketplace—to watch the television shows they reject with intellectualized disdain, to stroll through department stores and shopping malls, to listen to late-night radio call-in shows, to scan one consumer magazine for each trade magazine they read?

In my opinion, this makes the writer a far better keyboard gladiator than poring over a competitor's catalog. In my opinion, basing catalog copy on what a competitor writes is "me-tooism" that might help immortalize the competitor's mistakes. In my opinion, everybody in this business should spend as much time outside the insulated corporate walls as inside them.

Six magic words

Invariably, catalogers who quarantine themselves away from "those people" at whom their catalogs are aimed are unaware that what they think and like may not be the same as what "those people" think and like.

Go through the catalog, item by item, and ask the logical six-word question: What will this do for me?

Not only will you overcome the "feature isn't identical to benefit" mistake, but your own attitude toward catalog copy will begin to resemble the attitude of "those people" . . . and they're the ones who keep you in business.

The ultimate "ultimate"

Falling in love with a word is like falling in love with a vampire. Every kiss drains a little more strength out of your message.

You'd rather not shout. People listen better when you don't.

You prefer unpasteurized beer and your own french fries to seven courses at Quaglino's.

I think I have what you're looking for.

Cashmere Blazer. Classic single breasted. Three buttons. Keyhole buttonhole (for occasional outbreaks of jauntiness). Besom pockets with flaps (will actually hold things). Fully lined. Center vent. Rather like the best blazer you ever owned. Only better. Color: Real Navy or Black Forest. Pls. specify. Men's even sizes: 38 through 48 Regular, 40 through 48 Long. (Nº. AAQ8002.) Imported. Original price: $495. Sale: $349.

Guaranteed
under the tree Christmas Day if ordered by 12 noon Wednesday December 23, '98. (additional $12 by FedEx.)
1-800-231-7341

Floral Wool Rug (Nº. AAQ10469), rich handtufted pile. Small (3' x 5'), Medium (5' x 8'), and Large (8' x 10'), pls. specify. Original price: $250, Sale: $199; $495, Sale: $395; and $995, Sale: $789, respectively. Turns a garret into an atelier. Imported.

Art Nouveau Pewter Dish (Nº. AAQ10529) decorated with a lush protea blossom, 4 small ball feet on bottom; 6" x 4". Imported. Original price: $60. Sale: $44.

For potpourri, too (bowls and bowls of it throughout the Waldorf suite).
Italian Silver Ashtray (Nº. AAQ11506), a stable 5" square x 1-3/4" high, with glass tray that removes from silverplated base for easy cleaning. Original price: $178. Sale: $139.

Figure 23-2: When a catalog achieves a "personality position," as the former J. Peterman catalog did, copy can become personal and even puzzling, provided it also describes. On this page, one of the best bits of copywriting is the last sentence describing the floral wool rug: "Turns a garret into an atelier." The catalog eventually failed.

One of the better upscale catalogs has, in a single issue, a whole gaggle of "ultimates." A golfer can buy "the ultimate putter"; the young adventurer can buy "the ultimate remote-controlled off-road vehicle"; a dog can have "the ultimate defense against fleas" (this last shows a dog inside the house, his electronic collar probably driving the fleas deep into the carpet).

Like fine wine or good jokes, words such as *ultimate* or *supreme* or *beautiful* or *important* should be dispensed sparingly (see Chapter 11). Poured out in a glut, they sour the stomach.

Sure, a writer forgets which words he used yesterday. A catalog has two separate sets of problems: 1) More than one writer can contribute prose; 2) Copy might be written over an extended period of time, especially if some sections are picked up from previous catalogs.

The solution (as is true of all creative writing) lies in dispassionate proofreading. A person not connected to the origin of the copy reads it in a single sitting, looking for annoying duplications.

If copy comes out of a word processor, checking is a lot easier. The search key will pick up adjectival overuse. It's the ultimate defense against the ultimate gaffe, and ultimately it works to the ultimate benefit of the mailing.

And Just What Makes it "Ultimate"?

If we're saying what we mean, we won't use *ultimate* as the ultimate description anyway. Why? Because *ultimate* implies the end of the rainbow, the best, beyond further improvement. If, in fact, whatever we're selling actually *is* the ultimate, we'll sell more merchandise when our copy tells the reader just what it is that makes what we're selling "the ultimate" than we would by making an unexplained claim.

If you've been using *ultimate* and *important* as unexplained—ergo, unjustified—descriptions, a mild chiding: You're cheating the reader, whether your claim is true or not. If what you're selling really is the ultimate or if it really is important, you have more ammunition than you're using; if it isn't, you're using paper to cover a hole in the roof.

How to Give Prospects a Reason to Do Business With You

Visualize a selling situation in which a shopper wanders through an insane shopping center. A dozen stores have identical lines of goods. The shopper has one hour; each store gets a five-minute shot at the sale.

I can't believe, in such a circumstance, that a marketer would take the position so many catalogers take: "Here's what I have to sell. Do you want it or don't you?"

Oh, no: The winner of this little battle shrewdly sizes up the prospective buyer, saying, "Aha! I know what will appeal to him or her."

"But we can't be sure what they want"

Someone who sells women's shoes can't be sure all the catalogs go to women. Someone selling automobile parts can't be sure all the catalogs go to car owners.

That isn't the issue. Except for blind prospecting, catalogs go to two groups: 1) those who made a previous purchase or put down a cash deposit to get the catalog or are referrals; and 2) those whose appearance on a particular list, residence in a particular neighborhood, or job title within a particular area of business makes them logical prospects.

If we don't use this information, we wind up with bland, overgeneralized product descriptions based on the ridiculous complaint, "But we can't be sure what they want."

I suggest a conference, attended by merchandise manager, list buyer, and copywriter. The meeting should last no more than ten minutes because the purpose is to ensure congruency of viewpoint: What are we selling, and to whom?

Recognition of what we're selling and the individuals we expect to buy it will in one brilliant flash eliminate the gray sameness so many catalogs share.

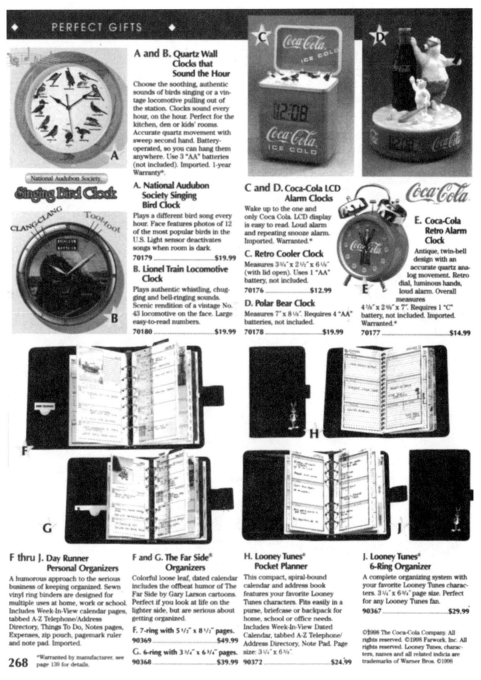

Figure 23-3: The page is headed "Perfect gifts." Neither clocks nor pocket planners are usually thought of as gifts; but the catalog supplies a mind-set that can tie these items to the theme and make individual copy blocks referring to the word "gift" unnecessary.

Give 'em a reason to buy

In my opinion, the only way you can go too far overboard in giving the reader a reason to buy is to have type running off the page.

Three sensible constraints are in order:

1. Only the most consummate master of wordsmithy can lecture or sermonize from an Olympian posture and not generate antagonism.
2. In catalogs, as in conversation, it's bad form to delve too deeply into the reader's shortcomings that we plan to correct.
3. Page after page of products for which the writer makes identical claims can kill credibility.

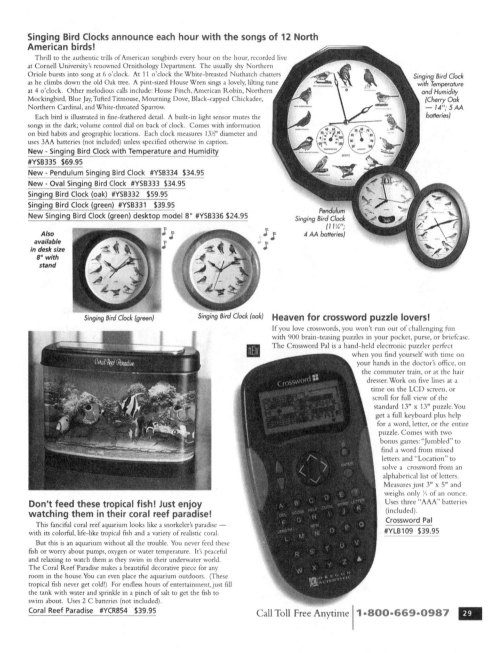

Singing Bird Clocks announce each hour with the songs of 12 North American birds!

Thrill to the authentic trills of American songbirds every hour on the hour, recorded live at Cornell University's renowned Ornithology Department. The usually shy Northern Oriole bursts into song at 6 o'clock. At 11 o'clock the White-breasted Nuthatch chatters as he climbs down the old Oak tree. A pint-sized House Wren sings a lovely, lilting tune at 4 o'clock. Other melodious calls include: House Finch, American Robin, Northern Mockingbird, Blue Jay, Tufted Titmouse, Mourning Dove, Black-capped Chickadee, Northern Cardinal, and White-throated Sparrow.

Each bird is illustrated in fine-feathered detail. A built-in light sensor mutes the songs in the dark; volume control dial on back of clock. Comes with information on bird habits and geographic locations. Each clock measures 13½" diameter and uses 3AA batteries (not included) unless specified otherwise in caption.

New - Singing Bird Clock with Temperature and Humidity
#YSB335 $69.95

New - Pendulum Singing Bird Clock #YSB334 $34.95

New - Oval Singing Bird Clock #YSB333 $34.95

Singing Bird Clock (oak) #YSB332 $59.95

Singing Bird Clock (green) #YSB331 $39.95

New Singing Bird Clock (green) desktop model 8" #YSB336 $24.95

Singing Bird Clock with Temperature and Humidity (Cherry Oak — 14"; 5 AA batteries)

Pendulum Singing Bird Clock (11¼"; 4 AA batteries)

Also available in desk size 8" with stand

Singing Bird Clock (green)

Singing Bird Clock (oak)

Don't feed these tropical fish! Just enjoy watching them in their coral reef paradise!

This fanciful coral reef aquarium looks like a snorkeler's paradise — with its colorful, life-like tropical fish and a variety of realistic coral.

But this is an aquarium without all the trouble. You never feed these fish or worry about pumps, oxygen or water temperature. It's peaceful and relaxing to watch them as they swim in their underwater world. The Coral Reef Paradise makes a beautiful decorative piece for any room in the house. You can even place the aquarium outdoors. (These tropical fish never get cold!) For endless hours of entertainment, just fill the tank with water and sprinkle in a pinch of salt to get the fish to swim about. Uses 2 C batteries (not included).

Coral Reef Paradise #YCR854 $39.95

Heaven for crossword puzzle lovers!

If you love crosswords, you won't run out of challenging fun with 900 brain-teasing puzzles in your pocket, purse, or briefcase. The Crossword Pal is a hand-held electronic puzzler perfect when you find yourself with time on your hands in the doctor's office, on the commuter train, or at the hair dresser. Work on five lines at a time on the LCD screen, or scroll for full view of the standard 13" x 13" puzzle. You get a full keyboard plus help for a word, letter, or the entire puzzle. Comes with two bonus games: "Jumbled" to find a word from mixed letters and "Location" to solve a crossword from an alphabetical list of letters. Measures just 3" x 5" and weighs only ¼ of an ounce. Uses three "AAA" batteries (included).

**Crossword Pal
#YLB109 $39.95**

Call Toll Free Anytime | **1•800•669•0987** **29**

Figure 23-4: Figure 23-3 included a Singing Bird Clock as one of a number of gift items. This catalog features the clock with a number of options and names each bird on its face. Two questions: 1) Which do you think will sell more clocks? 2) Why is that question unfair? (Answer to the second question: The question is unfair because it doesn't take into account the amount of dedicated descriptive space.)

Some catalogs implicitly answer the question "Why should I do business with you?" by their very content. Examples:

▶ You sell dresses to women who have "fuller figures."
▶ You sell sex aids to those who have paid to get your catalog.
▶ You sell prosthetic devices.
▶ You sell cigars to men who have asked for your cigar catalog.
▶ You sell computer software upgrades.

In such cases, recognition of the need reinforces the "who I am" recognition that prompted the original request.

For previous buyers, the problem doesn't exist at all; personal products always have a high buyer-loyalty rate because the buyers don't want to expose his weaknesses to outsiders any more than he must. Competitors have to find an extraordinarily compassionate approach to break the chain you've forged.

Don't overpower your own product

In a solo mailing, product can be secondary to its emotional match with the target reader. Catalogs need a more balanced copy slant.

This is because a catalog is more eclectic than a single-item mailing or an ad. Seldom do you find a customer who is wildly in need of *everything* in your catalog, and never can you prevent the various items you display from competing with one another for the buyer's favor.

So product descriptions are the floor under your selling argument, just as an uncooked, unseasoned steak is the floor under your dinner.

Which comes first, product or benefit?

I propose the Rule of Catalog Attention-Grabbing: Start the description with benefit—what the item will do for the customer. Then describe the product itself. Then recapitulate the benefit. Then list the specifics necessary to place an order.

The benefit/product/benefit/product sequence works well, in my opinion, because benefit grabs attention better than physical product description. Inserting the product description in the middle works well because this ploy softens the enthusiasm without breaking it, so the reader doesn't feel he's being "pitched." A final few words about benefit are a logical close, just before such product specifics as color, size, and price (which traditionally come last).

Can you do all this in one paragraph? Certainly. Some catalogers do it in twenty words.

A catalog cold-list impeller

Did you ever get a catalog from a company you had never bought from before, with this copy on the cover?

WE'RE SORRY, BUT . . .
Mailing costs being what they are,
this is the *last* catalog we can send you
unless you order *something* from these pages.
We hate to lose an old friend, so won't you please
look through this catalog right now,
while it's in your hands? Thanks much.

"The *last* catalog" from a company we don't know? This copy wasn't an accident. The mailer is exercising his right to add a free shot of guilt, larded with exclusivity, to the marketing brew.

The cataloger's last-chance target isn't the same as the solo mailer's second-chance target. But talking tough to those who have bought from a catalog within the past six months isn't a good idea at all. An individual who has made it to the golden plateau of your house list sees your catalog as a source, not as an impulse buy. He's easily outraged by your expression of disaffection, unless the time gap is a year or more.

The "ultimate" dressing room

A lot of people who should buy from us don't. Have you ever heard this comment?

"I just don't buy anything by mail order. Well, maybe from Eddie Bauer or L.L. Bean or The Sharper Image. Oh, yeah, and occasionally from the Neiman-Marcus catalog and Bloomie's by Mail. And we order office products from the Office Depot catalog, of course. But I'm not a mail-order catalog buyer." When the cryptographers decode this message, here's what we get: "I don't buy from you."

Some entire catalogs never devote a single line of copy to any of the gigantic advantages of buying from them by mail. They never do tell the prospective customer:

▶ When you order from a catalog, you get the exact size and color you want. You don't just pick over what happens to be in stock in the store.

▶ When you order from a catalog, you can return merchandise easily and without a hassle. You don't have to stand in line to get the department manager's signature and sour look; you send it back and you get your refund.

▶ When you order from a catalog, you can inspect the merchandise in your home or office and only then decide whether or not you want to keep it. You're not under pressure in a store, with someone else waiting to use the dressing room or the computer.

This boilerplate copy is yours to use if you want it. It lists only a handful of the obvious benefits of shopping from a catalog.

Freebies, Gifts, and Sweepstakes

Even now, when vigorous competition, including aggressive on-line catalogs, has catalogers scrambling for business, some old-timers refuse to believe excitement incentives exist. (An excitement incentive is a "booster" intended to generate orders you otherwise wouldn't have.) I remember sitting in a meeting in which the crusty entrepreneur, who for forty years has dictated the fortunes of his company, snorted, "If they want sweepstakes, let 'em play Powerball. If they want freebies, let 'em get food samples at Sam's Club."

I'm not lobbying for free gifts, and I wouldn't attempt to recommend a sweepstakes to any company that doesn't have the means to turn this whole promotion over to a specialist. My purpose is to analyze excitement incentives and to suggest some logical rules for their use—or avoidance.

The logic is obvious: Excitement incentives cost money, right? They're something of a pain to promote and implement, and they take up space you otherwise could use to sell merchandise, right?

So excitement incentives don't add image; their purpose is to add a competitive advantage by increasing dollar volume.

Then why doesn't every company use them? Even the most successful catalogers can use more business or they wouldn't be mailing their catalogs to speculative lists.

The answer lies in the First Rule of Excitement Incentives: Adding artificial incentives to generate sales invariably lowers the quality of buyer.

I think we'd better tack on the Second Rule of Excitement Incentives, before you draw the wrong conclusion: Lowering the quality of buyer is a detriment only if a promotion coincidentally lowers the image of the vendor with existing best buyers.

That last one means: Schlocking up your catalog a bit isn't necessarily an evil move. It may hurt you if it causes those who have been your customers to think, "We don't want to buy anything from someone who deals in freebies, gifts, and sweepstakes."

Want an opinion? With the exception of a handful of catalogs whose very existence depends on superexclusivity, it's impossible to alienate a buyer by offering him something extra. I think the additional business you'll write much more than offsets the infrequent "How could you do this?" reaction. (NOTE: Be sure to play up incentives on the cover.)

Proof of the validity of this type of stimulus is the number of once staid catalogs now using excitement incentives. Proof is the adoption of freebies and gifts by business-to-business catalogers (sweepstakes are complicated and often impractical for companies with a customer base smaller than 50,000). Proof is the establishment of popular-priced, promotional adjunct catalogs by some of the top-end merchandisers.

Where, how, and how much?

One of my clients had about a thousand inexpensive quartz watches left over from a space ad promotion. The retail price had been $29.95 to $39.95, but the markup had been large. And the market really didn't exist any longer because of a flood of bottom-end watches that could retail for less than $5.00.

We decided to give a watch with each order totaling $125 or more from the next catalog. Why $125? This number seemed to maximize the possibility of a customer who might have ordered only one item now ordering two or more.

Using this simple, uncomplicated promotion as an example, where and how would *you* have promoted the free watches? You wouldn't have had a great many choices. Chances are you'd have followed the same path we did: We put some high-powered teaser copy on the catalog cover; we peppered the body of the catalog with drop-in reminders; we showed a picture of the watches on the order form, where we also made a big deal of the promotion ("Did your order total $125 or more? Don't forget your FREE multi-function quartz watch!"); and we added a final reminder of what became, when the order form was folded up to make a business reply envelope, the point of no return—the gummed area some old-timers call "the lickin' spot."

Sure, we used up all the watches and, in fact, had to get some more. Actually our figuring hadn't been bad because most of the extra watches we had to round up were for orders filtering in after our proclaimed expiration date.

Which just happens to bring me to my next point, the Third Rule of Excitement Incentives, actually the easiest of all to implement: All promotions must have an expiration date.

This rule applies not only to catalogs but to many creative uses of media described in this book. An expiration date can bring a so-so promotion to life.

The Fourth Rule of Excitement Incentives isn't quite as easy, but it doesn't require an Einstein for implementation: Orders dribbling in after the expiration date should be honored as long as pre-bought supplies and computer programming make it possible, but remind the customer that you're doing him a favor.

The only machinery you need is a single form letter . . . personalized, if you have the equipment to do it. That letter, "To a Very Important Customer," says thanks for the order and expresses delight at being able to honor the request for the free gift, even though the expiration date has already passed.

I know people in this business who take the martinet position. If the expiration date was December 31, and a customer has the nerve to send in an order January 18 and still ask for the free whatever, they'll send the merchandise, but with a letter explaining he's too late to qualify for the freebie.

Oh, yeah? What happened to goodwill? Such a letter might even stimulate return of the merchandise. Instead, if the promotion is over and you're out of whatever it was, send a gift certificate good for an equivalent amount on the next order. You're dealing in paper, and the paper could bring a fast reorder instead of disappointment that degenerates into annoyance.

You can handle these situations in catalogs far better than you could in a retail store, as anyone operating both a store and a catalog operation can verify. A retailer whose specials expire on Saturday reprices goods on Sunday or loses both credibility and control. Catalogers don't share that problem because if your next catalog arrives with the timing and hoopla it should, your customer will order from the new catalog with its own new set of excitement incentives.

How sweepstakes differ

Sweepstakes are a different matter. Postal laws and some state laws prevent freewheeling use of sweepstakes promotions, which is one reason I suggest having professionals handle them. With a sweepstakes, a deadline is a deadline. The difference is, the buyer doesn't implicitly expect a bonus; it's *chance*, where freebies are a *certainty*.

Repeatedly, I get the feeling that many who use excitement incentives do so grudgingly—as though they're half-ashamed of it or want to keep it a secret.

Two more rules complete the sextet. An ancient saying, "In for a penny, in for a pound," is apt here because establishing an excitement incentive and then playing it down violates the Fifth Rule of Excitement Incentives: If the cataloger doesn't seem excited, the customer can't get excited.

Never forget who's in charge, giving the commands. This isn't a meeting of equals; the readers are unlikely to get excited unless you tell them to.

But don't run afoul of the final rule, the Sixth Rule of Excitement Incentives: Lack of clarity kills off excitement.

If you wonder how telling the reader you're giving something away can be unclear, take a look at some of the catalogs in your mailbox. You'll find free offers mentioned on the cover and nowhere else. You'll find an announcement of a giveaway claiming "2,500 Prizes!" and no foundation for that claim anywhere inside the catalog.

The Worst Scenario

Even as I was writing this chapter, I responded to a well-written candy catalog. I called the toll-free number. Uh-oh. "All our operators are busy. Your call is important to us. Please stay on the line." I did . . . for close to six minutes. Every minute or so, that same recorded message was repeated.

When I finally reached an operator and told her the SKU number of the item I wanted, she said, "That no longer exists." Huh? The catalog had arrived less than a week before.

What didn't exist was communication between the catalog's sales department and the outside telemarketing company, which had obsolete items. The dereliction came clear when I pointed out that because my order exceeded a certain amount, I was entitled to the quantity discount mentioned prominently in the text. "That no longer applies."

Wait a minute. It's a new catalog and the discount no longer applies? I hung up. Sale lost.

Check your order form. Make decoy calls to the telemarketing people, whether in-house or contracted. Business lost is a far worse crime than business never attracted.

Clarity and efficiency: mandatory

I suggest you make a big, pointed cover reference to the page number on which you list the specifics. I suggest you recapitulate the specifics on the order form. I suggest you use any vacant space on any page to remind the customer of the incentive. I suggest you educate your telemarketers to pitch and glorify upsells and ancillary benefits. Each succeeding reference adds to excitement, and each one also adds to clarity.

If sales are flagging, test an excitement incentive. As in any copy test, the offer has to be clearly visible or the results are muddy.

The Benefit of the Imperative

A business supply catalog has this descriptive copy for incentive builders:

You can mail copies to regular customers and logical prospects.

For generations we've lionized "You can . . . " as a motivating opener. Enablement is a key to reader acceptance.

But consider: Enablement is a weak and thoughtless motivator for an action we take for granted. Of course we can mail copies. We don't have any sense of accomplishment from being able to do this. Dropping letters into the mail is neither an achievement nor a triumph. "You can . . . " adds nothing.

Removing "You can . . . " does add something—viewpoint. We transform the copy from *declarative* into *imperative*:

Mail copies to regular customers and logical prospects.

Emphasis shifts. It's where it belongs—not on the act of mailing but on use and benefit.

"If" phrases are suspect because they're conditional. You might, as you look over your catalog copy, check "if" phrases. One I saw recently, selling a photoelectric light switch, could have benefitted from an "if-ectomy":

If you're out of town, leave it plugged in to discourage prowlers.

Replacing "if" with "when" makes item use universal, not dependent on forces beyond our control:

When you're out of town, leave it plugged in to discourage prowlers.

Are You a Writer or a Clerk?

The writer who describes a cordless phone as an electronic *device* instead of electronic *instrument* is like the store clerk who worked in men's shoes yesterday and was rushed down to ladies' hats today.

The copy chief or company head who mindlessly okays cover copy such as "Now is the time to stock up on those good things for your home" deserves to drown in the catalog clutter to which she has contributed so much.

The writer who puts on the order form "Please send me the referenced items" deserves to lose the orders he surely will lose from bewildered customers who just don't know what a "referenced" item is. This writer is a bookkeeper at heart, a dreadful attitude for a marketer.

The office-supplies-catalog writer who regurgitates *finest, the best, great, step-saver, heavy-duty, E-Z, built to give you a lifetime of service, adjusts to your needs,* and *unlimited flexibility* for several different brands and sizes of the same generic item, without explaining why these clichés are true, deserves to spend eternity in a limbo where no word from the Deity includes a single specific.

We expect the clerk, shifted unwittingly from department to department, to have only a fragmented product knowledge of what he's selling that day. We grant no such dispensation to the catalog writer.

The clerk at Kmart aims you at the auto supply section and stands by helplessly while you try to puzzle out the comparative benefit of detergent oil, multiviscosity oil, and synthetic oil. "The descriptions might be on the can," the clerk offers weakly.

The catalog writer whose copy leaves you trying to puzzle out those benefits has forgotten or has never learned why his medium of communication is the "ultimate dressing room." He, too, has descended the communications ladder to the level of clerk. His inability to transmit information is far more deadly than his fellow clerk's, who may destroy a sale to only one potential customer.

Oh, a parenthetical point: "Our best whatever" is salesworthy, where "The best whatever," unvalidated, is a wild generic claim.

Just answer two easy questions

Effective catalog copy is less a matter of creativity than of having answered two questions the catalog recipient may ask:

1. Why should I buy this?
2. Why should I buy this from you?

Product description is a specific. Lacking the ability to describe, no writer qualifies to generate catalog copy. Adding the dimension of selling, the buy-by-mail concept is an art. Fortunately for us all, it's a *learned* art, one catalog writers should practice until those income-earning fingers are as nimble as a concert pianist's and as strong as a wrestler's.

Don't write yourself into a corner

When writing turns cute or hyperpersonal, it's a violation of the First Statute of Novelty Burnout, that serviceable maxim applying to humorous radio spots, animated television spots, and mechanical production tricks in any print medium including catalogs. The statute: The impact of repeated messages decreases in exact ratio to reliance on novelty.

Copywriters can write clever lines in their spare time. At the for-pay keyboard, their copy has one purpose only—selling merchandise.

Is the reader in your family?

Down-home writing is reasonably easy to do. The technique has much to recommend it, principally inducting the reader into your family. But does the reader want to be a member of your family?

The company from whose catalog I drew the examples in this section is out of business, but the memory lingers on. Might it be that going bonkers with the down-home technique could have been the cause of its demise?

Product descriptions referred to the titular head of the company, her relatives, and her friends. I liked the copywriting in the catalog, but when the device became too prominent, it was ludicrous. And people don't buy from a source they regard as ludicrous.

Would you want to be in this group or be a neighbor of what seems to be a dysfunctional household in a dysfunctional neighborhood of a dysfunctional town? Let's keep score. All these references were in copy blocks selling merchandise:

▶ Pam, the salesperson, has an aching back.

▶ A favorite customer's son has the croup.

▶ The writer has an aching shoulder, sore feet, and a fractured wrist; has slipped while bathing; has constantly breaking nails; was late for an appointment because a hotel operator didn't wake her; had to take a pill in the middle of the night; and tripped on her mother's rug.

▶ The writer's husband sleeps on his side (I don't regard this as an ailment, but it seems to be one in this catalog) and has a twisted knee.

▶ A friend named Jerry has frostbitten toes.

▶ The writer's son has a cold bathroom.

▶ A neighbor's house caught fire.

▶ A neighbor named Joyce has worn-out stair treads.

▶ The town had a power failure.

▶ Friends Jackie and Fran have arthritis.

▶ Aunt Em had a stroke.

▶ Joe suffers from severe allergies.

▶ Aunt Sophie has arthritis.

▶ Marianne's mother hurt her foot.

▶ The writer's mother has osteoporosis, needs laxatives, and has trouble rising from the normal toilet-seat height.

▶ The writer's friend Lil has had a mastectomy.

▶ An unnamed friend is convalescing.

▶ Cousin Annette has lupus.

▶ Cousin Bob has spurs on his spine.

▶ Friend John has insomnia.

▶ One of the ladies on the staff has problems with chafing.

▶ Pregnant Meg couldn't bend down to feed her golden retriever, and her mother-in-law has a back problem.

▶ The writer's daughter is sensitive to wool and linen.

▶ Friend Barbara flooded her bathroom and the apartment below twice last year.

▶ Friend Sylvia put a kettle on the stove and melted the enamel.

Every one of these revelations (and there may have been others) is in a fifty-two-page catalog. We have enough problems here to fill a soap opera for two years.

What's my point? This: Personalizing copy for about 200 items resulted in a grotesque cataloguing of ailments and misfortunes. In my opinion, the word "lupus" has no place in any catalog other than one aimed at the medical profession.

"I Care About You"

Three motivators have driven many catalogers to dip their quill pens into the murky inks of first-person writing:

1. In solo mailings, most people read the letter first. This suggests that most readers accept the notion of exhortation first, product description second.

2. "I to you" writing is technically easier than dispassionate product description because personalization is implicitly emotional. Emotion outpulls intellect, a benefit in selling; "I to you" parallels the way we talk, a benefit in message composition.

3. Some catalogs separate themselves from the milieu by becoming an extension of an individual. "I to you" writing massages two egos at once—the buyer's and the writer's.

But does it work?

Personalized catalog copywriting gets tricky when, after writing a dozen descriptions-plus-personalizations has exhausted the thin storehouse of facile approaches, the writer begins to emphasize "I" over "You."

A ghastly error: The writer believes, naively or arrogantly, that the reader will follow every word of text. So when there are cross-references that remind the reader of a personal (to the writer) episode mentioned on a previous page, the connection between writer and reader can shake loose.

You can see what generates this gradual centering of attention on who's writing and not on who's reading: Instead of "I have this for you"—implicitly exclusive, implicitly personal, and therefore implicitly powerful—copy begins to slide inward: "I did this"; "I went here to buy it or to photograph it"; "I tried this and decided it's the best for you."

"I" becomes paramount, while "you" becomes subordinated . . . and yellow caution flags start to fly because this is the kind of copy that makes the reader feel patronized, subliminally or directly.

How can we get the benefit of personalization without risking the detriment of reader rejection?

First, we always have the inside-the-cover message. So, so, so many catalog writers waste the space dedicated to this message! They lapse into loose puffery instead of hammering down the "I to you" link.

Adding guts to the inside-the-cover letter can build the reader's acceptance of almost any kind of descriptive copy—first-person, third-person, and certainly second-person.

Another technique is available, and I've never understood why more personality-based catalogs don't use it.

A short, personalized message appears on each page, in a format paralleling the face of God peering out of a hole in the clouds. This message, made up of ten to twenty words, reinforces the "I found this for you, my dear friend" concept. Specific descriptive copy for each item on the page is released from the artificial first-person constraint so it can fight its own logical battle for attention.

Writer and reader both enjoy a benefit from this procedure. The writer shakes off the shackles of artifice and can use more space for description. The reader sees what he or she wants to see: an explanation of what's for sale unblemished by annoying puffery.

But I don't mean . . .

I'm not suggesting that a catalog writer pour word-bleach over the copy to fade it to colorless blandness. No, no. What I'm suggesting is an uncomplicated way to march around the pitfall of subordinating the message to the medium, still maintaining a facade of "personality."

Figure 23-5: Each description is a carefully created cameo. A book catalog cannot compete with a bookstore in terms of someone being able to handle and browse through a book; it competes on a higher level by building a reason to own a book . . . in this case, successfully.

Here's an easy copy test: If, instead of writing catalog copy for a pair of shoes, you were selling them in a store, how much "I" would you inject into your sales pitch? What would you say about those shoes to convince a casual shopper to buy them?

Use that same logic in catalog copy, and you're safe. The difference between retail head-to-head selling and catalog selling, whether in print or on-line, lies in the medium, not the message.

Why "we" is safer than "I"

Why is "We . . ." a safer copy-block opening than "I . . ."? Suppose the copy began:

> We've slashed the price on this one . . .

Or, carrying through the personality approach of some catalogs, suppose it began:

> I've slashed the price on this one . . .

A single instance may appear to be a "So what?" subtle difference. In bulk, "we" is an extension of the *company's* relationship with us, the prospective customers; in bulk, "I" is an autocratic group of fiats, unilateral decisions by a dictator.

So "I" becomes more dangerous than "we," which means that although first-person copy is easy to write, *effective* "I" copy isn't; it's a sales technique requiring scalpel-like delicacy.

A modest proposal

Here's a suggestion. Safe haven lies in what I call the "Episode-I, Buy-From-We" Indication. It's one of the simpler and more dependable tenets of catalog copywriting: If you're torn between *I* and *we*, use *I* only when referring to personal episode; use *we* for corporate suggestions that the reader buy.

Using this guideline, will your catalog be brilliant, establishing a personality of its own? Probably not; it'll be safely in a middle-of-the-road position.

If you're a bright light among catalog copywriters, ignore everything I've said here. You can carry off "I" copy with elan and effectiveness. But if you have a nagging fear that your own personality may become paramount over what you're selling, this rule of thumb can dry some of the sweat off your brow.

How about *you* in catalog copy? If that glorious word is tied to *benefit*, don't you dare change it.

How to Be Sure You've Described It

I'm looking at a photograph of a pair of cloisonné birds. This is the entire copy block:

> These lovely birds will grace any room of your home or office. Delicately designed and rendered in Oriental cloisonné, these ornate quails will add just the right touch to your decor.
> 1585-439 $149.95 Value . . . $89.95

So I read neutral copy such as "will add just the right touch to your decor," and I ask the writer, "Hey, is that for one bird or two?" The photograph shows two birds. Copy says "birds," not *bird*, but nowhere does it tell us whether we get one or two. So one of two situations will occur:

1. They'll ship two birds for $89.95, which means they've didn't state one of the key selling points in the copy.
2. They'll ship only one bird for $89.95, which means that readers who expected two birds won't be at all pleased.

Hifalutin dangers

The reason so much catalog copy loses its clarity is that literate catalog writers like to show off just how literate they are. By displaying their extensive education instead of projecting themselves inside the reader's mind, they lose contact.

The back cover ranks second only to the front cover in determining whether the catalog will be read. On the back cover of a lavishly produced catalog is a picture of a welcome mat on which, instead of *Welcome*, are the words *Essuyez vos pieds*.
Here's the copy:

> "ESSUYEZ VOS PIEDS" MAT
> A not-so-subtle command in French brings a smile to an otherwise mundane rainy-day chore. Sturdy natural fiber with non-skid rubber backing. (14″ × 13″)

In very small type, below this copy block, the words are unlocked:

> 9025C "Wipe Your Feet" Mat $30.00

Now, of course *we* all know "Essuyez vos pieds" doesn't mean "Fresh fish," but how about those guys down the street who didn't study French in high school? They might read the copy block, never get to the footnote, and conclude, "I don't want this mat because if someone asks me what the words mean, I won't be able to answer." Clarity calls for the translation *in the copy block*.

A visually magnificent catalog, using four different kinds of paper, full bleed, lamination, and gallery-quality photographs, has the following pomposity as its first copy block. The copy appears on an onionskin sheet inside the front cover (the inside cover itself is blank!):

> Perquisites are privileges earned by discrimination as well as by means.
> Superior design, superb engineering and exquisite taste are the perquisites of those who go beyond conventional expectations to demand excellence in everything that surrounds them.

To which I responded, "Huh?"
The first page has a single photograph of what appears to be bondage apparel, with this as the copy:

> LIVING WELL IS THE BEST REVENGE
> "I don't want to make myself comfortable,
> my dear, I want comfort to be made for me."

I guess this is profound, but I have to let the "Huh?" apply here, too. I'm being led into—what? What kind of catalog is this? To those of us in the business, it's plain that form has become paramount to substance. I don't object to this copy; I object to the *sequencing* because somebody is telling me he or she is superior to me without yet having given me a reason to become an admirer.

What a difference one word makes

My wife is a heavy mail-order buyer. She showed me a picture of a sweater in a catalog and asked me to read the description:

> WHO CAN RESIST soft, fluffy angora teddy bears and Marisa Christina's knit know-how? In a wool cardigan style. Sizes P(4), S(6-8), M(10-12), L(14). Imported. DG5716 Teddy Sweater $98.00 (5.25).

"What color is it?" she asked me. "I thought it was black, but it sort of looks like navy. Or is that a purple-black?"

Like the person who wrote this copy, I was no help, and she sighed and closed the catalog. "I'd better not take a chance on it," she said. And a sale was lost because one word—the color of the sweater, a primitive element of clarity—wasn't there.

We don't always have the luxury of being able to pretest copy. We surely do have the professional requirement of being able to build clarity, benefit, and verisimilitude into every block of copy in our catalogs.

Are you communicating . . . or showing off?

On a page in a women's fashion catalog were descriptions of six items. Each picture included a stuffed bear, which obviously wasn't one of the garments but (equally obviously) was, as the copy laboriously underscored, somebody's pet notion.

"Can You BEAR to Be Without This Bewitching Classic 'Little Black Dress'?" was the over-long heading for a relatively short copy block. A glassy-eyed model, hoisting a teddy bear the way an uncertain Statue of Liberty might hold a hot torch, was the accompanying picture.

I cringed twice: first at the emasculating effect "BEAR" had on "Bewitching," and second at the derailing effect the whole notion had on the "Little Black Dress," which lost position because pictorial emphasis was on the bear, not on the dress.

Un-bear-able?

Another picture on the same page had a bear peeking out of a purse, with this Trivial Pursuits heading:

> Urs-Satz? You'd Never Know It!

Ursus (or if you're a woman, *ursa*) is Latin for bear, get it? So it ties to vinyl, which is ersatz leather, get it? Huh? You don't get it? Aw, that's too bad.

Even before the typical reader reluctantly examines the photograph of a Lady in Red, her red-lacquered claw atop a kneeling muscleman whose only garb is a loincloth and a full bear's head mask, opinion is hardened in concrete: This writer has succumbed to the "That-Which-Is-Different = That-Which-Is-Better" cult. The heading:

> Queen of the Grizzlies

I find this whole creative concept un-bear-able, and to the creative director who planned this bugbear—and to anyone else who may be succumbing to the siren song of the unholy "That-Which-Is-Different = That-Which-Is-Better" cabal—I offer the Catalog Writing Truism: The purpose of catalog copy is to transmit an enthusiastic description of what's being sold to the best prospective buyers. Unless this purpose is achieved, the copywriter has failed, regardless of the cleverness of rhetoric.

For completeness, I offer the following two Catalog Writing Truism Footnotes:

1. The Catalog Writing Truism becomes truer when one writer has the responsibility for an entire catalog.
2. A catalog company can prevent its copy from becoming the extension of one person's personality by assigning eight-page sections to different writers.

To wordsmiths who may be rising up in wrath, I'll clarify and justify those footnotes: When a writer knows his or her copy is part of a whole, that writer is unlikely to project personality unrelated to what's being sold. Here's a thirty-two-page catalog. You're writing eight pages, I'm writing eight pages, and two other writers are writing eight pages each. Our instructions may be loose or they may be specific; whoever will approve our copy may or may not give us style sheets. But, invariably, this instruction supersedes all others: Our copy has to be stylistically similar so the catalog won't look like the product of four different writers.

I'm not assailing the notion of having one writer handle a complete catalog. No, I'm trying to stick a pin through the writer who falls in love with his vocabulary and thinks his words deserve more attention than the merchandise those words are supposed to describe.

Opinion: When a cataloger begins to crow about his or her copy *as copy*—"I write every word myself . . ."—hoist the danger flags. Description can give way to a rambling philosophy that can't sell as much merchandise because it's less in tune with benefits the reader wants to see.

At the very least, test clever copy against clearly descriptive copy. I offer the generalization that the larger the universe, the greater the edge for clear-cut description, but a test is always worthwhile.

Funny and pun-ny won't make you any money, honey

Suppose you're a salesperson in a store. A customer asks you about some sculpted candles, shaped like unicorns. Would you grin and show off your superior sense of humor by saying, "Don't myth these sculpted candles"? If you did, you wouldn't work for that store very long.

Why, then, would a catalog writer selling those same candles think cleverness with words works better than descriptive power? Here's the total description of what appear to be attractive candles:

Don't Myth These
sculpted candles—Unicorn
and Pegasus adrift on blue
clouds. Unicorn's horn is
clear plastic. 6×4½×7″H.
Unicorn 1807107
Pegasus 1807115, $15.00 ea.

If you have a spare five minutes, take a shot at this copy. What would *you* have written to sell those candles? Might you have emphasized their artistry, their novelty, their uniqueness as gifts, their translucency, their drip-free quality? What? My opinion: Any of these will outsell the weak pun.

I hold the same opinion about this copy for bedsheets:

Sheepy Time. 100% cotton flannel sheets for value, comfort, absorbency, to keep you warm in winter, cool in summer. Flat sheet is a perfect light summer blanket. Top quality imports. Wedgewood blue with white lambs and stars. Pre-shrunk. Machine wash/dry.

A couple of problems aren't germane to my point: 1) The spelling is *Wedgwood*, not "Wedgewood"; 2) "Sheepy" evokes the instant correlative *sheepish*, not *sheep*.

What *is* germane to my point is that the first two words, "Sheepy Time," generate a child-like image, which isn't what the writer intended. "Sleep Like a Lamb" might have satisfied the writer's desire to be clever *and* the reader's desire for information.

In Search of an Ombudsman

Some in the catalog business were surprised when an expensively produced oversize catalog company went out of business, but most weren't. If you believe the Catalog Writing Truism, you weren't, either.

What typified the violations of the Catalog Writing Truism? Headings like this one, positioned in the center of the page:

. . . at night I play second chef to my boyfriend.

To those who applaud the cleverness of this line, I ask the prosaic question: What does it mean? Nothing in the illustration suggests food. Rather, the picture is of a woman's "granny" outfit, laid out as though the model, like the witch in *The Wizard of Oz*, had melted out of them.

Most puzzling is the description of the first component of this bizarre ensemble, a cardigan sweater:

Textured stripe cardigan 75243 as shown
in smoke. See On The Model for details.

That's it. After some searching, I found a six-point heading on *another* page, "On the Model." In a listing of items, also six-point, was this copy:

Textured stripe cardigan has inky black
stripes down the front and at the cuffs.
Available as shown in smoke, it's made of
an acrylic blend and has a zip up front
with two small pockets. Imported. See
On The Figure for a closer look.
75243 Sizes S-M-L $90.00

Oh, it's a game! But how many readers, frustrated by the search for information, really want to play it to its end? Not enough, obviously, because the company went out of business.

And that's my point. An increasingly valuable tenet of effective catalog writing is one of the undeniable rules for all copywriting, the "Whose Message Is It?" Rule: Write within the experiential background of the reader, not yourself.

The writer, undoubtedly under goad from above, ignored this homily, bowed to art direction that worshiped the inscrutable, and didn't sell much merchandise.

An ombudsman might be a savior

I long have preached the doctrine of having an outsider—someone not involved in product acquisition and not involved in product description—check catalog copy for logic.

No, I'm not referring to a proofreader. I'm suggesting a designated ombudsman. I'd compare this with the role of independent counsel, although not in as dogged nor agenda-laden a mode as one hired by the government. The ombudsman is responsible to only the highest authority. The creative director, the art director, the head of merchandising—none of these should have any influence or control.

Why shouldn't they have any control? Because if they did, the job would be for window dressing only, not for serious reinterpretation of how what appears in print, or on the Web, represents the company. And how about clarity?

Yes, how about clarity? Here's catalog copy with a heading, "The skinny on bed and bath." They need an ombudsman.

Yes, I'm aware of current slang. I'm also aware that by the time it filters down to the bedrock over-35s, it's already worn out among its originators. To many—or maybe even to most—who see a king-size bed with a headline starting with "The skinny . . . ," the reaction has to be, "Huh?"

I'll bet whoever wrote that is younger than thirty. So the writer generated copy not for the catalog's readers but for the catalog's creative department. And somebody approved it. That's why the ombudsman shouldn't have to answer to a creative director or an art director, who may share the same attitude about the appropriateness of certain words.

Here's a catalog that, on page 2, offers "Pure & Simple Tropical Sampler." It's twelve 7-ounce bars of soap, made in Scotland. Regular price is $36.00, sale price $29.99.

Okay, that's page 2. Now, here's page 24, with a heading, "Pure & Simple Floral Sampler. Yep, it's twelve 7-ounce bars of soap, made in Scotland. Price is $38.00. To which the typical soap user puzzles, "Huh?"

They need an ombudsman. And what might that ombudsman have suggested, in this instance? If these two soaps differ—and from the photographs they don't seem to—he or she would have insisted that they be given adjacent positions, with the differences explained. If they don't differ, the ombudsman would have earned his or her salary for the month then and there.

Subtleties a proofreader might miss

Not every call on an ombudsman's talent is obvious. But certainly, anyone qualified to be a catalog ombudsman recognizes the necessity of a quick link from headline to body copy.

So a proofreader certainly would catch the ghastly grammatical error but might find nothing wrong with the logical error in this next example; in fact, *wrong* is too harsh a word. Rather, the proofreader might miss or discount the lack of linkage. The ombudsman wouldn't. The heading:

Get a light or vigorous workout with our electronic monitored Mini Stepper.

And the body copy:

Step up to better health in the convenience of your home as you tone waist, calves, hips, and thighs with this Mini Stepper. It's extremely smooth pulley system uses resistance from hydraulic cylinders to improve your endurance and cardiovascular performance as well as muscle tone. A built-in computer records elapsed time and counts number of steps taken. Made of durable steel . . . [rest of copy is mechanical].

I certainly hope you aren't wondering what the grammatical error is. Somebody who doesn't know the difference between "its" and "it's" is grammatically challenged beyond any help we might offer. The miniproblem an ombudsman would catch and rectify is the "light or vigorous" reference, never covered in the text although ample opportunity abounds. The elapsed-time computer provides a perfect opportunity for an explanation, such as: "Whether for a couple of minutes between conferences or for your daily tone-up . . . " And this should be first in line, since it's the headline reference.

Another example: As the century turned, "Titanic" mania was raging hot. Here's a ship model, and it isn't cheap. The heading:

Limited Edition TITANIC! $699.00 Length overall 24.5″

The picture is a ship model that doesn't quite look like the *Titanic* but has four stacks and the name *Titanic* on it. Any question about what this is? Keep reading. Here's every word of one of the strangest ombudsman-ready copy blocks you'll see today:

TITANIC! 15 April 1912! The ship that wouldn't sink . . . Amazing, the movie cost more than White Star Lines paid Harland & Wolff, Belfast to build the original. 46,439 tons, 882.5′ LOA, 92′ beam, triple screw, combination triple expansion engines and turbine, 23 knots. Her sister, *Olympic*, was also bad luck! Collided with HMS Hawke, 1911; rammed by German U-103, 1918; rammed and sank the Nantucket Lightship, 1934; demolished 1937. Tucher & Walther couldn't resist. Four funnels, but only twin screws, with big wind-up motor. Limited edition of 750, with Certificate and box. Hopefully proving that a pool is somewhat safer than the North Atlantic! Mea culpa! "Oops . . . , I goofed when I wrote the original copy. Titanic fans, please accept my sincerest apologies."—Slim

Okay, we'll accept your sincerest apologies if you'll accept the sincerest advice that you need an ombudsman.

A catalog of outdoor furniture includes the statement: "Both tables stand 28″ high and have a 2″ umbrella hole" but shows and lists a price for only one table.

The description of an "ElectriCruizer®" bicycle raises more questions than it answers.

A "Multi-purpose rug" never suggests any purpose, leaving the reader to wonder what the purposes might be other than just being a rug. Maybe you can place one in five different rooms.

I'll accept but never order the "Keep Food Cold or Hot Up to Three Days" bag that boasts, "This bag maintained the ice crystals on a frozen steak for 36 hours at 68 degrees." Does one brag about ice crystals on a frozen steak?

Parenthetically, the otherwise astute catalog company that thoughtfully sends a welcome letter to its customers . . . while thoughtlessly bypassing the opportunity to resell or at least offer *something* . . . needs an ombudsman.

Get the idea? Then it becomes your turn. Act as ombudsman for any catalog on your table. If you're in the business and are especially stouthearted, make it your own.

Whose Experiential Background?

Who's out there on the receiving end? I'll risk being called a fuddy-duddy by suggesting you'll sell more if you become the clone of the recipient instead of assuming, arrogantly, that he or she is *your* clone.

The difference is the comfort level while reading. A logical if disquieting equation: Discomfort = Wastebasket.

That's the challenge. We compete with retailers, with on-line deals, with solo mailings, and with what seems to be an avalanche of competing catalogs. If only the fit survive, how do we become the fittest?

The thoughtful catalog writer knows the answer. Copy matches the reader's experiential background, which gives us a whopping edge over catalogs that challenge the reader to a duel of wits. In the duel, the reader has the better weapon—a tightly closed checkbook.

Chapter Twenty-Four

THE ASTERISK EXCEPTION

The Asterisk Exception Defined

The Asterisk Exception is a device that seems to have been borrowed from politicians and diplomats. David Stockman, adviser to former president Ronald Reagan, lays claim to having invented the "magic asterisk," a technique for nonexplanatory explanation of how the federal government would save $44 billion. (In fact, the history of asterisks as an obfuscatory device far predated him.)

The Asterisk Exception works like this: An ad or a brochure makes a claim—a flat statement, unblemished by an "if" or "but" clause.

Then, at the end of the statement, we see the tiny symbol of contempt for the message we just interpreted too favorably: an asterisk. We *know* what we'll find as we look down the page: a disclaimer. "You collect only if you're in a goat cart in Mukden," or "Limited to the period from August 31 to September 1," or "Optional at extra cost."

In my opinion, the Asterisk Exception is a virus we have to fight; otherwise, it will add to the implicit skepticism already growing in our message recipients.

It's generic to financial mailings

A mailing from a credit card tells me I've been "Pre-approved." Oh, just a moment . . . I'm "Pre-approved †" . . . not quite the same. The envelope has a dagger symbol after the words "Pre-approved" instead of an asterisk. (See Figure 24-1.) Why the dagger? Because some may mistake it for an exclamation point. Inside, yep, there it is (Figure 24-2):

†Limitations apply. See Acceptance Certificate below and reverse side for details.

A bank mailing to an existing credit card customer has this legend at the top, in bold type:

This season use your card or access checks to do what you want with your limited-time 6.9% Annual Percentage Rate (APR)!*†

Wow! Three punctuation marks in a row! Well, let's see . . . at the bottom of the page, in tiny type, is a four-line explanation of the dagger:

†The promotional Annual Percentage Rate (APR) offer for Purchases, Check Cash Advances and Balance Transfers is 6.9% through your statement closing date in specified month]. Thereafter, the APR will be 28.99% (or the then prevailing APR if amended) and will be applied [blah blah blah]. . . .

GE SELECT PLATINUM CLASS MASTERCARD ®

The Benchmark of Success

4.9%
*introductory APR
on Balance Transfers
and Purchases*

- NO ANNUAL FEE

- PRE-APPROVED[†]

- CREDIT LINE UP TO $10,000

Figure 24-1: Lots of hedging here. The APR is "introductory"; the credit line is "up to" $10,000. See that little dagger symbol after "Pre-approved"? Figure 24-2 explains it, with more hedging.

GE SELECT PLATINUM CLASS MASTERCARD®

The Benchmark of Success

Invitation code: C 247351

4.9% *fixed*
*introductory APR
on Balance Transfers
and Purchases*

Reserved exclusively for you

CREDIT LINE UP TO **$10,000**

Herschell G. Lewis
340 N. Fig Tree Ln.
Plantation, FL 33317-2561

Reply by: 02/15/

PRE-APPROVED[†]

NO ANNUAL FEE

ONGOING VARIABLE APR AS LOW AS **11.9%**

$1 MILLION TRAVEL ACCIDENT INSURANCE

GE VACATION TRAVEL SERVICE WITH **2%** REBATE

GE INTEREST PLUS

YEAR-END CHARGE SUMMARY

† Limitations apply. See Acceptance Certificate below and reverse side for details.

* See Cardmember Benefits Guide for further details.

Dear Herschell G. Lewis:

Your superior financial management has allowed you to attain a level of success where you can begin to reap those benefits you so richly deserve. Among those benefits – The GE Select Platinum Class MasterCard.

You've earned an impressive credit line of up to $10,000, an outstanding 4.9% introductory APR on balance transfers and purchases until August 1998 and an ongoing variable APR as low as 11.9%.

The GE Select Platinum Class MasterCard eliminates your annual fee and offers exclusive benefits not available with other cards, such as:

- A 2% rebate credit on vacation purchases made through GE Vacations*
- Access to GE Interest Plus - a unique investment opportunity that pays higher rates than most banks and money market funds*

In addition, the GE Select Platinum Class MasterCard provides you with valuable convenience and security features at no charge to you, including:

- Purchase Protection and Extended Warranty Program
- $1,000,000 in Travel Accident Insurance

(over please)

▼ DETACH HERE AND RETURN IN THE POSTAGE-PAID ENVELOPE PROVIDED ▼

Figure 24-2: At bottom left is a dagger and an asterisk. The dagger says, "Limitations apply." The asterisk refers to the Cardmember Benefits Guide, not included.

The asterisk? Ah, there it is, hidden at bottom right:

*Over Please

If they didn't bother to separate those words with a comma, I'm not going to turn over the paper.

Yet another mailing, with "Congratulations!" on the envelope (followed by the flat statement "You're eligible for our *low, low* rate: 4.9% fixed APR," has an asterisk, two asterisks, and a set of

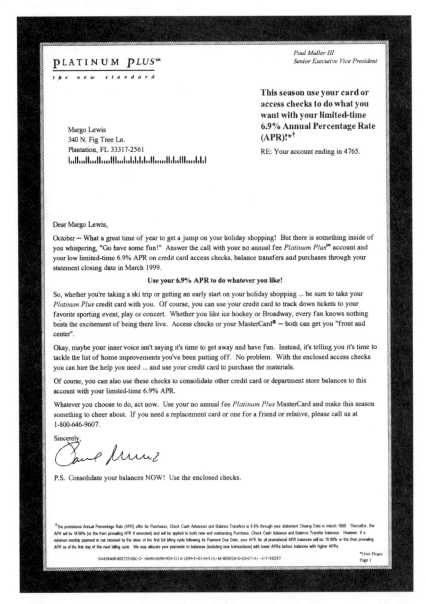

Figure 24-3: A wealth of symbols in that legend at upper right—an exclamation point, an asterisk, and a dagger. The dagger is a reference to four solid lines of mice-type, pointing out that the 6.9% becomes 18.99% after a short period. The asterisk says, "Over, Please"—where hard-to-read type says that credit card access checks "are processed as Cash Advances according to the terms of your Credit Card Agreement and are subject to credit availability." (Envelope copy says, "This season, you've really got something to cheer about." What?)

three asterisks qualifying the offer. The first asterisk reference is only mildly negative, but, to an unsophisticated recipient, puzzling after "Congratulations!" and "You're eligible" on the envelope:

*See Fee and Term Information on reverse side. Standard APR and credit line are based on your creditworthiness and income.

The explanation for the hedge is that names for almost all these mailings are cross-matched against credit bureau reports, so recipients *should* qualify, but occasionally people's fortunes change between the time the credit report is updated and the mailing. This is self-protection for the mailer.

The second asterisk group is brutal:

**Certain conditions, limitations, and exclusions apply. Details available when you become a cardmember.

Says the skeptical reader: "What is this? They ask for a commitment and won't tell me what I'm committing to?"

The third asterisk group is mechanical and has a typographical error that completely changes its meaning:

***The introductory period ends as of the first day or your billing cycle that includes July 1 of this year.

Yes, they mean "of," not "or" . . . but that isn't what the recipient reads. (Figure 24-4 shows the asterisk trilogy.)

Typos and legal requirements notwithstanding, what is demanded is completeness of explanation. I hope you can see how much more reader-friendly (and clearer) exclusions and definitions would be if they were inside a pair of parentheses *as each occurs* instead of being lumped at the bottom like a trio of evil bandits, eager to impede reading and add qualifiers to the promises.

Airlines are asterisk-happy, too

Although financial mailings are the cauldron from which asterisks seem to pour, a mailing from an airline is a textbook example of the Asterisk Exception.

The airline has a "Senior Class Travel Club" that offers benefits to senior citizens. A $25 fee enrolls the member; for $100, the member can add this generation's euphemism, a "companion." (Very modern: The member can change companions for each flight.)

Two facets of this package puzzle me. First, although membership is open to anyone age sixty or older, a 10 percent fare discount applies only to those sixty-five or older.

Second—well, judge for yourself:

THE PRIVILEGES
OF SENIOR CLASS
► double Frequent Flyer mileage credit for all flights
► a 10% discount on airfares for members 65 and older*
► special discounts on rooms at all participating Radisson Hotels*
► special discounts on rooms at all participating Stouffer Hotels*
► discounts on selected Hertz rental cars*

NationsBank Platinum MasterCard®

> ### WE BELIEVE A SUPERIOR CREDIT RECORD SHOULD <u>SAVE YOU MONEY</u>.
>
> - #### NO ANNUAL FEE
> - #### 4.9% FIXED INTRODUCTORY APR
> WHEN YOU TRANSFER BALANCES FROM OTHER CREDIT CARDS

Dear Dennis Tallyn:

People who pay their bills on time deserve to *get a better deal*. And that's exactly what you'll get with our Platinum MasterCard. It offers an unusually high credit line—from $5,000 up to $100,000—and *unprecedented savings*.* Here's how:

<u>**4.9% fixed APR.**</u> Available only to the most creditworthy individuals, this money-saving introductory APR is yours when you transfer balances from other credit cards right now. The rate is good until July 1, 1998***, and it applies to new purchases, too, to save you even more.

<u>**Easy Balance Transfer.**</u> Just complete the Balance Transfer Form above, and we'll handle all the paperwork once your request is approved.

<u>**No annual fee.**</u> You'll pay nothing to carry our Platinum MasterCard. Compare that to other platinum cards that charge an annual fee of $300.

<u>**Free Photo Security Card**</u>^{SM}. Enjoy the added security of having your photo and signature added to the front of your card, so everyone will know that *you* are the *only* person authorized to use it and you'll be safe if your card should fall into the wrong hands.**

<u>**Platinum MasterCard benefits.**</u>** You'll enjoy theft and damage protection plus extended warranties on most retail purchases, no liability for unauthorized charges, a free annual account summary, an interest-free grace period, toll-free travel assistance when calling from more than 70 countries, personalized concierge services, free travel accident insurance up to $1,000,000, complimentary rental car insurance, 24-hour road assistance, great savings on merchandise and travel, unsurpassed card acceptance at more than 14 million locations, access to cash at more than 450,000 places, and more!

<u>**Call now to enjoy the savings you deserve!**</u> Request your low 4.9% fixed APR NationsBank Platinum MasterCard and transfer other card balances right now! Our lines are open 24 hours a day, 7 days a week. (Or if you prefer, you can complete and mail the Request Certificate above.)

Sincerely,

Byron L. Ashbridge Jr.

Byron L. Ashbridge, Jr., President
NationsBank of Delaware, N.A.

P.S. Don't miss out on a low 4.9% fixed introductory APR! Request this money-saving, no-annual-fee Platinum MasterCard and transfer other balances before March 13. deadline.

* See Fee and Term Information on reverse side. Standard APR and credit line are based on your creditworthiness and income.
**Certain conditions, limitations, and exclusions apply. Details available when you become a cardmember.
***The introductory period ends as of the first day or your billing cycle that includes July 1, 1998.

NBPMCD-01/98

Figure. 24-4: Three asterisk exceptions here, and the 4.9% APR applies only when the applicant transfers balances from other credit cards.

▶ Quarterly Senior Class newsletters featuring vacation package discounts and other special offers.
* Certain restrictions apply.

I knew when I hit the first asterisk what the reference would be. As an old weasel-word artist, I'm sensitive to clues such as "participating" hotels, which tells me the ones I want aren't participants. And just who selects the "selected" Hertz rental cars? But those aren't my biggest objection to the technique of presentation.

We have six bullets. Four of them have that lethal asterisk. Nowhere in the mailer does an explanation appear. "Certain restrictions apply" is set in type about half the size of the other copy. In the Age of Skepticism, what must our logical conclusion be, even though only $25 or $100 is at stake?

Another airline, in a space ad, has this first sentence of body copy:

If you are 65 or over, you can get a 10% discount on any [NAME OF AIRLINE] air-fare, even low Ultimate SuperSaver fares.*

On the way downward to find what I knew I'd find, oops! Another asterisk:

A $25 Travel Voucher,* valid for one year, which can be used on any [NAME OF AIR-LINE] flight.

No surprises here. The asterisk at the bottom of the column was more forthright than the copy it amended: "*Some restrictions may apply." ("May"? I'll bet you the $25 voucher that some restrictions *do* apply.)

Another airline, describing its similar program, doesn't disappoint asterisk seekers:

From our travel partners, you will receive:*

I kind of like this one, more forthright than "Some restrictions may apply." The asterisk ref-erence says bluntly:

* Subject to Change.

The capitalization of *Change* suggests it isn't just a little change.

Is there a cure?

I offer, not as an antidote but as a map for exploration, this descriptive objection: A writer uses the Asterisk Exception when he or she has no confidence in 1) personal ability to convince the reader of benefit by putting all the facts in direct context, or 2) verity of the offer itself.

Either use tells us we have to train ourselves to overcome the Asterisk Exception the way we'd lick smoking or fingernail biting or a "You know" habit.

I'm looking at a space ad for a hotel. Here's the headline:

BEST LOCATION IN
WASHINGTON, D.C.
AT A CAPITAL PRICE
$39.50*

Uh-oh. Let's sneak a look past the hard-sell bullet copy. Yup. It's there. Yipe. It's worse than we expected, a *double* whammy:

* per person, double occupancy, per night, children under 16 stay free in parents' suite. Based on availability. Rate applies to all weekends and holidays.

This writer is no beginner. Look how that last piece of negative information came out posi-tively: "Rate applies to all weekends and holidays." A lesser scribe would have written, "Weekends and holidays only," which is what the copy really means. With this kind of talent, couldn't the writer consider options other than the Asterisk Exception?

Probably the answer is, "That's the way we write travel and leisure copy—the price is per person, not per room, and readers are trained to know most of these deals are for weekends only."

Oh, yeah? Then why did the ad run in a business publication targeted to government computer decision makers?

Why not a POSITIVE asterisk?

Why do asterisks always have to mean bad news, like a telegram from the Defense Department at wartime?

The coupon in a mail-order ad for a porcelain doll has this predictable use of the asterisk:

I will be billed prior to shipment for my deposit of $37; after shipment, I will be billed for the balance in four equal monthly installments of $37 each.*

At the foot of the coupon is the troll under the bridge:

* Plus a total of $5 for shipping and handling.

What if, instead of an asterisk, we had a pair of parentheses immediately following the price, so the copy would read:

. . . in four equal installments of $37 each (plus a total of $5 for shipping and handling).

We aren't just ridding ourselves of the asterisk, that negative and pedantic bugaboo. We're avoiding the unnecessary negative reaction we have to an increased price after we've digested what we think is a total.

It really would shake up the system if somebody used asterisks to present *positive* addenda! Not in our lifetime, we know, but maybe one day . . .

Help Stamp Out Asterisks

How many of these do you recognize?

* Plus sales tax, shipping, handling, insurance, and whatever.
* In pigskin only.
* Not available in colors other than white.
* Excluding purchase of sundries, beer and wine, and cigarettes.
* Not valid Dec. 15–Jan. 31.
* Subject to change without notice.

My point: It's out of hand. It's epidemic. It's the automatic choice of writers who think readers won't notice an unpleasant appendage to a message if it's relegated to asterisk status.

If you have a piece of copy in your word processor, hit the search key to see whether an asterisk has crept into the text. If it has, experiment with other ways of transmitting the same information. You may find El Dorado at the end of your search.*

---

* On the other hand, you may not. See how asterisks take the fun out of life?

Chapter Twenty-Five

A TIP A DAY—SO YOU CAN WRITE POWERHOUSE COPY WITHIN ONE MONTH

Thirty Nuggets to Help You Write Dynamite Copy
(Absorb and Use One Each Day for the Next Month)

Here are thirty nuggets to store in your word-pockets or -purse against that odd moment when you might need them. They're something like carrying garlic or a crucifix just in case Dracula shows up at your dinner party.

1. *Conditional words and phrases let the prospect off the hook (for fund-raising, senior citizens, nonproduct copy, and copy emphasizing deadlines or expiration).*

Here's the first pass at a paragraph in a mailing seeking contributions:

We squeeze every nickel and stretch every dollar, but we're desperately close to running out of money. If we did, we'd have to cut back on programs that might have been the only act of friendship for helpless children.

Sharp-eyed editing changed a couple of words, closing the loophole the first draft had given the reader:

We squeeze every nickel and stretch every dollar, but we're desperately close to running out of money. If we do, we'll have to cut back on programs that might be the only act of friendship for helpless children.

2. *"Staccato" copy calls attention to writing as writing. Except for headlines and bullet copy, it's more likely to irritate than to inform (for space ads, especially for consumer electronics, high-style men's fashions, and services).*

Staccato copy is a repeated burst of short thoughts, unfettered by grammar. The technique is used only in print and Web advertising; advocates say that's the way people talk. Detractors say people who talk that way aren't communicators, so why should we imitate them?

An example of staccato copy:

Move up. To a better way of life.

You have the opportunity. Now. Tomorrow? Too late. You'll love your neighborhood. Your neighbors. Not having to lock your door. Not having to keep your pup on a chain.

What do you say? Don't you deserve it? The freedom. The openness. The trees and streams. Sure you do. And you can have it. If you make your move now.

Did you, reading this short excerpt, feel off-balance? Those who embrace staccato writing say that's what you're supposed to feel.

My suggestion: Use staccato writing in small doses. For emphasis. Not for a whole message. You'll lose impact. Instead of gaining it. Because you overuse a gimmick. You.

3. *Don't use an incredible premise as your principal sales argument (for business-to-business advertising, first-person "I did it and you can do it, too" ads, and product puffery).*

A reader, listener, surfer, or viewer can identify with an episode he recognizes as probable and rejects an episode he recognizes as improbable. That's what's wrong with the idiotic television commercial that opens with a frazzled husband railing at his wife: "The most important conference of my life and you've switched deodorant soaps!"

The newspaper consistently ranked first or second in circulation in the United States sent me a message I reject implicitly as romantic fiction by a Horatio Alger pretender:

> On a beautiful late spring afternoon, twenty-five years ago, two young men graduated from the same college. They were very much alike, these two young men. Both had been better than average students, both were personable and both—as young college graduates are—were filled with ambitious dreams for the future.
>
> Recently, these men returned to their college for their 25th reunion.
>
> They were still very much alike. Both were happily married. Both had three children. And both, it turned out, had gone to work for the same Midwestern manufacturing company after graduation and were still there.
>
> But, there was a difference. One of the men was manager of a small department of that company. The other was its president.
>
> Have you ever wondered, as I have, what makes this kind of difference in people's lives? It isn't always a native intelligence or talent or dedication. It isn't that one person wants success and the other doesn't.
>
> The difference lies in what each person knows and how he or she makes use of that knowledge.
>
> And that is why I am writing to you and to people like you about *The Wall Street Journal* . . .

This letter has been used successfully for a generation. It's anthologized in compendia of famous sales letters. So what's missing here?

To a top executive, credibility.

Is the story true? In the words of Rhett Butler, "Frankly, my dear, I don't give a damn." It's just as possible that across the street from this "Midwestern manufacturing company" is another one twice as big. Its president is a functional illiterate and his junior clerk just celebrated twenty-five years of *Journal* subscriptions.

Accepting the argument that this letter has produced subscriptions, one might ask, *whose* subscriptions? The caliber of subscription this letter generates simply has to be bottom-end. To attract top executives, the letter might use the episode as a minor indicator, leaning on a more credible rationale to get the reader to subscribe.

4. *To generate guilt, suggest a positive act, not a negative act (for hard sell).*

The logic is unassailable: A negative act is more reprehensible than omission.
So we don't say:

 If you don't order something from the catalog . . .

Instead, we say:

 If you decide not to order something from the catalog . . .

5. *Careful with words that by their very nature will irritate some readers (for all advertising).*

Figure 25-1: (Nugget 5) The heading says, "18th Century France—Beheadings, Torture, Massacres, a great place to find inspiration for a butcher table." Would you want a blood-soaked table in your kitchen?

The writer whose space ad selling porcelain figurines used the phrase "hard-core collector" knows what this nugget means. A lot of readers older than fifty-five see the words "hard-core" and reach a set-in-cement conclusion.

Instead of arguing semantics, why take this risk? When I saw a promotional piece from a syndicated creative source, this nugget came into even sharper focus. A key sentence:

We make up a new ad each month and strip your name in it.

My own negative reaction to the word "strip" is a mechanical one. I don't want to be part of a creative cattle call, and this copy emphasizes my anonymity instead of massaging my ego. And I can see that others might reach a different but equally negative subliminal conclusion about the word. Why not *print* my name in it instead of stripping it in? (A better way of putting selling emphasis where it belongs: "Every month you'll get a new ad—with *your* name custom-printed in it.")

6. *Following "This is the best" or any other blanket claim of superiority with the self-disciplining word* because *will force you, the message originator, to structure a word-sell program designed to get those heads nodding (for general advertising, business-to-business ads, and subscription promotions).*

The people you'll sell with hit-and-run tactics ("This is the most important [WHATEVER]" or "You'll be interested in this," without any information justifying the claim) are those who already agree with you. Don't feel triumphant because these people reached their conclusion before your message arrived.

A publisher mailed me a well-produced offering for a one-year subscription to a market guide. The subscription costs $1,950, and in that stratospheric region I need a heavy injection of benefit to get me to open my checkbook.

The two-page letter begins rationally enough, if a little on the slow-moving and patronizing side:

Dear Mr. Lewis:

As the president of a direct marketing agency, we believe you will be especially interested in information on the size, characteristics and geography of the consumer market—basic structural data—that will provide you with important guidelines for designing sales strategy, developing new products and the planning of almost all your marketing activities.

The Conference Board's Consumer Research Center is designed to improve decision-making: (1) by keeping you abreast of current consumer trends and sentiment and (2) by placing at your fingertips the marketing data you require daily—at a price far below any alternative service you may now use.

Yawn. The letter goes on and on, always logical and always in a "Who we are, what we do" vein. What it *doesn't* tell me is why I need it. Instead of building, the letter winds down as it dips instead of peaks on the second page:

The Center's income service and expenditure series makes accessible to you the detailed facts and figures of continuous and extensive surveys conducted by the federal government—in a form designed to meet your decision-making needs in the most cost-effective fashion.

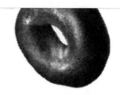

THERE'S AN ELEMENT OF RISK IN EVERYTHING.

Sometimes risks aren't so readily apparent. For example, you might not realize that thousands of people go to the emergency room every year for cutting their hands while slicing bagels.

Hidden risks also are part of investing. That's why Stein Roe Special Fund has a long history of looking beyond the obvious.

Special Fund seeks out stocks of financially strong companies that may be temporarily undervalued, underfollowed or out of favor. Stocks that we believe have limited downside risk relative to their potential for above average growth.

Like all Stein Roe funds, Special Fund seeks superior performance over the long term by pursuing a sensible balance between return and risk. Across six decades, Stein Roe has employed this strategy on behalf of its investors. In fact, the Fund's successful strategy has served shareholders across four decades and earned Special Fund a ★★★★ overall rating from Morningstar as of 12/31/97 (against 2,332, 1,292 and 676 domestic equity funds for the 3-, 5- and 10-year periods, respectively).

To find out more about Special Fund, do the one thing with no risk at all: call us or visit our web site at www.steinroe.com.

STEIN ROE SPECIAL FUND

Average Annual Total Returns as of 12/31/97

26.0% one-year **15.6%** five-year **17.3%** ten-year

Past performance does not guarantee future results. Share price and investment return will vary, so you may have a gain or loss when you sell shares.

 STEIN ROE MUTUAL FUNDS

SENSIBLE RISKS. INTELLIGENT INVESTMENTS.   **1-800-774-2314**

Call a Stein Roe account representative for a prospectus and more complete information. Please read the prospectus carefully before investing. Total return performance includes changes in share price and reinvestment of income and capital gains distributions. Morningstar's proprietary ratings reflect historical, risk-adjusted performance through 12/31/97 and are subject to change every month. The overall rating is calculated from the Fund's 3-, 5- and 10-year average annual returns in excess of 90-day Treasury bill returns with appropriate adjustments for fees and risk. The Fund received 4 stars for the 3-, 5- and 10-year periods ended 12/31/97. If a fund scores in the top 10% of its class, it receives 5 stars; if it scores in the next 22.5%, it receives 4 stars. Liberty Financial Investments, Inc., Distributor. Member SIPC.

Figure 25-2: (Nugget 6) One is hard-pressed to find a less relevant relationship than the one between bagels and investing. Is this the best the writer could come up with to show superiority? Pity.

The communication misses the target not because it sells something I can't use but because the thrust is analytical rather than inspirational. Copy that leans on phrases such as "basic structural data," "important guidelines," "the planning of almost all your marketing activities," "abreast of current consumer trends and sentiment," "makes accessible to you," and the ghastly "in a form designed to meet your decision-making needs" is the work of a textbook writer, not a commercial writer.

7. *When potency-draining "if . . . " follows the main clause, it twists the interpretation the reader—or, especially, the listener—already has reached, forcing a negative change. So an "if" clause is a better beginning clause than a follow-up clause (for all copy, especially spoken words).*

Here's a primitive example:

You can lose as much as five pounds the very first week, if you follow this simple weight-loss system.

We change nothing but the sequence:

If you follow this simple weight-loss system, you can lose as much as five pounds the very first week.

Can you see the difference? The residual image of the first piece of copy is the condition because that's the last part of the message. The residual image of the second piece of copy is the benefit because that's the last part of the message.

The "if . . . " clause unwittingly feeds skepticism when it follows a positive thought. Your listener thought he understood the benefit, then is forced to reevaluate because of a condition introduced after the benefit has been promised.

A more palatable version eliminates "if" altogether:

Just by following this simple weight-loss system, you can lose as much as five pounds the very first week.

8. *If you have to exclude the reader, explain why (for collateral literature, high-tech ads, and/or introduction of a product at a new lower user level).*

The ease with which you can couch the message should be equally obvious. A vendor of business software crows:

We have a special, private toll-free number for dealers.

What's wrong with this supposed benefit? The company makes the statement in a mailing to users rather than to dealers. How easy it would be to include the user instead of treating him like an outsider:

Have a question? Ask your dealer. He can call a special toll-free number and get the answer for you.

9. *When your claim is weak or hard to prove, enlist the reader as an ally (for self-improvement products and plain ol' country boy (P.O.C.B.) copy).*

An ad for a weight-reducing tea, whose claims might be hammered by the Food and Drug Administration if they were too strong, does a neat job of enlisting the reader as an ally with this headline:

If You Drink This Delicious Tea
You Just Might Lose Weight.
We're Not Sure Why.

Body copy reinforces the nonclaim:

READ THIS CAREFULLY

We make no specific claims for Oriental Slimtea, not only because it's against the law to do so but also because we ourselves aren't sure how or why this wonderful-tasting tea has the power to help you get rid of excess fat.

All we can do is offer you a *100% Absolute Money-Back Guarantee*. If it doesn't . . .

See how it works? No ammunition for the skeptic who wants to say, "I don't believe your claim"—and now can't say it.

10. *Don't risk the reader's wrath by using words with multiple meanings (for consumer advertising).*

A mailing from a financial institution has this headline copy on its brochure:

Put the Cash Hidden in Your Home
to Work for You.

What's wrong here? The word "Hidden." If I did have cash hidden in my home, I'd wonder how this savings and loan knew about it. *Hidden* has so many negative connotations that it's best used when telling someone what *not* to do.

All the writer had to do was hold the homeowner harmless:

Did You Know There's CASH Hidden in Your Home, Waiting to Go to Work for You?

11. *When you project an assumption, base it on a psychological truth or a known psychographic fact, not on a self-serving fantasy (for all copy).*

Measure this next example—presumption whose self-serving fantasy isn't even masked— against that nugget:

Dear Gold Card Member:
Like you, the Japanese love nature.

Of all the "So what?" statements we've read this year, this one ranks at the top. Maybe I'm a nature lover, maybe not. Even if I am, loving nature isn't among the 8,000 leading motivators of our time.

12. *If inconsequential fact doesn't enhance the possibility of response, don't introduce it. If you include copy that lowers the competitive position of what you're selling, use it to prove your integrity (for all copy).*

Figure 25-3: (Nugget 11) One word analyzes this ad—"Huh?"

You aren't an investigative reporter. Your job is to present a *selection* of facts, not an "If the truth hurts, so be it" confession.

A trade ad for a magazine that boasts about its superiority offers this statistical evidence:

A Solid SECOND
In Reader AND Advertiser Preference!

If I were a space buyer, this copy would motivate me, all right—to head for *Standard Rate & Data*, looking for the magazine that's a first. Think: How would a good copywriter have used

Figure 25-4: (Nugget 12) So what? A more dynamic statistic . . . if the writer has to use statistics . . . is in the text: The company already hosts 80,000 sites.

this same information to generate a positive image? Did Avis say, relative to Hertz, "A Solid SEC-OND"? Nope. They built a campaign out of their position: "We Try Harder."

You aren't writing an exposé or a learned treatise. You're writing forceful communication. What's forceful about this negative classic, a headline for a computer magazine?

Seven good reasons why you should subscribe to *Creative Computing*

The first reason:
Creative Computing
gives you things to
actually do with a
computer.

This is the top reason? What this does is make mashed potatoes out of the other six reasons. We can't accept this copy as projecting anything other than useless, comparatively benefitless fact. (The magazine went out of business.)

A copywriter asks me to buy art by a painter, but nonenhancing fact does the writer in:

Ms. Kuck is an exceptionally gifted painter. She has devoted her considerable talents to child-subject art for the past decade and as a result has sold more than 1,200 original paintings—and a number of her paintings have sold for over $1,000 each!

Count your objections. I find two. First, if this artist has sold more than 1,200 paintings over the past decade, she's sold 120 a year, or about one every two working days. That's about as exclusive as a caricaturist at a party. Second, $1,000 each is a barely respectable price for a painter of any consequence at all.

Think of the ways the writer might have made the point of desirability and value if the desire to introduce all the facts, negative as well as positive, hadn't interfered.

13. *Kick out extra words. Good copy is lean (for all copy except fashion and entertainment, and, conditionally, those also).*

The most common writing weakener is, happily, the easiest to correct. A writer fills his paper edge to edge with words. Some of those words are as useful as extra water in an overflowing bathtub because they add neither description nor selling power.

What do these typical lines of copy have in common?

The finest in sporting goods . . .
The best in electronic wonders . . .
Designed for the use of the novice and the experienced user alike . . .
Ours is a business of which it might be said that . . .

Right. Each has weakener words, just as this sentence would be weaker if I wrote, "Each *of them* has weakener words." Good writing is lean.

So, accepting the useless word "finest" as a descriptive word, which it isn't, the phrase unplugs its clogged artery when changed to: *The finest sporting goods.* Accepting the outrageous arrogance of "best," an unproved superlative, we still help drag the phrase back a foot or two from the abyss of somnolence when we drop a word so that it reads: *The best electronic wonders.* Exorcising the redundancy, we add at least fifteen miles per hour as we claim: *Designed for novice and experienced user alike.*

How about that fourth example? My suggestion: Drop the whole word-pile. As an exercise, you might complete that sentence, then eliminate the opening and see how much more power your words have.

14. *For the wordsmith, communication is more professional than grammatical correctness (for all copy except textbook promotion).*

No, no, I'm not saying it's okay to use *its* instead of *it's* or to misspell key words. I'm saying that you can use *ain't*, start sentences with *And*, and use *'em* instead of *them* . . . if circumstances make such constructions logical. You can end sentences with prepositions.

A force-communicator who puts grammar ahead of results is like the senator who puts *Robert's Rules of Order* ahead of legislation. It's a dedication to form instead of substance, means instead of end—a tribute to fogeyism.

If in the pursuit of grammatical excellence we let form take precedence over substance, we can cripple reader rapport. As an example, not long ago I okayed this sentence in a piece of selling copy:

Every man, woman, and child on this planet needs something to write with.

Try writing this without ending the sentence with a preposition. You'd have " . . . something with which to write," a weak way of putting a strong idea, and awkward as well. (Did you notice *okayed*? That word is okay in context.)

So "It's a book you'll never grow tired of" is superior to "It's a book of which you'll never grow tired." I write *formulas* even though I know the plural of *formula* is *formulae* because I'm writing to communicate, not to impress the English Department. If I have to use *graffiti,* I always stay in the plural because to most readers and all listeners the singular *graffito* seems odd. I sell tennis *rackets* even though proper usage calls for *racquets* because that's what readers of ads in tennis magazines expect.

Now for the big BUT—

15. *Don't lapse into illiteracy (for the same targets as Nugget 14).*

If you hire writers, you have applicants who hand you a test piece crawling with misspelled and misused words and who become annoyed when you chide them mildly about *to* instead of *too* and *it's* instead of *its.*

Don't let them give you the dumb argument that someone can write professional copy and not know there's no apostrophe in the possessive *its.* Don't let them tell you it's inconsequential that they haven't learned that the contraction for *you are* is *you're,* not *your.*

Apply, with as much vigor as the circumstance warrants, the Illiteracy Rejection: Communication in the Age of Skepticism is informal, but it isn't casual.

You know the next line of the specious argument defending casual use of wrong words: "Anyway, a proofreader will catch those little word changes."

I submit: If a proofreader can learn the English language, so can the writer whose words are being proofread.

16. *Don't use unexplained and unvalidated comparatives and superlatives (for all advertising).*

This is more than taking a look at your last ad or mailer, searching for and circling adjectives ending in *er* and *est* (see Nugget 6).

Have you crowed, "Compare!" without offering a specific comparison? Have you shouted at the reader or viewer, "I make this claim!" without validating that claim?

With the backing of solid information, comparatives and superlatives are potent selling words: Information + comparative/superlative = product or service superiority.

Without that backing, look out! You're making a lot of noise but firing blanks. (For silver bullets, reread Chapter 6.)

17. *When a sentence has too many commas, consider using parentheses instead of one pair of commas. You can speed up both reading and comprehension (for all print advertising and direct mail).*

A sentence read:

We think the combination of a successful history, going back to 1866, and such dynamic new trading techniques as *Commodex*, are unbeatable in today's pressure-laden economic environment.

The sentence seems sluggish. Comprehension isn't easy because all the elements set off by commas aren't parallel. A five-second revision had the copy reading this way:

We think the combination of a successful history (going back to 1866) and such dynamic new trading techniques as *Commodex* are unbeatable in today's markets.

The words flow past the eye faster, and changing the explanation of the company's history to a parenthetical phrase makes the third comma unnecessary altogether.

18. *Get rid of qualifiers (for on-camera testimonials and first-person ads).*

Flab can attack fingers as well as hips and thighs, when those fingers are writing copy. Can you spot the flabby qualifiers in these constructions?

You may be a bit surprised to learn . . .
We were rather pleased when . . .
I would like to take this opportunity to tell you that . . .

Why should I be "a bit surprised" when by dropping those two words the writer can have me flat-out surprised? The second copywriter is better off being pleased than being "rather pleased."

What was your conclusion about the third example? If it's anything other than throwing out the phrase altogether, go to the foot of the class and sit next to whoever wrote it.

Words such as practically, largely, somewhat—these are giveaways of a syndrome I call the Principle of Expository Uncertainty. Hedging stems from the writer's lack of assurance; the result is lack of message strength.

19. *Don't make the reader write your copy for you (for copy intended to generate a positive attitude).*

If you say, "For many reasons," name some of those reasons. If you say, "Among other things," name some of those things. If you use the word *important,* justify your claim, or it becomes arrogant. While you're at it, be sure it's important to the reader, not just to you.

One word that always tips off the reader that you're out of gas and want to siphon some from his imagination-tank is . . . *etc.*

Whenever I see this nonword, I draw two assumptions:

1. The writer is lazy.
2. The writer thinks whatever he's selling may have additional features, but he doesn't know what they are.

Never use *etc.* again, except in satire or parody.

20. *Don't use nouns as verbs (for financial, insurance, or computer copy).*

I admit this is a losing battle, but I include it after hearing, repeatedly, the word *architect* used as a verb.

Careful, now: Many words—*fish, cash, slip, pick, watch,* for example—*are* both nouns and verbs.

However, that group does not include *input, access, impact, network, reference,* or *window.*

It's probably a losing battle, but let's go down swinging. Such usage isn't terrible, and unquestionably it's going to wind up in the dictionary one day, but it isn't yet the way a professional should use language.

Take a look at some computer magazines and verify for yourself: The superior ads don't use in-talk.

21. *Keep copy references in character. Decide what state of mind you want to generate, then stay inside it (for print media).*

Figure 25-5: (Nugget 21) The cause of failure in this trade ad isn't the concept—that the cashier is using an old-fashioned cash register—but that the shopper and the cashier also represent bygone times. Instead of unearthing an old stock photo, the creative team would have bred greater impact by having a smartly modern setting highlight the anomaly of an antique register.

Your copy style might be grim. It might be funny. It might be olympian. It might be documentary. It might be plain ol' country boy. It might be frantic. Whatever it is, keep it consistent.

A piece of copy, selling recordings of vintage radio comedy shows, read this way:

> These timeless masters of wit and humor never had to depend on sight gags. Their exquisite timing and detailed observance of the human condition were their hilarious weapons to make us chuckle at ourselves.

What would *you* do with this piece of copy? You might be vaguely dissatisfied, but unless you can pinpoint *why* you're dissatisfied, you can't fire it back at the writer or rewrite it yourself.

Which words are out of key? Right! "[D]etailed observance of the human condition" reads like something out of a military medical manual. While we're at it, "timeless" doesn't help build a word image for us, so let's replace it, too:

> These are the giants of laughter, the masters of wit and humor. They never had to depend on sight gags. Their exquisite timing and sense of the ridiculous were their hilarious weapons to make us chuckle at ourselves.

Getting rid of "detailed observance" keeps the copy in character. Our choice of words no longer confuses the reader.

22. *Amputate your arrogance before you start to write (for business-to-business and occasional consumer copy).*

To whom can you say "You're lucky to do business with me" without generating antagonism?

I can think of two groups: 1) those who owe you money and whose payment is long overdue and 2) those who depend on you for livelihood or peace of mind.

The neighborhood pusher can say this to the addicts he controls, but the world of normal commerce blesses us with two kinds of choices: the choice between "yes" and "no," and the choice between you and a competitor.

How easy the choice becomes when we get a brochure with this copy:

> EVERYONE
> ELSE
> IS A
> PRETENDER
> We Hate to Say It, But . . .
> If You Pass Up
> Our "Sense Off" Sale
> You Deserve What You Get . . .
> Having to Buy from
> One of Those Other Guys.

Sure, "Sense Off" doesn't make sense, but we might forgive this sin if the advertiser hadn't jutted out his jaw and played General Patton with us.

The trickiness of this nugget is being able to amputate arrogance without cutting off muscle.

23. *Look for ways to inject* you *into the word mix (for all advertising).*

An insurance company had this piece of copy:

> We value your trust and confidence, and that is why we have worked so hard to make this unique coverage possible.

We have a not-dreadful, not-strong string of words. If the writer had considered Nugget 23, we might have had:

> We value your trust and confidence, and that is why we have worked so hard to make this unique coverage possible for you.

The final two words tie the benefit to the target individual, just as the opening tied the premise to the target individual.

24. *Coattail riding isn't terrible because it has a built-in identification factor but it probably isn't the best you can do (for consumer advertising).*

Bemused readers, listeners, and viewers are deluged with clever imitations whenever a catchy campaign takes hold.

One sample: Remember when Wendy's had a short-lived but popular campaign, "Where's the beef?" As the campaign burned out, we saw and heard the following imitations:

- ▶ "Where's the beep?" (for a paging system)
- ▶ "Where's the reef?" (for a scuba-diving cruise)
- ▶ "Where's the leaf?" (for a grass-catching attachment to a lawn mower)
- ▶ "Where's the thief?" (for a security system)
- ▶ "Where's the beach?" (for a time-sharing condominium)

Purists may mount arguments of piracy. One campaign fastens itself, leechlike, on the neck of another, better-known campaign. I say, what's wrong with that? We use "solid gold" and Rolls-Royce every day as touchstones; we have "platinum" credit cards. Why not a current ad fad?

The question is when to get off the communications train in which you're riding the caboose. All these coattail-riding campaigns *begin* when the coat-wearing campaign has already peaked.

No writer can become a communications guru scrabbling around for scraps in the wastebaskets of successful campaigns. Coattail riding is serviceable, but seldom is it the best approach you might have used. You're at the mercy of another advertiser for recognition value and you can't use the campaign for long; it has a self-destruct timer built in and clicking away even as it starts.

25. *If the reader feels proud to do business with you, you have a competitive edge (for all advertising).*

A less theoretical way of putting this nugget: You can shock to get attention, but a lapse into bad taste will cost you.

If we never get their attention, we're 100 percent losers. This alone is justification for writing whatever we must to get them to open the envelope or keep reading the page or to keep their finger off the "zap" button. But doesn't this ad, from the *Wall Street Computer Review*, make you feel the Treasury agents will come after you if you do business with the company?

If Al Capone
had our file-scrambler,
he might never have
done hard time.
PRIVILEGED
INFORMATION
Protects your files by enciphering them . . .

This next example, from a catalog, is actually funny:

Let's face it. There's nothing more disabling than a sinus attack.

Oh, yeah? I'll match my Colt .45 against your sinus attack any day. Why, oh, why is the phrase "Let's face it" in there? Those three words are supposed to enlist the reader as an ally; instead, they cause the reader to disagree, which would obviously weaken the delivery of the message.

26. *Hyphens are an underused tool of clarification (for all copy).*

Sometimes, reading a piece of copy, we aren't sure what it is that bothers us. It just doesn't read right. If the bothersome sentence has an adjective followed by an adjectival noun, you have the tip-off—a clarifying hyphen can eliminate the bother. An example:

Your attractive counter display . . .

What's wrong here is the word "counter," an adjectival noun. The rules of grammar work against us because "attractive" could modify either "counter" or "display." We seize firm control of the reader's interpretive potential by adding a hyphen:

Your attractive counter-display . . .

27. *As you make it easier for people to respond, the quality of responses goes down (for subscriptions and lead-generating copy).*

Those who toil on the treadmills in the murderous world of magazine subscriptions know the trap: Without incentives, you can't get enough subscribers, but as you add incentives, you drive down the buying level and subscription renewal rate of those you recruit.

Adding "free gifts," shipping before payment, tying the promotion to a sweepstakes, giving two for one—these venerable motivators bring bulk, which, regrettably, is the way we so often have to keep score. Our job is even tougher than it first appears because only by tracking the renewals or purchases over a year or more can we tell whether or not we've gone too far in order to get early action. (My own viewpoint may not coincide with that of a theoretician who would take the high road. I side with those who pull out all the stops to get a name. We can't milk the goat unless she's in our own barnyard.)

The value of Nugget 27 may be its role as governor on our copywriting throttle. If we begin to assume automatically that salvation lies *only* in freebies, ultimately we force downward the image and value of what we're selling. But I'd be more afraid of the "expert" who damns all incentives as undignified.

28. *A claim of superiority is in no way as convincing as ostensible evidence of superiority, and a feature is in no way as convincing as a benefit (for all advertising).*

We as writers too often face this dilemma: Someone for whom we're writing an ad or a mailing piece says to us, "What I want you to do is make it clear that this is the best on the market. And it is, it is!" We're given some background information that fails to prove that theory. No matter; our obligation is to regurgitate corporate philosophy. We come up with something like this copy for a cosmetic:

A Beauty Care Breakthrough!

Now there's a new and better way to help your skin look soft, supple, and inviting.

It's the ICE-BORN™ way. Our skin care products contain only *totally natural* ingredients that are deep-frozen for purity.

With ICE-BORN you can have beautiful skin—without any chemical additives.

What have we written? We've claimed superiority without offering evidence. *"Totally natural* ingredients" aren't benefits in themselves; it's what they do (if anything) that's the benefit. Does freezing something give it purity? If so, how? What does it do for the user?

Transforming features into benefits is what we're supposed to do, or we aren't going to sell much.

29. *When logic says you can, make the buying decision for the message recipient (for all copy).*

Phrases such as "You can . . . " or "If you . . . " suffer in a head-to-head battle for business against a direct statement. So instead of "You can make money . . . ," we drop the first two words and add vigor: "Make money . . . " Usually a nonconditional statement will come to mind once the writer wonders, "Could I write a stronger piece of copy?"

30. *Practice using words effectively. Don't let your copy run on tracks (for all copy, for the rest of your life plus six months).*

How many of us actually practice? Somebody needs a piece of copy by tomorrow noon; we do a workmanlike job, always with the hollow excuse, "I could have done it better if I'd had more time."

Is that really so? We work with words. If we had more time, would we find more exciting words, more motivational words, words our readers/listeners/surfers/viewers would find more credible and stimulating? Or would we just spend more time looking over the background materials and then write the same tired, trite descriptions marbled a little with puffery?

For those with true grit, I have a suggestion: Pretend, as you write every word and phrase, that you have only two inches of space in which to transmit the message. That pretense will result in your optimizing the impact. As a wordsmith, you'll have entered a new level of consciousness.

Welcome, friend!

Chapter Twenty-Six

A COMPENDIUM OF RULES FOR EFFECTIVE COPYWRITING

Rules are always controversial because an antagonistic practitioner can find an exception to almost any rule. This list of usable rules for the copywriter is no exception.

Here we begin an endless process, not only of unearthing and codifying rules but of refining exceptions. Future list makers may regard this beginning tabulation as primitive. It is, however, a beginning.

The Umbrella Rule

The Umbrella Rule is the most foolproof, universal rule in all copywriting. Copywriters who know and follow this master rule are at the top of the marketing mountain. Your copy must succeed if it has these three ingredients:

1. clarity
2. benefit
3. credibility

The Four Great Laws

The Four Great Laws override all other rules for force-communication. They're congruent and do not compete with the Umbrella Rule.

The laws are the key to copywriter survival during the Age of Skepticism, an era spawned by television, self-aware politicians, and universal backlash against unproved claims of superiority by a multitude of competing advertisers.

▶ The First Great Law: Effective force-communication reaches and influences, at the lowest possible cost, the most people who can and will buy what you have to sell.
▶ The Second Great Law: In the Age of Skepticism, cleverness for the sake of cleverness may well be a liability rather than an asset.
▶ The Third Great Law: $E^2 = 0$. (When you emphasize everything, you emphasize nothing.)
▶ The Fourth Great Law: Tell your message recipient what to do.

Within the First Great Law, don't overlook the qualified relationship of two elements, "reaches" and "lowest possible cost": A hopelessly underproduced advertising message may not "reach" its target.

The Fourth Great Law is mandatory for direct-response copy but becomes optional if the message has a purpose other than persuading the message recipient to act (not usually a good idea).

The Other Rules

Adaptation of the First Great Law for Fund-Raising and Political Campaigns. (See complete list under FUND-RAISING.) Effective direct-mail fund-raising reaches the most people who might contribute and avoids those who never would contribute.

BENEFIT

The John F. Kennedy Buyer Attitude Truism. In the Age of Skepticism, the prospective buyer's first question isn't "What will it do?" but "What will it do for me?"

The Benefit/Benefit Principle. First announce the benefit. Then tell the reader how the benefit benefits him.

The Benefit/Benefit/Benefit Principle. This is the "can't miss" approach to copy that sells, especially for catalog copy—a three-step procedure:

1. State a claim of superiority over others.
2. Relate superiority to the reader.
3. Tell the reader how your superiority will bring specific improvements to his life. (See SPECIFICS, *the Specifics Superiority Principle*.)

The Benefit/Feature Bloodline Comparative. Features are cold-blooded and benefits are warm-blooded, so benefits are more emotional than features. It follows directly that benefits outsell features.

The Rhetorical Benefit Error. Telling the reader a product or service is beneficial is in no way parallel to convincing the reader a product or service is beneficial. (See SUBTLETY, *the Second Rule of Negative Subtlety*.)

The Credible Benefit Proposition. Maximize benefits within the limits of credibility.

The First Nonargument = No Benefit Rule. Copy depending on a nonargument invariably omits reader benefit.

The Second Nonargument = No Benefit Rule. Details unrelated to the buyer's appetites become nonarguments that skew the reaction because of their irrelevance.

The Rule of Partial Disclosure. Tell the target individual as much as you can about what your product or service can do for him or her. If you have space or time left over, don't move down to the next information level (facts unrelated to benefit); instead, restate or illustrate some of the benefits. (See IMPORTANCE.)

The Profit-Killer Equation. Inability to specify benefit = lower response.

The Puffery-Defeat Inevitability. No amount of puffery or self-applause can sell as effectively as a listing of specific benefits.

BRAGGADOCIO

The Braggadocio Avoidance Procedure. Write headlines for space ads and first paragraphs for letters as though you have only two inches of space for your entire selling argument. For broadcast commercials, write the first two sentences as though the spot were half its actual length.

BUYER ATTITUDE
The Artificial Loyalty Rule. Personal products have a high buyer-loyalty rate because the buyer doesn't want to expose his weaknesses to outsiders more than he or she must. To break the chain forged by this rule, a competing advertiser of such products has to use an extraordinarily compassionate approach.

The Buyer/Seller Equivalence Equation. The Seller's Concern = What it is. The Buyer's Concern = What it will do for me.

The "Whose Message Is It?" Rule. Your message should operate within the experiential background of the message recipient, not within your own experiential background. (See BENEFIT, *the John F. Kennedy Buyer Attitude Truism.*)

CARD DECKS
The First Principle of Card Deck Copy. Your offer must be instantly identifiable.

The Second Principle of Card Deck Copy. Sell, coherently, what the headline promises, not a secondary service or product down the road.

The Third Principle of Card Deck Copy. Stress benefits. You don't have room to write poetry about features, and the reader has neither the patience nor the interest to read your poetry. Use a bulleted format, to save space and hold attention.

The Fourth Principle of Card Deck Copy. Assume your card is buried in a deck of offers, all of which are as good as yours or better.

The Fifth Principle of Card Deck Copy. Tell the reader what to do (a direct application of the Fourth Great Law).

The Sixth Principle of Card Deck Copy. Force the reader to respond immediately because delay will cost money, reduce benefits, or lose business to a competitor.

CATALOG WRITING
The Rule of Catalog Attention-Grabbing. Start the description with benefit—what the item will do for the customer. Then describe the product itself. Then recapitulate the benefit. Then list the specifics necessary to place an order.

The Catalog Writing Truism. The purpose of catalog copy is to transmit an enthusiastic description of what's being sold to the best prospective buyers. Unless this purpose is achieved, the copywriter has failed, regardless of the cleverness of the rhetoric.

The Catalog Writing Truism Footnotes:

1. The Catalog Writing Truism becomes truer when one writer has the responsibility for an entire catalog.
2. A catalog company can prevent its copy from becoming the extension of one person's personality by assigning eight-page sections to different writers.

The "Episode-I, Buy-From-We" Indication. If you're torn between "I" and "we," use "I" only when referring to personal episode; use "we" for corporate suggestions that the reader buy.

CELEBRITY USE
The Celebrity Matchup Principle. Matching your spokesperson to what you're selling accelerates your target individuals' acceptance of what the celebrity is pitching.

The Celebrity Waste Factor. Having a celebrity move out of context is an artifice that exposes itself to the viewer or reader. A professional athlete may keep credibility endorsing athletic equipment or beer, but not alkaline batteries; an actress may keep credibility endorsing fashion or beauty aids, but not machinery or automobile muffler installations.

CLARITY

The Clarity Commandment. When choosing words and phrases for force-communication, clarity is paramount. Let no other component of the message mix interfere with it.

The Say What You Mean Mandate. The reader invariably will apply a negative interpretation to statements that violate the Clarity Commandment.

The Concept of Reader Dominance. The writer's knowledge of the colorful words in a piece of copy is inconsequential. What matters is whether or not the reader knows them. (See SPECIFICS, *the Specifics Superiority Principle*.)

The Tightness Rule. Keep copy tight enough that it fits the reader's skimming without forcing a break in comprehension.

COMPARATIVE ADVERTISING

The Comparative Imperative. Good marketing strategy calls for Brand No. 2 to shout superiority over Brand No. 1; good marketing strategy calls for Brand No. 1 to shout superiority over all others without singling out any one of them.

The Touchstone Rule. A touchstone becomes effective when the reader, viewer, or listener recognizes the value of the original relative to the pretender.

CONDITIONAL WORDS AND PHRASES (See QUESTIONS.)

The First Rule of "If." Let *if* relate to your buyer, not to you, because *if* seems to take objectionable high pressure out of your sales argument without actually doing it.

The First Rule of "If" Subdecree. Logic stands behind the writer who makes an action conditional for the buyer, since buyer control is proper stroking, but to give this control to the seller through an "if" reference suggests seller superiority, which can provoke buyer antagonism.

The Second Rule of "If." Don't use *should* instead of *if*. The pomposity not only is less straightforward but also puts greater distance between seller and buyer.

The Third Rule of "If." Don't use the phrase "if you can," which suggests difficulty or problems. Linking *ability* ("can") to "if" is a *double* conditional.

The Principle of "If" Control. An "if" condition should imply a "then" promise.

The Conditional Declension Syndrome. The more conditional the statement, the weaker it is.

The Comparative Conditional Declension Syndrome. The conditional isn't as impelling as the imminent.

The Subjunctive Avoidance Commandment. Avoid the conditional. It denies actuality. (See next rule.)

The First Rule of Positivism. Stay out of the conditional and replace *can* with *will*. (See previous rule; see also PSYCHOLOGY.)

The Second Rule of Positivism. After telling the reader you've presented a logical argument, take acceptance for granted.

CONFUSION

The First Confusion Factor. Don't let any piece of copy off your desk until you can say without crossed fingers, "My mother would understand it."

The Second Confusion Factor. A message matched to the recipient can't be confusing. (See BUYER ATTITUDE, *the "Whose Message Is It?" Rule*.)

The Third Confusion Factor. A sales message that violates the Second Great Law inevitably adds confusion and lowers sales. (See MOTIVATORS, *the Rule of Copy Misdirection*.)

CONSISTENCY

The Consistency Command. Components of a mailing must reinforce and validate one another, or reader/viewer/listener response to *all* components will be lessened.

The Precept of Factual Agreement. When facts within a message are in disagreement, the reader disbelieves all of them, even though one of them probably is true.

The Rule of Word Matching. Use words that match the image you're trying to build. An out-of-key word changes the image.

DIRECT MARKETING (DIRECT MAIL, DIRECT RESPONSE)

Unassailable Loser Statute I. When seller and buyer both are uninvolved, the seller loses.

Unassailable Loser Statute II. Readers are more likely to pick holes in transparent shouts of importance than in projection of benefits.

Unassailable Loser Statute III. Illustration should agree with what you're selling, not with headline copy. (Also known as *the Illustration Agreement Rule*.)

Unassailable Loser Statute IV. Adding qualifying words to a statement of superiority is an admission of inability to claim superiority.

Unassailable Loser Statute V. Use only as much of the language as you know. Your dictionary is your verifier, not your originator.

Workmen's Noncompensation Rationale. Reciprocity is the key to have-the-reader-do-something decisions.

Workmen's Noncompensation Provision 1. The reader's pleasure from absorbing your message diminishes in exact ratio to the amount of work he thinks he'll have to do.

Workmen's Noncompensation Provision 2. Excluding contests, asking the reader to perform a task that requires talent, prior knowledge, or problem-solving ability will lose that reader if he or she resents, feels inferior to, or is annoyed by the unsought challenge.

Workmen's Noncompensation Provision 3. In a contest or sweepstakes that has reward geared to apparent talent, prior knowledge, or problem-solving ability, the reward justifies the challenge.

EMOTION VS. INTELLECT

Emotion vs. Intellect Rule I. When emotion and intellect come into conflict, emotion always wins.

Emotion vs. Intellect Rule II. Emotion outpulls intellect.

The Rule of Emotional Mandate. Unless you specifically want to avoid reader involvement in your message, always write in the active voice, regardless of the type of communication.

ENVELOPES

The Cardinal Rule of Envelope Copy. The carrier envelope has one purpose (other than preventing its contents from falling out onto the street): to get itself opened.

The Outer Envelope Function. The only purpose of graphic treatment on a direct-mail envelope is to impel the recipient to open that envelope.

FUND-RAISING

The First Rule of Fund-Raising. Effective direct-mail fund-raising reaches the most people who might contribute and avoids those who never would or could contribute.

The Second Rule of Fund-Raising (a version of *the "Whose Message Is It?" Rule*). Operate inside the experiential background of the person you're contacting, not inside your own background.

The Third Rule of Fund-Raising. Since you're operating inside the reader's experiential background, select and shape a selling argument you think will grab his or her emotional handles.

The Fourth Rule of Fund-Raising. Tell the reader how much to give.

The Rule of Fund-Raising Copy Length. The need for long copy is tied to the need to feed an implicit or expressed reader prejudice or belief.

The Fund-Raising Reminder Rule. When writing prior donors, remind them how much they gave last time and ask for a little more.

The Rule of Bulk Negation. Bulk doesn't create an emotional reaction. Episode does.

The Rule of Claimed Fund-Raising Success. Claiming success works if you credit that success to the prior donors you're contacting; it's a turnoff in contacts with those with whom you have no previous connection.

GENERAL RULES FOR WRITING

The Rule of Chromatic Imagery. Write in color, not black-and-white. Superimpose your imagination on your reader/viewer/listener's imagination to enhance receptivity.

The Rule of Concealed Ballooning. If you're trying to make something big out of something little, don't let the buyer know it.

The Dullard's Lament. The more a copywriter depends on mechanical tricks, the more that writer exposes a sterile imagination.

The Factual Edge. Teaser mailings and space ads, which don't tell the reader what the mailer has for sale, are almost always less effective and less productive than mailings that include facts on which the target individual can formulate a buying decision. (See IMPORTANCE.)

The Peripheral Pussyfooting Weakener Rule. Writing around a point drains excitement out. Copy loses impact in direct ratio to the percentage of information given indirectly instead of directly. (See CONDITIONAL WORDS AND PHRASES.)

The Power-Filter Effect. Surplus words are power filters, reducing impact.

The Reader-Fatigue Effect. Drama in writing is implicit, or it doesn't exist at all. Labeling isn't the same as colorful writing. Claiming "drama" or "excitement" is an uninspired and punchless substitute for using words to prove those claims.

The Stupidity Equation. Stupid questions and statements = lower response.

The "You First" Rule. Tell the reader, listener, or viewer what's in it for him, not for you.

GRAMMAR (See PUNCTUATION AND GRAMMAR.)

GUARANTEES

The First Rule of Guarantees. Unless a guarantee specifically offers a refund, it probably is a cynically inspired sales gimmick, not a true guarantee.

The Second Rule of Guarantees. When the buyer feels he is in total command, the offer becomes true regardless of its incredible nature.

The Third Rule of Guarantees. Deliver what you promise.

HUMOR

The Pagliacci Syndrome. Beginning writers want to write funny copy. Don't let them, and don't do it yourself.

The Humor-Avoidance Rationale. When writing to people who don't know you, humor is never the best possible approach and often the worst. When writing to people who do know you, almost always humor is at best no better than straightforward exposition; at less than best, humor can kill any impression of sincerity, verisimilitude, and credibility.

The Comic Exception. The "almost always" assertion in the Humor-Avoidance Rationale is tempered by this exception: When you apologize for a mistake, quiet humor (carefully handled) can defang a venomous buyer. You benefit from this paradox: Admitting you're a fool makes you less of a fool.

The Clown Nonequivalence Rule. The onlooker always feels superior to a clown.

IF (See CONDITIONAL WORDS AND PHRASES and QUESTIONS.)

ILLUSTRATION AGREEMENT RULE (See DIRECT MARKETING, *Unassailable Loser Statute III.*)

IMPACT

The First Statute of Novelty Burnout. The impact of repeated messages decreases in exact ratio to reliance on novelty.

The Redundancy Control Rule. Use redundancies only when you want the reader to know you've repeated or doubled words to show emphasis.

The Principle of Expository Uncertainty. Words such as *practically*, *largely*, and *somewhat* are hedges betraying the writer's lack of assurance. The betrayal results in a weaker message. (See GENERAL RULES FOR WRITING.)

The Shock vs. Dignity Decision. If you exchange your dignity for shock value, be certain the shock is positive for your best buyers. (See PSYCHOLOGY and SUBTLETY.)

The Shock Diminution Rule. Shock diminishes in exact ratio to repetition.

IMPORTANCE

The Rule of Importance-Determination. If you claim importance, prove it.

The First Rule of Implied Importance. Everything we do is important to us. Almost nothing someone else does is important to us, unless what he does directly affects us. (See BUYER ATTITUDE, *the "Whose Message Is It?" Rule.*)

The Second Rule of Implied Importance. Importance should relate to the state of mind of the reader, not the writer.

The Third Rule of Implied Importance. If the copy message following the word *important* is a letdown to the reader, the copy is more likely to breed rejection or contempt than to stimulate an urge to buy.

The Automatic-Importance Technique. Capitalizing a word makes it important.

The Nonimportance Fault. Calling something "important" when your best readers will know it isn't important will cost you some business you otherwise might have had. (See LOGIC, *the Phony Claim Mistake.*)

The First Rule of So-What Turnoff Control. Select as your key selling arguments those facts and suggested benefits that satisfy the intended buyer's probable psychological motivators. (See MOTIVATORS.)

The Second Rule of So-What Turnoff Control. Using a "so what" statement as a major selling point adds confusion in direct ratio to the reader/viewer/listener's own product/service interest/knowledge. (See MOTIVATORS.)

The Third Rule of So-What Turnoff Control. "So what?" becomes "Here's why I want it" if benefit is added to the rhetorical mix. (See BENEFIT.)

INCENTIVES

The First Rule of Excitement Incentives. Adding artificial incentives to generate sales invariably lowers the quality of buyer.

The Second Rule of Excitement Incentives. Lowering the quality of buyer is a detriment only if a promotion coincidentally lowers the image of the vendor with existing best buyers.

The Third Rule of Excitement Incentives. All promotions must have an expiration date.

The Fourth Rule of Excitement Incentives. Orders dribbling in after the expiration date should be honored as long as pre-bought supplies and computer programming make it possible, but remind the customer that you're doing him a favor.

The Fifth Rule of Excitement Incentives. If the cataloger doesn't seem excited, the customer can't get excited.

The Sixth Rule of Excitement Incentives. Lack of clarity kills excitement.

INTERNET

The First Rule of Internet Advertising. Stop the surfer in his tracks.

The Rule of Internet Ennui. If you state who and what you are instead of stating, quickly and dynamically, a recognizable benefit that will transform the surfer into a visitor, forget it.

The First Rule of Web Site Order Forms. Make ordering easy.

The Second Rule of Web Site Order Forms. Have an order form or "shopping basket" visible at all times.

The First Rule of E-Mail. Promise benefit in the heading and justify the promise in the first two sentences.

The Second Rule of E-Mail. Once you have justified the promise and specified a quick and easy means of response, end the message.

The Third Rule of E-Mail. Give the recipient an option for additional information. Don't force-feed that information.

LOGIC

The Bluster Mistake. The suggestion "You must . . . " backed by a reason the reader/viewer/listener doesn't regard as logical is bluster rather than logical sales argument because it has no factual core. Beginning the sentence with "This is why" forces the writer to add that core.

The Phony Claim Mistake. Those whom you most want as buyers are the same individuals who are most likely to see through phony claims. (See IMPORTANCE, *the Nonimportance Fault*.)

MOTIVATORS

The Five Great Motivators of our time:

1. fear
2. exclusivity
3. guilt
4. greed
5. need for approval

The "soft" motivators, working in concert with the Five Great Motivators:

1. convenience
2. pleasure

The Motivating Word-Choice Proposal. When choosing words, use terms and phrases your target buyer regards favorably unless you're using *fear* as a motivator.

The Rule of Contemporaneous Transmission. Unless the writer has a knowledge of his target prospect, copy can be a horrible psychological mismatch.

The "Diarrhea of the Keyboard" Syndrome. Details unrelated to the buyer's motivators slow down or kill the sale.

The First Rule of Fear. The reader must always know that you have the answer to the problem you expose.

The Second Rule of Fear. Unless your own fear of overkill suggests a weaker message, write a direct challenge, not a "What if . . ." subjunctive. (See CONDITIONAL WORDS AND PHRASES, *the Subjunctive Avoidance Commandment*.)

The Third Rule of Fear. Don't lose your nerve halfway through and begin polluting your "fear" approach with lightheartedness.

The Truth-as-Motivator Noneffect. Apparent truth is insignificant in a selling argument unless that truth is built around the target individuals' motivators. (See VERISIMILITUDE.)

The Rule of Copy Misdirection. Words that puzzle can't motivate. (See CONFUSION.)

The Rule of Statistical Deficiency. Readers respond less to cold-blooded statistics than they do to warm-blooded examples.

NEWS RELEASES

The First Canon of News Release Writing. The reader, viewer, or listener should be unaware that the message is sponsored.

The Second Canon of News Release Writing. Put puffery in quotes.

The Third Canon of News Release Writing. Replace or eliminate descriptive adjectives that suggest editorial viewpoint.

The Five Rules of Cutline Writing:

1. Repeat pertinent information even though it also appears in the release.
2. Don't be afraid to write long cutlines.
3. Write complete sentences, not bullets.
4. Set a maximum of twenty words per sentence.
5. If you include several pictures, write a separate cutline for each one, even if they're similar.

The Rule of News Release Information. Don't leave obvious questions unanswered.

PERSONALIZING

The De-Icer Rule. Personalizing helps melt the ice of skepticism and apathy.

The Capitalization-Loss Rule. Setting copy in all caps depersonalizes a message.

PREDICAMENT USE

The Predicament Method Principle. Establishing a predicament as a sales argument has these five sequential components:

1. Create a predicament the reader, viewer, or listener finds logical.
2. Put your target individual into that predicament, either by unmistakable association or by hard use of the word *you*.
3. Demonstrate whatever you're selling as the solution to the predicament.
4. Restate the circumstance with a happy conclusion.
5. Have the central character in the predicament state satisfaction.

PRODUCT IMAGE

The Rule of Buyer Defense. A product is what it is, plus what the buyer thinks it is.

PRODUCTION

The First Rule of Production-Reduction. Poor production won't destroy a good message.

The Second Rule of Production-Reduction. Lavish production that tries to mask an inferior message usually doesn't pay for itself.

PROFESSIONALISM

The Form Worship Maxim. The writer who puts form ahead of substance implicitly admits a creative deficiency. Communications with this deficiency call attention to format rather than to what they say. Invariably, the writer has a more effective way to transmit the message. (See GENERAL RULES FOR WRITING.)

Roget's Complaint. With all the specific descriptive words available, the writer who regards neutral, nonimpact words such as *needs*, *quality*, *features*, and *value* as creative nouns should agree to work for no pay.

The Professional/Amateur Differential. The amateur says: "Most people will get the idea, no matter how poorly I say it." The professional says: "Every word is our weapon, and anyone who thinks otherwise is an amateur."

The Ethics Rule. Keep your dignity.

The Fat Copy Procedure. Good writing is lean. Slice weak, forceless words out of your copy the way you'd trim fat from a steak.

The First Nonprofessional Revelation. The worst, most pompous, least imaginative, and most unprofessional advertising line of this decade is, "If you can find a better (WHATEVER), buy it."

The Second Nonprofessional Revelation. Forbidding words lock your target individual out. Familiar words and verbalisms, short of undermining your dignity, invite this person in.

The Third Nonprofessional Revelation. If you have to show off your erudition or use a foreign phrase, explain the phrase and also explain why you had to use it in the first place.

The Fourth Nonprofessional Revelation. Write on a level of mutual interest, rather than as instructor to student. At the very least, preface your verbal strutting and preening with the words "As you know."

The Fifth Nonprofessional Revelation. Eliminate adjectives that do nothing to further comprehension.

The Sixth Nonprofessional Revelation. The professional writer of force-communication has three areas of knowledge—basic psychology, vocabulary suppression, and salesmanship—roughly equivalent to that of a vacuum cleaner salesperson.

PSYCHOLOGY (See QUESTIONS.)

The "In Your Face" Message Rule. The effectiveness or annoyance of an "in your face" message depends entirely on its synchronization with the attitude of the message recipient.

The Challenge Response Principle. People respond to challenges that don't suggest incapability.

The Connotation Rule. Substitute words with a positive connotation for words with a neutral or negative connotation.

The Generic Determination Rule. The generic determines reaction more than the number.

Generic Determination Subrule "A." When the experiential background of your primary targets includes a date within the adult experience, numbers of years, months, or days are apparently longer ago than the date itself.

The Rule of Negative Transmission. Unless you want the reader or viewer to think you're the generator of the reason for negative information, don't put this information aggressively.

The "I'm Not Responsible" Stipulation. Second- and third-person writing which begins "There is" or "There are," "You have been selected," "It was determined that" and verbs in the passive voice are implicitly weaker than statements in which the message sender assumes responsibility for the action.

The "Only You" Blessing. You can search for a hundred years and not find a sales argument more powerful than "Only you . . . and only from us."

The Chosen People Effect. (See *the "Only You" Blessing*, above.) If what you're selling has any aura of rarity or scarceness, this three-step sales argument is an easy winner:

1. Everybody wants it.
2. Nobody can get it.
3. Except you.

The Renunciation Proposition. It's easier to renounce the obvious than to renounce the traditional. This human characteristic is grist for the sales promotion mill, but it can be a deadly attitude if the writer is caught up in an unrenounceable tradition of his own.

The Shock-Therapy Negation. If you exchange your dignity for shock value, be certain the shock is positive for your best buyers. (See GENERAL RULES FOR WRITING and PROFESSIONALISM.)

The Psychological Truth Injunction. When you project an assumption, base it on a psychological truth or a known psychographic fact, not on a self-serving fantasy. If the person you're trying to convince might regard your presumption as incredible, acknowledge the presumption as incredible. Then explain, with logic comprehensible to the reader, why it isn't incredible at all.

PUBLIC RELATIONS (See NEWS RELEASES.)

PUNCTUATION AND GRAMMAR

The Illiteracy Rejection. Communication in the Age of Skepticism is informal, but it isn't casual.

The Decimal Cheapener. Decimal-zero-zero after a dollar number has a cheapening effect without the accompanying effect of seeming less expensive. $500.00 has less class than $500. The effect is psychological, and some readers may be more comfortable with the cheapener; the better choice depends on the context.

The Quotation Mark Rule. Putting quotation marks around a word or phrase the reader may not recognize tells the reader we share the novelty of the idea . . . and helps him or her accept the unknown. Without the quotation marks, we say to the reader, "We know something you don't."

QUESTIONS (See CONDITIONAL WORDS AND PHRASES and PSYCHOLOGY.)
The First Rule of Question Asking. Don't ask a question that risks rejection by your best potential buyers.

The Second Rule of Question Asking. Don't be afraid to shake up borderline buyer-prospects by challenging them to make up their minds.

RADIO
The First Rule of Radio Spot Writing. Aggressiveness leaves a stronger residue than subtlety.

The Second Rule of Radio Spot Writing. If humor isn't directly related to what you're selling, scrap it.

The First Principle of Radio Clear Reception. Help the announcer's pronunciation and you'll help the listener's comprehension.

The Second Principle of Radio Clear Reception. Spell out numbers, symbols, and abbreviations. The words will come out the way you want them to.

The Mandate of Business-to-Business Radio Spot Writing. Break hard into the listener's usual apathy. Intrude on his easy-listening attitude. Grab his attention and then shake it so the listener knows what you want to sell him.

REMAIL
The First Remail Determinant. If a mailing has been successful, the only content change for a "second chance" remail to someone whose characteristics match your buyers is the information that this *is* a remail.

The Second Remail Determinant. Unless you're out of cold-list names, send second-chance mailings only to proved names. For prospect groups, sending additional mailings to cold lists probably will be more productive.

SALESMANSHIP
The First Canon of Salesmanship. When the prospect says yes, quit selling.

The First Rule of Upscale Selling. Reverence for what you're selling, not overblown descriptions, suggests exclusivity.

The Second Rule of Upscale Selling. Put yourself, as vendor, on a par with your buyers, not above or below them.

The Third Rule of Upscale Selling. For the upscale buyer, a credible benefit needn't be a product's usefulness; it can be the product's origin. "Only you" works when coupled with "Only from us."

The Fourth Rule of Upscale Selling. Because the words "classless society" are in quotation marks, the assumption that a single motivator works for all potential buyers is as specious as the assumption that all media or mailing lists pull with equal strength.

The Fifth Rule of Upscale Selling. Since "upscale" is a state of mind, not a homogenized group with parallel interests and knowledge, appeal to the state of mind and your sales argument is safe; appeal to an assumed common base of knowledge and a significant percent of target individuals won't have the information to decode the benefits.

The Sixth Rule of Upscale Selling. The Fifth Rule being true—that "upscale" is a state of mind—individuals move in and out of any particular group, motivated by factors the marketer can't control. So copy should include this reminder: You're indeed a member of our group.

The Seller/Buyer Differential. The seller's concern: What it is. The buyer's concern: What it will do for him. (See BENEFIT.)

SKEPTICISM
Fifteen Ways to Thwart the Age of Skepticism. (See *the Second Great Law,* BENEFIT, and VERISIMILITUDE.)

1. If you make a claim, prove it.
2. Don't lie.
3. Draw attention to what's being sold, not to a celebrity who's selling it.
4. Don't clown.
5. Imply bulk or community acceptance.
6. Personalize—"Only you . . . only from us."
7. Be positive and specific.
8. Cut down the puffery.
9. Don't assume the public knows your "in-terminology."
10. Showing innocence or artlessness can prove your sincerity.
11. Tie newness to an established base.
12. Don't make something big out of something little.
13. Tell the reader, early, something he already knows.
14. If you talk down to the reader, be gracious and benevolent, and observe point 15.
15. Don't be omnipotent; admit an Achilles' heel.

SPECIFICS
The Specifics Superiority Principle. Specifics outsell generalities. (See BENEFIT, *the Benefit/Benefit/Benefit Principle*; CLARITY, *the Concept of Reader Dominance;* and TESTIMONIALS, *the Second Testimonial Rule.*

The "Whoever You Are, Hello!" Principle. Since specifics outsell generalizations (*the Specifics Superiority Principle,* above), if you don't know who will read your message, you can't be as specific as if you do know. So the writer who doesn't have target data at hand can't sell as much as the writer who does.

SPEED FORMATS (MAILGRAMS, JET EXPRESS, et al.)
The First Law of Speed Formats. If the recipient becomes annoyed by discovering your ploy, the speed format has worked against you, not for you, because more conventional formats wouldn't have generated a negative reaction.

The Second Law of Speed Formats. The message must project timeliness, personalization, and possible loss of benefit, or it falls out of key with the format and violates the First Law.

The Third Law of Speed Formats. Open the message with compelling benefit.

The Fourth Law of Speed Formats. Don't let any distraction soften the "bulletin" copy approach.

The Fifth Law of Speed Formats. If your message is supposed to be one-to-one, keep excitement high by keeping adjectives down; your message will match the medium if its entire structure demands imperative action that produces benefit.

The Sixth Law of Speed Formats. Slash away mercilessly at hard-selling copy that leans toward the verbose. It destroys speed-format credibility.

The Rule of Implied Urgency. Stay in character.

The Ultimate Rule of Speed Formats. Stay in sync with yourself.

STATISTICS

The Rule of Statistical Failure. Statistics don't sell.

The Victim-Statistic Rule. In fund-raising copy, individual stories of victims are superior to statistics even though statistics represent bulk numbers.

SUBTLETY (These rules are aimed at violators of the Second Great Law.)

The First Rule of Negative Subtlety. The effectiveness of your message decreases in direct ratio to an increase in subtlety.

The Second Rule of Negative Subtlety. Don't mask benefit with subtlety. Benefit is why the recipient pays attention to what you've written, so state it clearly and directly.

The Teaser Complaint. Teaser mailings and advertising, which don't tell the reader what the mailer has for sale, are almost always less effective and less productive than mailings that include facts on which the target individual can formulate a buying decision.

SYLLABLES

The First Theorem of Word Construction. When naming or describing product or company, matching word sounds to the intended effect will heighten that effect until repetition blurs it.

The Second Theorem of Word Construction. One-syllable words are harder, tougher, and stronger than their softer, more reasonable multisyllabic equivalents.

The Third Theorem of Word Construction. Flat vowels are crisper and are spoken faster than long vowels, so the words they represent seem crisper and faster.

TELEVISION

The First Rule of Television Impact. If you open with a five-second episode excluding product, close with five seconds of hard visual and auditory emphasis on product.

Explanatory Subrule to the First Rule of Television Impact. Validity of the First Rule of Television Impact increases with a decrease in spot length.

TESTIMONIALS

The First Testimonial Rule. The relative value of a testimonial by an authority or expert, compared to a celebrity, is in direct ratio to the message recipient's knowledge of the product or service being sold.

The Second Testimonial Rule. In testimonials, as in all force-communication, specifics outpull puffery.

VERISIMILITUDE

The First Verisimilitude Commandment. Regurgitating all the facts, undigested, invariably results in a poorer selling argument than selecting facts the message recipient perceives to be 1) true and 2) beneficial.

The Second Verisimilitude Commandment. The most effective sales argument is not clinical truth, but, rather, what the reader, viewer, or listener perceives to be true.

The Third Verisimilitude Commandment. Consistency prevents the buildup of skepticism, which erodes verisimilitude. (See CONSISTENCY, *the Rule of Word Matching.*)

The Fourth Verisimilitude Commandment. Evidence is more credible than an unexplained statement of position.

The Fifth Verisimilitude Commandment. Use fact to make a point, not just for the sake of using fact. (See IMPORTANCE, *the First Rule of So-What Turnoff Control*.)

The Specificity Principle. Specific details build verisimilitude.

The First Rule of Cheating. To be acceptable from any viewpoint, an ad that cheats must be unassailable factually.

The Second Rule of Cheating. To be competitively preferable, an ad that cheats must boost the product or service beyond the ability of a conventional sales argument to do so.

The Third Rule of Cheating. Surrounding a thoughtful cheating argument with weak and thoughtless cheating arguments saps strength by thinning the base of reader credulity. (See *the Second Verisimilitude Commandment*.)

The Fourth Rule of Cheating. As cheating moves toward lying and betrays a lack of integrity, effectiveness among the best buyers vanishes proportionately.

The First Rule of Lie-Avoidance. A lie visible to the target individual is a symbol of a weak imagination.

The Second Rule of Lie-Avoidance. Lying is never necessary nor preferable in a sales promotion message.

The Third Rule of Lie-Avoidance. When the reader thinks you are not telling the truth about one point, he extends that opinion to include your entire sales argument. He rejects even the statements that *are* true.

WEASEL WORDS

The First Rule of Weaseling. An effective weaseled claim is written so the reader slides past without realizing it.

The Second Rule of Weaseling. The main purpose of writing weasel words should be credibility.

The Third Rule of Weaseling. "Parity" advertising—a statement of "We're as good as they are," worded to appear to mean "We're better than they are"—is an effective tactic whose impact is gradually weakening through competitive overuse.

The Fourth Rule of Weaseling. *Can* and *may* as substitutes for *will* usually are successful and acceptable weasel words. An unidentified accolade such as "One art authority says . . . " or "Consumers choose . . ." is weak and unacceptable.

Chapter Twenty-Seven

A Glossary of Communications Terms

AFTRA American Federation of Television and Radio Artists, the union for television and radio actors and announcers.

agate line A measurement of the depth of print ads—$\frac{1}{14}$ inch (14 lines = 1 inch). This measurement is almost obsolete, but some publications still use it.

bait-and-switch The unsavory technique of advertising a big bargain and then, when the customer comes to the store, switching to a similar but more expensive item.

bangtail An extra detachable flap on the backside of an envelope, on which an additional offer has been printed.

b.f. Boldface, referring to the weight of a typeface.

bingo card A reply card inserted in a publication; the reader circles the code numbers of items on which he wants information.

bleed Printing to the edge of the page, with no uninked border.

body copy The copy block of a print ad, excluding headlines, coupons, or signatures.

bounceback An enclosure with merchandise, offering additional merchandise for sale.

box An insert into a piece of copy, usually bordered by a thin rule.

b.r.c., b.r.e. Business reply card, business reply envelope.

broadsheet Standard newspaper advertising page, 21 inches deep and 13 inches wide (see **SAU**).

broadside A big, single sheet of paper, folded to mailing size; the standard size is 17 inches by 22 inches.

buckslip A small single-sheet enclosure with a direct-mail package, usually highlighting a special offer or additional benefit.

camera-ready A finished ad ready for reproduction (see **pasteup**).

caps All capital letters.

caps and l.c. Capitalized first letters, lower case for other letters.

caption Descriptive words above a photograph (see **cutline**).

click-through rate The rate at which individuals who land on a Web site click to the next page.

column inch Advertising depth measurement, one column wide by 1 inch deep.

comprehensive, "comp" An artist's layout, closely resembling the way the finished ad or literature will look. Type is in position. The layout probably has low-resolution images, replaced by high-resolution images in finished art.

computer personalization Insertion of individual's name and other personal information in a letter or mailing piece.

continuity Radio copy.

continuity program A direct-mail term for a series of items (for example, collectibles or books) shipped in sequence over a period of time.

copy test Testing one copy approach against another.

counter card   A point-of-purchase sign, usually set up as an easel.
c.p.m.   Cost per thousand.
CU   Close-up (television term).
cut   A printed illustration or halftone.
cutline   Descriptive words under a photograph (see **caption**).

dealer imprint   An area on a manufacturer-prepared brochure in which the dealer prints its name, address, and phone number.
demographics   Characteristics—for example, age, sex, education—of a target market group. Often tied to zip codes.
display ad   A print ad other than classified.
dissolve   In television, the gradual fading of one scene into another.
DVD   Digital video disk with higher-quality images and more content than prior CDs.
double truck   A two-page spread (facing pages).

ECU   Extreme close-up (television term).

force-communication   Delivery of an imperative message through mass media—print, broadcast, direct mail, or (on a campaign level) telemarketing (see **mass communication**).
four-color process   Full-color printing, a blend of the four standard colors—red, blue, yellow, and black—in hairline registration to give the photographic effect of many colors.
freestanding insert   A preprinted promotional piece inserted into a newspaper or magazine.

gimmick   A technique unrelated to the message, designed to create reader/listener/viewer interest in the message.
go to black   Fade out the scene (television term).
gutter   The inside margins of two facing pages.

hairline   (a) Perfect registration of colors in printing; (b) a thin rule used as a border.
halftone   A dot pattern that simulates a continuous-tone photograph. Reproduced in print, the picture is actually a group of individual fine dots, usually ranging from a coarse 65-line "screen" (newsprint) to a very fine 200-line screen (enamel paper).
HDTV   High-definition television, a 1,050-line screen planned to be the U.S. standard by 2006.
high-res   High-resolution art, ready for printing (see **low-res**.)
hitchhiker   A commercial at the end of a program, selling one of the sponsor's products not associated with program identification.
html   Hypertext markup language, a language for Internet communication.

ID   "Identification"—a short commercial delivered at a break between programs, just before or after a station's identification of its call letters.
impulse buy   Purchase of something the buyer hadn't intended to get when entering the store or picking up the mailer.
insert   See **freestanding insert**.
insertion order   The formal and specific written notice by an advertiser or advertising agency to a medium, requesting the insertion of a specific ad.
institutional advertising   Advertising designed to build image or goodwill rather than to sell something.
island   a) A store display unattached to any other display; b) an ad completely surrounded by editorial matter.

Java   An Internet language that allows animation and effects.
jingle   A musical composition integrated into a broadcast commercial, to give sound-identity to what's being sold.
justified   Type set so the right margin lines up evenly (see **ragged right**).

key   A code enabling the advertiser to determine the source of sales or inquiries (e.g., Department A).

leading   Pronounced "ledding." Spacing between lines of type to separate the lines from one another (see **set solid**).

lift note   An extra exhorting enclosure in a mailing package; sometimes called a "publisher's letter."

line   See **agate line**.

line shot, line drawing   A graphic element without halftone dots; solid areas are reproduced, but shaded areas become either solid (black) or nonexistent (white).

lip sync   Synchronized lip movements (television term). If the mouth movements don't match the words, the two are out of sync.

low-res   Low-resolution art, used for layouts. Low-res doesn't have the quality to be used for actual printing.

lower case (l.c.)   No capital letters.

LS   Long shot (television term).

magalog   Half-magazine, half-catalog—a sponsored magazine whose editorial content reinforces the items advertised.

mass communication   Delivery of a message to large numbers of people through mass media (see **force-communication**).

matte shot   Combining two elements, shot at different places, in a single shot (e.g., putting a studio announcer into a Parisian street scene)(television term). Sometimes called Green Screen.

MCU   Medium close-up (television term).

medium   An individual mass communications outlet, such as a radio station or a newspaper. Plural = media.

merchandising   Any technique for selling goods or services.

monitor   (a) To watch TV or listen to radio for the purpose of checking a particular segment or commercial; (b) a television set in the control room or studio.

montage   An illustration in which a number of images are laid over one another.

mortise   A hole cut in a reverse or illustration.

m.o.s.   Without sound (television term); literally, "mitout sound."

MS   Medium shot (television term).

negative option   A direct-mail continuity program in which the seller continues to ship and bill for merchandise until the customer asks for discontinuation.

newsprint   The soft, coarse paper used for most newspapers. Newsprint usually takes a 65-line to 85-line screen (see **halftone**).

news release   A self-serving statement whose format and writing style mirror that of a news story.

NTSC   National Television System Committee, source of the standard 525-line television screen standard in the United States, Canada, Central and South America, Japan, and South Korea (see **PAL** and **SECAM**). HDTV may cause NTSC to become obsolete.

optical   A special video effect (television term).

outline   A halftone in which all elements other than the main image have been cut away.

oxymoron   A phrase combining two contradicting words, such as "Icy Hot" or "Giant Midget."

package insert   A promotional or sales piece enclosed with a product shipment. Unlike a bounceback, it usually is supplied by a different company that pays for each enclosure.

PAL   Phase Alternation Line, the 625-line television screen standard in all countries except those using NTSC and SECAM.

pan   Left/right movement of the camera (television term).

Pantone   A chart of colors, enabling a printer to match exactly the color you desire.

pasteup   The original camera-ready art, in which elements are pasted onto a cardboard backing.

photostat   A copying process used for art and type.

pica   A measurement equaling $\frac{1}{6}$ inch.

p.i. deal Per-inquiry advertising, in which the advertiser pays the medium a fixed amount per inquiry or sale.

P.O.C.B. "Plain ol' country boy"—a technique of writing that uses "ain't" and "he don't" and other countrified verbalisms.

point A measurement used in typesetting; 12 points = 1 pica, 72 points = 1 inch.

p.o.p. Point of purchase—a display at a store.

press release Obsolete term for news release. (Broadcast media require a more generic phrase.)

psychographics Attitudinal characteristics—lifestyle, interests, and degree of sophistication—of specific groups of buyers, prospects, or nonbuyers.

public relations Organized sponsored activity or dissemination of selected information designed to improve the issuer's image and build goodwill.

Quark A popular computer program used to prepare art layouts.

ragged right Typeset so the right margin is uneven; spaces fall where they will.

reading notice, reader ad An ad structured to resemble the editorial content of the publication in which it appears. Some publications insist on the word *Advertisement* set in small type at the top of the ad.

recall A questionable but common way to measure the effectiveness of ads. Individuals who have had the opportunity to see the ad are given clues about ads, then asked to recall specifics related to those clues.

relative attention ratio (r.a.r.) The percentage of attention the reader, listener, or viewer focuses on the message. Under hypnosis, the r.a.r. might be 100%, with every external demand for attention excluded; but for a typical television commercial within a group of spots, it could be 20% or lower.

release A standard form authorizing an advertiser to use a person's statement or likeness.

reverse White-on-black or white-on-color—the reverse of standard typesetting, in which type appears in black or color on white paper.

Roman typeface Type that has serifs (see **serif**). Readership surveys indicate that Roman typefaces are easier and more pleasing to read than sans-serif typefaces. Examples: Goudy, Garamond, Times Roman.

rough layout A sketch showing position of elements in an ad but few details (see **comprehensive**).

S.A.G. Screen Actors Guild, the talent union for film actors and announcers.

sans-serif typeface Type without serifs. Examples: Futura, Univers, Avante Garde.

SAU Standard Advertising Unit, a system introduced by the American Newspaper Publishers Association that makes it possible to run 57 "standard" ad sizes in all full-size newspapers and 33 in tabloids. One-column width = $2^1/_{16}$ inches; two-column width = $4^1/_4$ inches. A full type page is 13 inches wide and 21 inches deep (six columns).

script Radio, television, and film continuity for program or ad.

SECAM Sequential Colour a Memoire, the French television system with an 819-line screen. Egypt and several French-speaking countries also use SECAM.

self-mailer A direct-mail piece that needs no envelope.

serif A decorative cross-stroke at the top and bottom of a character in a typeface.

set solid Type set at a height equal to the type size with no leading between the lines. Eight lines of 9-point type, set solid, would be 72 points high, exactly 1 inch. Eight lines of 9-point type leaded to 11 points would have exactly as many characters on each line, but the type block would be 88 points deep—almost $1^1/_4$ inches.

share of audience In broadcast, the percentage of sets in use tuned to a particular program.

spectacular A big, illustrated outdoor sign, often with motion or effects.

split-run Testing two ads against each other in the same issue of the same publication. A perfect "A/B" split prints each of two same-size ads on alternate copies.

spot announcement A broadcast commercial.

spread Two facing pages (see **double truck**).

SRDS   Standard Rate and Data Service, publisher of information on advertising rates and production requirements.

stat   See **photostat**.

statement stuffers   A printed piece enclosed with a customer's bill; the stuffer need not be from the company sending the bill.

stet   Literally, "Let it stand"; a proofreader's instruction to ignore a change marked on a proof.

storyboard   A series of sketches indicating how a television spot will look. Usually, the words are printed or typed below each sketch. A typical one-minute storyboard will have eight to twenty panels.

super   Superimposition of lettering over a scene (television term).

supplement   A special extra section in a publication.

tabloid   A newspaper whose size is about half the standard size. Most standard tabloid advertising pages are 14 inches deep and $10^{13}/_{16}$ inches wide; some, called "N"-size tabloids, are $9^3/_8$ inches wide (see **broadsheet**).

tag   An addition to a commercial, usually information of where to buy what is advertised. The tag may be live or separately taped or filmed.

tear sheet   The page on which an ad appears, taken from an actual copy of the publication.

teaser   An ad, or envelope copy, which transmits just enough information to "tease" the message recipient into looking for or waiting for more.

thumbnail   A rough layout in miniature size.

tilt   Up/down movement of the camera (television term).

trade publication   A magazine aimed at wholesalers or retailers.

trim size   Actual physical dimensions of a sheet of paper after trimming.

truck   Lateral movement of the camera relative to the subject being televised (television term).

type page   The area within a nonbleed page actually occupied by type or illustration (see **bleed**).

type weight   The degree of blackness of type, from lightface to extra-bold.

typo   Typographical error.

U-matic   Professional-size videotape, usually ¾-inch wide.

unaided recall   A method of determining advertising effectiveness in which individuals who saw or heard an ad are asked to answer questions about the ad without having another look at it (see **recall**).

upper case (u.c.)   All capital letters (see **lower case**).

URL   Uniform resource locator . . . computerese for on-line address.

velox   A paper copy of a complete ad with halftones in position, usually made up to send to publications for reproduction.

VO   Voice-over—narration by an unseen announcer (television term).

VTR, VCR   Videotape recorder.

widow   A single word or short line ending a paragraph that falls at the top of a page or column.

window envelope   A mailing envelope with a die-cut opening in the front, through which the name and address of the recipient (usually on a response form) are visible.

wipe   Replacement of one scene by another that wipes out the first scene vertically, horizontally, or diagonally (television term).

Zip disk   A high-capacity computer disk, often used to transmit finished advertising to publications or printers.

Zip pan   A blurringly fast pan (see **pan**) (television term).

zoom   A lens that enables the camera operator to change the apparent distance from the subject without actually moving the camera (television term).

Addendum

WHICH WATCH IS WORTH WATCHING?

Invariably, advertising faces a litmus test—comparison with the competition.

Here, without lengthy or major comments, are thirty-four full-page ads for wristwatches. What makes the comparison valid is that *all thirty-four* appeared in the same issue of *The Robb Report*.

The reader draws four assumptions:

1. The purpose of most of these ads is to maintain image, not sell watches here and now.
2. History is a valid selling point.
3. Contemporaneousness that leans on history is an even more valid selling point.
4. A high price can be a selling point.

Here they are, not in the order in which they appeared in the magazine but alphabetically (by surname when the watchmaker uses an individual's name). They aren't, by the way, all the wristwatch ads in that issue; only full-page ads are included here.

Which would attract you, as a potential buyer?

ALAIN SILBERSTEIN CRÉATIONS · 5 avenue Cusenier 25000 BESANÇON, FRANCE · Tél. (33) 3 81 83 14 06 · Fax (33) 3 81 83 22 95
E-mail : asc@a-silberstein.fr · http://www.a-silberstein.fr

Figure Add-1: Pure image here. Note the oblique statement of purpose.

Bell & Ross

VINTAGE COLLECTION

Model : Vintage 123 B . Information and catalog : Tel (305) 674 9464 . Fax (305) 674 7993
e-mail : bellross@bellsouth.net . website : http://www.bellross.com

Figure Add-2: "Vintage collection" can mean estate watches or new watches with a "yesterday" design. Obviously, the intention here is the latter.

Figure Add-3: A marvelous piece of photography emphasizes the glamor of this watch.
"Inspired by the natural beauty and shape of pebbles" is an odd encomium.

Figure Add-4: This watchmaker believes the watches speak for themselves.

Invented for you

Conceived by Breguet in 1780, the automatic movement featured an oscillating weight that rewound the mainspring. Today the craftsman's hand decorates the weight with fine guilloché engraving to complement the beauty of the movement.

The celebrated "pomme" hands in blued steel are now known the world over as Breguet hands. Created in 1783 by Abraham-Louis Breguet, they symbolise the flawless craftsmanship and style of the Breguet you select today.

A Breguet watch has a unique responsibility; it comes to you carrying the name of Abraham-Louis Breguet, the greatest watchmaker ever known. You will recognise it by the legendary "Breguet" hands, the shimmering guilloché dial, and the finely fluted case band that give your Breguet its strong character. Most important, it will house a hand-finished movement, as inimitable and inventive today as two hundred years ago. Wear it with pride, you have chosen an exceptional watch.

Breguet
Depuis 1775

By inventing the tourbillon device around 1795, Breguet eliminated the influence of gravity on the accuracy of the watch. This pivotal invention is seen at its best in the current collection, which has a number of fine tourbillon watches.

de Boulle
214.522.2400

Breguet LLC Sole Distributor for the USA, Canada, Mexico, South America and the Caribbean.
For further information and the dealer nearest you please call, 1-888-BREGUET or 1-888-273-4838.

Figure Add-5: Much information here, combining a venerable history with contemporary style.

www.breitling.com

LIMITED EDITION OF 25

MONTBRILLANT QP IN PLATINUM

Designed for connoisseurs first and foremost, the perpetual-calendar wristwatch remains one of the most challenging of all timepieces to build. Today, only a few master watchmakers possess the skills to assemble more than 500 components that enable this masterpiece to run for over a century without any adjustment to its day, date, week, month, season, year or moon-phase displays. This intricate mechanism is also programmed to self-adjust automatically to leap years as well as to months with 28, 30 and 31 days. In platinum on a crocodile strap with a folding clasp. $48,250

OROLOGIO

Your Complete Watch Store®
GARDEN STATE PLAZA PARAMUS
THE MALL at SHORT HILLS

INSTRUMENTS   FOR   PROFESSIONALS®

Figure Add-6: Breitling states a unique selling proposition—the watch will "run for over a century without any adjustments to its day, date, week, month, season, year or moon-phase displays." This is the first of the group to state a price: $48,250.

Pasha® Chronograph
38mm. Solid steel.
Automatic movement.
Water-resistant to 30 meters.

JEWELS BY
VIGGI LTD.
FINE JEWELRY AND WATCHES

26 MIDDLE NECK ROAD • GREAT NECK, NY 11021 • TEL: 516.829.6161 • FAX: 516.466.8110

Figure Add-7: A retailer places an ad for a Cartier chronograph. Unlike many retail ads, this one avoids any mention of cost.

Figure Add-8: The photograph has the watch typifying a mood.

Figure Add-9: Enlarged image emphasizes the watch's unusual display.

Figure Add-10: Small type at the bottom lists many features. Set in black over a dark gray tint, the listing requires concentration to read.

DANIEL ROTH

ESTHETICS, PRECISION, ULTIMATE CRAFTSMANSHIP: EACH DANIEL ROTH WATCH IS A MASTERPIECE THAT BREATHES NEW LIFE INTO THE GREAT TRADITION OF WATCHMAKING.

The "GMT" Automatic has a push-button at 2 o'clock used to select the time zone of choice; which is displayed in a window at 12 o'clock. The date can be seen in an aperture at 6 o'clock. Available in 18k Gold or Stainless Steel.

For information: The Hour Glass USA, Inc.
38 East 57th Street • Suite 300 • New York • 10022 • 212.207.4673

Figure Add-11: Elegant watches have both boilerplate puffery at upper left and solid features at lower right.

Figure Add-12: Specifics are stated firmly, with no puffery.

"Tabogan". On your wrist or on your dresser. A contemporary watch, a travel companion.

Available in solid 18K gold or stainless steel with mechanical or quartz movement. Registered model. The collection, from $2,990. As shown, $7,900. Corum Watch Company, 125 Chubb Avenue, Lyndhurst, NJ 07071. www.corum.ch.

Figure Add-13: Shown on a wrist, with the name upside down, the watch tells its price: "As shown, $7,900."

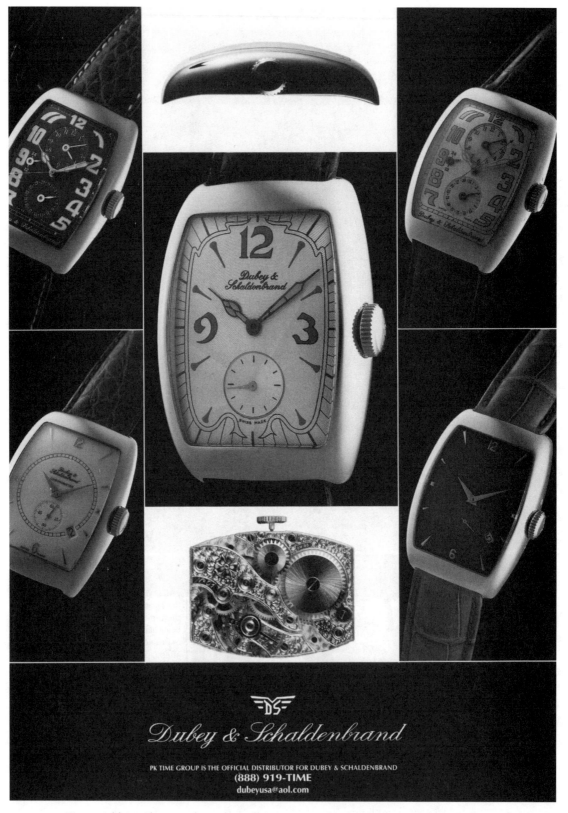

Figure Add-14: Photographs replace all copy except for the name, a toll-free number, and a Web address.

Figure Add-15: Selling copy does sell. Eight styles are shown and a single dealer's name (perhaps one who placed the ad with co-op money) is listed.

gĕrald genta

THE LIVING LEGEND

RETRO : A WORLD PREMIERE IN THE HISTORY OF TIME

The inventiveness, audacity and creative genius of Gerald Genta have marked the history of watchmaking through each of his creations and innovations. Staunchly faithful to his legendary acclaim, Gerald Genta revolutionizes timekeeping today by creating an ingenious automatic movement with jumping hours and retrograde minutes, double window and hand system. A world premiere protected by international patent, the Retro watch embraces an original alliance between mechanical watchmaking and digital display at the crossroads of yesterday and today.

To accommodate this new geometry of time, Gerald Genta has designed a case of sober elegance chiseled in gold or steel with mother-of-pearl dials of particular elegance. In his search for geometry, mechanical craftsmanship and attention to detail, Gerald Genta has once again illustrated his watchmaking genius and reinvented timekeeping with his Retro creation.

ЯeTRO

For information: The Hour Glass USA, Inc.
38 East 57th Street Suite 300
New York • 10022 • 212.207.4673

Figure Add-16: Heavy selling copy here, based on a "retro" watch.

Figure Add-17: "1997 Vintage" heads an ad that appeared well after 1997. Deliberate? Possibly, because of the word "Vintage."

Figure Add-18: No copy, except for identification of the same retailer named in the Fortis ad.

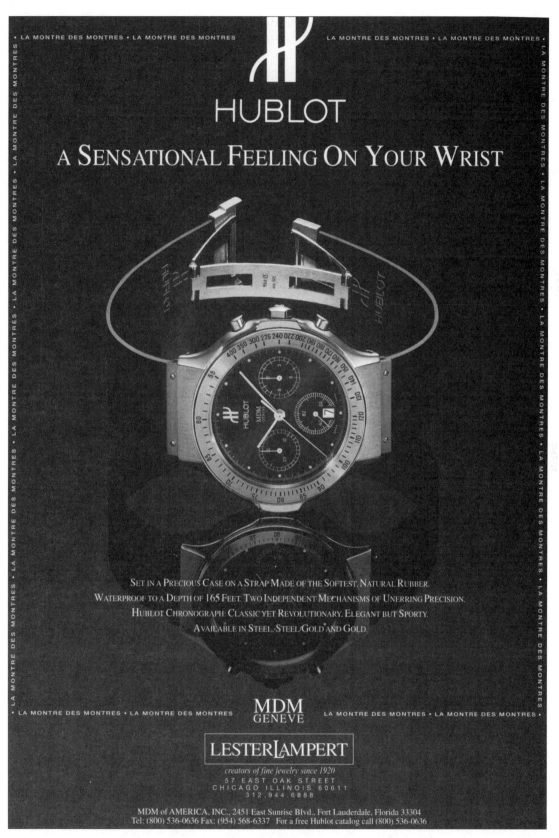

Figure Add-19: Strong selling copy with many adjectives.

Sport a lighter profile.

Ref. 3707

The GST Chrono-Automatic.
Case and bracelet in rugged,
non-irritating, ultralight titanium.
Also available in steel and
yellow gold. From $ 3995.–

IWC

International Watch Co. Ltd. Schaffhausen . Switzerland
Since 1868

EXTRAORDINARY WATCHES

10800 W. Pico Blvd., Los Angeles, CA 90064 (310) 470-1388

For complete IWC catalog please call (800) 432-9330
http://www.iwc.ch

Figure Add-20: The word "Sport" is the key word, even used as a verb. Price is
mentioned as "From $3995."

Figure Add-21: Watches are combined with bracelets. The retailer may have placed the ad.

Haute-Performance.

The Kriëger Velocitá.™ In high-polished stainless steel. It is the only Swiss-certified quartz Chronometer Chronograph available today. Which means it has no rival in terms of performance.

The Velocitá™ features four time recorders including a one-tenth second timer, tachymeter, tachymile and rotating bezel along with a sapphire crystal and water resistance to 200 meters (660 feet).

Technically accomplished it is. Yet it is also a masterpiece of European design, a felicitous fusion of high-fashion and polished performance.

The Kriëger Velocitá.™ For information, or the official Kriëger agent nearest you, call 1-800-441-8433. Fax: 305-861-1807. Or write Kriëger Watch Corporation, 300 Seventy First Street, Miami Beach, Florida 33141. Or visit us on the world-wide web at www.kriegerwatch.com.

KRIËGER®
CHRONOMÈTRES SUISSES

Also available in a combination of 18k gold and stainless-steel. Shown: C705P.2.136 suggested retail $1,495. Other models from $795.00-$1,995.00. Made in Switzerland.
©1998 Kriëger Watch Corporation

Figure Add-22: Copy makes specific claims of superiority—"The only . . . "

Figure Add-23: Paralleling the Jaeger-LeCoultre ad, the same retailer combines watches and jewelry.

Maurice Lacroix. Tomorrow's Classics.

Masterpiece Phase de Lune No 37757-1121

Masterpiece Phase de Lune:
Automatic movement ML 37, stainless steel case,
scratch resistant sapphire crystals (see through back),
water-resistant to 50 m, available in Ladies and Mens sizes. As shown $ 1990.
For more information: Toll Free 1-800-SWISS-DO pst (1-800-794-7736)
Fax 818-609-7079 • www.mauricelacroix.com

Figure Add-24: No-nonsense copy with many specifics, including price—$1990.

MICHEL JORDI
THE SPIRIT of THE WEST

A LEGENDARY TIMEPIECE
THAT CAPTURES
THE PIONEERING
SPIRIT OF AMERICA.

AVAILABLE ON LEATHER STRAP OR METAL BRACELET.
FOR MORE INFORMATION/CATALOG, PLEASE CALL 800-823-8340 OR 972-960-0335

Figure Add-25: The cattle skull sets a mood for the watch, with its "Lone Star" face
and western leather-band option.

Figure Add-26: Best known for pens, this company includes them, plus cufflinks, in a dealer-placed ad.

Figure Add-27: The illustration, a scuba diver, underscores a feature of the watch, water-resistance to 300 feet.

Cindy Crawford's Choice

Constellation
Stainless steel with diamond-set bezel.
OMEGA — Swiss made since 1848.

Ω
OMEGA
The sign of excellence

WESTIME
EXTRAORDINARY WATCHES
Westside Pavilion - Third Floor
10800 Pico Boulevard
Los Angeles, CA 90064
(310) 470-1388

http://www.omega.ch

Figure Add-28: The sole watch using a celebrity tie, this one makes no other claim.

You never

Actually own a Patek Philippe.

You merely take care of it for the next

generation. *The new men's Travel Time with dual*

hour hands. One local time. The other, home. Begin your *own* tradition.

PATEK PHILIPPE
GENEVE

's Travel Time ref: 5034. For information: Patek Philippe, Dept. 117, One Rockefeller Plaza - Suite 930, New York, New York 10020. Tel: (212) 581 0870. www.patek.com

Figure Add-29: Image, stated in a classic manner, plus an explanation of the dual hour hands.

Timeless.

Perhaps only Porsche can interpret time in such a timeless fashion. After all,

it has been the crucible by which we've measured our success for a half

century. Now, we pay homage to our race against time the best way we

know how – by creating something of enduring quality. An ultra-precise sports

watch built by the world's finest craftsmen. And styled after the legendary

Porsche 911. Each is individually numbered from our limited edition of only

1,911 worldwide. To place an order, receive more information or locate an

authorized Porsche dealer near you, visit us on the Web at porsche.com or

call 1-800-PORSCHE and discover why, time after time, there is no substitute.

911 Limited Edition Chronograph
This stainless steel automatic chronograph features 12 hour, 30 minute, 60 second
and 1/100 second counters, luminous hands and face, scratch resistant sapphire
crystal, tachymeter and date display. Water resistant to 50m.

Figure Add-30: The watchmaker ties the watch to a better-known product carrying the name—the Porsche 911.

Figure Add-31: Showing three watches of substantially different appearance, the
watchmaker also lists seven dealers.

The Ulysse Nardin GMT±

An Exclusive Mechanical Development

When traveling to another time zone, press the "+" or "-" button to adjust the hour hand instantly to the new local time. A jump hour window at 11 o'clock keeps track of the time at home.

24-Hour "home time" or second time zone

Local time adjuster "-"

Local time adjuster "+"

Available in 18 ct gold or steel with a strap or a bracelet and a dial of white, blue or black.

Each GMT± is hand-crafted in our workshop in Le Locle, Switzerland and individually numbered. The mechanical movement is self-winding. The case is water resistant to 100 meters and fitted with a screw-down crown.

ULYSSE NARDIN
since 1846

CORNER OF 55th STREET
700 FIFTH AVENUE · NEW YORK, N.Y. 10019 · TELEPHONE (212) 597-9000

For a free catalog and the dealer nearest you,
call 800-457-5309.

Figure Add-32: Callouts clarify the features of this watch. It is the only one in the group that fully explains how it works.

Figure Add-33: The watch is shown clearly against a distorted soft drink can. Many dealers are listed.

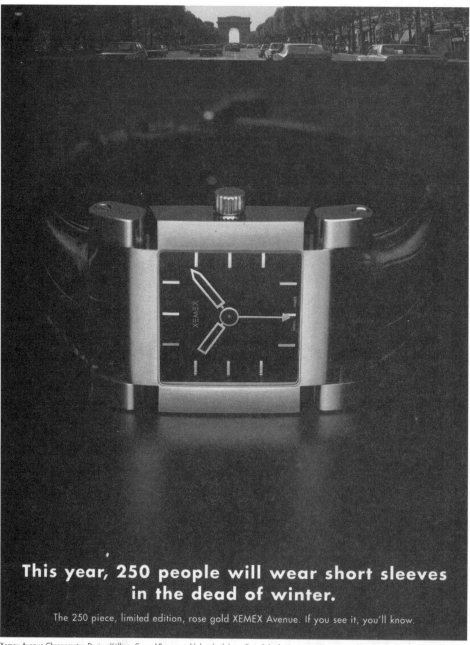

Figure Add-34: This is the only "wry humor" ad in the group. In mice-type are specifics, including price—$6,500.00, $12,950.00 in platinum. Note the use of double zeroes (".00").

INDEX